A time and a place

Two Centuries of Irish Social Life

A time and a place

Two Centuries of Irish Social Life

NATIONAL GALLERY OF IRELAND

Published on the occasion of the exhibition,
A Time and A Place. Two Centuries of Irish Social Life
at the National Gallery of Ireland, Dublin
18 October 2006 – 28 January 2007

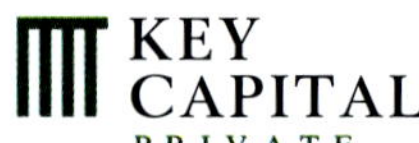

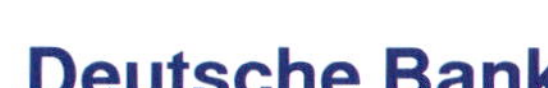

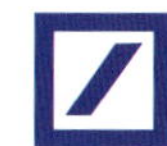

Distribution in Ireland by the National Gallery of Ireland
Worldwide distribution by Paul Holberton

Copyright © 2006 National Gallery of Ireland and the authors

ISBN 1-904288-17-0
ISBN 978-1-904288-17-6

Edited by Brendan Rooney

Catalogue designed by Vermillion Design
Printed in Dublin by Hudson Killeen

Note: every effort has been made to trace the copyright holders of material in this book. The Gallery apologises if any material has been included without permission, and would be pleased to hear from anyone who has not been consulted.

Cover image: cat. 80 (detail)

Contents

Director's Preface

Apart from their purely art historical and aesthetic value, paintings can also be significant because of what they can tell us about society and the way communities lived. They complement descriptive narrative and provide a visual basis for better understanding not only great historic events but also how people went about their daily lives and how they relaxed and enjoyed themselves. Before the advent of photography, painting is the most bountiful source of visual information on the lifestyle of previous generations.

The visual arts constitute a remarkably informative testament about Irish society. The works on display in this exhibition cover an exceptional gamut of activities which reflect vividly how Irish people, from all echelons of society, escaped from the drudgery and demands of work and sought to indulge themselves when they had a moment to spare - a quality which has not diminished with the passing of time. Looking at these images we get a real sense of just how seriously Irish people took their recreational activities down through centuries, from field games to race going and music making to dancing, from religious festivals and traditions to civic celebrations.

Coordinated by Fionnuala Croke, Head of Exhibitions, the show has been curated by Dr Brendan Rooney, who has drawn on the support of gallery colleagues and various eminent experts, who have worked together to assemble this wonderful panorama of Irish life down through the centuries. The essays and individual commentaries in this publication which relate to each exhibit provide an almost encyclopaedic survey of everyday life over the centuries as represented by some fifty artists. That the range is so comprehensive is in great part due to the generosity of the many lenders, both private and institutional, who have consented to contribute to the display, and the National Gallery of Ireland is immensely grateful for their support.

The Gallery is also deeply appreciative of the support provided by Deutsche Bank AG and Key Capital Private, who have provided sponsorship for this major survey of Irish social life over two centuries.

Raymond Keaveney
Director
National Gallery of Ireland

Sponsor's Foreword

We are delighted to be associated with this exhibition celebrating the richness and diversity of Irish recreation across class, community, geography and generation as recorded by some of the finest artists that have worked in Ireland. In revealing Ireland's rich social fabric as seen by its own artists, the curators of this exhibition have captured a perfect time and place for us all to celebrate the irrepressible spirit of Ireland.

Deutsche Bank's own art policies are socially motivated. Back in the 1970s we decided to buy art to involve our employees in the community and to support the art of our time. This has led to the purchase of 50,000 works of art. The strength of contemporary Irish art has ensured that many stimulating works by Irish artists hang on the walls of our offices around the world.

This exhibition is a great occasion to celebrate the recently announced association between Deutsche Bank, one of the largest financial institutions in the world, with Key Capital, the Irish specialist financial adviser, in the area of wealth management.

The impressive success of the Irish economy in the past decade has opened truly exceptional opportunities in the field of wealth management. We believe that combining the strong local expertise contributed by Key Capital and Deutsche Bank Private Wealth Management's global product reach will create a leader in the Irish market. Key Capital Private will not only be able to offer the full range of services offered in the Irish markets, but bring to the fore unique investment solutions and ideas sourced through Deutsche Bank's global network.

Deutsche Bank as a truly European institution is committed to the Irish markets, and is pleased through its extensive involvement in the diversity of the Arts world to support the National Gallery of Ireland.

We hope that you enjoy the exhibition and that this catalogue stands as an enduring testament to the wonderful event!

Pierre de Weck
Member of Group
Executive Committee
Deutsche Bank AG

Conor Killeen
CEO
Key Capital

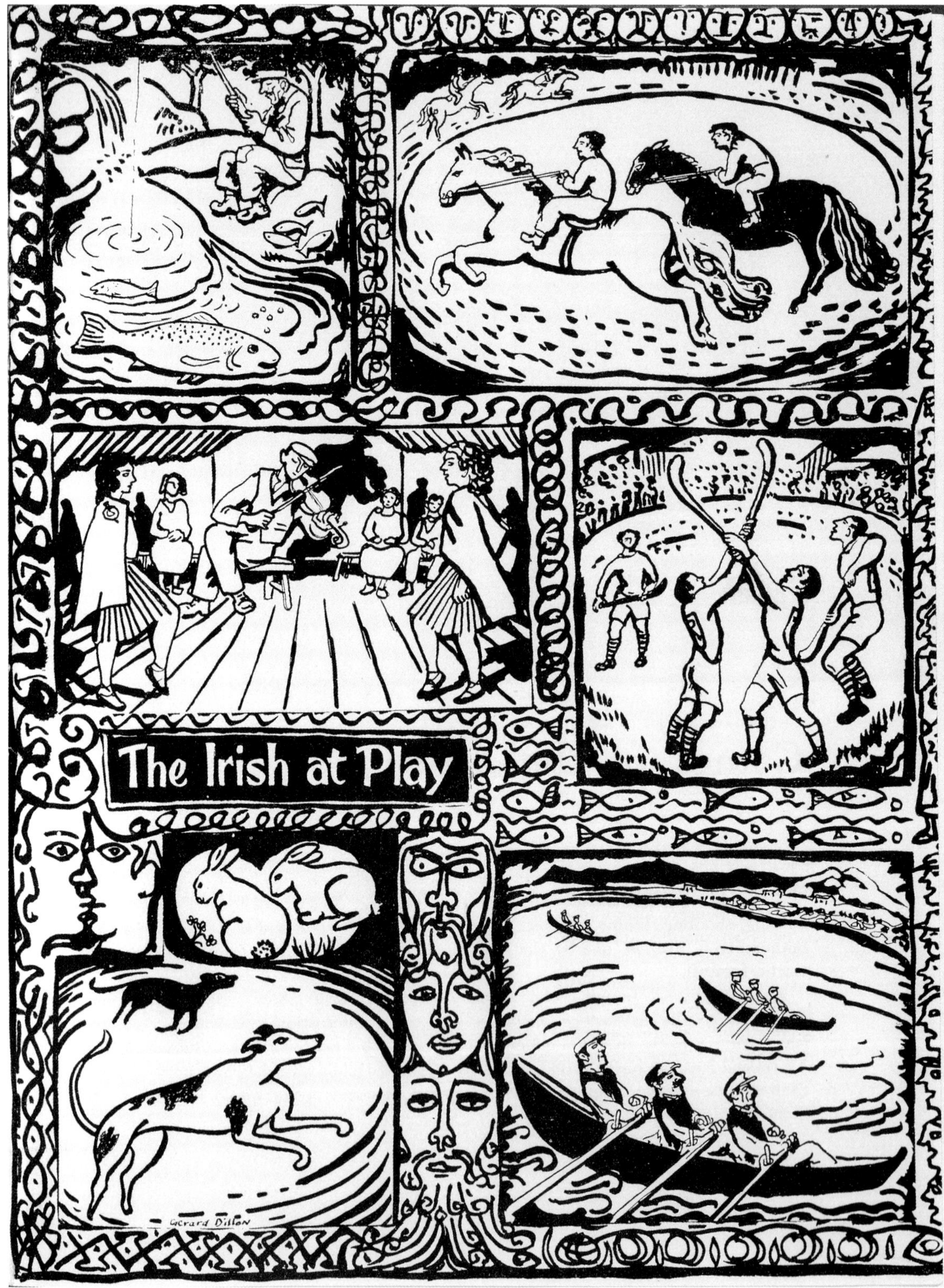

Gerald Dillon, *The Irish at Play*, pen and ink on paper. Design for An Tóstal Official Souvenir Handbook, 1953.
Published by Fogra Fáilte, Dublin. Courtesy of Bord Fáilte

Acknowledgements

The breadth of subjects encompassed by this exhibition has meant that I have relied greatly on the expertise and generosity of scholars and enthusiasts outside the National Gallery of Ireland in addition to the assistance and support of my colleagues within the institution. It has been an enormously satisfying project that has presented the opportunity of investigating and bringing together the work of a large number of Irish and Irish-based artists in whom I have long been interested. It is an opportunity that has also been facilitated by the generosity of private individuals and the custodians of other public collections, and to these collectors and institutions I am hugely grateful.

I would like to thank Fionnuala Croke, Head of Exhibitions at the National Gallery of Ireland, for overseeing the project with the assistance of Susan O'Connor, Exhibitions Officer.

My colleagues in the Library and Research Services Department, particularly Leah Benson, Margaret Donnelly, Dr Roisín Kennedy, Andrea Lydon and Catherine Sheridan, deserve special mention as they have been involved in the development of the project since its inception. They have provided welcome assistance in practical aspects of the exhibition and have been generally supportive of the endeavour throughout.

The staff of the Registrar's Office, Kim Smit and Felicia Tan, endured countless questions, and managed with consummate skill the complicated logistics involved in assembling an exhibition of this size. The care, assessment and preparation of the works were expertly undertaken by Ele von Monschaw, Michie Konishi, Muirne Lydon, Ranson Davy, Pat McBride and Mariateresa Pullano. I am also grateful to the art handling team of Kevin Kelly, Andrew Moore and Sheila Dooley for their skillful work with the pictures.

Dr Síghle Bhreathnach-Lynch, Curator of Irish Paintings and Anne Hodge, Curator of Prints and Drawings, endorsed the exhibition generously by allowing me to draw zealously from their collections. I would also like to acknowledge the enthusiastic contributions and advice of Sergio Benedetti, Marie Bourke, Niamh Gogan, Valerie Keogh, Niamh MacNally and Orla O'Brien.

The production of a detailed catalogue is a rare luxury, the realisation of which, from design and photography to proof-reading, was facilitated by a large number of my colleagues, notably Lydia Furlong, who managed its publication, and Roy Hewson, who with the assistance of Chris O'Toole, was typically exacting in photographing the works and preparing material for the catalogue. Marie McFeely's and Louise Morgan's sleuth-like abilities at sourcing illustrations and individuals were outstanding. I am also enormously grateful to Janet McLean and Adriaan Waiboer, who were generous and good-humoured in giving of their time, experience and expertise.

Prof. Mary Daly, Dr Claudia Kinmonth, William Laffan and Donal Maguire furnished me with texts that are at once erudite and accessible. Their scholarly contributions and insights have enriched the exhibition and associated catalogue tremendously. I am also very grateful to Caroline Delahunty for providing selfless assistance in the preparation of the catalogue text.

The knowledge of experts is an endlessly rich resource on which to draw, and the project benefited from the assistance of a number of scholars. Some were disarmingly forthcoming when approached by me for the first time, while others showed remarkable tolerance in indulging me yet again. Several mentioned below were similarly helpful to my fellow contributors. I think it is important to acknowledge that the interactive and interdisciplinary nature of projects such as this is fruitful but also hugely enjoyable. Among those to whom I owe a particular debt of gratitude are Linda Ballard of the Ulster Folk and Transport Museum, Dr Toby Barnard, Dr Eileen Black and Anne Stewart of the Ulster Museum, Nicholas Carolan of the Irish Traditional Music Archive, Mairead Dunlevy, Dr S.B. Kennedy, Dáithí de Mórdha of the Blasket Island Heritage Centre, Peter Murray, Dawn Williams and Colleen O'Sullivan of the Crawford Municipal Art Gallery, Cork, Eimear O'Connor of the Humanties Institute of Ireland, UCD, Sean Sexton and Barry Walsh of the Monasterevin Historical Society.

I would also like to extend my warmest thanks to Bruce Arnold, Bruce Bailey, David Britton, Katherine Cahill, Edward Chandler, Frances Christie, Joanne Clarke of the GAA Museum, Croke Park, Bernadette Cogan of Dublin City Libraries and Archives, Deirdre Conroy, Dr Riann Coulter, Anne Crookshank, Prof. Tom Dunne, Jane Eckett, Honora Faul, Desmond FitzGerald, Knight of Glin, Prof. Roy Foster, Fionnuala Gallagher of NUI Galway, James and Therese Gorry, Dan Hayes, Alan and Mary Hobart, Seamus King, Fiona Loughnane, Pat McLean, Dr Edward McParland, Dominic Milmo-Penny, Dr Barry Monahan, Maureen Porteous, Charles Reeve-Tucker and Stephen Reeve-Tucker, Karen Reihill, Orna Roche of the Tiernan McBride Library, Irish Film Archive, Sara Smyth, the Stopford-Sackville family, and Prof. Nancy Weston. Thanks are also due to Adam's, Christie's, Sotheby's and Whyte's Auctioneers.

Finally, I would like to thank my wife Alice, who has withstood with grace the vagaries of my project and received with similar good humour unsolicited information on everything from eighteenth-century court dance to the history of the Railway Cup.

Brendan Rooney

Contributors

Mary E. Daly is Professor of History and Principal of the College of Arts and Celtic Studies at University College Dublin. She was educated at UCD and Nuffield College Oxford, and has held visiting positions at Harvard and Boston College. Her most recent publication is *The Slow Failure. Population Decline and Independent Ireland, 1920-1973*, published by Wisconsin University Press (2006).

Claudia Kinmonth (CK) trained at the Royal College of Art and has worked at the Victoria and Albert Museum in London. Specialising in art history and material culture she is the author of *Irish Rural Interiors in Art* (2006) and *Irish Country Furniture, 1700-1950* (1993), both published by Yale University Press.

William Laffan (WL) is the editor of *Irish Architectural and Decorative Studies*. Educated at Oxford and the Warburg Institute, he has recently compiled editions of Hugh Douglas Hamilton's *Cries of Dublin* (2003) and Samuel Chearnley's *Miscelanea Structura Curiosa* (2005).

Donal Maguire (DM) is CSIA Assistant at the National Gallery of Ireland. A graduate of The National College of Art and Design, he has published recently on the illustrated letters of William Orpen and is a practising artist who has exhibited at the Royal Hibernian Academy.

Brendan Rooney (BR) is Administrator of the Centre for the Study of Irish Art (CSIA) at the National Gallery of Ireland. He received his doctorate from Trinity College Dublin and his publications include *The Life and Work of Harry Jones Thaddeus* (2003) and, with Nicola Figgis, *Irish Paintings in the National Gallery of Ireland, Volume I* (2001).

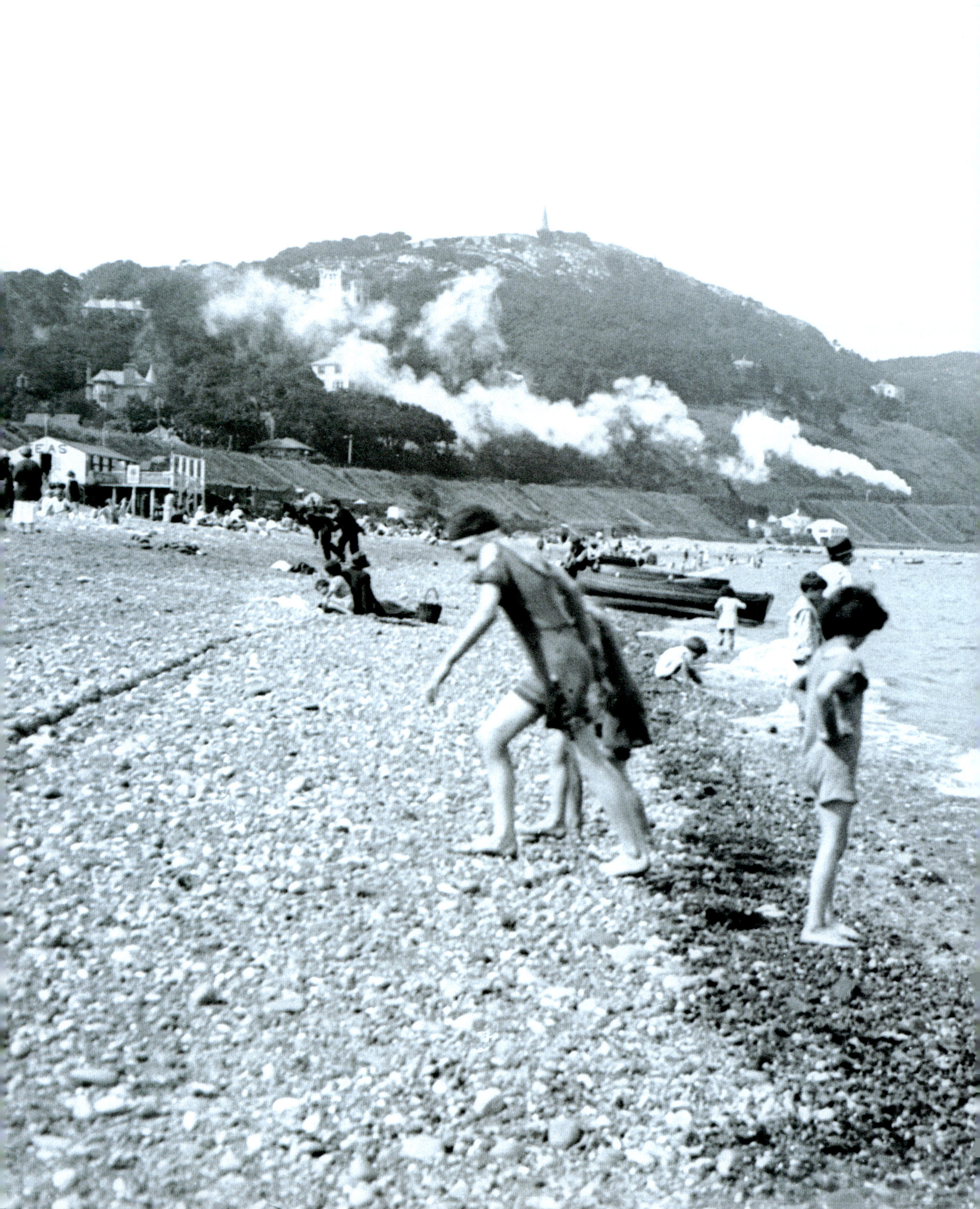

Essays

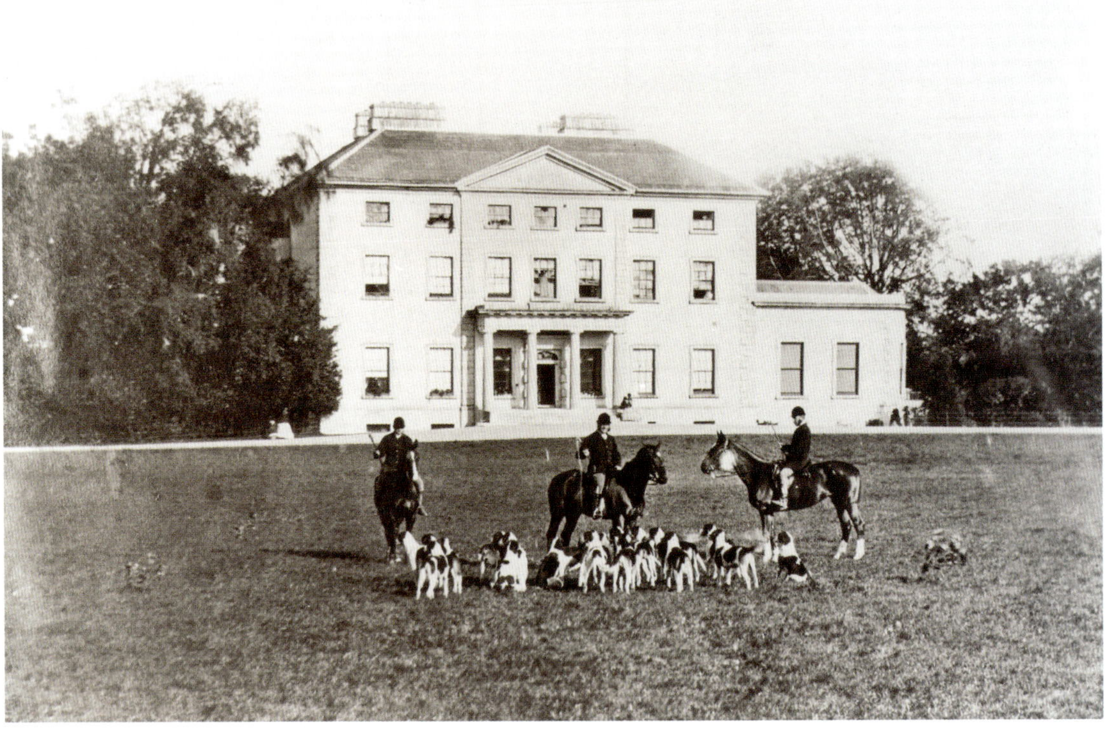

Fig 1. Attributed to **Augusta Crofton**, *Clonbrock, County Galway*, c.1867.

Two Centuries of Irish Social Life

Prof. Mary E. Daly

Ireland has undergone enormous changes over the past two centuries. At the beginning of this period the majority of the people lived in acute poverty; they were illiterate and often Irish speaking and they earned their living either from farming or from a combination of farming and domestic spinning. A small but influential network of landed gentry set the tone for fashionable social life in Dublin and the countryside. Irish society was divided by class, religion and politics. Over time Ireland has become much more prosperous and more urban, and the landed gentry are now confined to history. Social life today tends to be divided on the basis of money and age-cohort. Technology and economic prosperity have made it possible for people to enjoy a range of leisure activities inconceivable to former generations: cheap foreign holidays, international sporting events, giant pop concerts, cinema and music in the home. Yet there are some themes that were common to all periods and to all social classes: an interest in sport, Music & Dance, and conversation– though this may now be via mobile phone rather than in person.

This short essay does not attempt to give a comprehensive picture of Irish social life over the past two centuries. However I have highlighted a number of broad themes that are relevant to the subject matter of this exhibition: work and leisure; respectability and religion; politics and parades; sport; music and popular entertainment.

Work and Leisure:

Today, most people, who are in paid employment draw a rigid distinction between work and leisure, but in the past this line was less clearly drawn. Farming was the most common occupation in Ireland until the second half of the twentieth century, and farm work was not governed by fixed times for starting and finishing work. This was equally true of many people working in shops, pubs, small workshops, and it remains the case for women working in the home. Working time adjusted to meet seasonal and weekly pressures; leisure activities were often fitted in when work was slack. For example in the Irish countryside, there was very little work done in the fields during the winter, so January and February were a time for visiting and especially for match-making. In contrast the high summer was not a time for holidays on the farm, because it coincided with hay-making or the grain harvest. The tradition of farmers holidaying in

Lisdoonvarna or Ballybunion in September ties in with the farming cycle: with holidays coming after the busy summer/early autumn farming season. In the towns workers would be busiest on market and fair days. Dublin businesses stayed open late on Saturday nights, knowing that workers who were paid at the end of the week would have money to spend. To compensate for this busy period coming up to the weekend many tradesmen celebrated 'Saint Monday'– starting work late or perhaps not working at all– because business was slack and the next deadline for making shoes, suits and other goods was four to five days away.

A lot of social activity was spontaneous: farm workers stopping work to follow the hunt, when it happened to pass through their fields. Time spent chatting at the creamery when they delivered milk – one of the reasons why some farmers were reluctant to have milk collected from the farm. But other events held a firm place in the calendar; fair days, whose dates were set by law; race meets and traditional religious dates. There were religious dates of universal significance such as Christmas Day, Shrove Tuesday, Easter; national religious days, such as St Patrick's Day or St Brigid's Day and others commemorating local saints or religious occasions, whose origins might go back to pre-Christian times. Hallow'Een – a major Irish festival, whose origins are lost in pre-history – marks the end of autumn and the onset of winter. It was a time for feasting, because food was plentiful, and a time for playing traditional games. St Brigid's Day, the (optimistic) first day of spring, marks the beginning of a new growing season, and an end to the lack of milk that marked the winter months.

Only a minority of workers received a regular weekly or monthly pay packet. Servants working in private houses or as live-in farm labour were generally paid only twice a year, and it was not uncommon for the money to be given to their parents, who would then dole out a small amount for pocket money. In 1943 one clergyman described 'more than one instance where young men of 25 years still go to their father (or in one instance their mother) to ask for the price of a smoke or the cost of a ticket to a dance or cinema'. Farmers got money when they sold produce at a fair, though with the coming of creameries dairy farmers could expect a regular monthly cheque. When people had money to spare, they generally splurged a little. A trip to the fair to sell cattle was commonly followed by a visit to the local grocery to pay off part of the outstanding shop bill, and then to the pub, which was often part of the grocery store. Women who sold eggs, butter or other produce might splash out on a new table-cloth, small toys for the children and shop goods, including white baker's bread– as a change from the home-made soda bread. When a farmer recruited a teenage boy or girl at a hiring fair, he gave them a small cash payment that they probably spent buying ribbons, trinkets, or indulging in fun fair games. A fair day brought fortune tellers, travelling show people, second-hand clothes stalls and fiddlers to a town.

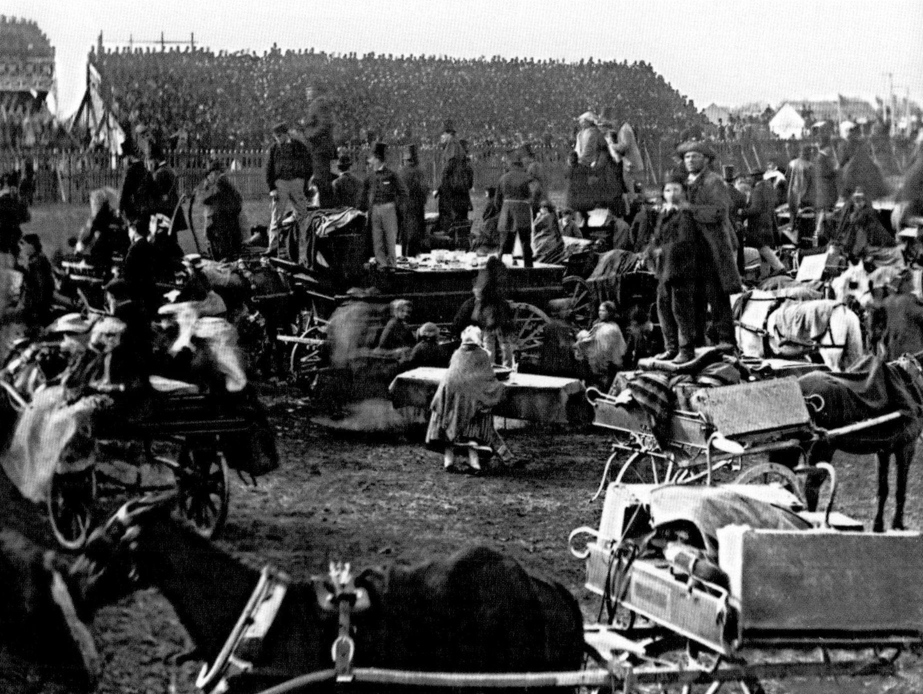

Fig 2. Anonymous, possibly **Frederick Holland Mares**, *Dublin, Punchestown Races*, c.1864.

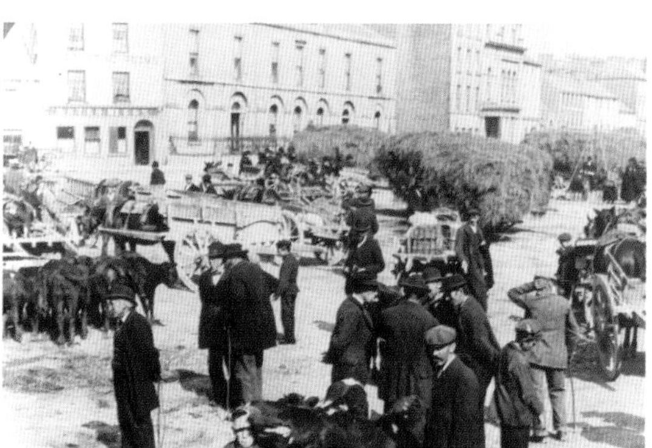

Fig 3. **Charles Johnston**, *Market, Eyre Square, Galway (detail)*

In Britain, the coming of the Industrial Revolution with its large factories created the need for a more sober and punctual workforce: men, women, boys and girls who would come to work every day on time. The economic pressures of a modern industrial society were in conflict with older traditions such as 'Saint

Monday' or taking time off for local festivals and fairs. Ireland outside Ulster was slow to experience the industrial revolution. When factories opened in various small towns in Ireland during the 1930s a number of employers complained that workers invariably arrived late, if at all on Mondays, after Sunday night dances, and it was common for them to vanish for a couple of days without permission to attend a local race meeting. In the early factory system working hours were extremely long by modern standards – often a twelve-hour day for six days a week. Hours gradually became shorter – initially only for women and children, but then also for men. By the end of the nineteenth century work finished early on Saturdays (say 4 o'clock), and by the 1930s the Saturday half-day was the norm. It was only in the early 1960s that most Irish workers secured a five day week.

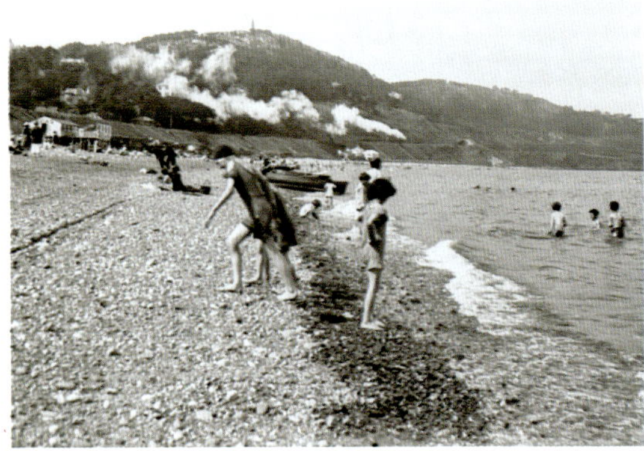

Fig 4. **Fr Frank Browne**, *Killiney Strand*, 1925

Public holidays or bank holidays were a means of standardising free time for working people. The first Bank Holiday was introduced in Britain in 1871. Because Ireland was part of the United Kingdom from 1801 to 1922, Irish public holidays are secular holidays (bank holidays) rather than religious holidays; many European countries observe major church holidays, such as Ascension Thursday as a public holiday. Farmers and farm workers tended to celebrate church holidays rather than bank holidays.

Although travel and transport was much more difficult than today, some people did make long journeys, both within Ireland and abroad. The landed gentry have a long tradition of travelling for pleasure in Ireland and overseas; indeed the Grand Tour was often a rite of passage for young men. During the nineteenth century many Irish landlords found that it was less expensive to travel on the Continent than to maintain the lavish lifestyle and open house that was expected of them in Ireland. Travelling scholars, musicians, tramps, story-tellers and beggars moved through the Irish countryside, getting food and some modest board from farmers, and occasionally (if they were good musicians or scholars) from a landlord. In return they transcribed manuscripts, played music, carried out odd jobs, or offered prayers. By the 1840s Ireland had an excellent road network that reached into remote Connemara, and west Cork. Bianconi's coaches, based in Clonmel, carried thousands of travellers at very cheap prices from one town to another. From the 1840s the railway made it possible to travel relatively cheaply and speedily to Dublin to attend the funeral of Daniel O'Connell (1847), to visit the International Exhibition (1853) or for a holiday in Killarney, which was already well known for its scenery. Most working people first used trains, not to take holidays, but for day trips perhaps to the seaside, or to race meetings. Seaside holidays became fashionable because of their alleged health benefits. During the Victorian era, middle-class men often sent their wife and family away from the city to the seaside in order to avoid the infectious diseases that flourished in the warm, unsanitary city streets. Limerick families favoured Kilkee; some Dubliners rented houses in Killiney, Bray, Skerries or even Sandymount. Bank holiday excursions to the seaside were popular with all classes. Swimming was a popular pastime with many Dubliners. The tradition of nude bathing at the Forty-Foot recalls the time when many Dublin swimmers could not afford to buy swimsuits. By 1900 the bicycle had opened up new travel possibilities for younger people; youth hostels, popular on the Continent began to open in the 1930s. In 1935 most Irish workers became entitled to one week's paid holidays; today most workers have in excess of one month paid holidays– something that distinguishes European workers from those in the USA. However, it is only in recent decades that the idea of taking holidays away from home has come to be seen as the norm.

Respectability and religion:

In the eighteenth century the social lives of the gentry and the poor alike were characterised by heavy drinking, gambling and general raucousness. Social behaviour changes over time, and the long reign of Queen Victoria (1837-1901) saw a concerted drive for respectability in British and Irish society, the influence of which lasted up to the 1960s. Since that time social behaviour has become less strait-laced – indeed more akin to what prevailed two hundred years ago. In Ireland the drive for respectability marched in step with the growing influence of the churches. Travellers who visited Ireland before the Famine described a society of impoverished, improvident peasants, who married early, had lots of children without any consideration for their upbringing; drank freely (often illicitly distilled liquor), and spent a lot of time lazing around and gossiping rather than working. The French writer Gustave de Beaumont, who toured Ireland in the 1830s, claimed that Ireland was one of the most violent societies in Europe – a claim that is not borne out by statistics. These highly exaggerated and inaccurate stereotypes were embarrassing to the Catholic middle-class, and most especially to the Catholic clergy, who were determined to secure their rightful place within Irish society. In the years immediately before the Great Famine there was a serious campaign to clamp down on drinking and on social gatherings associated with drinking, faction fighting and other forms of disreputable behaviour, and this campaign persisted for much of the nineteenth century. By the 1840s many bishops and priests were working hard to stamp out disreputable 'religious' practices, such as the games and customs associated with wakes. Held in the home, they combined prayer with story-telling, drinking, tobacco and games – some very bawdy indeed – and even match-making. The origins of these practices probably pre-date Christianity, but they suggest a wish to affirm that life goes on, despite the inevitability of death. The traditional Irish wake, where neighbours and friends visited the house of the dead, talked, smoked clay pipes and drank tea, stout or whiskey survived, but in a much more decorous form. Patterns – traditional pilgrimage to a site associated with an Irish saint – such as Glendalough (St Kevin) were another target for the Catholic clergy. Held on a specific date they offered a combination of prayer, penance, perhaps a cure for ailments, plus drinking, music, dancing and faction fights. When Thomas Crofton Croker visited Gougane Barra (Cork) in 1813 he commented how 'drunken men and the most depraved women mingled with those whose ideas of piety brought them to this spot; and a confused uproar of prayers and oaths, of sanctity and blasphemy sounded in the same instant on the ear'.

Clergy of all persuasions worked hard to alert people to the evils of drink. The most famous temperance crusader, Cork priest Fr Theobald Mathew could attract thousands to his meetings in the years immediately before the Famine. Evangelical Protestant clergy were even more determined temperance campaigners. The Great Famine of the 1840s made it easier to reform social behaviour. Most Famine victims were poor and illiterate people who believed in the cures and prayers associated with patterns or holy wells. The survivors tended to be the middling and larger farmers, literate English-speaking people who aspired to a respectable, 'modern' lifestyle. Whiskey or illicit spirits were the traditional peasant tipples, but during the 1850s, the British chancellor of the Exchequer William Gladstone jacked up taxes on spirits and reduced taxation on beer, which helped to persuade many Irish drinkers to change to Guinness. A law passed in 1878 ended Sunday drinking except in the major cities, and restrictions on Sunday drinking remained in force in the Irish Republic until 1959, and much later in Northern Ireland. St Patrick's Day, a traditional day of drinking and merry-making in the eighteenth century, when gentlemen's clubs organised special dinners (now surviving mainly through the Irish-American Friendly Sons' of St Patrick and other groups such as the Eire Society of Boston), was gradually brought into line as a 'respectable' day. In 1927 the Dáil imposed a ban on public houses opening on St Patrick's Day, prompting a new interest in visits to the Dog Show at the RDS, or cruises on Dublin Bay – because alcohol was available at both venues.

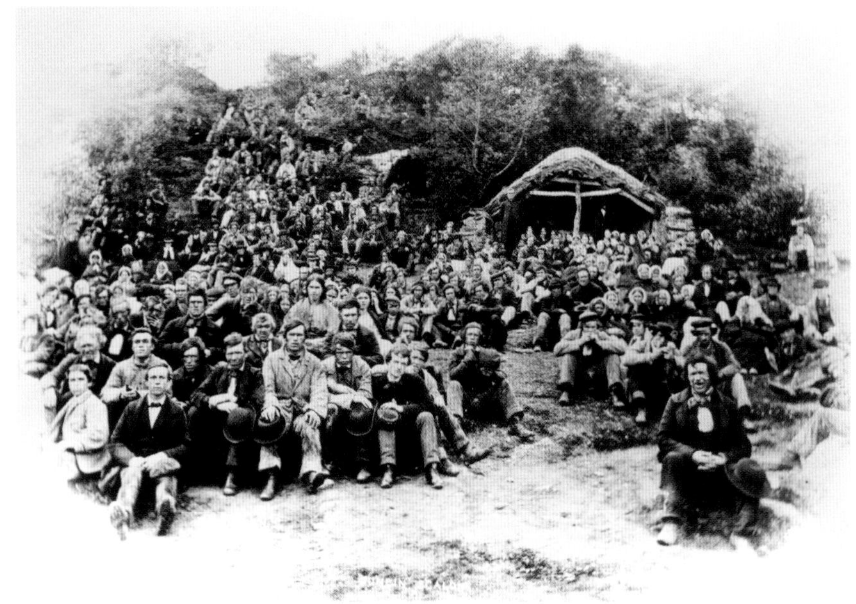

Fig 5. Attributed to **A. Ayton,** *Open Air Mass at Bunlin Bridge, County Donegal*, 1867

Donnybrook Fair, held in late August, was another casualty of changing social mores. In the 1820s, according to Fergus D'Arcy, 'it was still a place where high and low, rich and poor came together to enjoy a good boxing match, wrestling contest, or to take part in the dancing or to listen to the Rakes of Mallow played by a fiddler getting steadily drunker'.

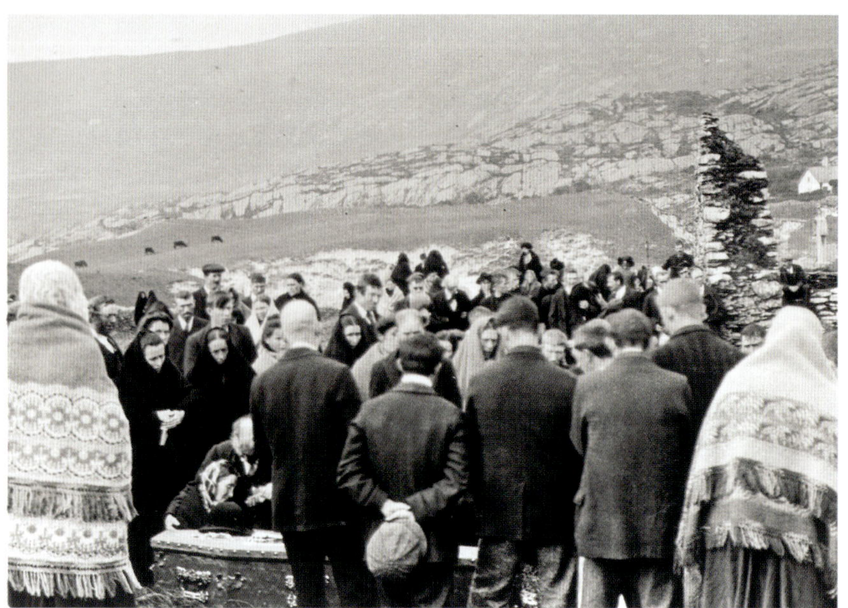

Fig 6. **Christine Chicester**, *Funeral, County Kerry*, c.1910

By the 1850s a group of prominent Dublin businessmen and Catholic clergy determined to bring an end to the fair. Following a number of lacklustre attempts to revive it following its abolition in 1855, the last fair took place in 1868; the official opening of the new Catholic church in Donnybrook in 1866, across the road from the Fair, was deliberately held on the opening day of the Fair.

The century or so after the Famine saw a significant rise in church-going, through all sections of Irish society. In the 1830s many poor people, especially in remote areas, did not attend church on a regular basis (often because they lived too far from a church or did not have respectable clothing), though they did frequent religious events such as patterns, or stations – masses said in a private house. The Catholic church replaced the traditional religious occasions with more solemn events, such as missions, confraternities, sodalities and Corpus Christi processions; rituals that owed more to Counter-Reformation Europe than to Irish traditions. Some traditional pilgrimages did survive, notably Lough Derg, one of Europe's great pilgrimage sites, which is mentioned in Dante's *Inferno*. The reformed Lough Derg pilgrimage became a determinedly penitential exercise, consisting of fasting, sleep deprivation and prayer, but the numbers participating fell. By the early twentieth century, however, many Lough Derg pilgrims had reinstated the traditional combination of prayer, penance and play by leaving the island after the pilgrimage and taking the train to the sea-side resort of Bundoran. The tradition of climbing Croagh Patrick, the Reek on the last Sunday of July – an event that commemorates the traditional Gaelic festival of Lughnasa – was another surviving ritual. But by the 1930s Knock, in County Mayo, the site of a Marian apparition in 1879, had become Ireland's largest pilgrimage destination: an Irish Lourdes.

Religion continued to offer a combination of prayer, penance and sociability, though in a much more respectable form than in the past. Mass-going and other religious services provided an opportunity to meet friends and neighbours. But the travelling stalls selling religious objects that accompanied many missions were a poor substitute for the fiddlers, strong men and poitín sellers found at traditional patterns.

Irish Protestantism also changed. The growth in evangelicalism – an approach to religion that emphasises personal conversion based on the Bible– resulted in new churches and chapels, home Bible groups, and increased religious attendance. In the summer of 1859 Ulster experienced a wave of religious hysteria during the first in a series of evangelical revivals. Open-air preaching, targeted at the 'unsaved' became a feature of Ulster summers; such gatherings often attracted large attendances.

The churches were the primary focus of social life for many Irish people. Choirs, amateur dramatics, badminton teams, debating groups and lending libraries were often attached to a parish or a particular church or chapel. A glance through local newspapers during the 1950s, especially during the summer months or at Christmas, throws up notices or photographs of numerous excursions to the sea-side, picnics, and parties organised by various church groups. Bazaars, garden parties and concerts to raise funds for churches, convents or missionary work formed a major part of social life in provincial Ireland, for Catholic and Protestant alike. By the 1950s carnivals and dances – held for church fund-raising - were a major part of Ireland's summer calendar, and the Catholic Church also brought whist drives and later bingo to many parishes.

Politics and Parades:

Until the Act of Union suppressed the Irish Parliament the Dublin social season was determined by the parliamentary cycle; social life was at its most glittering when the parliament was in session. After 1801 the Dublin social calendar was determined by the vice-regal court at Dublin Castle, where the premier event was the St

Patrick's Day Ball. The Dublin Horse Show, held on Leinster Lawn – part of the site is now occupied by the National Gallery - was another landmark event. In provincial towns, the timing of major balls or other gatherings was often determined by the dates when the assizes or the grand jury were sitting, because most landed gentry served as magistrates and jurors.

Since the 1820s, when Daniel O'Connell launched his campaign for Catholic Emancipation, politics has provided unending scope for conversation, meetings, drinking and outings. Elections were major social occasions. During the nineteenth century polling lasted for weeks, not one day. Candidates were expected to 'treat' voters with free food and entertainment as well as drink. All day pub opening; dancers, fiddlers and other musicians plus open barrels of beer on the street were the norm, leaving candidates with very large bills. Although women did not have the vote until 1918, they were actively involved, cheering a candidate or booing his rival, as were other non-voters. Fights between rival factions were common. The 1828 Clare by-election, which returned Daniel O'Connell to parliament was noteworthy because many Catholic voters pledged to abstain from alcohol.

Tens of thousands travelled to attend O'Connell's monster meetings at Tara or Mullinavat, or to attend public meetings organised by Parnell and other Home Rule leaders. The Ulster Unionist leaders William Carson and Sir James Craig also attracted huge crowds to their meetings. Mass outdoor political meetings remained a feature of Irish elections until the late 1960s, when the combination of television and security fears from the Troubles brought them to an end; but traditional bonfires and blazing tar barrels still greet some newly-appointed cabinet ministers, and victorious football teams.

Political parades are both social gatherings, and a means of defining identity, and of asserting control of the public space. The victory of William III at the Battle of the Boyne on July 12th 1690 was marked by a major parade in Dublin until the early nineteenth century, and it continues to be celebrated throughout Northern Ireland. The rituals associated with July 12th – elaborate banners commemorating historic events; the regalia worn by members of the Orange Order, who march to tunes played by fife and drum bands – are well-established. Most political parades in Dublin from the mid-nineteenth century commemorated nationalist events. The funerals of Daniel O'Connell, Charles Stewart Parnell, or the veteran Fenian Jeremiah O'Donovan Rossa followed clearly thought-out rituals – passing 'sites of memory' such as the Irish parliament in College Green or St Catherine's Church in Thomas Street where Robert Emmet was hanged. The marchers included political and religious dignitaries; nationalist or republican clubs and other organisations, and the inevitable marching bands, who played appropriate patriotic tunes. Thousands of onlookers watched from the footpaths. At O'Connell's funeral a group of traditional Irish women keeners gathered at a particular spot and broke into a traditional wail as the funeral passed. Parnell's funeral was watched by an estimated 50,000 people. These public displays were used as a means of asserting the growing strength of Irish nationalism. Today's marches tend to be held to highlight a particular cause; they continue to follow similar rituals – banners, marching bands, and the combination of campaigning with a social occasion.

Sport:

Interest in sport was and still is common to all walks of life, though until very recently women were relegated to the status of bystanders. Landlords and peasants shared a common interest in horse racing, and in ball games such as cricket and hurling; indeed many landlords supported teams on their estate, backing them against the teams of rival landlords. Traditional race meetings attracted people from all walks of life. During the nineteenth century, sports fixtures were gradually subject to more formal regulations, with a view to standardising rules for players and controlling anti-social behaviour. Traditional hurling games, such as the game played annually by Blasket islanders on the beach during the Christmas holidays – one half of the island against the other – could last a long time and result in many injuries. Faction fights were a

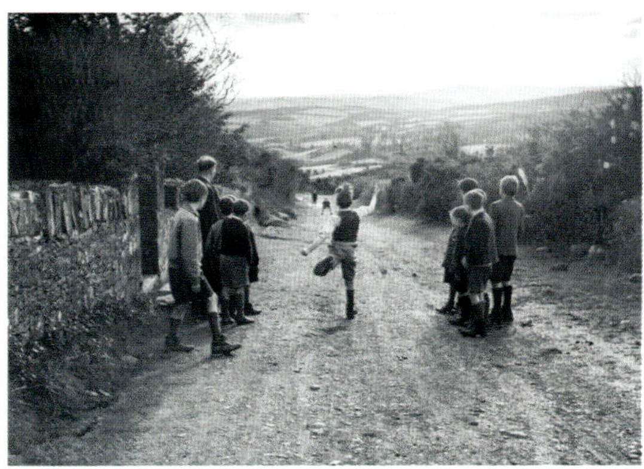

Fig 7. **Anonymous**, *Boys Road Bowling in Tipperary*

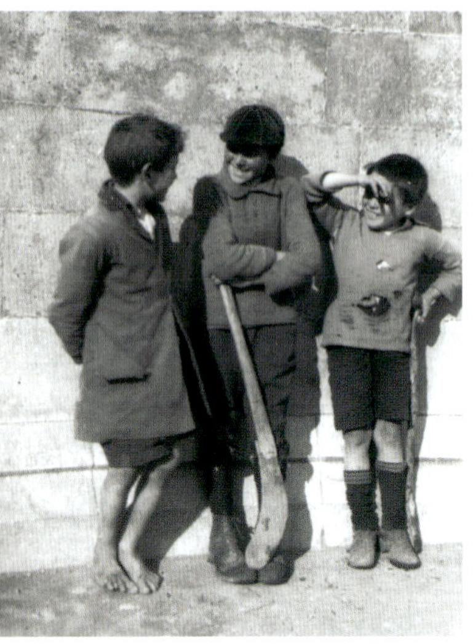

Fig 8. **Fr Frank Browne**, *Kilkenny Boys with Hurley Sticks*, 1920s

common feature of race meetings at Limerick in the early nineteenth century. By 1900 most race courses were enclosed, with fences designed to keep people out, and stands or enclosures catering for the more exclusive attendees.

The first standardised rules for hurling (1870) appear to have originated with the hurling club at Trinity College Dublin though the real impetus came with the establishment in 1884 of the Gaelic Athletic Association (GAA), an organisation soon represented throughout the country. The introduction of rules and regulations was closely linked with the emergence of sporting clubs and formal teams. Railways played a major role in creating national sporting events. Successful race courses tended to be located close to railway lines. Horses and punters travelled to race meets, the latter generally on specially reduced tickets. The development of national GAA competitions was also dependent on rail travel; many country youth first came to Dublin to watch their county play in an all-Ireland competition. Soccer was brought to Ireland by English skilled workers, especially those involved in railway engineering. By the eve of World War One, soccer attracted considerable support among urban workers. Golf was also becoming popular with the urban middle and professional classes. Sport, and supporting a county, a specific soccer team, or a national team were not just past-times; they helped to create a sense of identity.

Music, Dance and Popular Entertainment:

People have played and enjoyed music from the earliest times. Giraldus Cambrensis, a Welshman who came to Ireland with the Normans in the twelfth century, and who was no admirer of the native Irish, claimed that they were 'incomparably more skilled' musicians 'than any other people I have seen'. By the nineteenth century the harp- the national symbol – had been superseded by the much more portable fiddle and the pipe or flute. Music formed part of the entertainment in public houses, fairs, farm kitchens, cross-roads and the best drawing rooms. Church choirs, marching bands– often aligned to political organisations– were part and parcel of Irish life. Most middle-class families and respectable farmers wanted their daughters to show how accomplished they were at singing and playing the piano. Indeed some girls schools attracted pupils, not on the basis of examination results, but by the standing of their music teachers. The fashion for things Celtic helped to make traditional Irish airs respectable. Moore's melodies were played in the best drawing rooms throughout Europe. But airs from well-known operas or Gilbert and Sullivan were also popular. Touring opera companies filled theatres in Dublin and Cork, and amateur musical societies were found in most towns. Patriotic ballads have a long history; broadsheets giving the words could be bought for a penny or less at most fairs, and well-known tunes were often recycled with new words to honour a new hero or a new achievement.

Spontaneous dances were held in houses, at crossroads and other public places, with the music provided by a fiddler and perhaps one or two other musicians. Dancing masters, who taught the steps of set dances, polkas and jigs were a part of Irish social life that was common to the landlord's big house and the farmhouse alike. Landlords hired local musicians to play at weddings and other festive occasions. By the 1920s, however, dances were increasingly being held in public halls rather than in the home and dancers increasingly preferred jazz and quicksteps to more traditional polkas and reels. Church and state feared that there would be a decline in moral standards, because young couples would no longer be dancing under the watchful eye of parents or neighbours, so they were determined to introduce regulations. All dance places had to be licensed, and the state regulated when they could be held (no dances during Lent), and how late they could last. House dances – where those attending paid a small sum to the musicians – survived in some parts of Ireland until the 1950s, but most young people danced in parish halls, summer marquees and increasingly in large purpose-built ball-rooms.

Fig 9. **W.A. Green**, *'Wedding Maskers'. A Sligo Marriage Custom*, c.1910

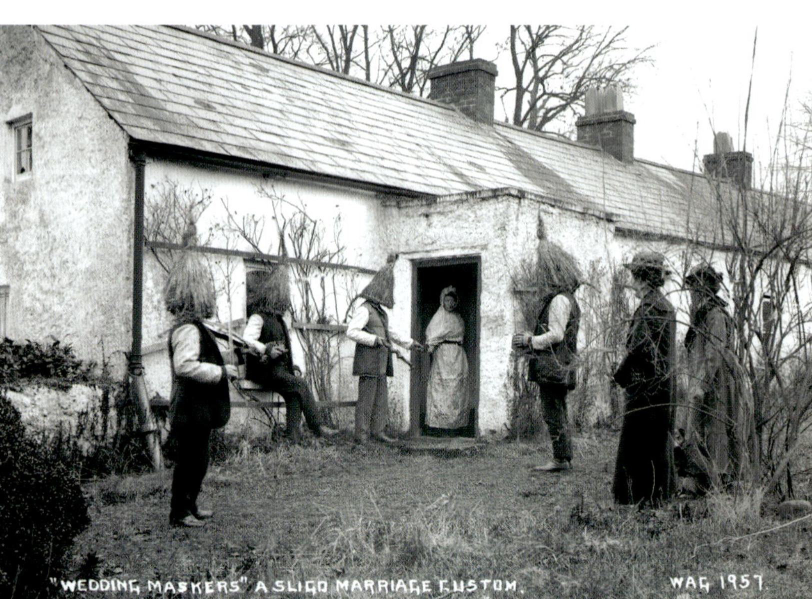

Bicycles and motor cars (often hackney cars hired for the evening) made it possible to travel some distance to a dance. When young people in rural Limerick were asked about dances in the early 1960s they explained that they preferred attending dances a long distance from home, where they would be free from the prying eyes of their neighbours.

During the 1920s dance halls were seen as unwelcome harbingers of modern culture, and it was widely feared that they would introduce jazz and other undesirable forms of modern music in place of Irish traditional music. By the 1960s Irish dance-halls had given birth to the showbands, and to a distinctive Irish variant of popular music. Irish traditional music was not a static entity; indeed it evolved to meet changing times and changing needs. During the 1920s ceilí bands with more than ten musicians began to replace the smaller two to three-man group, because they were better suited to playing music in public halls. The state-owned Radio Éireann, the only radio station broadcasting in Ireland, played an important role in keeping Irish traditional music alive. By the 1960s traditional music was attracting keen interest from younger people, who flocked to *fleadhanna cheoil*, and there was a revival of small groups, better suited to playing in pubs. Ballad singing also took on a new lease of life; part of an international ballad craze.

Cinema-going soon became one of the most popular Irish pastimes. Films were shown in purpose-built cinemas, in village halls and by the travelling cinemas that toured Ireland up to the 1950s. Dublin acquired a reputation as a major cinema-going city. Most films screened were made in the USA or in Britain, and they came under attack for promoting alien values, whereas many of the plays staged in Dublin theatres or by amateur groups were written by Irish playwrights.

The Irish tradition of the *cuaird*, where a group of men would meet regularly in a neighbouring house gradually disappeared during the twentieth century. The *cuaird* was an occasion for story-telling, gossip and card games, and perhaps for reading aloud from a local or national newspaper. These gatherings were dominated by men, with primacy given to older men. They occupied the most comfortable seat, near the fire. Younger men who were present were expected to listen to them in silence and with respect. The *cuaird* could be regarded as a rural version of the men's clubs that were found in cities and larger towns: working men's clubs, and clubs catering for professional men or landed gentry. They offered newspapers, card games, billiards and drink; an exclusively male environment and select membership.

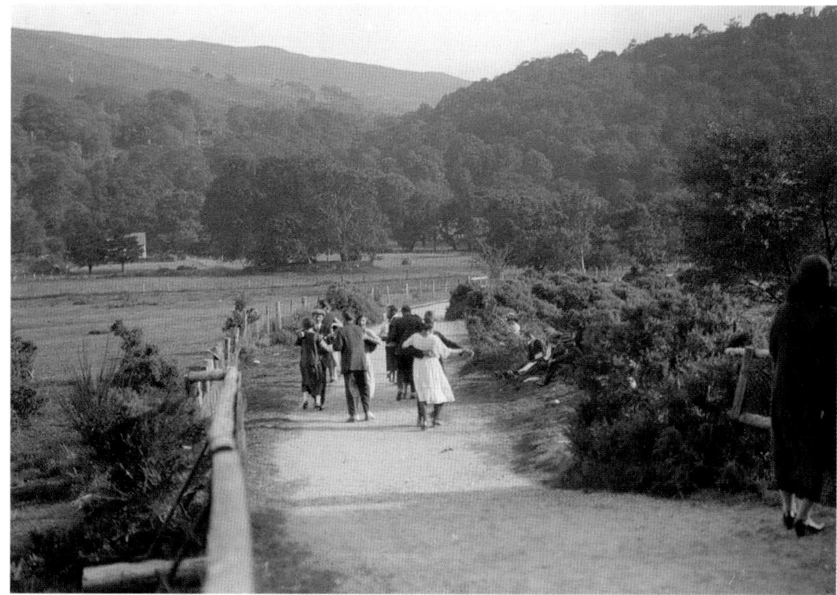

Fig 10. **Valentine & Sons**, *Dancing on the road, Glendalough, Co. Wicklow*

Women played no part in the *cuaird*: indeed some women actually resented the intrusion of male neighbours, with their muddy boots, into their family kitchen to spend the evening. In rural Ireland women did not traditionally pay casual visits to neighbours' homes, but they did visit on specific occasions– during the Christmas holiday period, or to attend a wake. When Rosemary Harris spoke to farming families in Ulster in the 1950s she was told that women loved a funeral, because it provided an opportunity to visit a neighbouring house and meet their neighbours. The Irish Countrywomen's Association and the Mothers' Union were among the few groups to provide outlets for respectable women to meet in a public place. It was only during the 1960s that it became common to see women in the lounge bars of public houses.

Young people traditionally met under the watchful eye of family and neighbours. The Irish tradition of match-making did not rule out couples falling in love, but for a marriage to go ahead with parental blessing the marriage partner generally had to be someone from a similar social standing. Parental disapproval could mean no dowry, and perhaps disinheritance from the family farm; in some cases this could prevent a couple from marrying. It was relatively easy for parents to control their children's social life and courtship when dances were held in neighbouring houses, and when the social occasions took place within the parish and the immediate community. One of the alleged attractions of Gaelic League classes around the turn of the century were the opportunities that they gave for young people to meet. It is uncertain when match-making disappeared in rural Ireland, but there were several factors that contributed to its decline. Motor cars, commercial dance halls and cinemas provided greater opportunities for young people to meet away from the control of parents or neighbours. Changes in work patterns were also important. As increasing numbers of young men and women found work outside the family farm or the family business, they gained both economic independence and a more independent social life.

Two Centuries of Irish Social Life:

One of the most interesting features of the past two hundred years has been the long cycle of increasing respectability and social conformity, and the gradual easing of these trends. At the beginning of the nineteenth century social life tended to be marked by drunkenness and rather unruly behaviour. Over the course of the nineteenth century however, respectability gained the upper hand, ably enforced by both church and state. Because of the slow pace of social change in Ireland, it was not until the 1960s that these forces were reversed. The *fleadheanna cheoil* or rock concerts of recent times have a lot more in common with Donnybrook Fair than with any mass gatherings in the early twentieth century. The Victorian Sunday, characterised by church-going and an absence of public entertainments (with the possible exception of a GAA match), has receded and Sundays now offer race meetings, shopping opportunities and busy pubs. Another important change can be seen in the more equal social lives of today's women, and the emergence of a very lively social life targeted at young people.

Fig 11. **Anonymous**, *Belfast Children Play in the Street*

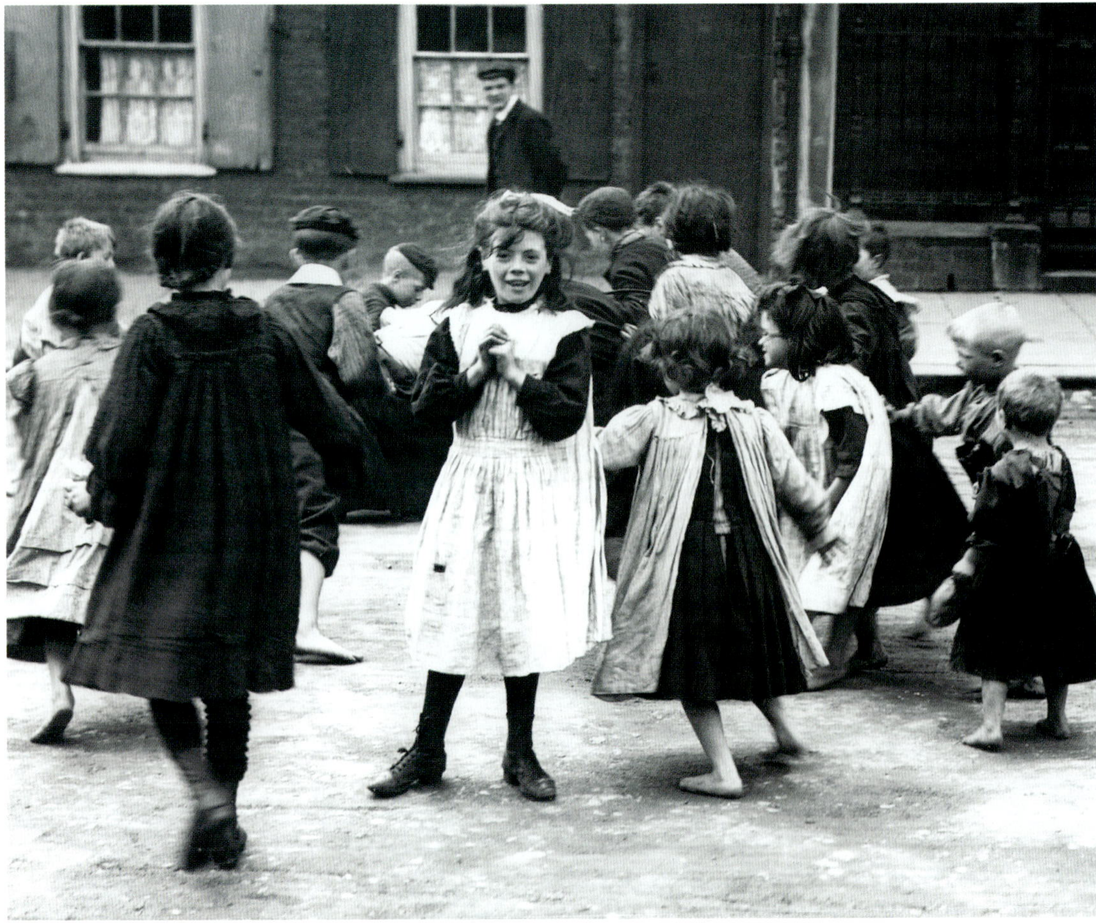

Books cited and further reading:

Conrad Arensberg,
The Irish Countryman,
(Gloucester, Massachusetts 1937).

Conrad Arensberg and Solon T. Kimball,
Family and Community in Ireland, second edition, (Cambridge, Mass. 1968).

Dominic Bryan,
Orange Parades: The Politics of Ritual, Tradition and Control, (2000).

Sean J. Connolly,
Priests and People in Pre-Famine Ireland,
(Dublin 1982).

T. Crofton Croker,
Researches in the South of Ireland, illustrative of the scenery, architectural remains , and the manners and superstitions of the peasantry,
(London 1824).

R. V. Comerford,
Inventing the Nation. Ireland,
(London 2003).

L.M. Cullen,
Six Generations: Life and Work in Ireland from 1790,
(Cork 1970).

L.M. Cullen,
Life in Ireland,
(Cork 1968).

Mary E. Daly, Mona Hearne and Peter Pearson,
Dublin's Victorian Houses,
(Dublin 1998).

Mary E. Daly.
The Slow Failure: Population Decline and Independent Ireland, 1922-1973
(Madison, Wisconsin 2006).

Kevin Danaher,
In Ireland long ago,
(Cork 1962).

Kevin Danaher,
The Year in Ireland,
(Cork 1972).

Fergus D'Arcy,
'The Decline and Fall of Donnybrook Fair: Moral Reform and Social Control in nineteenth-century Dublin',
Saothar, vol. 13, (1988).

Fergus D'Arcy,
Horses, Lords and Racing Men. The Turf Club 1790-1990,
(Dublin 1991).

Gustave de Beaumont,
Ireland: social, political and religious,
(Cambridge, Massachusetts 2006).

James S. Donnelly and David W. Miller, eds,
Irish Popular Culture, 1650-1850,
(Dublin 1998).

James S. Donnelly, Karl S. Bottigheimer, Mary E. Daly, James E. Doan and David W. Miller, eds,
Encyclopaedia of Irish History and Culture,
(New York 2004).

Tony Farmar,
Ordinary Lives. Three Generations of Irish Middle Class Experience,
(Dublin 1991).

Diarmaid Ferriter,
A Nation of Extremes. The Pioneers in Twentieth-century Ireland,
(Dublin 1999).

Rosemary Harris
Prejudice and Tolerance in Ulster. A Study of Neighbours and 'Strangers' in a Border Community,
(Manchester 1972).

Janice Holmes,
Religious Revivals in Britain and Ireland, 1859-1903,
(Dublin 2001).

K. Theodore Hoppen,
Elections, Politics and Society in Ireland, 1832-1885,
(Oxford 1984).

Jeremiah Newman, ed.,
The Limerick Rural Survey, 1958-1964,
(Tipperary 1964).

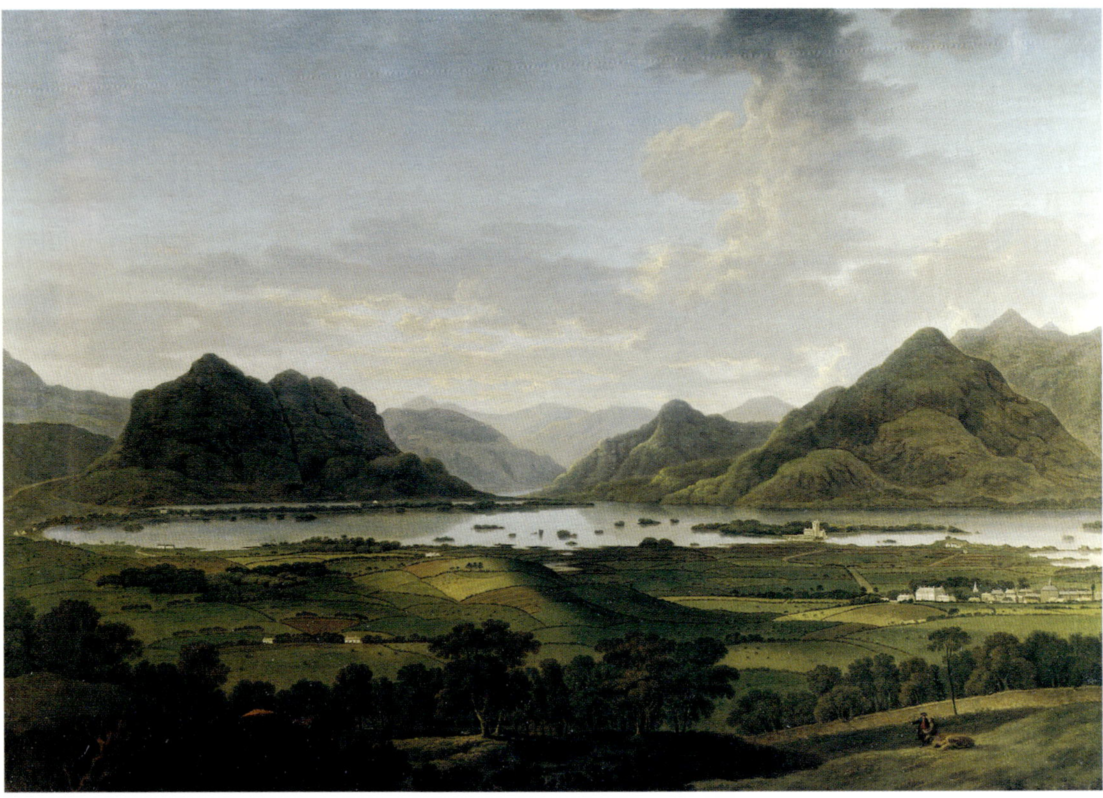

Fig 12. **Jonathan Fisher**, *View of the Lake of Killarney, from the Park of Kenmare House*, c.1770, oil on canvas, private collection

'A Very Minor Virtue'?

The Notion of Accuracy in Scenes of Irish Social Life

Brendan Rooney

From the eighteenth to the twentieth century, genre and landscape painters became increasingly preoccupied with affirming the veracity of their work. Many sought to demonstrate or imply in their pictures that they were familiar with a scene or had borne witness to an event, though traditionally the means by which they could do this were limited and controlled. The preeminence of concerns regarding the picturesque or dramatic qualities of landscape, the empirical requirements of topographical views, physiognomic exactitude of portraits, or the appropriate dressing, didacticism and in some cases decorum of history painting transcended any notion of personal experience.

The tradition by which artists included themselves in their paintings (apart from self-portraits) was longstanding but codified. Whether prominent or peripheral, malign or endorsing, this pictorial signature could be deliberate but not intrusive. Artists in Ireland adhered to this code, though over time the proposition 'I am a gentleman' in landscape painting and portraiture became in genre painting, variously, 'I have been here', 'I know these people', 'I have witnessed this event'. It is interesting to trace this gradual change from the eighteenth century onwards in the context of representations of Irish social life in particular because of the inclusive or participative nature of its subjects and the authenticity that proximity to them suggests. Moreover, it is worth considering the artistic consequences of this notion of bearing witness and the ultimate relevance of the authenticity or accuracy of pictures.

In Jonathan Fisher's panoramic view of the lower lake at Killarney of the late 1760s (fig.12), he presents himself sketching from a vantage point high above his subject while beside him a companion in tricorne hat appears to discuss his endeavour, gesturing with an outstretched hand at the surrounding countryside. The figures' isolated, diminutive presence communicates not only the expanse and picturesque splendour of the landscape, but also crucially proclaims the artist's familiarity with his subject and his integral role in its pictorial capture. Here the figures supplant the aristocratic characters that more commonly appear surveying such grand landscapes and demesnes.

Significantly, this claim to accuracy was not simply a personal impulse but a quality stressed in the

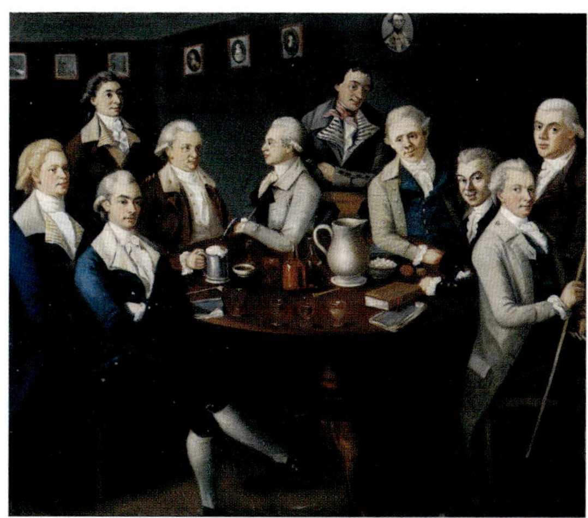

Fig 13. **Joseph Wilson,** *The Adelphi Club, Belfast*, 1783, oil on canvas, private collection

promotion of such work at the time. An advertisement in *Faulkner's Dublin Journal* of 5-8 November 1768 specified that Fisher had produced related prints 'having spent the greatest part of last Summer in Killarney taking Views of the much admired lakes'.[1] It was a judicious qualification, as many years later in 1801, the artist Joseph Farington recalled in his diary that while his friend Harden had thought Walmsley's views of Killarney 'by no means faithful' he considered Fisher's 'the most like'.[2]

Similarly, Gabriel Beranger depicted himself sitting comfortably and well dressed while engaged in the more empirical process of producing detailed drawings of Ballymount Tower and Castle for his 'Collection of Drawings of the Principal Antique Buildings of Ireland'. Though the purpose of these topographical drawings differed from Fisher's more elaborate views, here too the artist guaranteed their accuracy by asserting that they were also 'Designed on ye spot'.[3]

In some cases, artists used this device to claim more than mere intimacy with their physical surroundings, allowing their presence to denote social realities or aspirations. Anthony Chearnley appears in the foreground of his view of Kinsale not passively isolated but seated sketching in the company of modishly dressed women and similarly elegant men. Lest this desire to promote himself pictorially as a gentleman was not clear enough, he made sure to inscribe a print of Kinsale with 'Anthony Chearnly, Gen.'. Here, then, Chearnley presents himself not just as artist-witness, but as a gentleman, who both appreciated and shared the sensibilities of his elevated patrons.[4]

Joseph Wilson's group portrait of the Adelphi Club, for its part, is an unambiguous declaration by the artist of his membership of a social elite (fig.13). Gentlemen and high ranking artisans in the eighteenth century seized on any opportunity to commune, partly because of the freedom and ribaldry such social interaction afforded, but also because of the opportunities for attracting patronage it provided. Association of this kind was vital to an artist's professional prospects and, appropriately, Wilson portrayed himself prominently, mahlstick and palette in hand, among his fellow members of the Belfast club.

The desire to count oneself among one's elevated patrons found full expression in the latest known self-portrait by Nathaniel Hone, in which he appears as a country squire (fig.14).[5] Where before he was satisfied to present himself as a confident, successful practitioner, here he celebrated what he saw as his arrival among the elite that constituted his clientele. A hunting dog at his elbow and walking stick in hand suggest gentlemanly pursuits, while the pedestal against which he leans and the classical building in the background point to erudition and refined sensibility. Most significantly perhaps, Hone places himself implausibly in an Italianate landscape to which, assuming a pose akin to that of the Apollo Belvedere, he appears to lay claim. He also classicises and immortalises his wife on the plinth against which he rests his elbow.

This image is, of course, fanciful. Urban by nature and circumstance, Hone never became the squire he presents, and the landscape is patently capricious, but the picture resonates with the artist's desire to position himself socially.

Fig:14. **Nathaniel Hone**, *Self-portrait*, oil on canvas, National Gallery of Ireland

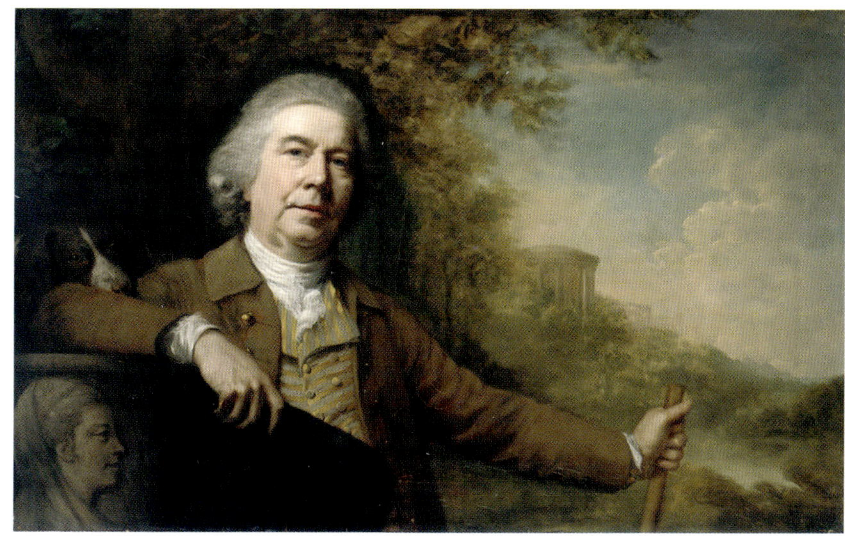

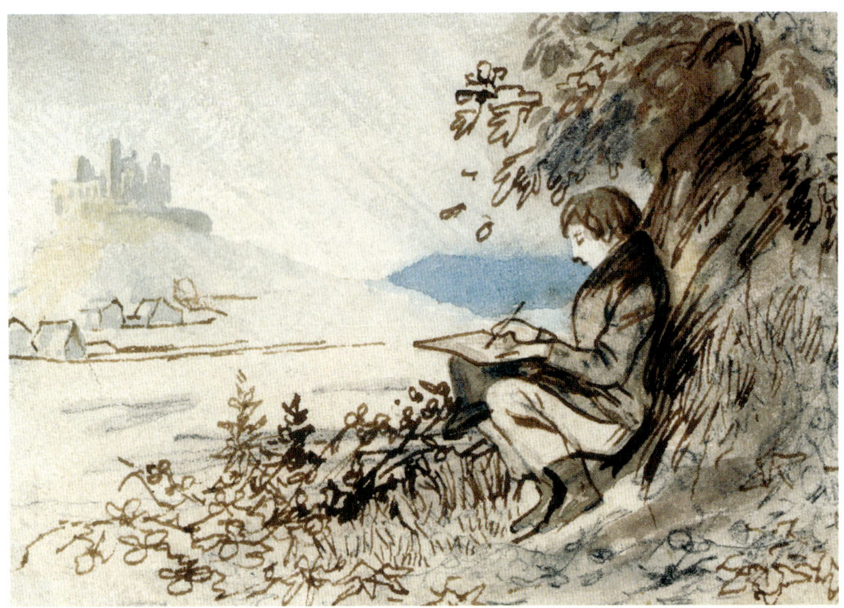

Fig 15. **Daniel Maclise**, *The Artist Sketching the Rock of Cashel*, c.1826, pen and ink wash on paper, V&A

These landscapes and portraits, while affording artists the opportunity to claim familiarity with and access to the subject, were also exercises in self-aggrandisement and demonstrations of social standing. Painting grand demesnes and gentlemen's clubs, and by extension enjoying the associated patronage, were privileges enjoyed by few. The visible presence of the artist at this point did not, however, indicate for those with their eyes fixed firmly on the upper echelons of society an engagement with any of the so-called 'lower orders'.

As patronage and artistic tastes and patterns changed in the nineteenth century, however, so did the professional opportunities presented to artists in Ireland and the emergence of their role as chroniclers. The dissolution of traditional lines of demarcation between genres gave rise to new hybrid picture types that drew on landscape, genre and history painting traditions. In Ireland this transition coincided with a burgeoning interest in antiquarianism and Ireland's ancient history, the popularisation of scenes of everyday life through prints and book illustration, the flux that characterised Irish politics and society, and a significant shift in the nature of patronage following the Act of Union. This move towards subjects drawn from everyday life was more sizeable than sudden - Nathaniel Grogan among others had anticipated it decades earlier - but gathered momentum as the century unfolded.

The naturalism and apparent authenticity of Daniel Maclise's and James Arthur O'Connor's studies of themselves sketching outdoors are consistent with the incipient image of the practising artist as independent and free-spirited (figs.15 and 16). Differences in media and scale notwithstanding, these pictures, Maclise's depiction of himself immersed in the landscape in particular, differ fundamentally from Fisher's and Chearnley's placement of themselves in grander views. While in those earlier pictures the presence of the artist is emblematic, qualifying both the scale of the surroundings and the status of the artist, Maclise and O'Connor's sketches focus on their practical occupation. The credibility of Maclise's study lies to some extent in the rather arbitrary and uncomfortable-looking station he assumes under a tree in the Tipperary countryside. No such element of chance is evident in Fisher's or Chearnley's pictorial manifestoes. Moreover, Maclise's study tallies with what is known of his early activity. Thomas Crofton Croker recalled Maclise's accounts of visits to local landmarks in Cork with his fellow student Samuel Forde, which included all-day sketching excursions to Kilcrea Friary and Carrigrohane Castle. [6]

The importance of accuracy and authenticity for artists remained, but was now manifest in an increasingly documentary or narrative approach to subject matter that echoed inclinations among writers, poets and playwrights to record everyday life in Ireland. Writers like William Carleton and Mr and Mrs Hall sought, with varying degrees of success and conviction, to describe in detail the lives of ordinary people, those unheralded and previously often lampooned labourers, merchants, clergy and local professionals of rural Ireland. Carleton, who Barbara Hayley identified as a 'peasant author' who 'knew [his] subjects from within' might have provided an interesting model for artist contemporaries.[7] He set himself vehemently against the 'gross and overcharged caricature' of the stage 'Paddy' that had been promulgated and popularised in England by writers over generations.[8] Moreover, his resolve was borne of first-hand experience, and his activities in his early years represent an animated profile of Irish social life. He recalled:

I now mingled in the sports and pastimes of the people, until indulgence in them became the predominant passion of my youth. Throwing the stone, wrestling, leaping, foot-ball, and every other description of athletic exercise filled up the measure of my early happiness. I attended every wake, dance, fair, and merry-making in the neighbourhood, and became so celebrated for

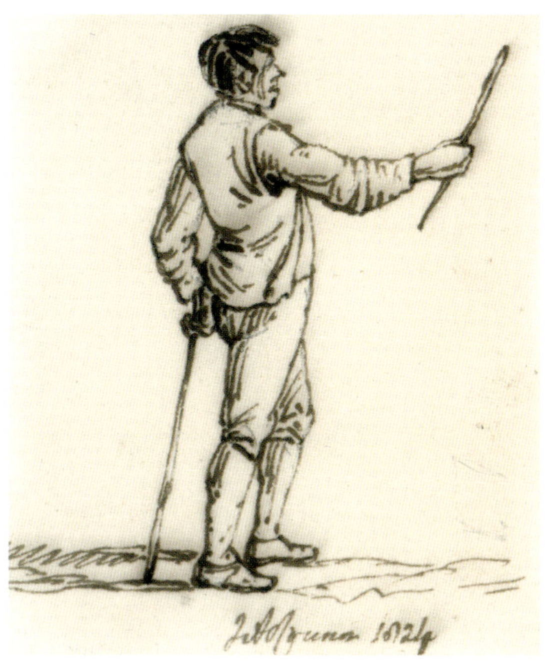

Fig 16. **James Arthur O'Connor,** *Self-portrait*, 1824, pen and ink on paper, National Self-portrait Collection, University of Limerick

dancing hornpipes, jigs, and reels, that I was soon without a rival in the parish.[9]

Though some authors, like Carleton, expressly desired to avoid clichés, the scenes they described, and their pictorial equivalents, were often contrived, melodramatic, and at times pejorative in tone, but they also bore, either implicitly or explicitly the fingerprint of those who committed them to paper and canvas. Thus, where Fisher and Chearnley had made a *general* claim to familiarity with their subjects, a new generation of artists began to mimic their literary contemporaries by invoking specific experience, or at least attempting to do so. Mrs Hall was conscious of the artistic potential of such enterprise, opining that 'perhaps no country in the world is so rich in materials for the PAINTER; nowhere can he find more admirable subjects for his pencil, whether he studies the immense varieties of nature, or human character as infinitely varied'.[10] Rural Ireland, she maintained, was a place in which 'every peasant the artist will encounter, furnishes a striking and picturesque sketch'.[11] As Tom Dunne has pointed out, several writers of the early nineteenth century, from Maria Edgeworth to Gerald Griffin and Lady Morgan endorsed this notion further by introducing itinerant artists into their popular novels.[12] These characters, however, like the writers themselves, were normally portrayed as observers, outsiders, practical voyeurs whose contact with rural life was relatively superficial. Samuel McCloy (cat.3) and Trevor Thomas Fowler (cat.4), among others, catered unapologetically for the appetite among the art-buying public for sentimental and picturesque Irish genre scenes. Genuine though their intentions may have been, the veracity of their records was predicated by their own expectations and the appetite of their audience. They resemble the playwright Dion Boucicault, who 'devoted a vigorous lifetime to giving the people what he believed they wanted- an extravaganza of melodramatic plots, comic characters, and music-hall entertainment' and attributed deficiencies in his work to the limitations of his audience.[13] Vestiges of this phenomenon lingered, and such was the draw of the west of Ireland by the 1920s, for example, that many naturalists, travel writers, poets, painters and polemicists discovered the primitive, pagan, Christian, Gaelic and elemental qualities that they expected to find there.

It would be simplistic to dismiss the accuracy of pictorial testimony merely on the grounds of theatricality and the demands of the market, however. Several works by accomplished painters point to a genuine desire to capture the actuality of personal experience. Maria Spilsbury Taylor lived in privileged circumstances and encountered everyday life in Ireland from the sequestered confines of the country house. Numerous stately piles, including Cronroe Lodge, Ballycurry and Glanmore Castle, and portraits of their resident families and servants feature within the pages of her sketchbooks and informed her more elaborate oil paintings. Significantly, however, these sketchbooks do not record exclusively the elevated social circles of which she was a member, but also record contiguous local communities.[14] The scope of her themes may be limited, but her sketchbooks and oil paintings, such as *John Wesley Preaching in Ireland* (cat.32), *Wedding Dance at Rosanna* (cat.33) and *Pattern at Glendalough, Co. Wicklow* (cat.81), testify to a sincere curiosity about those social junctures at which life in the big house and that in the surrounding communities overlapped. Furthermore, in her depiction of John Wesley preaching, Taylor, in a predictably polite and understated way, sought to bear witness to this convergence. Her placement alongside recognisable local figures of members of her own family celebrated a shared community and sense of location. Contrived, and wholly unhistorical- Wesley had died over two decades earlier- this was nevertheless an interesting artistic gesture. As Wesley was one of a number of preachers invited by Mrs Tighe to preach in Wicklow, her work is as much genre as history painting, recording a familiar episode in the lives of a local community rather than an historical event *per se*.[15] It is also interesting that at a time when numerous writers were more inclined to

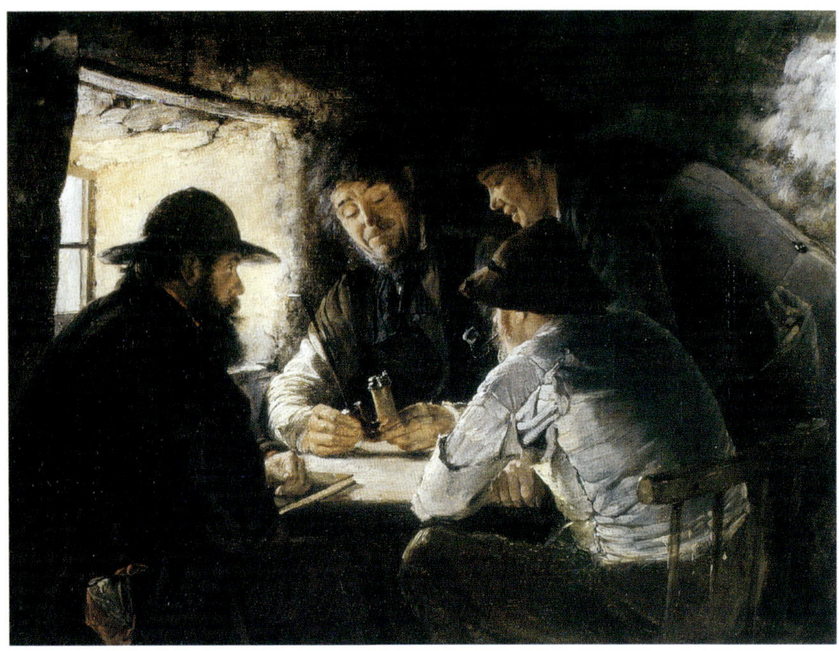

Fig 17. **Erskine Nicol,** *An Interior, Westmeath Cabin*, oil on canvas, private collection

indulge the stereotype of Irish rural society as inherently picturesque but unruly, Taylor, in keeping with her evangelical background, depicted one small section at least as gregarious and devout.[16]

Erskine Nicol's relationship with Ireland and related works have arguably been misunderstood in recent years. His name is invariably invoked in discussions of the pictorial popularisation of the 'stage Paddy' in Victorian art and illustration. It has been suggested, for example, that as Nicol was 'neither a member of [Irish-speaking] society nor sympathetic toward it', he was 'hardly inclined to give us an accurate ethnographic presentation of an Irish *seanchaidhe*'.[17] Projecting views expressed in contemporary Scottish journalism and literature on to Nicol on the basis of nationality alone, this argument concludes that the artist was thoroughly convinced of the inferiority of the Gaelic race, whether Scottish or Irish. Admittedly, much of Nicol's work betrays a tendency towards indulging that particular stereotype, but several other pictures within the oeuvre of this prolific artist suggest a more ingenuous and considered view. Nicol enjoyed not a passing encounter with Ireland, but rather a longstanding relationship, and it appears that he was most sensitive when representing people, places and events well known to him personally.[18] He built a lodge and studio on the island of Clonave in Lake Derravaragh, County Westmeath, and painted various local genre subjects and landscapes.[19] At least five of the twelve paintings that Nicol included in the Exhibition of Fine and Ornamental Arts in Dublin in 1861 were scenes of Westmeath,[20] and such was Nicol's affection for this spot that he called his residence in London 'Clonave Villa'.[21]

Nicol was less inclined to distance himself from the community that he knew well than is implied by many of his commercial paintings. Most notably, in a signal painting, *Interior, Westmeath Cabin* (fig.17), Nicol placed himself amongst locals in a scene of relaxed and convincing *bonhomie*.[22] Sitting with his back to the viewer and a sketchbook in front of him, he observes his company intently, as they in turn study a meerschaum that one assumes belongs to the artist. One might argue reasonably that the meerschaum is presented as something sophisticated when juxtaposed with the simple clay pipes of the locals, just as the artist seems urbane in humble company. Similarly, Nicol's clothing, fine and intact, contrasts starkly with the ragged attire of the man sitting opposite. However, the picture represents a significant departure in Nicol's work and more generally in Irish genre painting in terms of the subjects that might now be considered worthy of attention and the proximity of the artist to them. Fisher and Chearnley would certainly not have entertained such a subject. Daniel Maclise, for his part, having been delayed on his return from a day's sketching with Forde, was invited to share a supper with a peasant family that they found 'assembled round a table of smoking potatoes'.[23] He described graphically to Croker that he and his fellow artist had stayed with the family, sleeping on a 'miserable bed, covered with a ragged piece of patchwork', but this mundane episode would have been for Maclise the stuff of anecdote not art.[24] The setting of Nicol's social, interactive scene within a local cottage tells us as much perhaps about the complexity of his relationship with Ireland as do his vulgarly phonetic titles (which themselves owe a debt to the likes of Boucicault and Mrs Hall) and commercially-oriented images of the gormless 'Paddy'. In the context of this and other more serious paintings and studies in watercolour by Nicol, Lional G. Robinson's faint praise of the artist's ability to depict 'with telling vigour the wretchedness of the Irish peasantry' seems strangely inadequate.[25]

The accommodation of a conservative audience, meanwhile, did not itself denote an obfuscation of physical reality. Richard Thomas Moynan, like Taylor, was an inveterate sketcher, who filled pocket-sized notebooks with dynamic ideas for poses and compositions, and was meticulous in his description of detail while appearing to have maintained a professional distance from both his rural and urban subjects.[26] His sketchbooks, which indicate rapid but careful application, informed his naturalistic, if anodyne salon works like *A Travelling Show* (cat.40) and the perennially popular *Military Manoeuvres* (NGI). Despite the presence of many ostensibly rural subjects within his oeuvre, Moynan cut a distinctly urban figure. He epitomised the pragmatic, professional artist: well-connected, reliable, accessible and alert to the wishes of his audience. His capacity to gauge prevailing tastes in Dublin was evinced by the consistently laudatory manner in which his contributions to the annual RHA exhibitions were discussed by critics in the major Irish broadsheets. He held a firm position within Irish art establishment circles, sitting on the committee of the Dublin Art Club, serving as president of the Dublin Sketching Club and contributing regularly to the Royal Hibernian Academy. He was also a member of the Grand Lodge of Freemasons.[27] Holding such positions ensured that he avoided distancing himself from his clientele and peers.

Conversely, familiarity with subjects did not necessarily lead to works of human interest. G.M.W. Atkinson's intimate acquaintance with the maritime world did not inspire him to record its social diversity but rather the landscapes and engineering associated with it. The human interest in *A Boating Party in Cork Harbour* (cat.54) is revealing, but almost incidental in the context of Atkinson's work. His professional background and amateur artistic training rather than any desire to adhere to or reject artistic orthodoxy underpinned his approach to maritime subjects drawn from a world of which he was a part. He was born in Cobh, a harbour town he painted on many occasions, and trained as a ship's carpenter, a capacity in which he spent many years at sea.[28] On his return to Cork, he served as Inspector of Shipping and Emigrants, and developed further an advanced understanding of boats and shipping, from fabric to function. Occasionally, his desire to describe vessels meticulously outstripped his technical abilities, but his importance as a conscientious recorder of Ireland's maritime history is beyond question.

Subjects that one might imagine would invite an investigation of human experience did not always do so. Lough Derg, for example, did not inspire Sir John Lavery artistically in the way that his written accounts might suggest (cat.36). This may well have been attributable to the fact that, on his own admission, he found it difficult to engage with the social dynamic that prevailed there, conceding that as his faith 'did not tempt me to follow the example of the pilgrims', he contented himself with the idea that the Prior saw his artistic endeavour as a 'another way of showing the grace of God and another of His great mercy'.[29]

As subjects in Irish figurative painting became more democratic in the twentieth century, empathy or the desire for it might be said to have exercised a greater influence on painters. In assembling the most comprehensive pictorial record of troubled vibrant, industrial and social Belfast of any artist of his generation, William Conor proved himself irresistibly drawn to the human, social realities of everyday life. A 'city man' (though of a kind quite different to Richard Thomas Moynan), he captured a sense of community and camaraderie that transcended the austerity of the times and the hardship endured by those working in city industry or on the land. [30] This was often achieved through the recording of times of leisure, respite or recreation, which may not have been considerable but were essential to community spirit and to the maintenance of ties of friendship and family. Conor's corpus of work, though uneven, represents a resolute commitment to recording ordinary life, particularly in Belfast, in all its richness, adversity and humanity.

Curiously, however, though he too was an habitual sketcher, Conor appears to have kept a discreet distance from his subjects. Chronicling life unobtrusively, he left a voluminous collection of drawings that Jonathan Bell has said 'leaves the impression of detached scrutiny, rather than impassioned engagement'.[31] He is even understood to have employed such clandestine methods of observation as sketching subjects from behind a newspaper.[32] John Hewitt's bold claim for Conor's ability to mediate between viewer and subject is one to which many figurative artists would have aspired.[33] But it was perhaps Conor's apparent facility in removing himself from the subject that marked him as a social observer. Admittedly, it is a quality that to the contemporary eye is often strongly redolent of photography. In some of his studies of urban characters, such as *Ready for Action* (Queen's University Belfast Art Collection), in which a group of young girls sit on a park bench clutching tennis rackets, and *Queue for the Picture House* (fig.18), his subjects giggle and squirm at the attentions of the painter as they might under the inanimate purview of a camera. However, as Bell has argued,

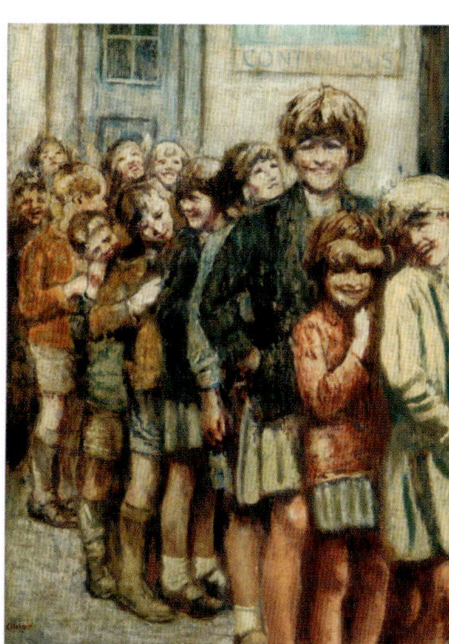

Fig 18. **William Conor,** *Queue for the Picture House (Shankill Road, Belfast)*, 1930-34, Oil on canvas, Ulster Folk and Transport Museum

what is particularly interesting about Conor's drawings, produced surreptitiously in many cases, is that through them one is 'looking at the artist's view of observed reality, rather than a reality which is also mediated by the way in which human subjects presented themselves to the artist'.[34]

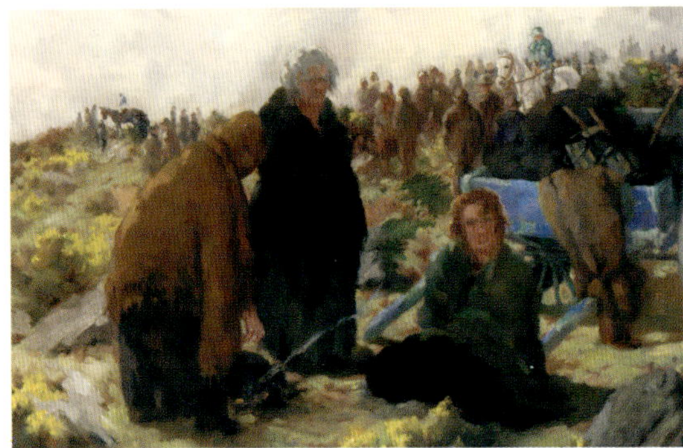

Fig 19. **Lilian Lucy Davidson,** *The Country Races*, oil on canvas, private collection (detail)

It has been suggested that due to the material hardships endured by Lilian Lucy Davidson and her family compared with the comfortable circumstances of most of her fellow female artists, she empathised with her peasant and working-class subjects.[35] Speculative though this may be, it is interesting to note the manner in which Davidson appears to have included herself sitting by a cart and wrapped in a shawl in a distinctly melancholy painting entitled *The Country Races* (fig.19). She presents herself as neither indigent artist nor transient visitor but as just another member of the crowd, thereby making an apparently genuine claim to membership of the rural masses.[36]

Fig 20. **Gerard Dillon,** *Island People*, oil on canvas, Crawford Municipal Art Gallery, Cork

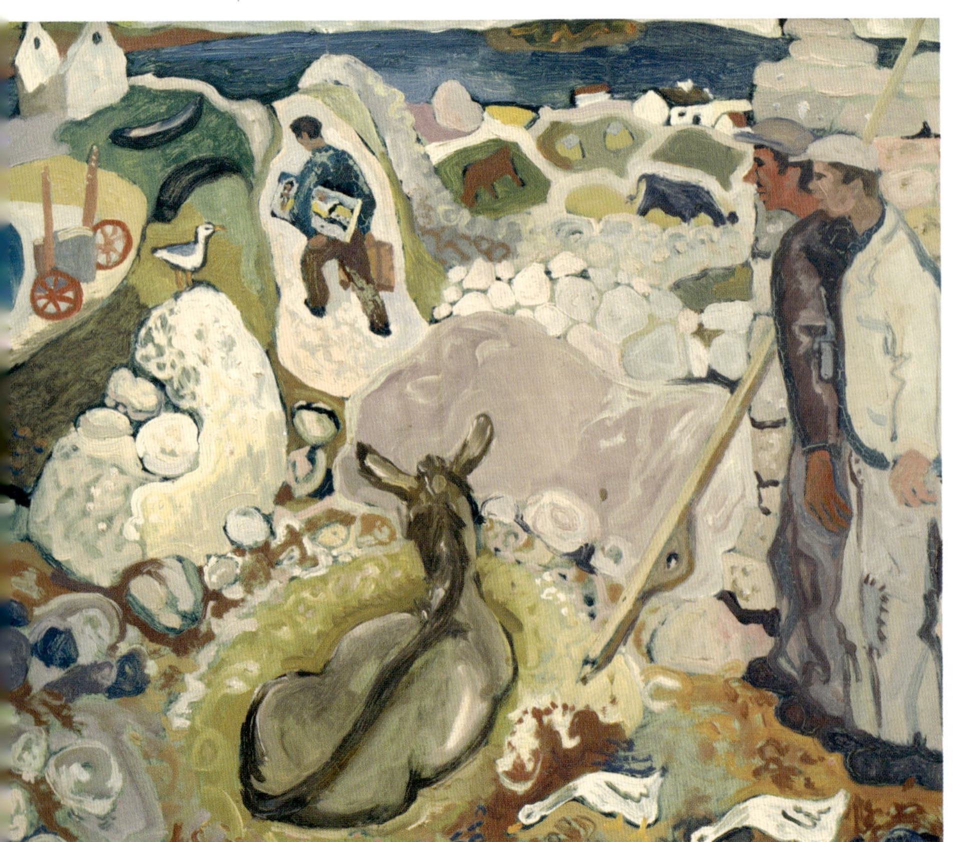

The search for reality or accuracy in art is a subjective and inconclusive one. For example, the authenticity of the artist's experience was not necessarily diluted by inaccuracies in local detail. Indeed, artistic licence allowed artists in many instances to enrich and broaden their testimony. Letitia Hamilton included donkeys tethered to the wall in her view of Monasterevin despite the fact that the market square, the setting for her picture, remained entirely open until the 1950s (cat. 78).[37] However, her inclusion of the animals as an integral part of the scene is wholly consistent with her memory of both the place and the social event.[38] Similarly, Jack B. Yeats depicted the Liffey Swim under a blue sky despite the fact that it had rained throughout the event in the year in which he painted the picture (fig. 21).

Yeats's experience as an illustrator for the popular press and his innate curiosity about people and community undoubtedly influenced his development as chronicler and actualist. However, it is clear that he appreciated the mediated nature of painting, the principle that the recording of everyday life was not an unconscious act but the product of numerous judicious choices, memories and experiences. 'A picture which is true,' he declared 'is the memory of a moment which once was as it appears to the artist'.[39] Nor did this necessarily mean verifiable memory. Yeats did not draw exclusively on his own experience, but seemingly on accumulated evidence and the testimony of others, such as his friend J.M. Synge. Hence, for his representation of a funeral on the Blaskets he appears to have drawn both on his own knowledge of Kerry and the descriptions of Synge (cat. 37).

Yeats responded principally to the social, collective nature of these events and communicated it skillfully in his work. In both *Before the Start* and *An Island Funeral*, he involves the viewer in the event, and in *The Liffey Swim* seems to place himself in the heart of the crowd, simultaneously bearing witness to the event and affirming his role as recorder of Dublin life.

Elizabeth Rivers's *Stranger in Aran*, with its unambiguous title and evocative and distinctly

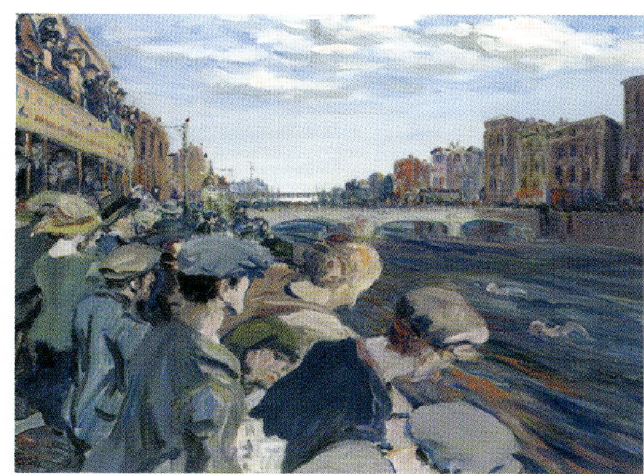

Fig 21. **Jack B. Yeats,** *The Liffey Swim*, 1923, oil on canvas, National Gallery of Ireland

pictorial style, complements her paintings. Indeed, much of it reads like an intentionally corroborative text, composed to legitimise her pictorial output and demonstrate further her experience of the islands and their inhabitants. Moreover, it also seems to confirm the veracity of the work of some of Rivers's close contemporaries, such as James Humbert Craig, whose people walking and cycling to mass (cat. 35), for example, seem reminiscent of the characters Rivers describes collecting seaweed on the shore at Cowrugh[40] or the working men she mentions whose pale clothes 'were lost in the distance being much like the walls'.[41]

From 1950 to 1951, Gerard Dillon spent a year working on the Island of Innislaken, accompanied by George Campbell.[42] While Campbell frequently wore a beret, a familiar item of artistic garb, Dillon adopted the image of the western islander, even going to the lengths of making his own tweed caps, which he wore almost at all times. The west suited him: as an artist, he was drawn to pattern, colour and texture, with which it abounded, while as a personality he was gregarious and a talented raconteur and ballad singer. He was professionally astute, recognising that patronage often resided in cities, and exhibited accordingly, but returned as much by instinct as volition to the rural areas that were such a rich quarry for him.

However, though Dillon was fascinated by the culture and character of people of the west, Connemara and the Aran Islands in particular, he like Rivers was conscious of his alien status among them. Rather than disengaging from his subject or feigning inclusion, however, Dillon chose to communicate this experience unambiguously in his painting *Island People* (fig. 20) in which he presents himself walking along a *bóithrín* with the ostensibly incongruous trappings of the artist, a case in one hand and an easel under the other, as two island fishermen watch him curiously from behind a wall.[43] This sense of difference was among the principal factors that drew artists like Dillon, Henry and Lamb back to the west, to a world that though geographically close was socially and physically different, but Dillon's expression of his alien status is both novel and disarmingly honest. Historically, Irish artists seemed disinclined to acknowledge their separation from their subjects. Worsdale and Yeats placed themselves among the crowds they recorded, while others implied their presence merely by the proximity of their viewpoint.

In twentieth-century figurative painting in Ireland, it was common for artists to circumvent the notion of belonging by merely implying presence and involvement in everyday scenes through the composition and orientation of viewpoint. Many of the works in this exhibition celebrate activities as distinctly social events by acknowledging, and in numerous cases emphasising their observational as well as their participative dimensions. Thus Paul Henry marks the inclusive nature of a local dance in Achill by producing what one can read as synchronous images of a single event, observed from within (cat.8, 9 and 10).

In *The Olympia*, Maurice MacGonigal bore witness to Dublin theatre as if by proxy, depicting his friend Harry Kernoff in the shadows near the stage (fig 22). Indeed, the performance, which conventionally might have been the subject of the picture, is strangely peripheral. As if to emphasise his and Kernoff's intimate knowledge of the theatre, MacGonigal has rendered the actors pictorially only as important as the fabric of the auditorium, the musicians and the audience.

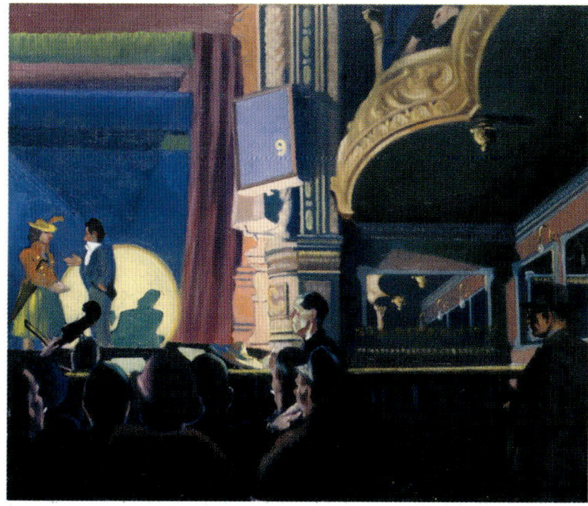

Fig 22. **Maurice MacGonigal,** *The Olympia*, oil on canvas, Ulster Museum

Fiction and theatricality underpin many of these images of social life, just as they did the above mentioned exaggerated texts of the nineteenth century. Traditionally, genre and history compositions could be said to be theatrical in the sense that fundamental principles of display applied, which included making sure that the chief protagonists or figures of interest faced the viewer or at least did not obscure each other. A simple example of this is the orientation of figures around three sides of a table so that they are all visible to the audience, as is the case from Wilson's *Adelphi Club, Belfast* (cat. 66) to Kavanagh's *Gambling for a Goose* (cat. 47) and Hanlon's *Recreation* (cat. 48). Lamb was fascinated by the people of the west of Ireland, in whom he believed was to be found 'the national essence', but his picture *Dancing at a Northern Crossroads* (cat. 7) was unapologetically theatrical and painted far away from the world that inspired it.[44] Elsewhere, this tradition was eschewed by the interruption of the view by figures with their backs to the viewer, as one sees in Lilian Davidson's *Fashions at the Fair* (cat. 77). Paradoxically, though this is more naturalistic in theory, it can have the effect of placing the viewer outside the activity, notionally observing from within the same physical space but actually excluded from it.

Curiously, some early twentieth-century Irish art criticism was defined by a demand for witness and accuracy that would have been more readily satisfied in the nineteenth century. Thomas MacGreevy, for example, was unnerved by Paul Henry's peasants, referring to them as 'those hideous elementals standing on a hilltop'. [45] They were not peasants, he maintained, but 'wanderers from that world of Neo-Romanticism, or unreal Realism, to which the characters of Strindberg's plays belong'.[46] As S.B. Kennedy has pointed out, MacGreevy would have been happier perhaps with Keating's and MacGonigal's Social-realist manner, the origins of which date back almost a century, but which was in fact equally theatrical.

Just as one is encouraged to perceive Erskine Nicol's images as fundamentally flawed, in the case of other conspicuous artists, one is faced with the problem of embracing the authenticity of their work out of hand. Paul Henry's work provides an interesting case, as the Irish audience has grown used to accepting its verisimilitude. However, as S.B. Kennedy has acknowledged, 'there is no way of either depicting, or reading, the world except by depicting it *in a certain style*'.[47] This truism makes Dorothy Walker's blunt conclusions on Henry's work all the more interesting. 'There are days,' she wrote 'when the Irish landscape does look like a Paul Henry, undoubtedly, but his paintings never look like the Irish landscape'.[48] The same might be said of all the figurative painters represented in this exhibition in the sense that their works are necessarily mediated records or personal impressions.

Jack B. Yeats maintained that 'those painters who have the greatest affection for their country and their own people will paint them best', a principle that transcends stark notions of accuracy of detail.[49] Nor was Yeats alone in this belief. Thomas Bodkin maintained that the 'pervading harmony of outlook' identifiable in the individuals represented in Victor Waddington's *Twelve Irish Artists* (1940), who conspicuously did not include Yeats, was attributable in part to the fact that they drew their inspiration 'from scenery and human types which are to them familiar and beloved'.[50] It is interesting to consider if, ultimately, such claims are in fact so far removed from Nicol's conceit in placing himself in a Westmeath cabin or Beranger's guarantee of the authenticity of pictures produced on the spot.

Considering the multiplicity of factors that determined artists' access to and interpretation of subjects, from patronage and taste to class and professional ambition, authenticity and accuracy become deeply complex considerations. One must always make allowance for the singular vision of the artist. 'How could I see things the same as another man?' wrote William Conor, ' And why should I? With a piece of charcoal in my hand I might make a drawing of a woman's arm, but no other human being could make a drawing exactly similar, because something of me had gone into the making of that drawing. And what does accuracy mean in any case? It is a very minor virtue'.[51] None of the recorders of Irish life featured in this exhibition can be said to have approached their subjects with an innocent eye, despite their documented familiarity with the subject, or the authenticity afforded by their physical or implied presence. The variety of testimony that these scenes of social life represent and the relativity of their pictorial language are fascinating subjects in their own right.

Footnotes

1 Quoted in Laffan 1999, p.40.

2 Farington 1978-85, vol. IV, p. 1482 (14 January 1801). Quoted in Figgis and Rooney 2001, p.145.

3 National Library of Ireland, MS 1958 TX. The artist's benign presence is mitigated somewhat by the fact that a musket lies by his side in both drawings.

4 Elsewhere, Chearnley included the 'neat residence he built for himself' in a view of the ruins of the castle of Burnt Court, County Tipperary that was engraved for Francis Grose's seminal *Antiquities of Ireland* of 1791-95. See Crookshank and Glin 2002, p.75

5 For further discussion of this picture, see Figgis and Rooney 2001, p.235-36.

6 Thomas Crofton Croker, *Recollections of Cork*, c.1833, unpublished MS, TCD, pp.276- Library, MS No. 1206.

7 Barbara Hayley, 'Foreword' in Carleton 1990, p.5.

8 *ibid*, p.i.

9 *ibid*, pp.xv-xvi.

10 Hall 1843, vol.3, p.392.

11 *ibid*, p.393.

12 Dunne 2006, pp.53-54.

13 Krause 1972, p.12.

14 Among her sketches is one starkly inscribed 'An Irish rebel who threatened to murder Mrs Tighe'.

15 For a comprehensive discussion of the relationship between Taylor and the Tighe family, see Yeldham 2005.

16 For a discussion of the notion of the picturesque in the repre sentation of the Irish peasant, see Dunne 2006.

17 John T. Koch, 'When a Seanchaidhe is not a Seanchaidhe and a Paddy is not a Paddy', in Dalsimer and Kreilkamp 1996, p.23.

18 Nicol travelled to Ireland first in 1846, and during this initial four-year sojourn taught art in Dublin. Over subsequent decade, he returned many times.

19 Nicol's landscapes in Ireland range from views in Meath, Wicklow and Connemara.

20 All but one of these were lent by Andrew Amstrong MRIA, Nicol's faithful patron who delivered a speech at the opening of his studio on Clonave in 1862. Wallace 1987, p.240

21 See Brendan Rooney, 'Erskine Nicol', in *Gorry Gallery, Dublin*, exh. cat. (June 2001), pp.14-17.

22 See Brendan Rooney, 'Erskine Nicol', in *Gorry Gallery, Dublin*, exh. cat. (February 2003), pp.30-31.

23 Thomas Crofton Croker, *Recollections of Cork*, c.1833, unpublished MS, TCD, pp.277.

24 *ibid*.

25 Robinson 1884, p.343.

26 A number of these sketchbooks are in the collection of the National Gallery of Ireland.

27 O'Regan 2004, p.61.

28 For an overview of his work, and a thorough investigation of his works in the Crawford Municipal Art Gallery, see Murray 2005, particularly pp.85-132.

29 Lavery 1940, p.205.

30 Bell 2002, p.7.

31 *ibid*, p.8.

32 Wilson 1977, p.65.

33 Hewitt 1977, p.121.

34 Bell 2002, p.11.

35 Cahill 1999, p.40.

36 Cahill does suggest that Davidson's Protestant background and social network meant that she was in fact 'not one of them'. *ibid*.

37 Animals were usually tied to the railing at the entrance to Moore Abbey a short distance away, just beyond the picture plane.

38 Barry Walsh, letter to the author 2006.

39 Quoted in Pyle 1993a, p.95.

40 Rivers 1946, p.13.

41 *ibid*, p.30.

42 Since his first tour around Connemara in 1939, Dillon travelled extensively around Ireland, from the Boyne Valley and Conlig, County Down (where he stayed with Dan O'Neill and George Campbell) to the Aran Islands, seeking out subjects.

43 See Murray 1997, pp.64-65.

44 Quoted in Power 1969.

45 Quoted in S.B. Kennedy 1989-90, p.47.

46 *ibid*.

47 S.B. Kennedy 1999, p.107.

48 Walker 2003, p.61. First printed in *Hibernia* magazine, 1973.

49 Quoted in Pyle 1993a, p.95.

50 Thomas Bodkin, 'Introduction', in Waddington 1940, p.7.

51 Quoted in S.B. Kennedy 1999, p.99.

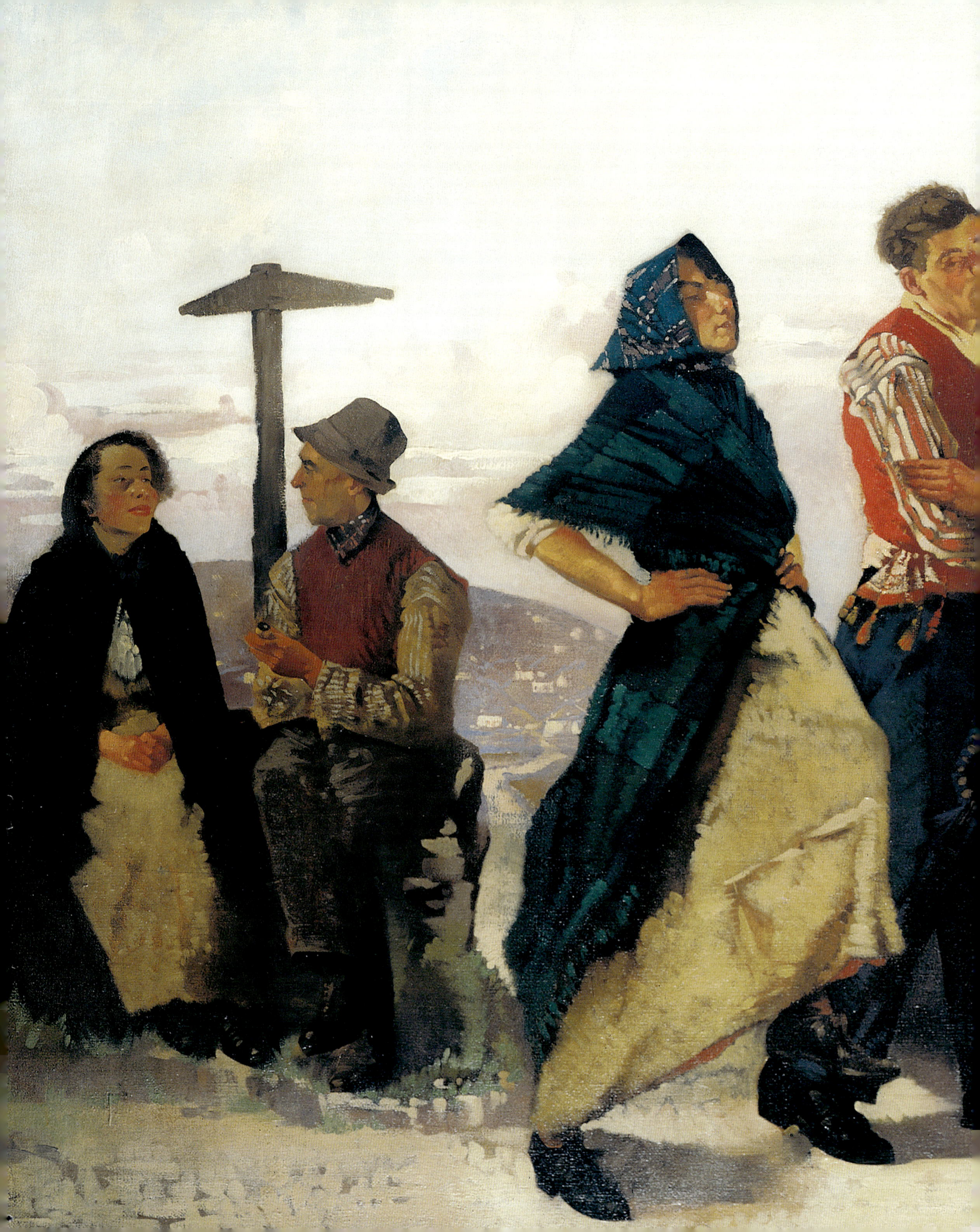

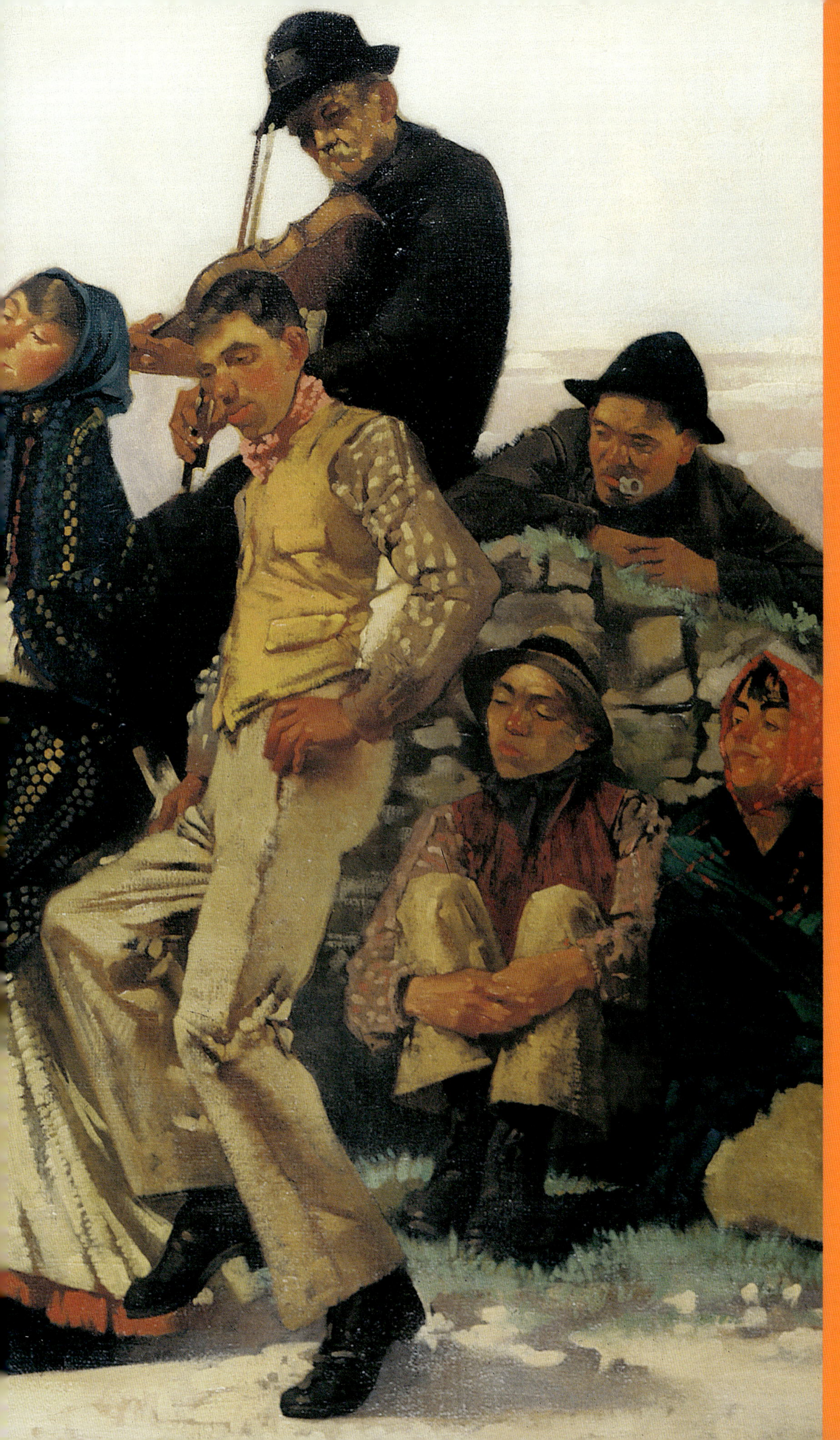

Music & Dance

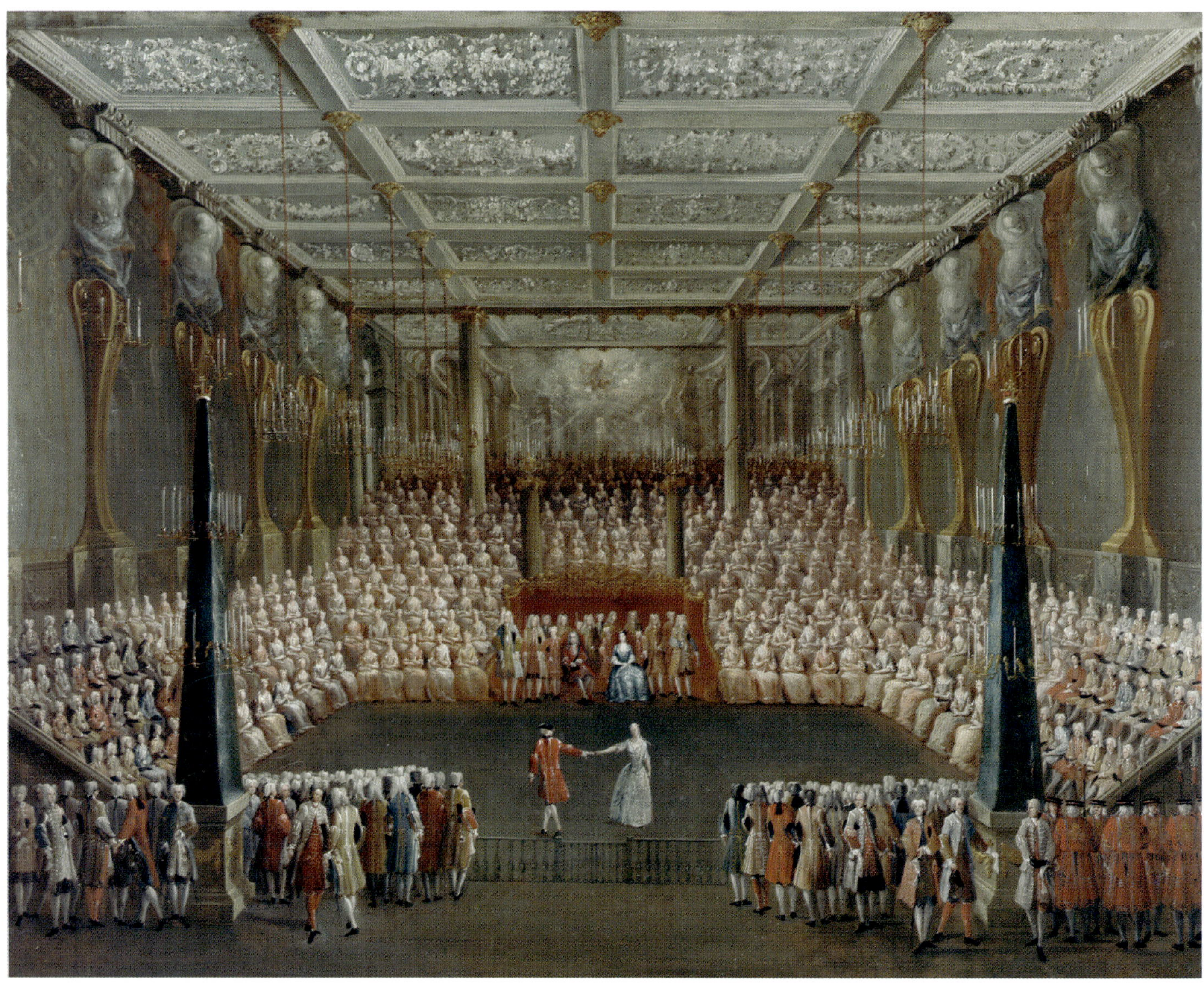

William van der Hagen (fl.1720-45)
1. State Ball at Dublin Castle
1731
Oil on canvas
122 x 145 cm
Private collection

1. State Ball at Dublin Castle

William van der Hagen

As Toby Barnard has described colourfully, Dublin Castle was 'a place to be seen' for the privileged in seventeenth and eighteenth-century Ireland.[1] Image was everything, and from the hosts' point of view, 'décor, design and decorum quickly decided the standing of a viceroy'.[2] Consequently, functions at Dublin Castle, during the incumbency of certain viceroys in particular, could be relied upon to be extravagant affairs. Ceremony and the provision of entertainment were important means of maintaining support for the government among influential Dublin society, though some viceroys proved more willing and adroit hosts than others. Lords Chesterfield and Carteret, for example, were eager to exploit this particular part of the 'propaganda offensive', while Lord Buckinghamshire, by comparison, was distinctly parsimonious.[3] Lord Townshend, for his part, possessed a bacchanalian appetite for food, drink and company, and caused quite a stir during his incumbency in the 1760s and 1770s with his sociability. As if to justify his predilection for entertainment, Townshend observed that 'a social hour did no hurt sometimes to the King's service'.[4] Lionel Sackville, duke of Dorset, was viceroy at the time that Van der Hagen painted this scene. His personal consumption was rather moderate when compared to that of his predecessor, Lord Carteret, but the social events he hosted, particularly during his second administration, were grand affairs.[5]

Mrs Delany, a regular at Castle functions, was present at the event recorded by Van der Hagen, and her gleeful description of the evening corroborates the artist's depiction:

...on the first of March we went to Court in the morning, heard a song of Dubourg's [Matthew Dubourg, leader of the viceroy's musicians], (not so pretty as the last) after that compliment was over and we had refreshed ourselves by dinner, we went again at seven.

The ball was in the old beef-eaters hall, a room that holds seven hundred people seated, it was well it did, for never did I behold a greater crowd. We were all placed in rows one above another, so much raised that the last row almost touched the ceiling! The gentlemen say we looked very handsome, and compared us to Cupid's paradise in the puppet-show. At eleven o'clock minuets were finished, and the Duchess went to the basset table.

After an hour's playing the Duke, Duchess, and nobility marched into the supper-room, which was the council chamber. In the midst of the room was placed a holly tree, illuminated by an hundred wax tapers; round it was placed all sorts of meat, fruit, and sweetmeats; servants waited next, and were encompassed round by a table, to which the company came by turns to take what they wanted. When the doors were first opened, the hurly burly is not to be described; squawling, shrieking, all sorts of noises; some ladies lost their lappets, others were trod upon. Poor Lady Santry almost lost her breath in the scuffle, and fanned herself two hours before she could recover herself enough to know if she was dead or alive.[6]

In another letter, Mrs Delany described a similar event with equal zeal and attention to detail:

...on Monday at eight o'clock we went to the Castle. The room where the ball was to be ordered by Capt. Pierce [Sir Edward Lovett Pearce] finely adorned with paintings and obelisks, and made as light as a summer's day. I never saw more company on one place; abundance of finery, and indeed many pretty women. There were two rooms for dancing. The whole apartment of the Castle was open, which consists of several very good rooms; in one there was a supper ordered after the manner of that at the masquerade, where everybody went at what hour they liked best, and vast profusion of meat and drink, which you may be sure has gained the hearts of all guzzlers![7]

The decorations described by Mrs Delany were discovered in the late twentieth century hung up in the attic at Knole, the duke of Dorset's seat, and Crookshank and Glin have speculated that Van der Hagen may have executed them to Edward Lovett Pearce's design.[8] The decorations were evidently used on more than one occasion, as an article in the *Dublin Evening Post* of 1733 described them at some length:

The Great Hall below Stairs was fitted up for the Ball in a most Magnificent manner, the Sides were covered with Hangings painted in perspective, at the Entrance stood two obelisks, on which were Coronets, and other devices in Candles, the Seats were rais'd on each side... with Pillars stuck full of Candles, and placed at such proper distances as to Deceive the Sight, and make the Hall look much longer than it was. The lights are very numerous and placed with great Taste and Order.[9]

The attribution of these elaborate and ambitious decorations to Van der Hagen is based, reasonably, on the fact that the artist worked for many years as a scene painter for Smock Alley Theatre. Van der Hagen, described as 'lately arriv'd from London', was among the first scene painters of note to work in the Dublin theatre, designing and executing the scenery for *Alexander the Great* at Smock Alley Theatre as early as 1722.[10] He had a major influence on the following generation of Irish painters, a number of whom, including Joseph Tudor, John Lewis and Robert Carver, also became scene painters for the Dublin theatres.[11]

Van der Hagen, then, was already well-established by the time he painted the State Ball at Dublin Castle. As well as theatre scenery and decorative works for the Castle, he is understood to have undertaken commissions for altar pieces, panoramic landscapes (including Beaulieu and Carton), and even produced designs for six tapestries for the Irish House of Lords in 1728 at the behest of upholsterer and tapestry maker Robert Baillie.[12]

The dance being performed by the couple at the centre of the hall is a minuet similar to that illustrated and described in detail in Pierre Rameau's manual, *Le maître à danser*, published in 1725.[13] Translated by dancer and instructor John Essex in 1728 as *The Dancing Master,* Rameau's manual, which covers etiquette and deportment as well as dance steps, is exacting in the extreme, and is a measure of the precision with which these dances were expected to be performed. Rameau maintained that 'the menuet [sic] is become the most modish Dance, not only for the easy Dancing of it, but for the easy Figure used at present'[14]. Minuets were the most popular of the baroque duets, for which such composers as Jean-Baptiste Lully (for the French Court), Bach, Haydn, and Mozart had written.

Van der Hagen's familiarity with his subject is evident from a comparison of the movement of his principal couple with the text of Rameau's manual:

Corner of the Room or other, looking upon one another, present your right Hand in your Step forwards.

But that you may better apprehend it, when are going over, that is at the End of your last Step returning to the Left, raise your right Arm to the Height of your Breast, the Hand turned as represented by the two Arms: The Head being turned to the right, looking at each other, you make a little Movement of the Wrist and Elbow raised up, with a slight Inclination in presenting the Hand, and still looking at one another, make a Turn quite round…[15]

The splendour of this event is best appreciated in the context of the city of Dublin as a whole, which Mrs Delany herself described as 'bad enough, narrow streets and dirty looking houses, but some very good ones scattered about'.[16] BR

1 Barnard 2004, p.17.
2 ibid, p.16.
3 Powell 2005, p.146.
4 Quoted in Powell 2005, p.147.
5 *ibid,* p.153.
6 Letter from Mrs Pendarves (later Mrs Delany) to her brother, Bernard Granville, 7 March 1731/2, in Llanover 1861, vol.I, p.337.
7 Letter from Mrs Pendarves (later Mrs Delany) to Mrs Anne Graville, 4 November 1731, ibid, p.309.
8 Crookshank and Glin 2002, p.71.
9 *Dublin Evening Post*, 30 October-3 November 1733.
10 *Harding's Impartial Newsletter*, no.46 (29 September 1722).
11 Coincidentally, the duke of Dorset was an enthusiastic patron of the Dublin theatre, an admirer of Peg Woffington, and subsequently a member of Thomas Sheridan's (ostensibly non-political) Beefsteak Club, founded in 1852.
12 Of these six just two were actually executed.
13 Crookshank and Glin 2002, p.71. A minuet is a slow stately dance for two in triple time.
14 Essex 1728, p.48.
15 *ibid,* pp.49-50.
16 Llanover 1861, vol.1, p.300.

Joseph Tudor (fl. 1739-59)
2. View of Dublin from Chapelizod
Oil on canvas
117 x 150 cm
Private collection
See Foldout opposite page 39

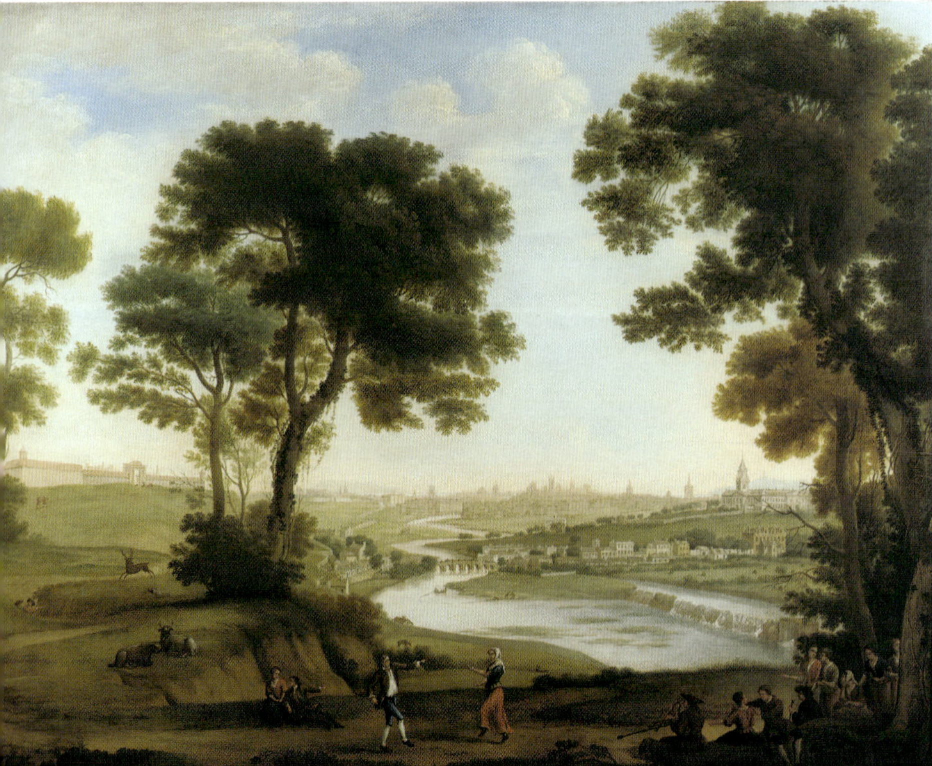

2. View of Dublin from Chapelizod

Joseph Tudor

Tudor's magnificent panoramic view has justly been described as 'the most important mid-eighteenth century depiction of Dublin'.[17] However, while the cityscape dominates the distance, much of the interest of the picture lies in the festive scene of Music & Dance in the foreground. Tudor worked as a scene painter in Smock Alley Theatre, and here Dublin rather acts as a painted backdrop to the light-hearted intermezzo being acted out on the fringes of the Phoenix Park.

Dublin is shown from the west at the mid-point of the eighteenth century. Tudor's ambitious oil painting had been preceded by a pen and ink drawing (private collection) which was engraved in 1753, giving a *terminus ante quem* for the drawing and, presumably, the painting. At the same time, the oil cannot have been executed until after 1741, the date of the Mapas obelisk which, rather improbably, can be seen perched on Killiney Hill to the right of the composition. The city is generally quite accurately depicted, although topographical exactitude is on occasion sacrificed for artistic effect. In the centre of the composition appears the village of Islandbridge and to its right the weir at Chapelizod, which is included here, if not quite accurately, by a slight change of viewpoint from the preparatory drawing. Other landmarks include the spires of the city's two cathedrals, the Royal Hospital, Kilmainhaim and Dr Steeven's Hospital with its recently erected wooden clock tower. The other end of Dublin Bay is clearly marked by Howth Head. In selecting this viewpoint to depict the city, Tudor had been preceded some fifty years earlier by Francis Place (NGI) and Thomas Bate (Bath Preservation Trust). However, Tudor's view, widely circulated by engraving, was to be influential on later portrayals of the city, notably by William Ashford (NGI) and William Sadler.

Framed on either side by the Magazine Fort and the Royal Hospital, the foreground scene is set within the Phoenix Park. Although Dublin is very much the subject of the picture, the action takes place in the indeterminate ground between city and country. The cattle who rather insouciantly observe the figures in the foreground emphasise this bucolic, suburban location, away from the noise, smells, poverty and crime for which eighteenth-century Dublin was known. The Phoenix Park, seemingly named from the Irish *Fionn uisce* (referring to a stream of clear water), rather than from the mythical bird, formed part of the estates of Knights Hospitallers until the dissolution of the monasteries. Under Charles II it was turned into a deer park, and the startled deer in the left centre ground (directly paralleled in Ashford's NGI picture) bears witness to the herds, which from that time until the present have been kept in the park. Through the first half of the eighteenth century, the park was noted as a place of refined entertainment. This is evident in a letter from Mrs Delany written in 1731, shortly after her arrival in Ireland:

The chief entertainment of this week I have forgot to mention, which was the review on Friday morning last. The park, justly called Phoenix Park, was the place of show....The Duchess of Dorset was there in great state, and all the beau monde of Dublin. The weather favoured us, and we were very pleased with the sight. But I must not pass over in silence the beauties of the park, which is a large extent of ground, very fine turf, agreeable prospects, and a delightful wood, in the midst of which is a ring where the beaux and the belles resort in fair weather; indeed, I never saw a spot more to my taste, it is far beyond St James or Hyde Park.[18]

Tudor's oil, showing rather less refined figures than Mrs Delany's beaux and belles, dates, perhaps significantly, from shortly after the Phoenix Park had been opened to the public by the then viceroy, Lord Chesterfield. This provided Dublin with a remarkable amenity. Covering almost 1,762 acres it remains one of the largest enclosed city parks in the world. Changes between Tudor's preparatory drawing and the oil are instructive. In the foreground of the drawing, a well-dressed family promenades, the father wearing a tricorne hat, the mother in broad oblong hoops and a young girl in a bonnet.[19] Although in essence the viewpoint remains the same between drawing and oil, significantly, Tudor completely changes the staffage. These prosperous Dublin citizens are replaced by a scene of music, courtship and dance. The humble attire of the figures may perhaps allude to the democratisation of the park, by the admittance of the public. However, although details such as the pipes played by the seated musician are accurately depicted, and recognisably Irish, these are far from ordinary Dubliners coming to make merry in their new open space. The dress of the dancing woman is generically rustic and the figures recall the staffage of Claude's landscapes, specifically, his celebrated *Landscape with the Marriage of Isaac and Rebecca* (National Gallery of London).[20] At the same time, compositional aspects of the picture, such as the *repoussoir* trees that frame the city, suggest that in contrast to Place's more prosaically accurate rendering of the same view Dublin – and Dubliners – are here mediated through the classical tradition of Italianate landscape painting.

The reality of the poor at play – or at least the perception of that reality – was quite different from the elegant bucolic figures of Tudor. Certainly not everybody welcomed the opening of the Park to the public. A report in *Freeman's Journal* bemoaned the innovation: '[Previously] ill looking strollers of either sex could never get admittance at the gate except on public occasions....But now the gates are opened wide to Tag, Rag and Bobtail. The Sabbath is abused by permitting a hurling match to be played there every Sunday evening, which is productive of blasphemous speaking, riot, drunkenness, broken heads and dislocated bones...'.[21] In the next century the portrayal of the Catholic Irish at play was largely effected through the vocabulary of caricature. *Freeman's Journal's* account would no doubt have inspired pictures along the lines of the Donnybrook Fairs of Samuel Watson or Erskine Nicol. However, this approach would not accord with the decorum of the Claudean landscape tradition in which Tudor here works. Instead he imbues his humble figures with the grace of myth and the precedent of Claude. A similarly distorting process no doubt, if one that lacks the bitter edge of nineteenth-century caricature.

A similar process of idealised reordering can be found in a poem from later in the century. In 1772 John Leslie dedicated to the Lord Lieutenant, Lord Harcourt, an allegorical eulogy, *Phoenix Park: a Poem,* which has many points of direct similarity with Tudor's painting. The Horatian tag 'ut Pictua, Poesis' on its title page specifically invites a link being made between its topographical description and paintings such as Tudor's, which would have been familiar to Leslie through its engraving. The inhabitants of the park are again seen in mythic terms:

Widely diffus'd below, the nymphs and swains
Indulge their sports on her Elysian plains.
Islandbridge is conjured up thus:
Where curv'd the salmon springs, the glassy ridge

Pours steep, and foamy, to the antique bridge,
Through the arch'd vistas, swift the currents glide,
And lose their sweetness in the briny tide.[22]

As in Tudor's painting, the poem progresses outwards from the park, along the river towards the city. From Islandbridge the Liffey 'creep[s] obscure' and, as it leaves the world of the pastoral and enters Dublin, it is suddenly 'choak'd, embrown'd [and] polluted'.[23] However, though thereby acknowledging, if in poetic form, the urban reality of Dublin, Leslie, like Tudor marvels at the distant prospect of the city from the park. 'Lo! Fair Eblana's lofty towr's ascend, And swelling fabricks, far and wide extend!'[24] Leslie's poem, just like Tudor's distant horizon, culminates with Howth which the poet classicises as a new Capri. A direct link between poem and picture is uncertain; indeed it is unnecessary. The point is that they display an identical method of viewing Dublin from the Phoenix Park, the city and its peoples filtered through a classical lens. It might be noted, however, that in Tudor's view, perhaps uniquely in its depiction in topographical art, Howth Head does indeed look rather like Capri. WL

17 Crookshank and Glin 2002, p.73.
18 Day 1991, p.25.
19 See the account of the picture by B. Rooney in Christie's Irish Sale 17 May 2002, pp.32-35.
20 *ibid*, p.34.
21 Quoted in Gwynn 1938.
22 Leslie 1772, p.16.
23 *ibid*, 17.
24 *ibid*.

3. *The Arrival of Phadrig na pib*

Samuel McCloy

Samuel McCloy frequently recorded the gentler side of youth and rural life, producing many rather saccharine images of rosy-cheeked children working and playing.[25] Here, Phadrig na pib arrives like an 'Irish Pied Piper',[26] to whom the young children of an Irish community seem irresistibly drawn. The picture represents a rural idyll, in which healthy, good-humoured folk, most of them young, look forward excitedly to the Music & Dance that the piper's arrival promises at the end of their working day. In the background, locals continue to stroll in from the fields, the haystacks behind them a testament to their labour. A general feeling of *bonhomie* pervades the scene, and only the idle mischief of over-zealous suitors and teasing boys threatens to disturb the harmony. This atmosphere is complemented by the hazy light of a late summer evening, and the local peasants' excitement echoed by the dog in the foreground skipping joyously around the group of children and pipor. This Ireland of healthy, fresh-faced youths, ample harvests and benign weather would have been much more palatable in London, where the picture was shown at the Society of British Artists in 1873, than the country frequently described otherwise in the national press.

The piper appears to enjoy unmitigated popularity among children and adults, though the reality of such a lifestyle could be rather harsher. The peripatetic existence of the travelling musician was precarious, Mr and Mrs Hall reflecting in the 1840s that a decline in faction fighting and local dances, and the rising popularity of 'the "brass bands" of the Temperance Societies' meant that the piper found it 'a hard matter to live by his music'.[27] Nevertheless, pipers proved a popular subject in their own right for artists in Ireland in the nineteenth century, by which time pipes had replaced the harp as the principle classical instrument for Irish music. Previously, pipers had appeared as regular but peripheral figures in Irish pictures (see, for example, Tudor's *View of Dublin from Chapelizod* (cat. 2), though Hugh Douglas Hamilton's detailed study of *Blind Daniel the Piper* of 1760 (private collection) anticipated later artists' response not just to the widespread popularity of the pipes themselves, but to the celebrity of their exponents.[28] Daniel Fitzpatrick, a gifted musician in Cork, was the subject of a poem published in *The Rover* in 1796, while Pádraig O'Briain, the popular Limerick piper, was painted by Joseph Haverty on at least two occasions. Other artists to depict pipers included George Grattan, Samuel Lover and Frederic William Burton, whose watercolour of Paddy Connelly, a Galway piper, was engraved for the *Irish Penny Journal* in 1840. A blind piper also features prominently in Charles Henry Cook's *St Patrick's Day* (cat. 3). These pipers often appear in a distinctive ensemble, comprising a hat (often tricorne), knee breeches, frock coat, waistcoat and stock, which corresponds loosely to gentlemanly fashions of the 1760s and belies the penury endured by many of these musicians.[29]

Within McCloy's idealised scene, there is evidence of a commitment on the artist's part to accuracy of detail. The musician, for example, holds genuine Irish pipes, complete with bellows, chanter, three drones and three regulators. Typically, these pipes were made from robust, durable woods such as elder, ebony and blackwood, allowing them to be carried by travelling musicians, as demonstrated by McCloy's character.[30] The Irish pipes are thought to have developed in the eighteenth century, though mouth-blown pipes are

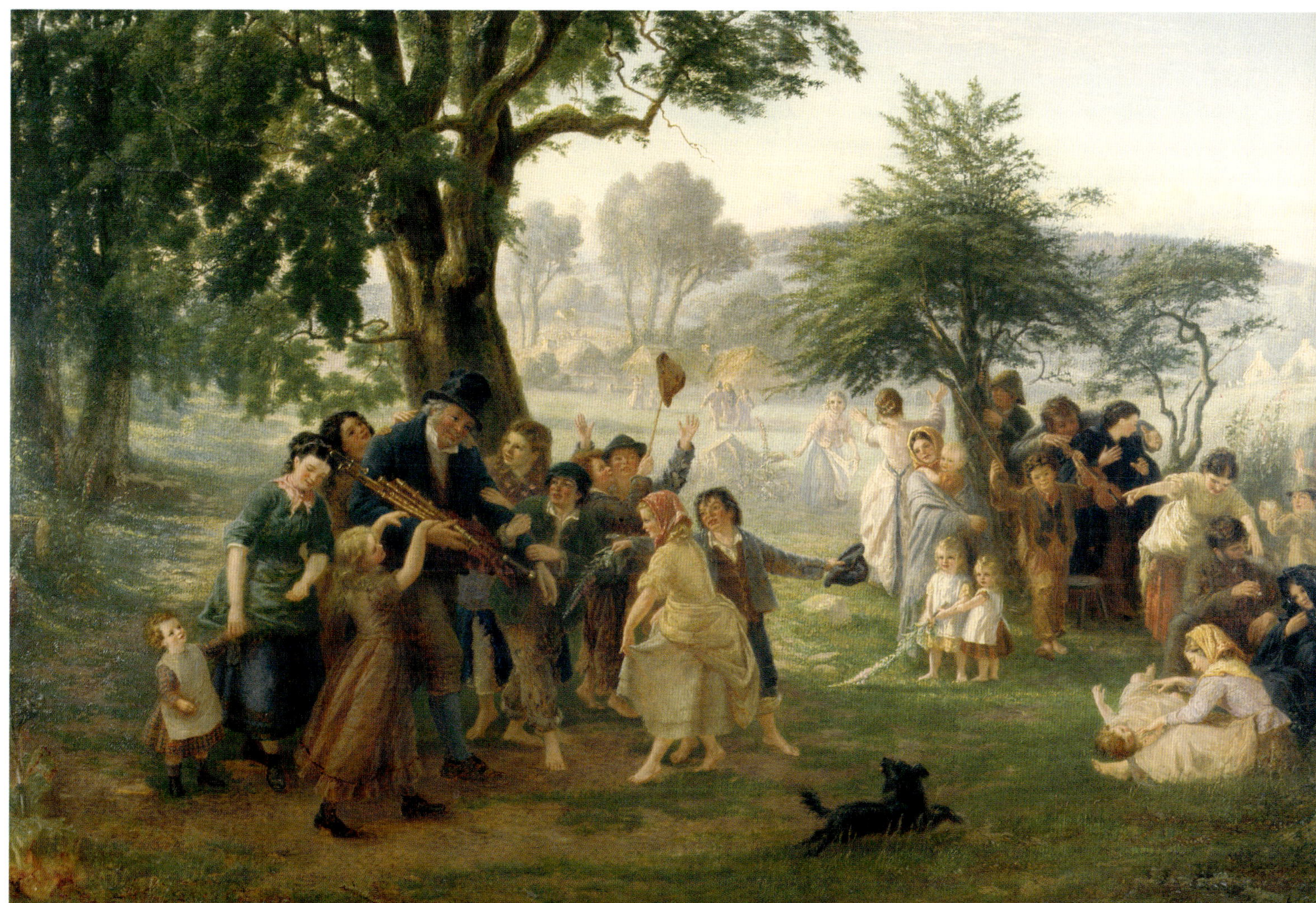

Samuel McCloy (1831-1904)
3. The Arrival of Phadrig na pib
1873
Oil on canvas
71 x 96.5 cm
Irish Linen Centre & Lisburn Museum collection

known to have been played in Ireland since the Middle Ages. By the 1790s they were known commonly as the union pipes, not for any social or political reasons, but rather more prosaically due to the 'addition of a regulator in the main stock'.[31] Inflated by a bellows rather than mouth-blown, they were a uniquely Irish instrument, albeit derived from pipes that had been known in Europe since at least the sixteenth century.[32] The instrument's preferred title by the twentieth century was 'uilleann pipes', a term believed to be attributable to confused etymology. The pipes suffered a decline in popularity towards the end of the nineteenth century, but their fortunes were reversed through the work of committed enthusiasts and the foundation of such bodies as the Cumann na bPíobairí Uilleann (1944) and Na Píobairí Uilleann (1968). BR

25 This picture was purchased in 1987 with the assistance of the National Art Collections Fund of the United Kingdom.

26 Pyms 1986, p.15.

27 Hall 1843, vol.III, p.421.

28 See Laffan 2003a, pp.134-35.

29 This image appears to have extended to behaviour. The countess of Fingall remembered that Burke, a blind piper who played at crossroads dances and weddings, 'had manners that any of us might have envied'. Fingall 1991, p.30.

30 The author is grateful to Nicholas Carolan for his analysis of these details.

31 *Irish Traditional Music Archive* 1992, p.5.

32 In 1773, 1774 and 1783 the term 'Irish Organ' was employed in advertisements for concerts by the Cork piper Mr MacDonnell. Brooks 1999, p. 10.

4. Children Dancing at the Crossroads

Trevor Thomas Fowler

Trevor Thomas Fowler's *Children Dancing at the Crossroads* seems to anticipate what Terence Brown has described as 'de Valera's Gaelic Eden' in the same way that Keating and Lamb's paintings might be said to illustrate it.[33] In the picture, children imitate the traditional and well-documented adult practice of dancing at crossroads. Comically, the only adult supervision, so to speak, is provided by

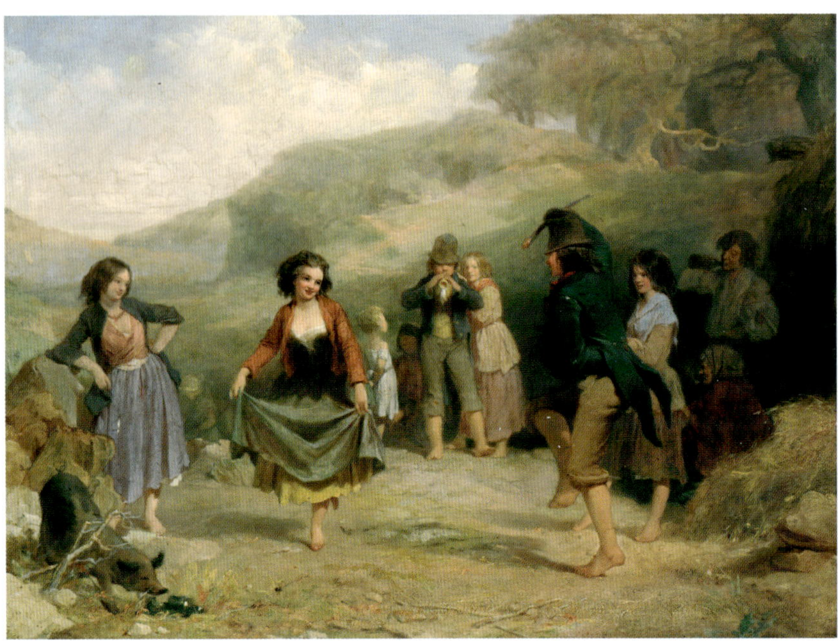

Trevor Thomas Fowler (1800-81)
4. Children Dancing at the Crossroads
c.1840
Oil on canvas
71 x 92 cm
National Gallery of Ireland

an elderly woman who sits smoking a clay pipe disinterestedly to the right of the composition. The children appear to be dancing a *pultóg*, a type of jig in which the male dancer holds a stick, which he incorporates into the dance. The impromptu, makeshift nature of the children's dance is emphasised by the fact that the music is provided by just one instrument. Played by the barefoot boy in the background, this appears to be a home-made or toy instrument. Advertisements for such musical toys, which were usually made from cast iron or brass alloys, were common in eighteenth and nineteenth-century newspapers. These were often approximations of shawms (medieval instruments that evolved into oboes), and some featured a bell at the end of the tube and holes similar to those found on an oboe or clarinet. The position of the young musician's fingers in Fowler's picture suggests strongly that his instrument features such holes. The sound produced by these toys was unpredictable and often noisy and unmelodic, but generally good enough to approximate a recognised tune. [34]

William Carleton, writing around the same time as Fowler was painting, recognised the importance of music in the community in Ireland, though one presumes he was concerned more with the tunes propounded by finer musicians than those represented in Fowler's painting. He opined that the music of any nation was 'the manifestation of its general feeling and that which creates it'.[35] 'It is no wonder then,' he continued 'that the domestic feelings of the Irish should be singularly affectionate and strong, when we consider that they have been, in spite of every obstruction, kept under the softening influence of their music and poetry'.[36] Not unusually, Fowler's is an idealised view of rural Ireland in as far as it acknowledges materially the poverty of the peasantry but suggests nothing of the concomitant anxiety and hardship. Fowler's barefoot boys and girls, like those in McCloy's picture (cat. 3), call to mind the boisterous children of the Kelly family described fancifully by Mrs Hall, who 'moved about, a miscellaneous mass of brown-red flesh, white teeth, bushy elf locks, which rarely submitted to the discipline of a comb, and party-coloured rags; yet were, nevertheless, cheerful, strong, and healthy'.[37]

Fowler and McCloy practised a kind of selective realism. Many of the figures in Fowler's painting, for example, wear recognisably home-spun garments, such as shawls, hats and waistcoats 'made from a mixture of frieze, flannel, coarse linen and wool'.[38] Fowler evidently shared an interest in local dress with many artists and writers who travelled through Ireland in the nineteenth century. Some appear to have been struck more by the vernacular subtleties of costume than by the poor quality of these garments or the often wretched conditions in which their wearers lived. Thomas Crofton Croker, for example, observed regional differences in costume and appearance during his travels in the 1840s, maintaining that in County Limerick 'the men's dress is invariably of a gray (or pepper and salt colour) produced by a mixture of black and white wool without any process of dying' while in the eastern parts of Cork 'dark blue is the predominant colour' and in the west and Kerry 'light or powder blue is almost universally worn'.[39] While Fowler's painting features no landmarks to identify the scene, it may have been set in or at least inspired by a scene in Carlow or Kilkenny, where the artist is known to have worked. However accurate the setting may be, it is certainly consistent with the untamed Irish landscape type propagated and popularised in early nineteenth-century romantic literature and art. BR

33 Quoted in Hill et al 1988, p.58.
34 The authors are grateful to Nicholas Carolan for his assistance in identifying the dance.
35 Quoted in Glew 1870, p.27.
36 *ibid.*
37 Hall n.d., pp.210-11.
38 Bourke and Bhreathnach-Lynch 1999, p.100.
39 Croker 1969, p.222.

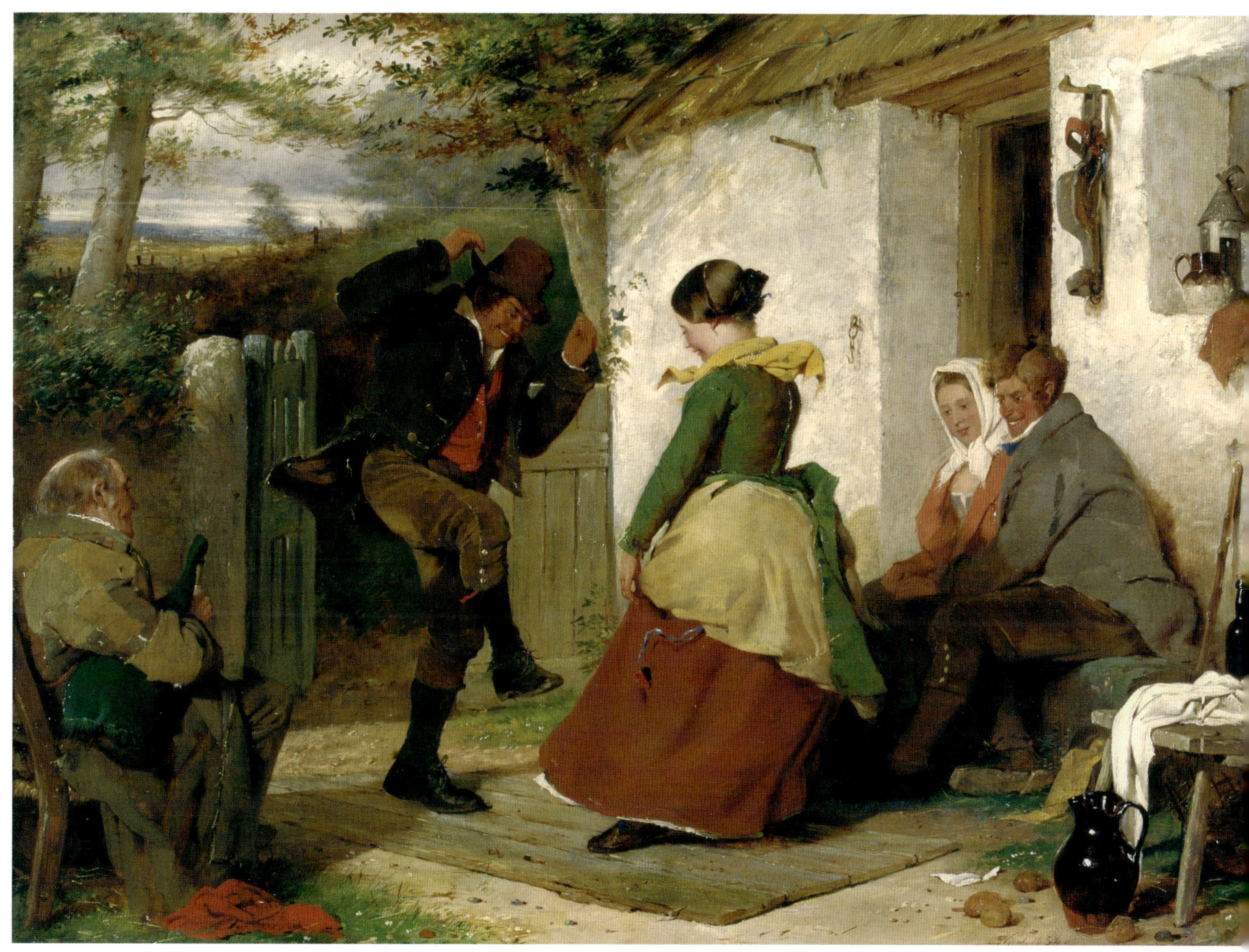

5. Cover the Buckle

Erskine Nicol

Nicol, a Scottish artist, was well known for his depictions of the rural Irish at play, and this light-hearted, humorous scene is typical of many others in which Nicol shows people dancing, carousing, playing cards or gathering for meals by the turf fire. This painting makes an interesting comparison with Helmick's *The Country Dancing Master, West of Ireland* (cat. 6), which shows the quiet formality of measured instruction. Here we are shown the comparatively noisy exuberance of adults dancing upon a door. A door was often removed from its hinges for this purpose as it gave audible resonance to dance-steps in houses where the beaten earth floors were prone to damp in winter and dust in summer. It was also typical to place glasses of water on the corners of the door as a challenge to the dancers. In this case, the dancers perform on a full door, though it would have been more typical to do so on a half door. In a country chronically short of timber, those who could afford to have part of the floor boarded added boards near the hearth, and sometimes buried a horse's skull beneath them when the house was built to add resonance to jigs and reels with rapid foot tapping and audible rhythm. Contemporary Irish dance competitions and displays with elaborately turned out children wearing weighted shoes still involve an element of improvisation, with boarding laid down outside, or a stage created from the wooden flat bed of a truck.

Nicol chooses to arrange his uilleann piper and the older couple watching the fancy footwork outside

Erskine Nicol (1825-1904)
5. Cover the Buckle
1854
Oil on canvas
45 x 60 cm
Courtesy Gorry Gallery

the front of a thinly thatched farmhouse. The working horse's winkers (or blinkers) and the storm lantern on the windowsill suggest farming rather than fishing as a livelihood. The female dancer's petticoat is typical of the west, where women spun the wool from their own sheep, then dyed it with madder (for its distinctive red hue) before weaving it.[40] The meeting of function and fashion is apparent in the way her apron is tucked up over the petticoat, and her hair fashionably tied back. She is unmarried, unlike the woman sitting and watching, whose white bonnet denotes her elevated married status. In poor working families the luxury of shoes was reserved for the men, who needed them most for working in the fields and amongst horses and bulls. If women owned shoes, they treasured them. In the 1840s, Thackeray observed women walking to church in Skibbereen carrying their footwear, then stopping to wash their feet and don their shoes just before going in.[41] Likewise Irish artists such as Daniel Maclise and Edmond Fitzpatrick show girls in the act of slipping on their shoes just before dancing, if there was a board to dance upon. Conversely, images of people dancing without a board or a door, such as *New Year's Night in an Irish Cabin* by Francis W. Topham, often show them barefoot.[42]

Nicol falls just short of accuracy in his portrayal of some of the detail. His arrangement of the piper, for example, is idiosyncratic as he has mistakenly placed the arm strap on the musician's right arm. Instead it should be on his left arm and connected to the bellows for leverage, rather than to the bag under the right arm which, being very light, would have required no support.[43] Although this is a somewhat idealised scene, it suggests relative prosperity within the rural hierarchy, where few people aspired to owning shoes or horses. The title was until recently thought to be *Over the Buckle*, and was described thus in a Dublin sale in 1995. However it seems more likely to be correctly titled *Cover the Buckle*, which was the name of a piper's double jig, a dance or a song. The phrase was used by the Halls in the 1840s, who mention Kate Cleary, the object of the affections of a local youth, 'covering the buckle, and heel on toe on the flure' opposite a rival suitor at a dance,[44] and O'Keefe and O'Brien record 'Cover the Buckle' as a double jig played by a nineteenth-century American piper.[45] It seems that the title derived from a dancing master's ability to hide the buckles of his shoes by the rapidity of his dance. Mrs Hall describes how one of her characters, Tom Corish, 'after "covering the buckle" to admiration, and beating his partner at the "highland fling," made "a remarkable genteel bow"' to his dancing partner.[46] The style of dancing, whether 'heavy' or 'light', and the choice of steps, from shuffle to grind to batter and double-drum, were commonly determined by a dancer's ability, the preferences of the dancing master, and local tradition and taste. Often, masters would devise their own particular steps, which would subsequently become associated with them and established as part of a recognised local or national repertoire. In Nicol's painting, the male dancer's exuberant stance and raised arms suggests that his dancing is less than serious. The emphatic use of the arms was discouraged in the nineteenth century, so Nicol's dancer is at least over enthusiastic. CK

---

40 Madder is a dye extracted from a herbaceous climbing plant of the same name.

41 William Makepeace Thackeray and Crofton Croker quoted in Kinmonth 2001, pp.173-74, figs.3-4, 6-8.

42 See Kinmonth 2006, figs. 185, 188 and 194.

43 Information courtesy of Nicholas Carolan of the Irish Traditional Music Archive.

44 Hall 1843, vol. I, p.350.

45 James George O'Keefe and Art O'Brien, *A Handbook of Irish Dances*, (1902).

46 Hall n.d., p.222.

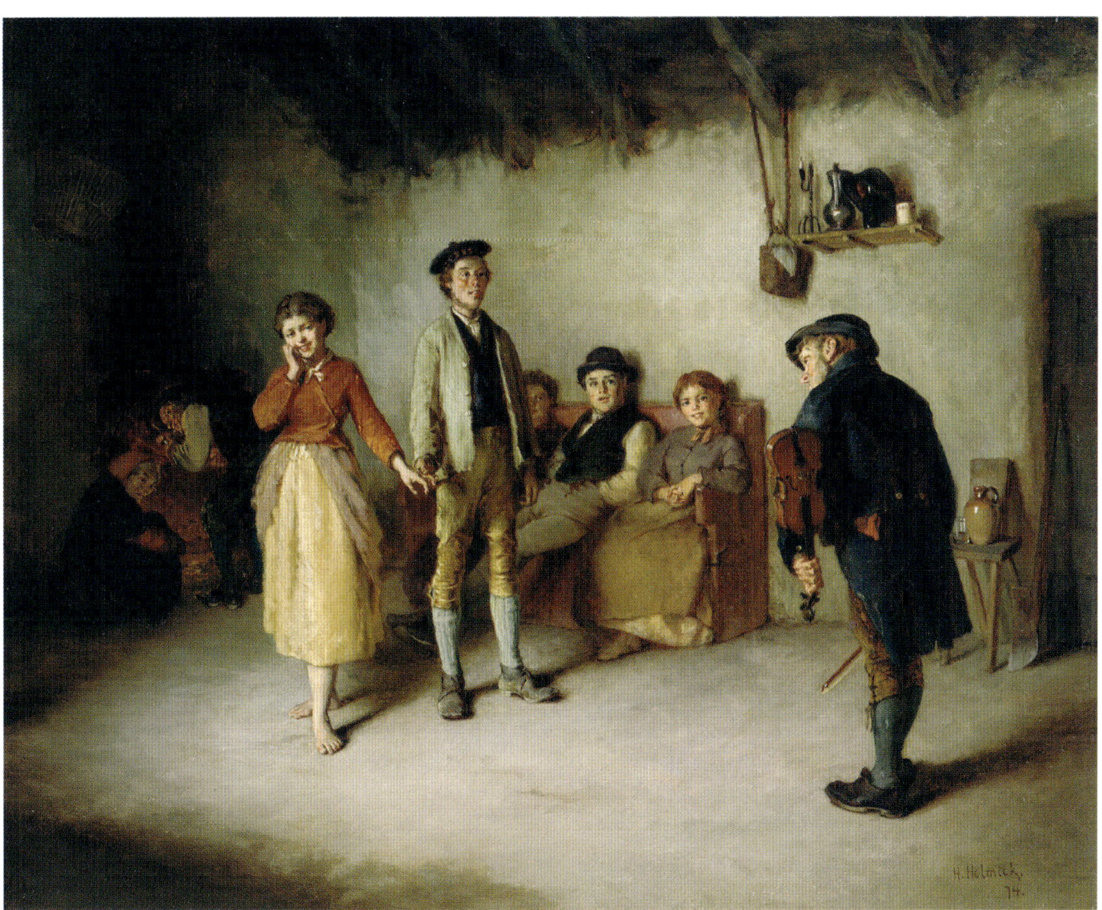

Howard Helmick (1845-1907)
6. The Country Dancing Master, West of Ireland
1874
Oil on canvas
60 x 67.5 cm
Private collection

6. The Country Dancing Master, West of Ireland

Howard Helmick

This gathering is typical of Helmick's genre paintings, and contains none of the polemics of his *News of the Land League* (cat. 68), a slightly later work. Here Helmick shows us the interior of a thatched single-storey farm kitchen, exaggerating slightly the light and width of the place to allow for his composition and to accommodate the group that centres on an awkward young couple waiting to dance. The young man wears on his head the Tam'O'Shanter which can be seen in other paintings of the west,[47] and the audience sits to wait their turn on a settle bed, a bed disguised as a bench. Settle beds were generally made out of pine, and this one is painted red in imitation of more fashionable mahogany. This dual purpose design saved precious timber as well as space, stored its own bedding within the seat, and was nearly always placed beside the hearth. Versions of settle beds were found in farmhouses throughout Ireland, and this one with its solidly boarded ends is most typical of the style found in northern and western counties.[48] Helmick has observed closely how such beds were kept closed, carefully including the long wrought iron hook below the girl's left wrist. The girl wears a long-sleeved fitted bodice, with her petticoat tucked up and her hair tied up, as was fashionable. Her head is uncovered and her feet are bare, as was customary for all but married or elderly women. The specific style of settle bed and the Tam'O'Shanter would both have been regionally typical of the area around Helmick's studio in County Galway.

In the background, the elderly parents sit in the place of honour right next to the hearth reflecting their seniority. The father looks over his shoulder while stooping to light his pipe from the glowing turf fire. The woman, meanwhile, echoes other observant figures who feature in the background or sidelines of Helmick's paintings.[49] The relatively bare space, lacking paint except on the settle bed, and with a beaten earth floor, is a realistic depiction of how such small, darkly-lit homes looked. Beside the door is a turf slane, the type of spade that was used to extract from the bog the turf that was later dried and stacked as fuel. The small chair on the right beside it is not of a type that has survived, although similar versions do appear in Helmick's other paintings.

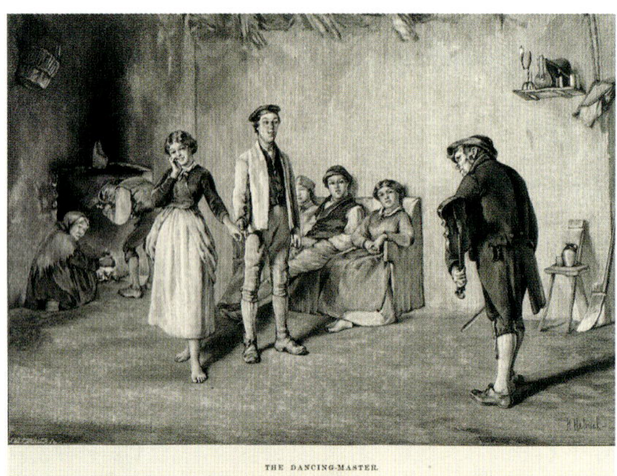

Fig 23. **Hermann Werdmüller after Howard Helmick,** *The Country Dancing Master, West of Ireland,* engraving, *The Magazine of Art* , vol.11, (1888), p.23.

This is one of a few images that were used in their engraved form by the nationalist poet and novelist Katherine Tynan to illustrate a series of articles that she published in the highly-respected *Magazine of Art* in 1888 (fig. 23). Not unusually, the engraver, Swiss-born Hermann Werdmüller, made a number of small alterations to Helmick's original, perhaps to refine the composition.[50] Werdmüller altered the little chair so that instead of having two back legs it has a single broad slanting one. This would have been impossible to construct. He also misunderstood and omitted the crucial long hook that holds the settle bed closed, and one can only conclude that such misunderstandings render his engravings after paintings a disappointingly unreliable source for small details of design.

The important status of professional dancing masters in Ireland was well-established by the time Helmick came to paint this picture in the 1870s. Contracts survive that record the formal activity of a dancing master in West Cork as early as 1718.[51] Dancing masters commonly took it upon themselves to teach not just the current repertoire of dances, but also manners, ballroom etiquette, and what Helen Brennan has described as 'deportment'.[52] One Mr Trench of Wexford, for example, who travelled in the early nineteenth century in the company of a blind fiddler, undertook to produce dancers who could 'mingle with the quality as though it was the next door neighbour's child you had for a partner'.[53] Not all masters were comfortable instructing young men and women together. Some would teach men and women the same steps, while, in the interests of decorum, others would not admit women to their classes at all.[54] As a consequence, women would often end up learning the steps from male friends and brothers.

Helmick's painting is an authentic depiction of a dancing master instructing two young pupils. It was just as common for instructors to play the music themselves while instructing as it was for them to be accompanied by a musician.[55] In Dublin, dance masters often taught French and other Continental dances using a small type of violin called a kit or 'pochette' fiddle, which would fit between the hand and elbow, thus affording the instructor more physical freedom. The instructor here, however, carries a full-size violin.

A peripatetic existence meant that masters could become known among numerous communities, albeit normally in a localised area, and could trade upon a good reputation. Many were held in high esteem and sometimes enjoyed considerable celebrity. Towards the end of the eighteenth century, Arthur Young recorded that dancing masters exercised an 'absolute system of education' travelling 'through the country from cabbin to cabbin with a piper or a blind fiddler'.[56] Though often conducted in less than salubrious surroundings, the teaching was a disciplined practice that could draw heavily on classical and balletic models. Classes were held during the winter months, from October to March, and masters could charge either by lesson or term, depending on circumstances. Generally, they stayed with the family of one of their students or relied on cheap lodgings. They could also be territorial, a tendency that might lead, as William Carleton recorded, to animated disputes and dancing contests. CK

47 Kinmonth 2006, fig.115.

48 Kinmonth 1993, pp.82-91, figs 117-132.

49 See, for example, Kinmonth 2006, figs 129 and 160.

50 Brendan Rooney in Laffan 2002, p.68, cat.16 and fig.17.

51 Brennan 1999, p.45. The contract specifies the dances that Charles Stanton should teach the children of William Bayly, a gentleman landowner in West Carberry.

52 Brennan 1999, p.46.

53 P. Kennedy 1863, p.430.

54 Brennan 1999, p.55.

55 The author is grateful to Nicholas Carolan for his assistance in cataloguing this work.

56 Young 1892, p.146.

7. Dancing at a Northern Crossroads

Charles Lamb

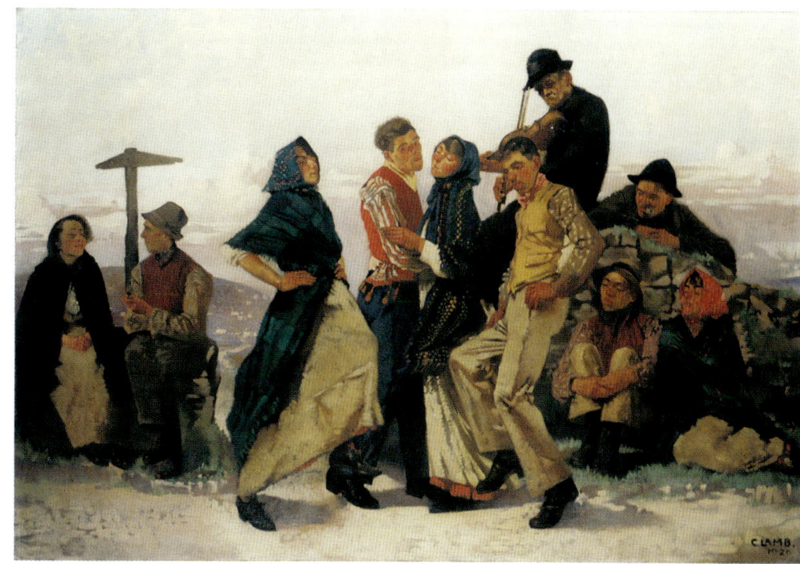

Charles Lamb (1893-1964)
7. Dancing at a Northern Crossroads
1920
Oil on canvas
132 x 191 cm
Private collection

Born in County Armagh, Lamb, like so many other artists of the period, was drawn instinctively to the west where he hoped to find the 'essence' of Ireland. He first travelled to the Aran Islands in 1914 at the suggestion of his fellow artist Harry Clarke and found it instantly arresting. When still a student, Lamb had been introduced to the writer and poet Pádraic Ó'Conaire and the two men became firm friends. Lamb was inspired by Ó'Conaire's work, which drew on the writer's familiarity with his native Connemara and a keen knowledge of Irish folklore and language. As he later reflected, this was a world quite different from the red-bricked streets of Portadown in which he had grown up. While primarily a painter of modestly-sized landscapes and rural scenes, often with boats going to and from the islands in the broadly empirical tradition of artists such as William Bartlett, here, and in *Pattern Day in Connemara* (cat. 82), his figures take on deliberate, if slightly obscure, emblematic significance.

Two couples, pensive and self-absorbed, dance to the music of a fiddler, while five further figures to the left and right choose to watch or ignore them. There is an elegant symmetry based around the dancing couple placed slightly off centre, while a series of diagonals converge on the topmost head, that of the fiddler. When the picture was exhibited at the St Stephen's Green Gallery in 1924 George Atkinson's review drew attention to the 'control of design and arrangement' unusual, he noted, 'in a landscape painter'.[57] It is an extraordinarily ambitious work for a twenty-seven year old artist.

The depiction of traditional rural dancing at crossroads was already well rooted in Irish art. Trevor Thomas Fowler's *Children Dancing at the Crossroads* (cat. 4) turned the subject into a quaint genre scene. In contrast here, Lamb's monumentality of scale suggests that his picture is a deliberately programmatic work. There is a staged theatricality to the composition and the comparison often made between the work of artists such as Lamb and the drama of Synge seems inevitable.

Significantly, Lamb's *Dancing at a Northern Crossroads*, painted in 1920, precedes by a number of years his erstwhile master Sean Keating's *Dun Aengus: Fisherfolk on a Galway Quay* (private collection), which resembles it closely. Both pictures have been described as 'ritualistic exercises' in which the artists appear 'as interested in the audience as in the performers'.[58] The paintings, particularly Keating's, owe a debt to the work of Sir William Orpen, who had charged with allegorical significance simple episodes from life in the west of Ireland in pictures such as *The Western Wedding* and *The Holy Well* (NGI). However, it must be acknowledged that Lamb and Keating lack the element of constructive ambiguity that gives Orpen's work in this tradition its strength. In a way inconceivable with Orpen's work, paintings such as Lamb's specifically anticipated, and possibly even inspired de Valera's own image of a utopian Ireland, articulated in a radio broadcast in 1942, although the much quoted ideal of an Ireland 'joyous… with the laughter of comely maidens dancing at the crossroads' seems never to have been uttered in quite these words.[59] No doubt reflecting the uncertain conditions of 1920 when it was painted, there is a distinct absence of laughter in the scene.

Dancing at a Northern Crossroads is a picture very much of its time. For Lamb and a number of his contemporaries, images of such communal, longstanding activities encapsulated a singularly Irish experience and, following a new tradition of Irish literary and theatrical endeavour, and in the wake of the Easter Rising, contributed to a collective, indigenous redefinition of Ireland. Nor did the significance of such paintings as *Dancing at a Northern Crossroads* reside in their broad subjects alone. Lamb, like his literary and artistic predecessors and contemporaries, was attentive to local detail, although he allows himself a certain artistic licence in its depiction. One can identify anomalies in both the costume and the dance. The position and waltz-hold of the figures suggests that they are engaged in neither a set nor a céilí dance. [60] Similarly, the costume appears to be a composite of items that Lamb may have seen in different parts of the country. It would have been unusual, for example, for the women to have worn skirts over their red petticoats, while the central male figure's bright red waistcoat is more likely to have originated in the north of the country. The striped shirts, broad tartan and crocheted shawls are also rather incongruous.[61] These inaccuracies must be attributable, at least in part, to the fact that Lamb painted the picture in Dublin and relied on fellow students at the Metropolitan School of Art, rather than Galway locals, to pose for the bronzed, rangy dancers.[62] While dance was necessarily regimented, customs in costume, particularly everyday clothes, were not so binding that garments were not transported around the country. The artist certainly appears to have been *au fait* with, or at least had observed closely, musicianship. The fiddler's posture, which evolved from the baroque tradition, is consistent with Irish practice. At this time fiddles, which would not have included a chin or shoulder piece, would have been played downwards on the shoulder rather than under the chin.

Dancing at a Northern Crossroads demonstrates that the tradition illustrated by the children in Trevor Fowler's painting (cat. 4) continued into the twentieth century. It was represented continually as a practice defined by courtesy and order. Constance Battersea demonstrates this in her reminiscences of travels in Ireland. On the Newtown Anner Estate in Tipperary, she and her sister:

...watched the dancing one Sunday afternoon at the four cross roads, and were much flattered when one young Irishman after another came up shyly but civilly inviting us to dance. Upon my saying that I had not learnt the steps of a jig, I was told in the most delightful brogue that I could be taught, and that it would be an honour to teach me.[63]

Many decades earlier, Elizabeth, countess of Fingall had described the dancing at the crossroads that she had seen 'in some red and dark dusk of a Connemara evening' as 'a strange rather melancholy stately dancing... two long lines of men and women facing each other, their arms folded their bodies swaying'.[64]

It has been argued that Lamb's paintings, which elevated local subjects and celebrated indigenous character, folklore and landscape, contributed to a pervasive and increasing sense of national consciousness.[65] It is not, however, an empirical, unmediated snapshot of life in the west of Ireland. It is, rather, a contrived, romanticised, almost theatrical view. However, the colour and activity, regardless of accuracy, certainly suggest the vibrancy and vigour of an emergent nation, albeit one caught in 1920 in the throes of the War of Independence and destined to endure a pernicious civil war. As James White observed, Lamb 'chose the people and the places west of the Shannon possibly because they were decorative and therefore paintable but more probably because they seemed to offer an alternative to the vulgarity of city life, speed, noise and profit searching'.[66] This dichotomy, perhaps even more apparent today than when White wrote, is problematic and certainly very much a city dwellers' view. However, in the context of this exhibition, it is ironically instructive that 'one of the archetypal images of the New Ireland', and particularly a picture painted in the troubled year 1920 should, in contrast to Paul Henry's figures of Achill labour, depict the Irish at leisure.[67] While the size of the canvas and the monumental frieze-like composition suggest a certain heroic quality to the dance, it has been noted that the painting, perhaps unwittingly, bears evidence more to 'the idleness existing in economically impoverished communities.'[68] A few years after the picture was painted, the practice was used by George Russell as a metaphor of the material and cultural poverty of the country (see cat. 56 and 57)[69] WL

---

57 *Dublin Magazine* April 1924, quoted Snoddy 1996, p.249.
58 McConkey 1990, p. 152.
59 The text of de Valera's St Patrick's Day address reads: '...a land whose countryside would be bright with cosy homesteads, whose fields and village would be joyous with the sounds of industry, with the rompings of sturdy children, the contests of athletic youths and the laughter of comely maidens, whose firesides would be forums for the wisdom of serene old age. It would, in a word, be the home of a people living the life that God desires that man should live.'
60 Bourke 2000, p.33.
61 *ibid*.
62 The couple sitting under the signpost to the left were based on studies executed on location in Connemara.
63 Battersea 1922, p.103.
64 Fingall 1991, p.30.
65 See, for example, Bourke 1999 and Bourke 2000.
66 James White, 'Charles Lamb', in Municipal Gallery of Modern Art 1969.
67 Kenneth McConkey in Pyms 1986, p.68.
68 Berkeley Art Museum 1998, p.168.
69 AE, 'Rural Clubs and National Life', *Irish Statesman*, 12 Jan 1924, quoted in McConkey 1990, p.63.

8. An Irish Dance

Paul Henry

10. The Dancers

Paul Henry

9. Old People Watching a Dance

Paul Henry

The Dancers, *An Irish Dance* and *Old People Watching a Dance* were painted on Paul Henry's first visit to Achill.[70] Indeed, they can be regarded as companion pieces to one another, as all are set in the Achill Knitters Hall in Dooagh, and were exhibited at the Royal Hibernian Academy in 1911.[71] Moreover, the trio can be read as simultaneous views of a single event, recording in turn dancers, musicians and observers. *Old People Watching a Dance* is one of the paintings illustrated in *Twelve Irish Artists*, Victor Waddington's influential publication of 1940. In the introduction Thomas Bodkin claims that the artists (including William Conor, Paul Henry, Sean Keating, Harry Kernoff and Charles Lamb) whose work featured in the book, were indicative of a 'national school' in that they were 'affected in their outlook by a persistent national or local tradition of culture'.[72] Henry had recently been reading Synge's *Riders to the Sea*.

Old People Watching a Dance presents some of the older members of the local community watching silently, and rather seriously, others engaged in an activity in which they themselves are unable to participate. The restricted, almost monochrome palette binds these three individuals together, and in its earthiness connects them tangentially with the land on which they have probably worked all their lives. Boldly modelled and thickly painted, and lacking facial detail,[73] these figures can be said to represent more their generation than themselves as individuals. This is consistent with the general 'sturdiness of character and dignity of manner' that Henry identified in the pensioners on the island.[74] Like Lamb's *A Quaint Couple* (Crawford Municipal Art Gallery), they exemplified a world that was disappearing, while embodying the stoicism on which an emerging nationhood might be built. Discussing Henry's *An Irish Dance*, the reporter for the *Belfast News-Letter* referred tellingly to the 'ancient fiddler sitting back in

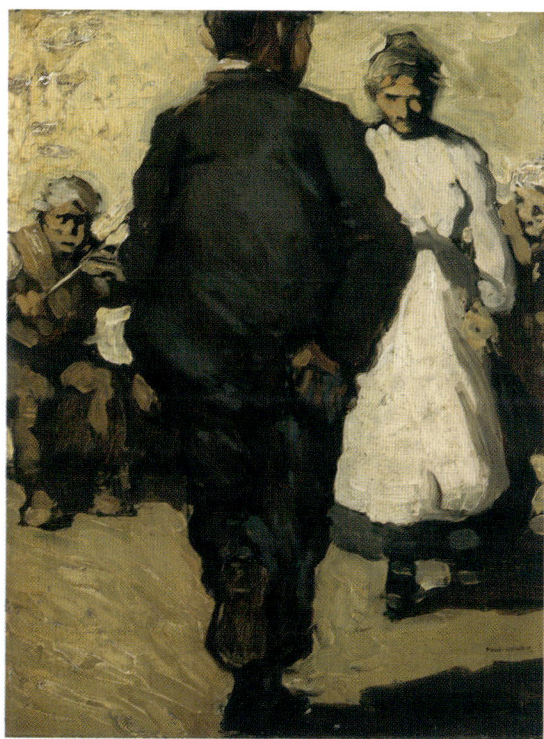

Paul Henry (1876-1958)
8. An Irish Dance
1910-11
Oil on board
31 x 23.5 cm
Jack & Sandra O'Neill- London

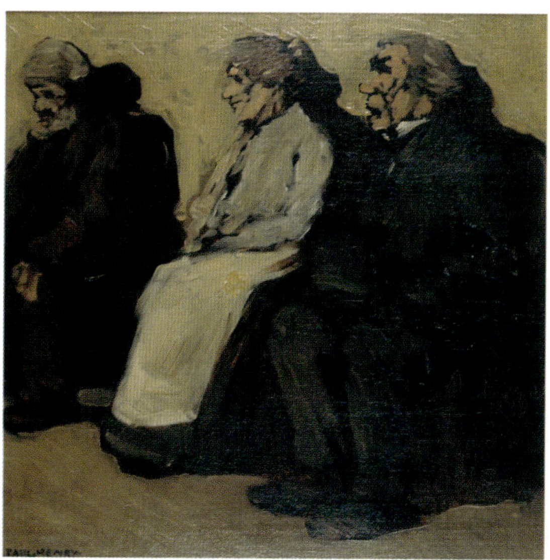

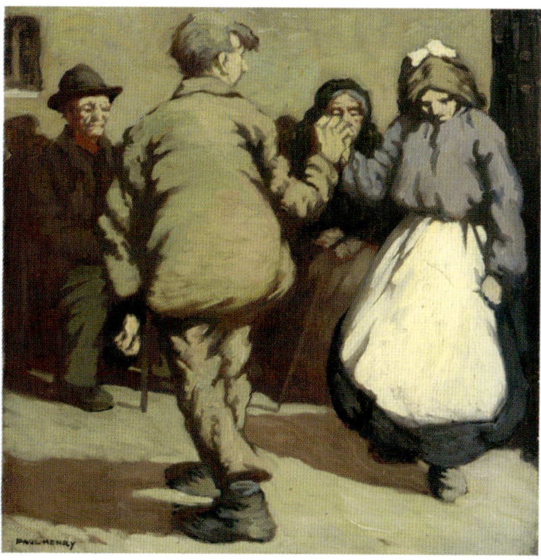

Paul Henry (1876-1958)
9. *Old People Watching a Dance*
1910-11
Oil on canvas
30 x 29 cm
Mr & Mrs F. Hughes Collection

Paul Henry (1876-1958)
10. The Dancers
1910-11
Oil canvas
40.5 x 35.5 cm
Anraí ó Braonáin

the shadows', a description that bears a deliberate duality.[75] Similarly, the *Northern Whig* declared somewhat melodramatically that *Old People Watching a Dance* demonstrated that 'dignity does not depend on the subject but on the manner in which it is treated'.[76]

Dancing in their slightly ill-fitting, ready-made clothes, Henry's figures resemble those in Lilian Davidson's *Fashions at the Fair* (cat.77) and many of the even more stylised characters that are the subject of paintings by Grace Henry. They inhabit a relatively simple, subsistence world, where the niceties of tailoring that might have concerned the pictures' wealthier audiences were beyond their concern. These people embodied the rural lifestyle which Henry instinctively favoured over its urban equivalent. Significantly, both the *News-Letter* and the *Northern Whig* remarked on what they saw as the clumsiness of the figures in *An Irish Dance* and on the cottage's earthen floor.[77]

Paul Henry is most closely associated with landscape painting, to the point that he is commonly regarded as having created the most recognisable images of the west of Ireland of any Irish artist. Indeed, his views of Achill and the west have become so archetypal that their accuracy is practically assumed, and they retain the nostalgic appeal that they had during the artist's own lifetime and that was cleverly exploited for advertising campaigns. Henry's econonomical compositions, modulated tonal palette and bold modelling certainly lent themselves to reproduction and impressed themselves upon the Irish public's collective memory. Henry was also, however, an accomplished painter of human activity, who used similar technical devices, including impasto, to monumental effect in modelling his figures. It seems reasonable to assume that in doing so, he looked to the work of his wife Grace, as his characters echo the more stylised, solid figures of the west that inhabit her paintings.

All three pictures included here are modestly sized, and their frontal, cramped compositions echo the restricted domestic surroundings in which the dances take place. Neither in the space afforded the dancers themselves nor in their stiff, inhibited movement is there any suggestion of expanse. In this respect they differ greatly from the almost recklessly whirling figures in William Conor's *Stepping Out Together* (cat.11) and, indeed, with Henry's own later landscapes, in which the sky often occupies over half of the composition.

Both in terms of manner and subject, these pictures owe a debt to Jean François Millet, whose work Henry had known since his youth and actually seen in Paris when he travelled there in about 1898. In fact, as S.B. Kennedy has pointed out, it was specifically the visit to Achill that reawakened Henry's interest in Millet.[78] The pictures also suggest the peasant subjects of Daumier and Van Gogh, who Henry is also known to have admired. Unlike the better-known contemporaneous painting *The Potato Diggers* (NGI), which can be usefully and closely compared to images of toil on the land by Millet such as *The Diggers*, *The Sower* (Museum of Fine Arts, Boston) or *The Man with the Hoe* (J. Paul Getty Museum), this trio of paintings seems, by nature of its subject, uniquely Irish.

While it is true that Henry's figurative pictures, unlike Millet's (or indeed MacGonigal's and Keating's), were not individually didactic, collectively they suggest an awareness of the social realities and austerity of life on the land in the west of Ireland. Henry later reflected that he was 'yet to see people who worked so hard for so little gain'.[79] He does not use them as a means of salving a social conscience or expounding on a social theory, and was, in that sense, a strict observer. One must be careful not to make an analysis of his work too superficial, however. As was true of Jack B. Yeats, an acutely prudent process was at work behind Henry's figurative painting, though his interest in human themes was relatively short-lived, as he gradually relinquished peasant subjects from about 1915 in favour of pure landscape.

These pictures predate Henry's more Whistleresque, tonal landscapes, but their even light anticipates that later manner to some extent. The strong contrasts evident in them are redolent of illustration, in which Henry specialised at the beginning of his professional career in London, and charcoal drawing, in which the artist was also proficient. *An Irish Dance* has been exhibited under various titles, from *The Irish Dance* (1912) to *Dance in a Cottage* (1914). BR

---

70 Henry travelled to Achill for the first time with first wife Grace (née Mitchell) in summer 1910. The couple had married in 1903 but separated in 1930. Henry married his long-term partner Mabel Young shortly after Grace's death in 1953.

71 The author is very grateful to Dr S.B. Kennedy for bringing two of these pictures to his attention and for his assistance in cataloguing them.

72 The other artists to feature in the book were Grace Henry, James Humbert Craig, Maurice MacGonigal, Frank McKelvey, Dermod O'Brien, Seán O'Sullivan and Leo Whelan.

73 The same observation was made in S.B. Kennedy 2003b, p.48.

74 Henry 1951, p.108.

75 *Belfast News-Letter*, 13 March 1911.

76 'Paintings of Irish Life', *Northern Whig*, 13 March 1911.

77 *Belfast News-Letter*, 13 March 1911, and *Northern Whig*, 19 February 1914.

78 S.B. Kennedy 1989-90, p.45.

79 Henry 1951, p.57.

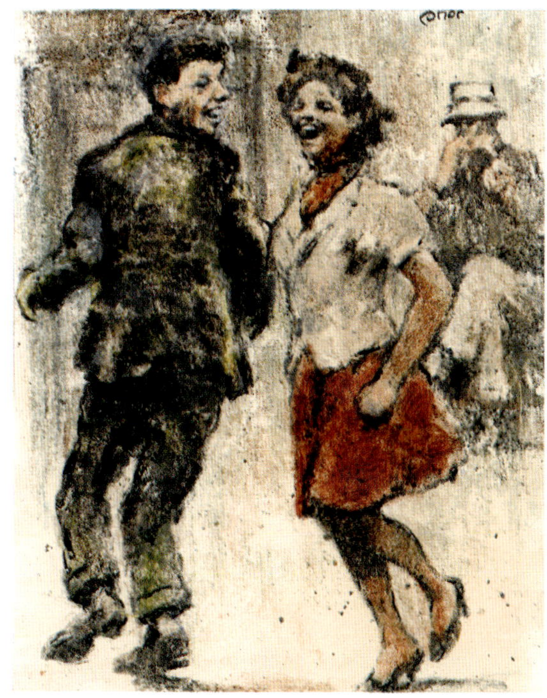

11.Stepping out Together

William Conor

William Conor (1881-1968)
11. Stepping out Together
Wax crayon on paper
45 x 34.5 cm
Private collection

William Conor's success in communicating abstract human qualities in his pictures often transcends his apparent technical shortcomings in drawing anatomy. Here, the young man's legs are noticeably odd, and his overall pose awkward, but Conor, as he had done in his *Queue for the Picture House* (cat. 42), focuses on capturing his young subjects' abounding energy rather than on the precise delineation and modelling of form. The unevenness in the technical quality of Conor's drawings may be attributable to the fact that he was a prolific and apparently compulsive draughtsman, who committed scenes and ideas to paper that, crucially, would inform many of his more highly finished paintings in oils but were not necessarily intended as fully finished works in their own right. In a letter of 1923 to Lawrence Haward, Director of Manchester City Art Galleries, Conor claimed that he had developed the habit of carrying a notebook with him at all times in which he would 'note down any happening which strikes me as interesting and significant'. [80] Jack B. Yeats, among others, employed a similar method. Conor added that by hiding his sketching block behind a newspaper, he had been able 'to garner many happy impressions' which he subsequently worked up into full easel paintings.[81] Conor's prolificacy in drawing translated to finished works, as he exhibited almost two hundred pictures at the Royal Hibernian Academy alone.

This is essentially a picture of humour and youthful abandon, in which the dancers have apparently departed from any formality to kick up their heels. As such, the picture differs greatly from the stiff, stylised form of dancing in Charles Lamb's *Dancing at a Northern Crossroads* (cat. 7), a painting underpinned by altogether more serious considerations. As demonstrated elsewhere in this exhibition, Irish artists have often been highly selective in their choice and representation of particular forms of dance, but the movement of the gleeful couple in this picture is noticeably less definitive. Indeed, the style of music to which they respond seems equally uncertain, and merely suggested by the figure in the background who appears to be playing a tin whistle (the instrument is indistinct). Admittedly, this reflects the increasingly eclectic nature of dance in Ireland in the twentieth century, driven by the introduction of various Music & Dance styles and instrumentation from abroad. Couples dancing was a subject to which Conor returned on many occasions, and this pair's movement is, admittedly, reminiscent of set dancing, a style derived from French dance (specifically 'set of quadrilles' introduced into Ireland in the eighteenth century). Set dancing survived uncertain times in the twentieth century, disapproved of and ultimately banned by the Gaelic League on the grounds that it was foreign and had been popularised initially in Ireland by the military, and viewed with comparable suspicion on moral grounds by the authorities of religious denominations.[82] Despite such censure, set dancing survived, healthily in the west of Ireland in particular, and enjoyed a revival from the 1970s onwards.[83]

Specificity was, in any case, often of secondary importance in Conor's work. Music & Dance often caught his attention but it was the energy and interaction associated with them that were invariably the real subjects of his pictures. Holbrook Jackson presciently opined that 'if a modern manufacturing town could have folk-songs and if those folk-songs could be translated into pictures, or if the feelings which inspired them could be pictorially represented, they would take the form of the art of William Conor'.[84] By an amusing coincidence, it was while sketching on a wall as a child, as he waited for a friend's music lesson to finish, that Conor's artistic talent was allegedly first recognised.[85] BR

80 Snoddy 1996, p.76.
81 *ibid*.
82 Vallely 1999, p.347.
83 Bell 2002, p.73.
84 *The Studio*, October 1925, p.76.
85 J. Wilson 1977, p.2.

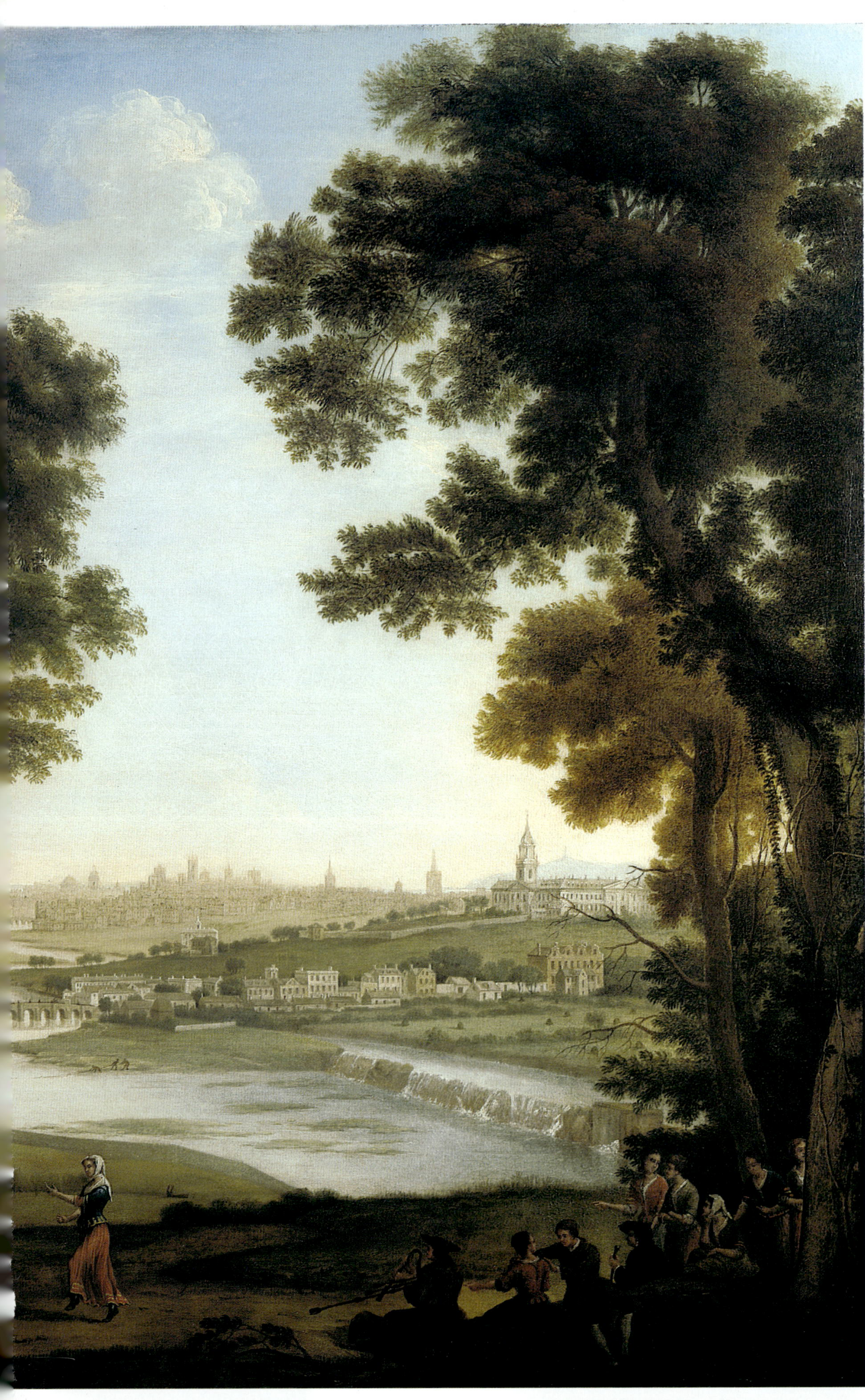

Joseph Tudor (fl. 1739-59)
2. View of Dublin from Chapelizod
Oil on canvas
117 x 150 cm
Private collection
See page 27

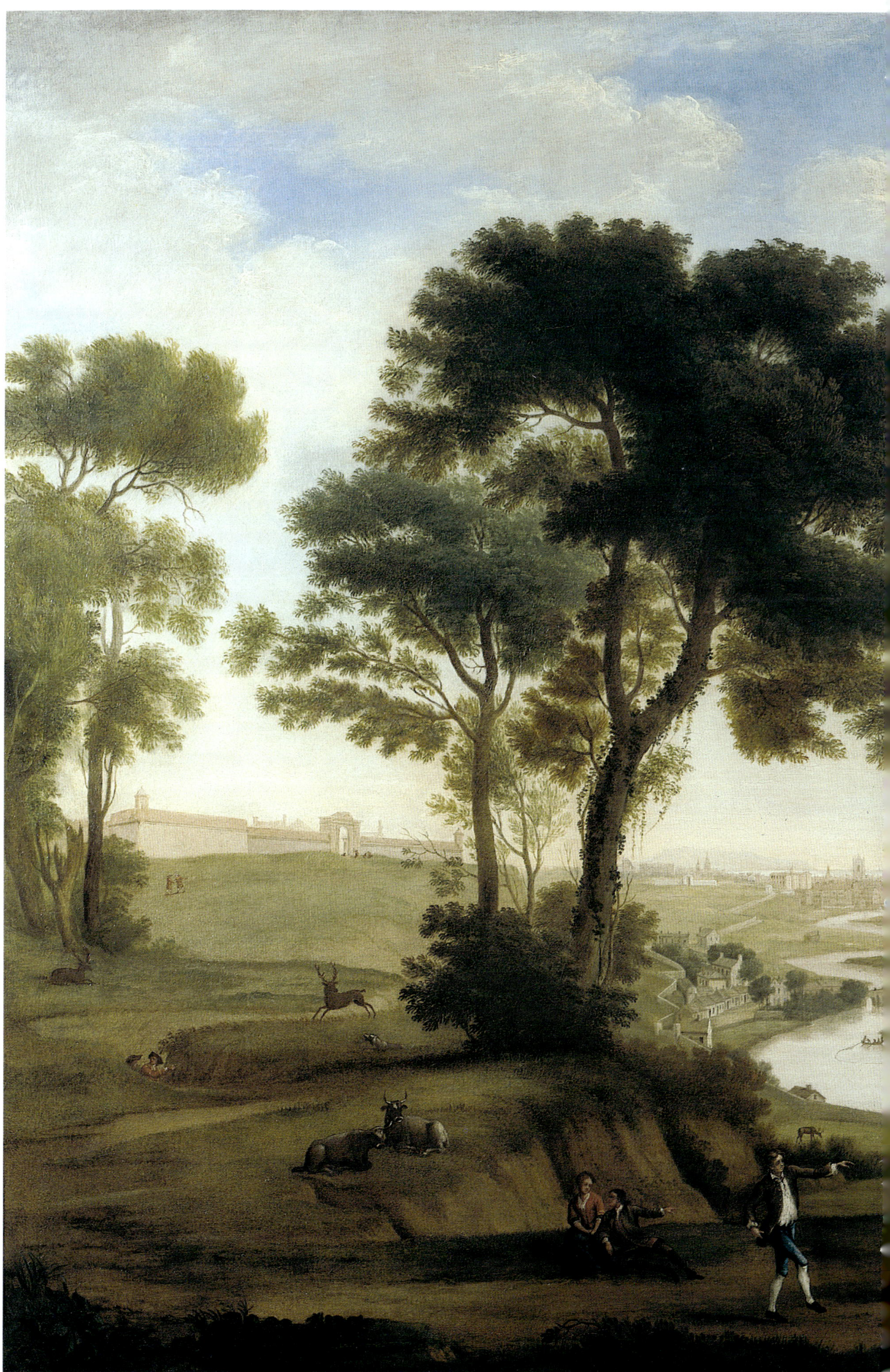

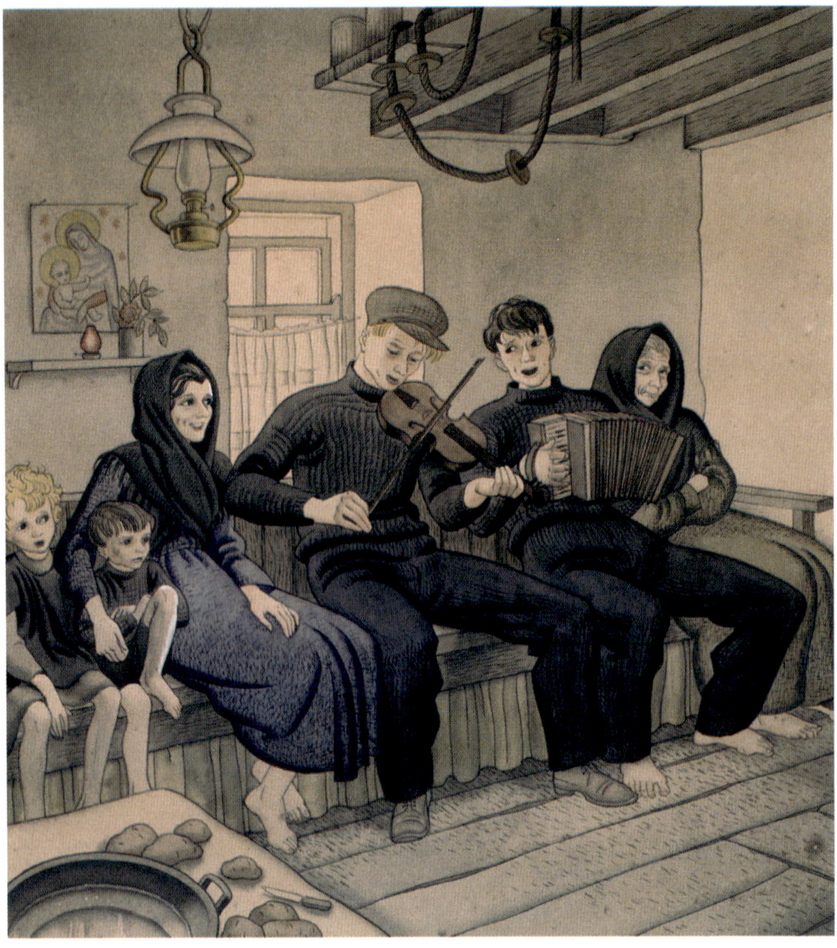

Christine Hurlstone Jackson
(fl.1933)
12. Music on the Great Blasket
c.1933
Watercolour on paper
33 x 27 cm
UCD Delargy Centre for Irish Folklore and the National Folklore Collection

12. Music on the Great Blasket

Christine Hurlstone Jackson

The Western Island, as the Great Blasket was also known, lies three miles off the Kerry coast, and in the 1930s was still home to about 150 inhabitants. They subsisted on a Spartan combination of fishing and small-scale farming, and entertained themselves chiefly with music, dancing, storytelling and poetry. Christine Hurlstone Jackson would have known about the visits of Robin and Ida Flower up to 1930, although Robin's book was not published until 1944.[86] Robin tapped into the tradition of Gaelic storytelling epitomised by islanders such as Peig Sayers and Tomás Ó Crithin, whose autobiography was published in 1929. His English translation came out the year after Jackson's visit to paint this picture. She travelled there with her brother, who was himself a collector of folklore, so she would have been aware of the community's cultural awakening.

Jackson presents a musical gathering in a kitchen interior of the old, traditional island type with a floor of beaten earth and boards (often salvaged from shipwrecks). The family are seated on a long settle, and the floor-level turf fire would be on the right, closest to the grandmother. Above her head is one of the two kitchen lofts. Flower describes how this '*cúllochta*, the back-loft, over-hangs the hearth...heaped with implements of the Island existence: nets, bags of wool, sails, oars, ladders, boots, and concertinas, shears for sheepshearing and panniers for turf carrying, an epitome and index of all that simple life'.[87] The furniture of such kitchens was 'all for use, not luxury; a settle which can be used as a bed, and has infinite capacity as a seat in the daytime, a table equally accommodating when there is call for seats, a dresser boarded in below to serve as a hen coop, and a few chairs either of wood or woven cords.'[88] Keeping hens in kitchen coops encouraged them artificially to continue laying eggs during winter, thus providing an important variation to a family's monotonous diet.[89] Significantly, Jackson shows potatoes, which formed an even higher percentage of the diet here than on the mainland at this time, being prepared on the table.

The position of the mother and her smallest son on the settle deliberately echoes the portrait of the Madonna and child, behind their heads. Flower's description enlightens us further:

The same wall decorations appear with monotonous regularity in all the houses. There are religious pictures bought from travelling pedlars, a Virgin and Child, or a Christ with sorrowing eyes and rent and flaming heart... before which a tiny brass lamp burns always with a thin red flame showing through red glass.[90]

The simple holy shelf shown here also has a tiny vase of flowers on it, following the tradition of decorating it on special days such as Ascension Day that endures in some households. The shelf was the focal point of family prayers, and more elaborate versions held plaster statues and incorporated pitched roofs or decorative fretwork.[91] The musicians play the accordion or melodeon and the fiddle and the sound they made would typically have been 'very much in the style of West Kerry music, rich in polkas and slides and designed for set dancing'.[92] CK

86 See Flower 1973.
87 *ibid*, p.44.
88 *ibid*, p.43.
89 Kinmonth 1993, pp.118-23, figs 181-90.
90 Flower 1973, p.42.
91 Kinmonth 1993, pp.192-94, figs 308, 310-13.
92 Bo Almqvist, quoted in Kinmonth 2006, pp.70-71.

13. Ceilidh at Dunboyne

Eva Henrietta Hamilton

Unlike those pictures by Fowler and Conor that represent impromptu dancing, this painting by Eva Hamilton seems to depict a more formal demonstration of the art. Though in the northern counties, the term ceilidh (ceilidhe or céilí), traditionally referred to a social visit, it is more readily associated with social evenings that were popularised following the Gaelic Revival after 1897. In response to the burgeoning interest in Irish Music & Dance among the Irish community in England and Scotland, these events drew on 'the revival, reconstruction and composition' of indigenous, old-Irish dance forms and music and were soon attracting large numbers in Ireland as well.[93] The form known as céilí dancing did not develop until decades later.

Both Eva Hamilton and her artist sister Letitia would have been throughout their youth familiar with pictures of everyday life, albeit within privileged and rarified circles. Their great-grandfather Charles Hamilton married Caroline Tighe of Rosanna, County Wicklow, who had executed many pencil and watercolour monochromes of 'elegant scandals and absurdities in the contemporary life of the Irish great house'.[94] These pictures hung on the walls in Hamwood, the Hamilton's family home.

Interestingly, the scene depicted by Hamilton evokes more immediately the Scottish céilí, which constituted an on-stage concert. In fact, the formality of the scene suggests that the young dancer may be taking part in a feis, a music festival involving competition, or at least a dance demonstration. This is suggested by various details. The young dancer, for example, wears a dance costume, dances alone on a raised platform, and is flanked closely by an accordion player on one side, and a dance mistress on the other, who watches intently while clapping out time. It is a spirited picture appropriate to the subject and perhaps indeed to the formidable personality of the artist, who Mary Swanzy referred to as having 'red hair and a temper to match'.[95]

The title indicates that the picture records a scene in Dunboyne, County Meath, the nearest village to Hamwood, the Palladian-style house built by Charles Hamilton in the 1770s, where Eva and her younger sister Letitia grew up.[96] The sisters had a close if sometimes tense relationship, travelling and exhibiting together on several occasions. For example, they exhibited a selection of Venetian pictures together in Dublin in 1924.[97] Though the Hamilton sisters were well-travelled and showed works of various subjects at major exhibitions in Ireland and abroad during their lives, local themes featured in both their oeuvres. *Dunboyne Village* (private collection), for example, was one of the paintings Letitia, the more accomplished painter of the two, contributed when she first exhibited at the RHA in 1909, while *The Moor of Meath* and *Dunboyne* were among the paintings Eva contributed to the Irish International Exhibition in Dublin in 1907 and the RHA in 1911 respectively. As a scene of recreation, however, this is a relatively unusual choice of subject for Eva, who when not painting portraits and landscape, tended towards scenes of domestic activity and outdoor work, such as *Haymaking in Connemara* (private collection). Nor is there obvious evidence of the influence of Sir William Orpen, her teacher at the Dublin Metropolitan School of Art, which features conspicuously elsewhere in her early work.[98]

Despite the number of figures involved and the animated subject, Hamilton's picture is consistent with the taste for simplicity that the artist displayed in much of her mature work. The summary technique makes it difficult to decipher some of the

Eva Henrietta Hamilton
(1876-1960)
13. Ceilidh at Dunboyne
Oil on canvas
56 x 52.5 cm
Private collection courtesy of James Adams Salerooms

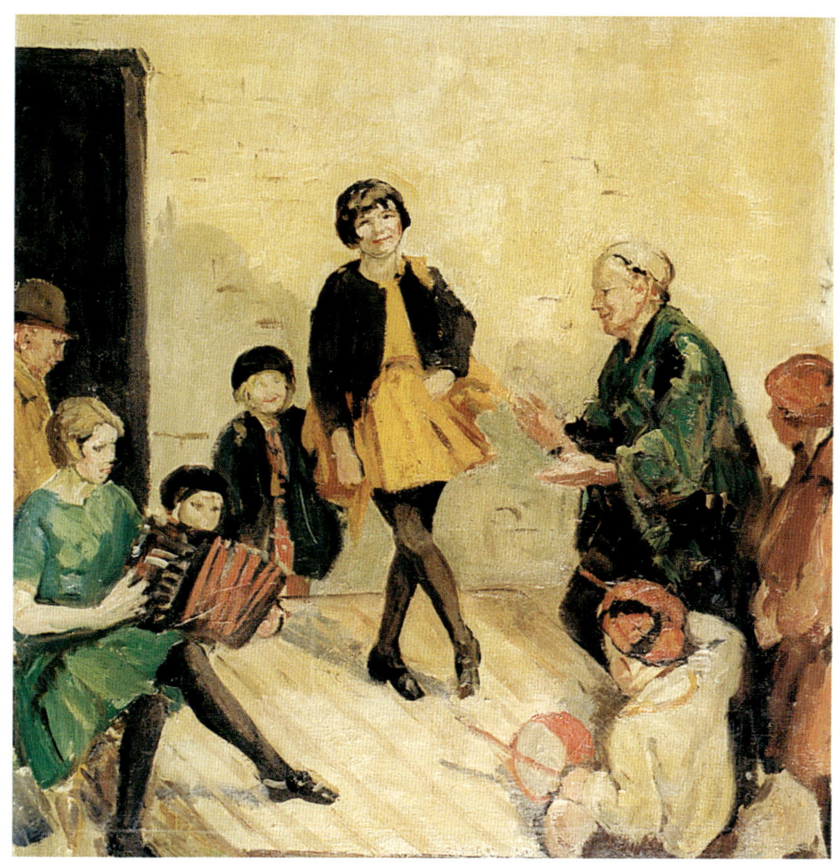

detail in the picture, particularly on the costume and musical instruments. However, one can clearly make out that Eva has placed the keys on the correct side of the accordion. More importantly, however, in the context of a record of a public performance, one can see that the young woman, appropriately, plays the accordion fully extended (rather than in small movements) to achieve a louder, stronger sound. Playing it this way would usually require the musician to support the instrument with a shoulder strap, though this is not always the case.[99] A comic counterpoint to the apparent formality of the scene is provided by the young boy in a hat in the foreground, who beats a drum perilously close to the dancer's feet and rather too vigorously. BR

---

93 Vallely 1999, p.60.

94 Pyle 1997a, p.123.

95 Snoddy 1996, p.162.

96 Maria Spilsbury Taylor was a visitor to Hamwood in the early nineteenth century.

97 *The Studio*, vol.87, (1924), p.169

98 See, for example, Eva's portrait of c.1910 of her mother, Louisa Hamilton in the drawing room of the family's winter residence, 40 Dominick Street, Dublin. Pyle 1997a, p.125.

99 Information courtesy of Nicholas Carolan.

14. An Interval in the Ceilidhe

Elizabeth Rivers

Though known recently under the title *Onlookers at the Ceilidhe*, it seems likely that this is the painting *An Interval in the Ceilidhe*, exhibited by Elizabeth Rivers at the RHA in 1936, at which time she was living on the Aran Islands. The term ceilidhe or céilí has come to be understood popularly as an event involving Irish dancing, but it traditionally referred to a social gathering that could include music and song.[100] Moreover, it was common practice at céilís for singers to perform between dances, either unaccompanied or assisted, as here, by musicians. The arrangement of Rivers's figures and furniture would have been consistent with common experience. As céilí nights were usually taken up principally with dancing, relatively few chairs would have been kept in the hall or house. As a consequence here, most of the men stand, while the group of women crowd together on the limited seating available, some sitting on each other's laps.

This painting betrays the artist's fundamental concern for the formal, aesthetic qualities of the picture rather than its strictly documentary function. This is partly attributable to Rivers's sojourn in Paris, during which she trained under Severini and André Lhote, who introduced her to Synthetic Cubism.[101] She has adopted a more reductive approach than her nineteenth-century predecessors, composing her picture with blocks of colour and simplified shapes rather than concerning herself, like Maria Spilsbury Taylor, Erskine Nicol and Howard Helmick, with the minutiae of the scene. This is clearly evident in the case of the concertina played by the seated figure on the right hand side of the composition. Described by a few judicious lines, it seems to fuse with the musician's similarly simplified hand. The picture anticipates the 'modern abstract approach' identified in her much later work by the *Dublin Magazine* in its review of the Dublin Painters exhibition of 1949.

Among Rivers's relatively few conspicuous concessions to vernacular detail is the representation of the flat caps of the men, though these too, forming an arc opposite the head of the singer, serve a formal function in the overall pattern of the picture. Human expressiveness too has been simplified, though not eliminated. The close attention of the women seated behind the singer is communicated economically by the manner in which they lean gently inwards towards the singer as if transfixed by her song.

Just as William Conor's clearly delineated compositions appear to owe a debt to his training as an illustrator, Rivers's painting possesses a flatness and angularity redolent of the woodcut printing technique in which the artist specialised in her early career. In any case, her schematic approach to the subject is perhaps to be expected. Rivers appears to have been compelled to see the Aran Islands in pictorial terms. From the beginning of her book, *Stranger in Aran*, she talked expressively of the colour of the island, from 'gentians of a blue so intense it draws the eye to find its single flower' to immense areas of limestone 'the colour of elephants hide'.[102] Elsewhere, she likened men toiling in the fields to 'notes on a stave of music', such was the rhythmic nature of their work, and described their newly dug fields as 'works of art'.[103] Elsewhere, her recollection of a gathering in a bride's house the day before a wedding compares neatly with the present painting:

The heat inside was stifling and there was little space in the crowded room, people sat or stood in a crush by the walls and in the few square feet of space in the middle of the room four people were dancing a set. A youth sitting near the fire played the melodeon the sweat pouring down his face.[104]

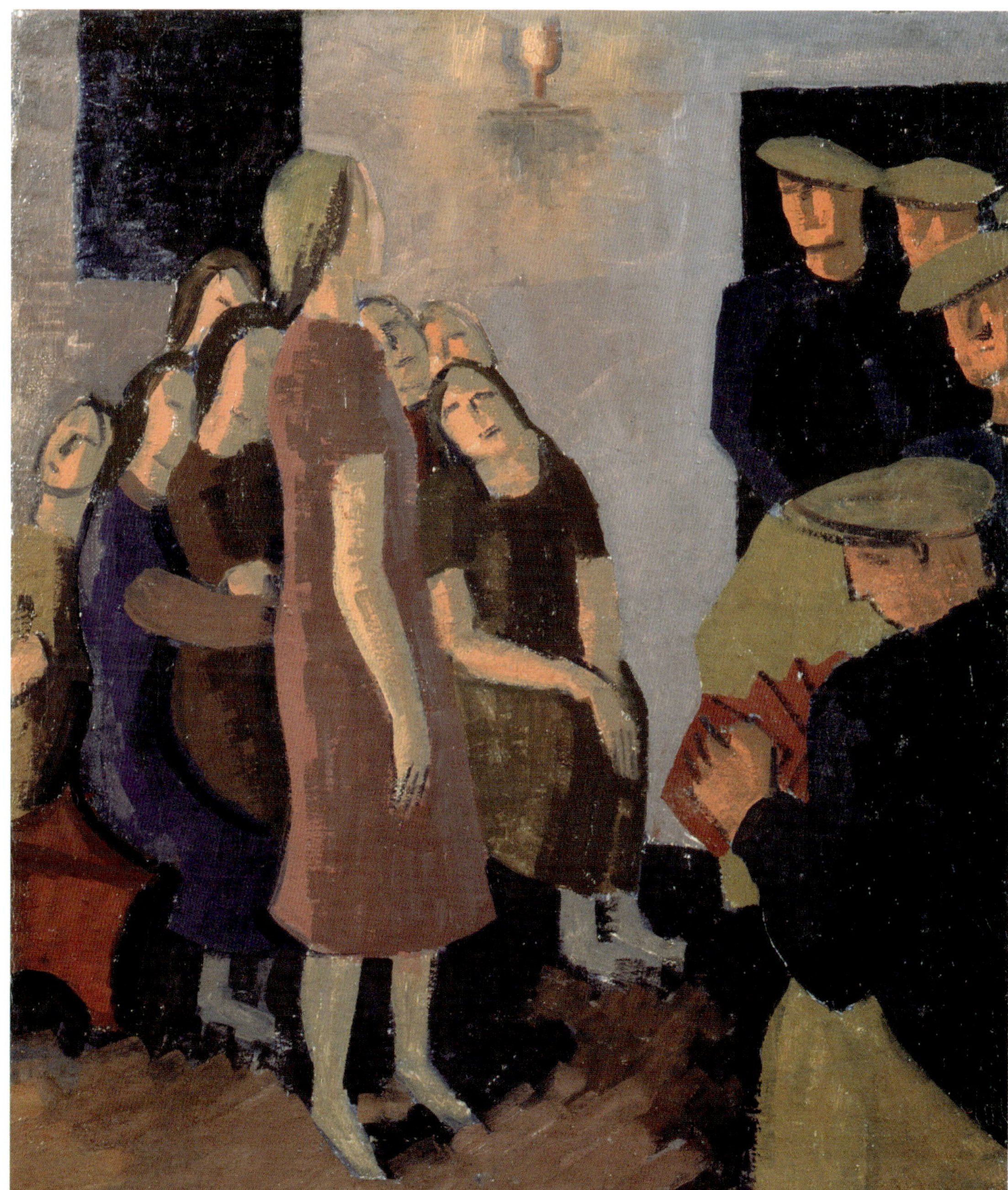

Elizabeth Rivers (1903-64)
14. An Interval in the Ceilidhe
1935
Oil on canvas
60 x 50 cm
AIB Art Collection

Later, she remembered:

The dance was over and the melodeon player, taking a moment's respite, went to the door. A handsome woman started to sing, one of the old songs that rise and fall in a long chant. Gripping her neighbour's hand she held it on her knee and looked up to the rafters as she sang; every now and again one of the audience encouraged her until, as suddenly as it had begun, the chant ceased and there was a burst of clapping.[105]

Rivers, who was born and received her initial training in England, painted *An Interval in the Ceilidhe* on her first visit to the Aran Islands in 1935. Intending to remain for just three months, she stayed for nine and the following year returned to live on Inis Mór for seven years. She embraced island life and her home, a cottage built for Robert J. Flaherty for his film *Man of Aran* (1934), was always open to visitors.[106] The works she produced during this period, such as *Dawn-Aran Islands* and *Unloading the Catch- Aran* (both in private collections), evince her affection for the lifestyle and landscape there. Her sojourn was not, however, entirely without complication. Theo Snoddy has recorded that Rivers's life on Inis Mór 'was initially shadowed by a parish priest who was somewhat agitated by women who wore trousers'.[107]

Despite moving back to England in 1943, Rivers maintained contact with Ireland, returning on several occasions, contributing to various groups and exhibitions, including the Watercolour Society of Ireland and the Irish Exhibition of Living Art, and collaborating on stained-glass projects over a nine-year period with her friend Evie Hone. The Aran Islands in particular clearly left a lifelong impression on her. *Stranger in Aran*, of 1946, which she illustrated with pen and ink drawings, was the last book to be published by the Cuala Press, while six of her wood engravings featured in Victor Waddington's *Ireland: The Aran Islands* of 1952. She also illustrated with wood engravings her friend Ethel Mannin's *Connemara Journal*, published in 1947. BR

100 Information courtesy of Nicholas Carolan
101 Mainie Jellett also studied under Lhote.
102 Rivers 1946, p.1.
103 *ibid*, p.2.
104 *ibid*, p.38.
105 *ibid*, pp.41-42.
106 S.B. Kennedy 1989, p.14. Her regard for community was exemplified by her decision to return to London to work as a fire warden during the blitz.
107 Snoddy 1996, p.426.

15. Yellow Bungalow

Gerard Dillon

Gerard Dillon lived most of his life in the urban environments of London, Dublin, and particularly his native Belfast, but developed during lengthy visits an affinity with the west of Ireland that he communicated powerfully through his art.[108] For these images of everyday life in the west, which are often at once idiosyncratic, evocative and monumental, he drew on memory, direct observation, whimsy and an appetite for pattern making. George Campbell's description of his friend Dillon as a 'simple complex' character might just as effectively describe his pictures.[109]

Yellow Bungalow, however, represents a departure from his early, matter-of-fact representations of simple life in the west. While the other pictures of Music & Dance in this exhibition imply or illustrate collective enjoyment and recreation, this painting introduces the notion of dislocation. It provides, in that sense, an arresting counterpoint to the gregariousness exemplified by these other paintings. The woman in the corner of the room sits insouciantly with arms folded, and the cat asleep on the chair appears as inert as the fish on the plate in the foreground. As if in consequence, the young boy with the accordion engages the viewer rather than the woman in the room with him. His music, it seems, is a personal indulgence. The silence of the accordion seems all the more loaded when one considers that Dillon was a music lover, who greatly enjoyed taking part in sessions during his stay with George Campbell on Innislaken just a few years earlier.

Dillon amplifies the awkwardness that attends the scene by distorting the interior space and presenting it from a bird's eye view. The painting also subverts the longstanding perception, perpetuated textually, pictorially and aurally, of the hearth as the fulcrum of the home. It was the point at which families met, storytelling took place, clothes were dried, meals prepared and sick animals cared for. It was even believed that if the fire in the hearth went out the soul of the family would be extinguished with it. It was synonymous with warmth and hospitality and its turf fire would normally have been kept alight at all times, through winter and summer. Compositionally, Dillon's picture is redolent of other scenes round the hearth, such as Sir William Orpen's *Old John's Cottage, Connemara* (private collection), Michael Powell O'Malley's *Himself and Herself* (Crawford Municipal Art Gallery) and Sean O'Sullivan's *The Old Couple* (private collection). However, here a sense of distance or absence has replaced the conviviality normally associated with the setting. Indeed, even the traditional hearth itself has been supplanted by a stove. The stove does glow, and the supply of turf beside it promises heat in the future, but a cold inertia seems to pervade the room. The sheet in the young boy's hand, perhaps a letter from abroad, and the prominently placed wicker chair occupied by the cat, might suggest that an important member of the household has emigrated.[110] The modest furnishings, supply of fuel for the stove and cooking utensils are indicative of a comfortable and ordered life, but the demeanour of the inhabitants suggests otherwise.

Dillon's liberal use of primary colours, normally employed to communicate a brighter, more positive atmosphere (as, for instance, in Lamb's *Dancing at a Northern Crossroads* (cat. 7), further confounds the viewer.[111] In this sense, the painting conveys more complex human emotions than is more usually associated with the artist's decorative landscape and genre pictures in the west of Ireland, with which, in the tradition of Gauguin and his predecessors in Brittany and elsewhere, he sought to 'express with modern naïveté the untainted simplicity' he saw there.[112] *Yellow Bungalow* has been compared plausibly to Van Gogh's *Le Café de nuit à Arles* (Yale University Art Library), not least on account of its bright palette and distorted perspective.[113] However, beyond these formal similarities, the paintings share a disorientating atmosphere at odds with their subject. Both represent social spaces devoid of interaction. BR

108 Dillon travelled to Connemara first in 1939.

109 Stairs 1990, p.64.

110 Susan Stairs has proposed that the sheet in the boy's hand, the fresh fish on the table and the supply of turf indicate that the couple in the painting anticipate an imminent arrival to their home. Stairs 1990, p.64.

111 Lavery felt that the 'red, blue and yellow' donned by the people of Connemara were more typical of Russia than Ireland. Lavery 1940, p.204.

112 Murray 1997, p.64. Dorothy Walker has described Dillon aptly as a 'genuine primitive'. Walker 1997, pp.41-42.

113 Stairs 1990, p.80.

Gerard Dillon (1916-71)
15. Yellow Bungalow
1954
Oil on canvas
76.8 x 81.2 cm
Collection Ulster Museum, Belfast

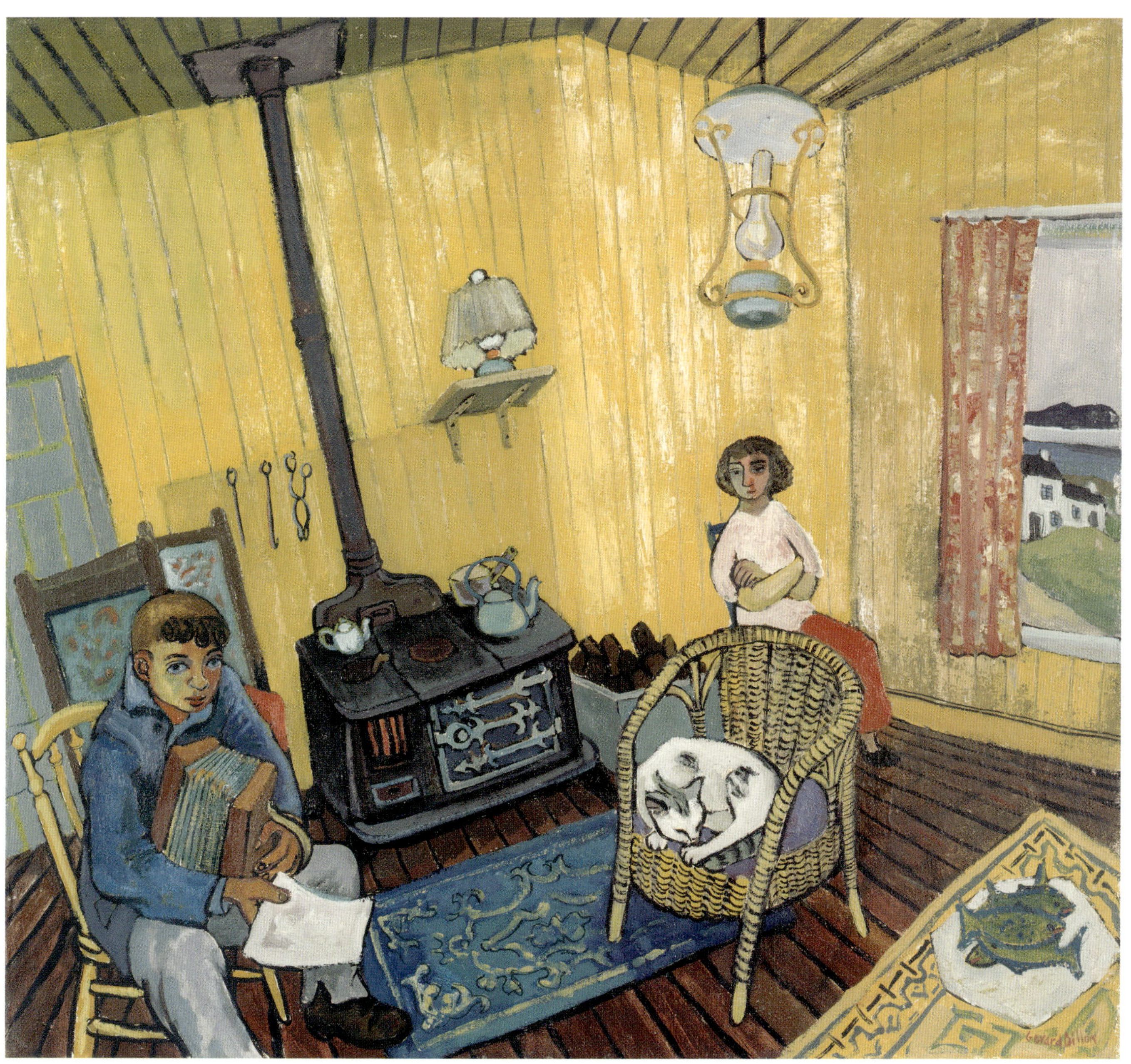

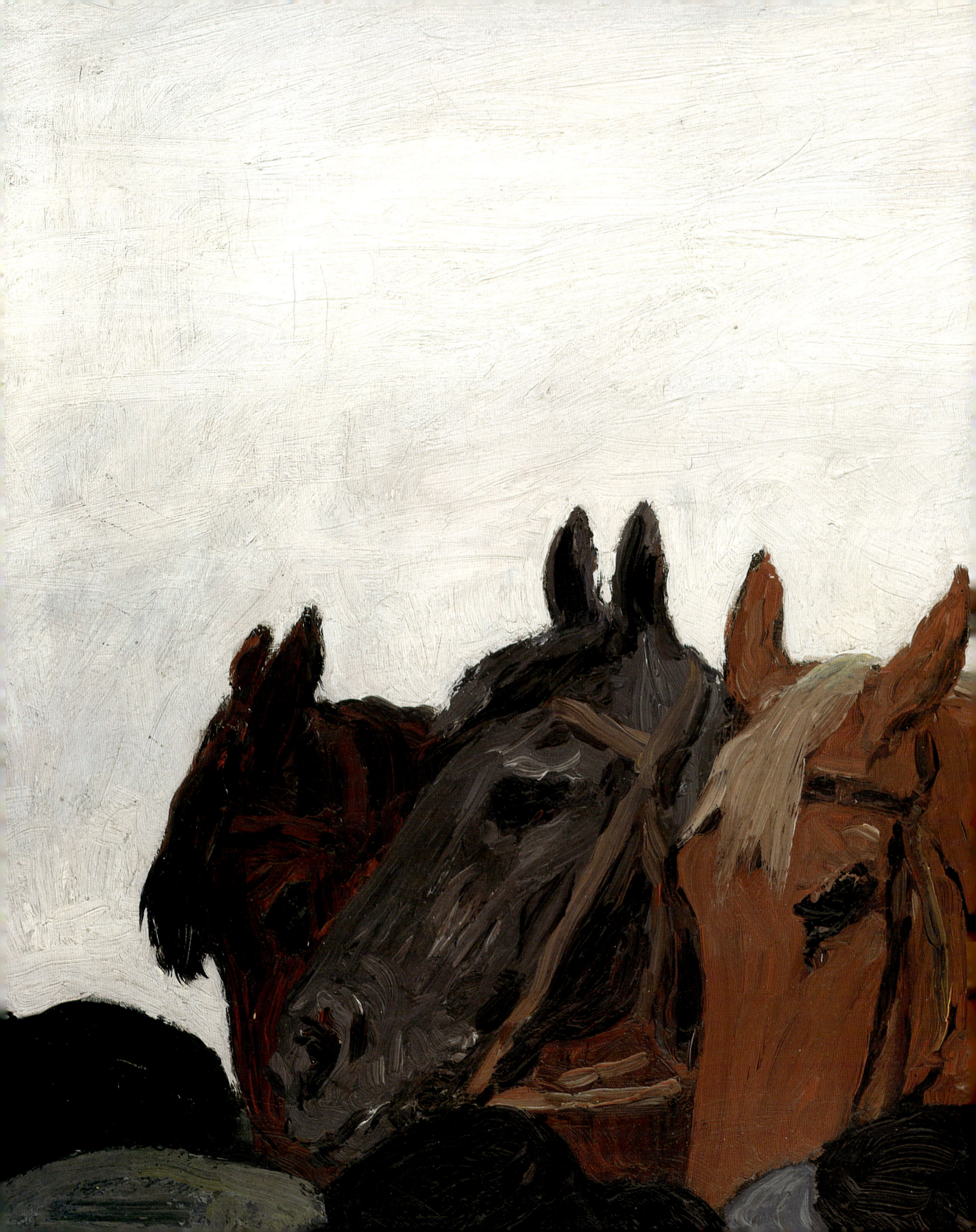

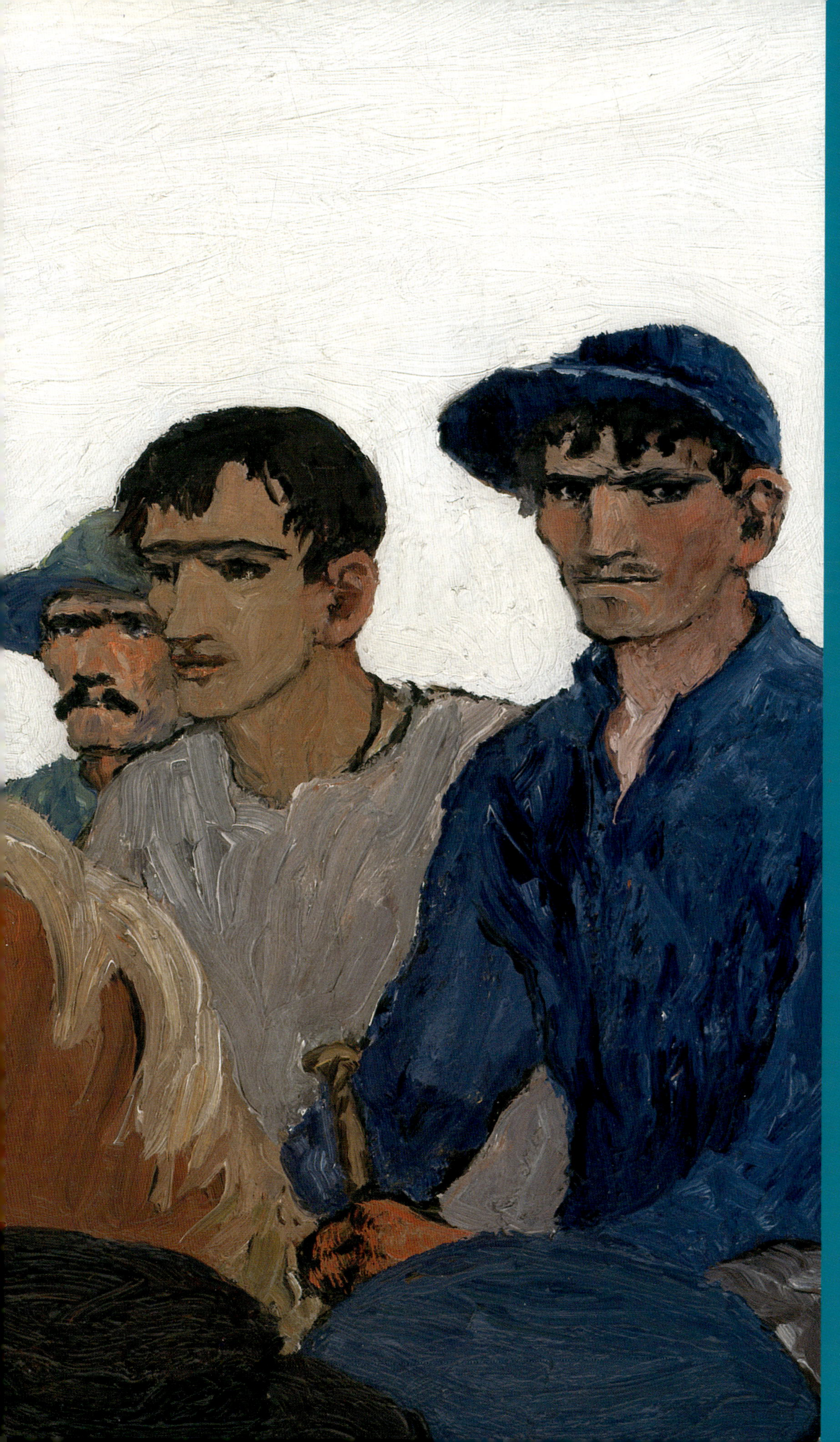

Sport

After **John Fogarty**
(19th century)
Robert Havell the Elder and
Robert Havell the Younger
16. Derrynane Abbey, Co. Kerry, home of Daniel O'Connell
1831
Etching and hand-coloured aquatint
52 x 64.6 cm
National Gallery of Ireland

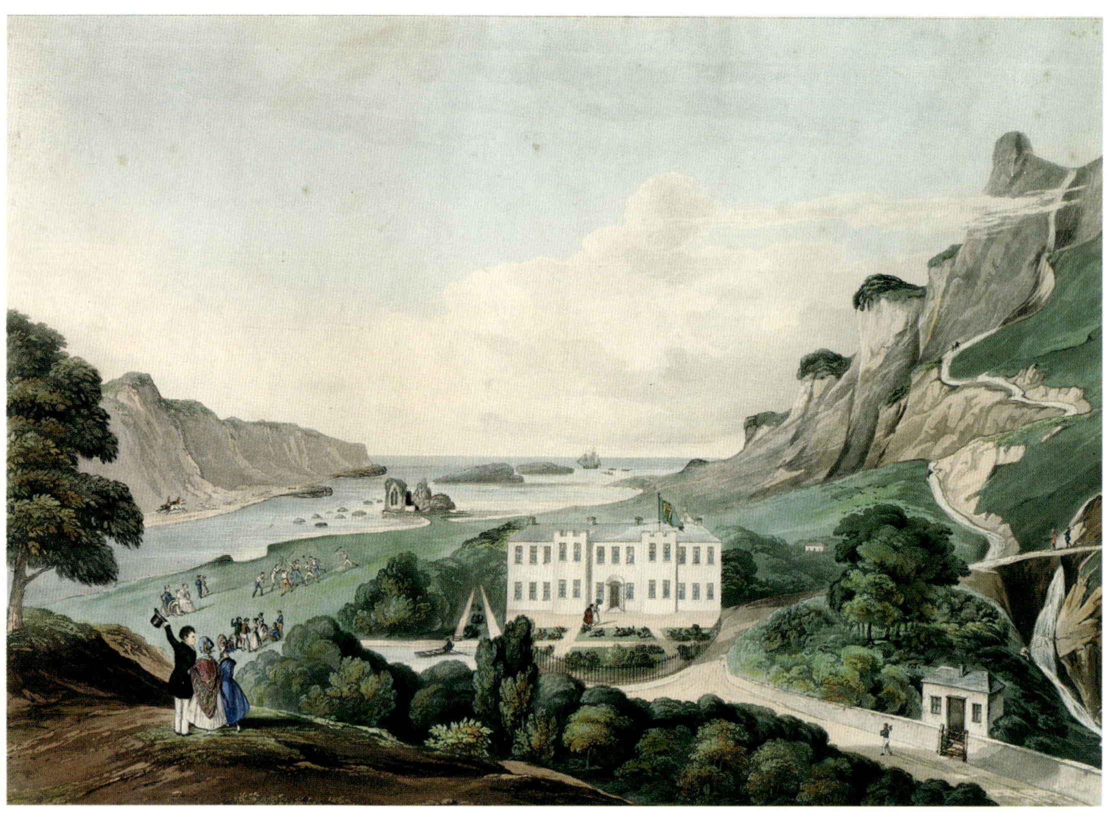

16. Derrynane Abbey, Co. Kerry, home of Daniel O'Connell

After **John Fogarty**

In Fogarty's naïve view of Daniel O'Connell's Kerry home, the figures may seem out of proportion with one another and their surroundings, and the detail, such as the mountain road, idiosyncratic, but the picture does present Derrynane and its local terrain as a place of considerable grandeur, quite unlike the 'half-lordly, half-slovenly State which [O'Connell] kept in Kerry' referred to retrospectively and ungenerously many years later by *The Times*.[1] Equally, the place seems more social than one would expect of 'the most deserted region of Ireland' as it was described by Prince von Pückler-Muskau in 1828.[2] Pückler-Muskau's journey on horseback to Derrynane was treacherous and eventful, but the area appealed to him as did its 'poor, good-natured' people,[3] who, Pückler-Muskau wrote, did not live 'gathered together in villages but scattered among the mountains and, unspoilt by the bustle of towns, lead a patriarchal life'.[4] The Halls recorded that Derrynane was 'originally a farm-house' but had been 'added to from time to time, according to the increase of the property, or family, of its possessor'. While they maintained that defining its architectural style was difficult, they conceded that it was 'beautifully situated; and in its immediate neighbourhood are the picturesque ruins of an abbey, founded in the seventh century by the monks of St Finbar'.[5]

Fogarty's composition can be read as a compendium of social, sporting and recreational pursuits, many of which feature elsewhere among the pictures in this exhibition. The activities represented include hunting, fishing, shooting, hurling, music making, dancing, and boating. Reference to labour is minimal.

Hurling as depicted by Fogarty differs markedly from the game described with typical hyperbole by Mr and Mrs Hall. To them it was a sport of unusual attrition, in which games that might have begun with as many as fifty or sixty players could continue until darkness fell and were 'often attended with dangerous, and sometimes with fatal, results'.[6] Writing just a few years after Fogarty produced his picture, the Halls portrayed hurling as admirable and popular, but somewhat akin to heroic, war-like, chaos. 'It is a fine manly exercise,' they wrote 'with sufficient of danger to produce excitement; and is indeed, par excellence, *the* game of the peasantry of Ireland. To be an expert hurler, a man must possess athletic powers of no ordinary character; he must have a quick eye, a ready hand, and a strong arm; he must be a good runner, a skilful wrestler, and withal patient as well as resolute'.[7] Fogarty's depiction, which features two balls and no goals, is a mere approximation of the game.

O'Connell himself, standing in the foreground, raises his top hat aloft as if in recognition not just of his own property but of the animated and contented social life that exists on and around it. The unmitigated harmony described in the picture is likely to be as fanciful as the exaggerated landscape that contains it, but points perhaps to the Arcadian Ireland to which O'Connell and his political allies aspired. With the inclusion of hurling, and the prominent figure of O'Connell himself, Derrynane can be read as a post-Act of Union, Catholic equivalent to the grand demesnes of the eighteenth century that had been laid out specifically to accommodate pastimes appropriate to their owners, such as 'walking, riding, playing bowls, boating, fishing and hunting'.[8] Moreover, these outdoor activities suggested a robust, even virile quality. Traditionally, field sports (including hunting) were seen and promoted by their exponents as manly alternatives to the effete diversions (such as opera and theatre) in which urban dwellers indulged.[9] Significantly, however, though the prosperous and powerful in the eighteenth and nineteenth centuries often endorsed and facilitated football and hurling, they preferred to engage in the less confrontational exertions of riding, hunting and shooting.[10] BR

1 *The Times*, 22 July 1775.
2 Pückler-Muskau 1987, p.211. Pückler-Muskau provides an entertaining and melodramatic description of his eventful journey to Dennynane.
3 *ibid*, p.214.
4 *ibid*, p.222.
5 Hall 1843, vol. I, p.269.
6 *ibid*, p.258.
7 *ibid*, p.257.
8 Barnard 2004, p.190. Admittedly, not all Protestant landowners distanced themselves from pursuits associated more readily with the poorer Catholic majority. Pole Cosby and Richard Edgeworth, for example, openly supported hurling, football and older forms of music. See Barnard 2004, p.250.
9 *ibid*, p.244-245.
10 *ibid*, p.250.

17. Two Boys on a Height

Estella Solomons

Two Boys on a Height is an enigmatic picture that is at once disquieting and curious. It is unclear, for example, whether the expressions of the two young boys are of anxiety, resignation or indecision. Also uncertain is their activity. One does not know if they are waiting, resting or perhaps, more dramatically, pondering their fate. Even the suggestion that one of them might be carrying a hurley stick is merely speculative and based on the minimum of pictorial evidence. Are they, as Hilary Pyle has proposed, young recruits of the Countess Markievicz, 'probably as well acquainted with a rifle' as with a hurley stick?[11] Solomons was a member of Cumann na mBan, through which she learnt signalling and prepared to administer first aid during the Easter Rising of 1916.[12] Alternatively, are the boys simply children of poverty similar to those in Solomons's marginally more optimistic *Street Urchins with Bird Cage* (private collection)?

Technically, the painting is quite unusual for an artist associated more readily with colour and light. Solomons's instinctive understanding of the dramatic potential of light and shade found full expression in her superlative etchings, many of which depict Dublin street scenes. She particularly favoured views into sunlit areas from places of shadow, such as alleyways, underneath bridges and archways. The manner in which the house on the right hand side of *Two Boys on a Height* is picked out against a brooding sky is vaguely reminiscent of those etchings. Similarly, in *Street Urchins with Bird Cage*, a painting comparable

Estella Solomons (1882-1968)
17. Two Boys on a Height
Oil on canvas
45 x 70 cm
Private collection courtesy of Karen Reihill Fine Art

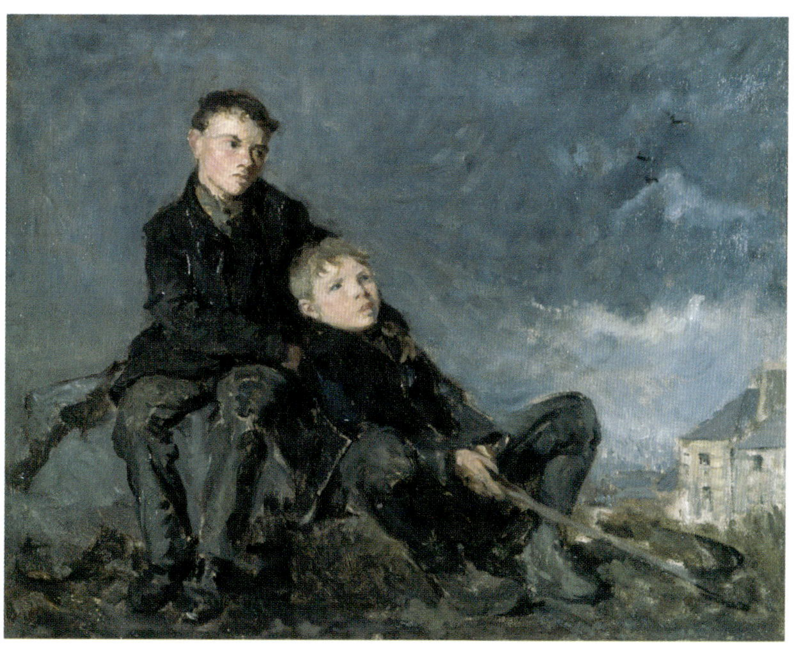

to *Two Boys on a Height* in both form and theme, a young girl squints in the sun that illuminates an otherwise gloomy setting. These pictures are particularly interesting as Solomons typically enlivened her landscapes in oils with rich, fresh colours. She also applied paint liberally and confidently, regardless of the location or nature of the subject. Like George Russell, she had a deep affection for Donegal, producing some of her most arresting, joyful landscapes around Dunfanaghy and Marble Hill, but also worked in north County Dublin, Kerry and elsewhere. The colour range she preferred for portraiture tended to be more subdued and austere, but also hinted occasionally at her predilection for contrasts in light and shade.

If the boys are indeed hurlers at rest, it is curious to reflect on how perceptions of gaelic games had changed over successive decades. William Carleton, writing in the 1840s, identified a tendency among the rural community to identify sport as the antithesis of piety and reflection. In his story 'The Station' a parish priest urges one of his local congregation to encourage his young son to attend a station in the man's home, assuring him that it will open the boy's eyes. 'Do you hear that, Briney?', the father says with appropriate urgency 'you must give up yer hurling and idling now, you see'.[13] In retrospect the association of sport with indolence seems extraordinary. By the end of the nineteenth century, the Gaelic Athletic Association (GAA), established in 1884, had harnessed a latent enthusiasm for football, hurling and athletics with such success that the games were played and promoted in an organised fashion throughout the country. BR

11 Pyle 1999, p.6.
12 Solomons made her home a safehouse for fugitives during the Easter Rising and Civil War. She also produced portraits of some of Ireland's foremost political and cultural figures.
13 Carleton 1843, p.147.

18. The Tipperary Hurler

Sean Keating

The Tipperary county hurling team was hugely successful in the early years of the Irish Free State, winning almost all their games between 1922 and 1927. In 1926 alone, the team won the inaugural National League title, embarked on a ten-week tour of the United States, which took them as far as San Francisco, and defeated Cork in the replay of the final of the Munster Championship in Thurles, the first game ever broadcast on national radio.[14]

Though not strictly an amalgamation, Keating's portrait appears to have been inspired by two notable characters, John Joe Hayes and Ben O'Hickey. Both men came from farming backgrounds in County Tipperary and bore a strong physical resemblance to one another. Hayes, born in Ballyerk in 1895, was a member of the Tipperary county team that won the All-Ireland Senior Hurling Championship in 1925 and that went on tour to the United States the following year.[15] It has been suggested that Keating sketched him during a break in the final at Croke Park in 1925. Hayes also played in the inaugural Tailteann Games in 1924.[16]

O'Hickey was a firebrand member of the Bansha Company of the IRA. Having been arrested in 1919 and jailed in Cork, he was transferred to Derry, but escaped to join Tom Barry's 'flying column'. He was wounded during one of the column's attacks, captured and subsequently sentenced to death. This sentence was commuted to penal servitude for life, however, and O'Hickey was imprisoned in England. On his release following the signing of the Anglo-Irish Treaty of 1921, O'Hickey entered the Dublin Metropolitan School of Art, and subsequently enjoyed considerable success as a professional artist. While at the school, he modelled for a number of Sean Keating's paintings, including *Race of the Gael* (NGI).

The figure's distinctive jersey seems similarly non-specific, but is consistent with the style of shirt worn by players at the time. The letters 'CHC', clearly visible on the sash, are likely to have been deliberately obscure, suggesting many possible towns or clubs in the county.

Typically, in Keating's contrived painting, studio and theatre converge in a dramatic display of props and backdrops. In the tradition of academic Victorian and Edwardian portraiture, and drawing particularly on the example of Sir William Orpen, Keating concerns himself with corporeality rather than verisimilitude *per se*. Formally, the picture is relatively straightforward, lacking the elaborate *mis-en-scène* and wistful air of many of Keating's politically loaded group portraits. Like a statesman or confident writer, the hurler engages the viewer directly with a curious turn of the head and knowing expression. The scale and composition of the picture lends Keating's figure a profound physicality that is consistent with the artist's general approach to figure painting and his concern with the construction of the figure.[17]

As Keating would have wanted his subject to be emblematic of a new, singularly Irish heroism, it is appropriate that he should have based it on the valiant figures of a champion athlete and an erstwhile militant nationalist. He presents his hurler as the

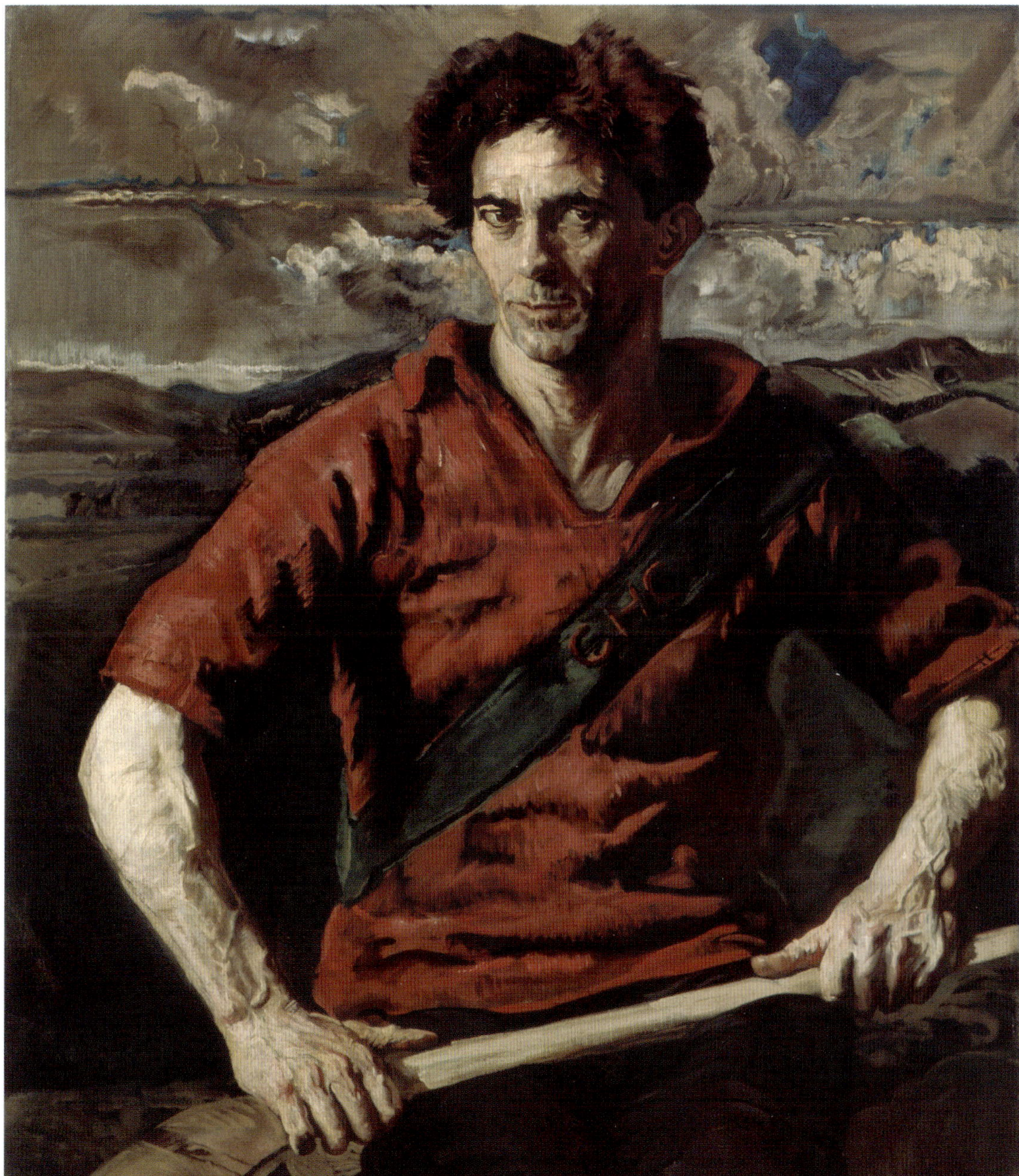

Sean Keating (1889-1977)
18. The Tipperary Hurler
1928
Oil on canvas
91.5 x 76 cm
Dublin City Gallery the Hugh Lane

sporting equivalent to the robust and upright characters elevated in *Race of the Gael* and *Men of Aran* (private collection), who battled with the elements.[18] This portrayal of hurling is consistent with both the public perception of its mythical origins and nineteenth-century accounts of the manner in which it was played. Keating's hurler appears to reinforce the connection between sporting prowess and masculinity that was well-established, and corroborates the notion of hurling as the game of warriors and heroes, of Cú Chulainn and St Colmcille. However tenuous these links might be when considered from a strictly historical point of view, the image certainly would have had resonance in the new Irish state, not least because of the strong identification of the GAA with political nationalism.[19] *The Tipperary Hurler* was exhibited at the XVIII Olympiad in Amsterdam in 1928 and in New York the following year. BR

14 2RN (later Radio Éireann) had been launched the same year.
15 See Kenny 1928, p.33.
16 The author is grateful to Eimear O'Connor for her generous assistance in the cataloguing of this work.
17 See Turpin 1988-89, pp.201-11.
18 Pyms Gallery 1993, p.62.
19 For a detailed discussion of this area see Cronin 1999, pp.72-111.

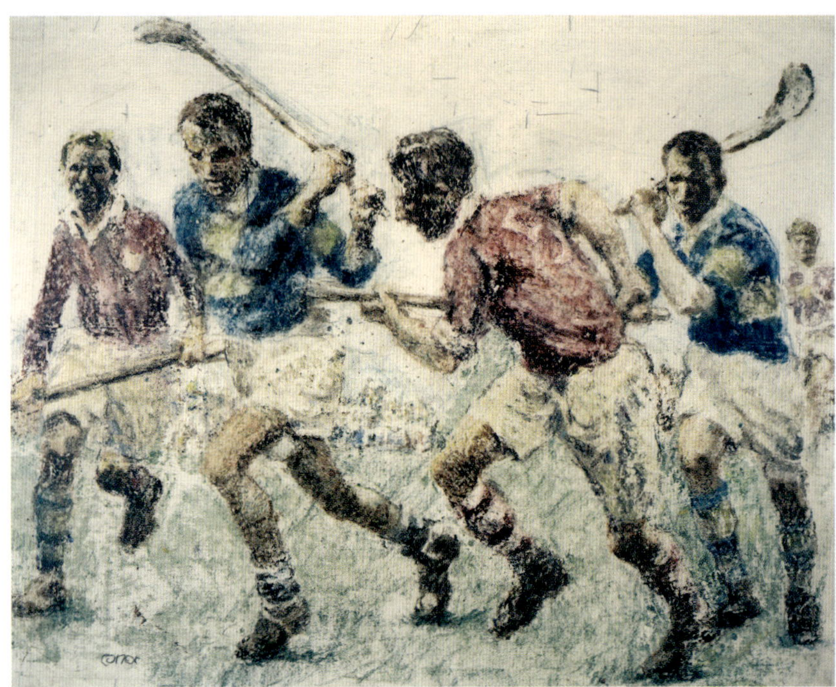

William Conor (1881-1968)
19. The Hurley Players (Falls Park, Belfast)
1948
Wax crayon on paper
50.8 x 61 cm
Ulster Folk & Transport Museum

19. The Hurley Players (Falls Park, Belfast)

William Conor

Given the ever-increasing popularity of hurling and gaelic football throughout Ireland in the early decades of the twentieth century, their poor representation in painting is conspicuous. Indeed, it is interesting that Conor, an artist who addressed in his work a myriad of social and participative activities across cultural divides in Ireland, from theatre and horse racing to children's games and parades, should himself have exhibited just one painting of Gaelic games, *The Hurley Boys*, during his lengthy and prolific career.

Though the jerseys worn by the players in Conor's picture suggest a Cork versus Tipperary clash, the picture actually records a local game in Falls Park, Belfast. Conor executed this work on paper at a particularly interesting juncture in the history of Gaelic games in the northern counties. The South Antrim GAA Board's stipulation of a few years earlier that each club should field a hurling as well as a football team had been met with consternation by many, as the latter code had been dominant in the county, but hurling soon proved extremely attractive to members. This popularity was galvanised in 1943 when Antrim reached the Senior All-Ireland Final, beating Galway and Kilkenny *en route*. Defeat to Cork in the final did not diminish enthusiasm, and clubs were soon campaigning for improved facilities (up to that point, just a handful of grounds, including Falls Park, were available). No county from the northern half of the country has yet won the All-Ireland senior hurling title, but Antrim can boast a sizeable hurling population and in some parts of the county that code is still favoured over football. Grass-roots support for the games was epitomised by the success of St Paul's Gaelic Athletic Club, who practised in Falls Park, in acquiring jerseys during rationing in the early 1940s by appealing to the local community to pool coupons.

Opened in 1873, Falls Park in West Belfast was the city's second public park. The park today occupies some forty-four acres, and as well as gaelic grounds, features a bowling pavilion, playground, cycle track, senior citizen pavilion, soccer pitches, pathways and horticultural displays.

In this study, Conor overcame the problem he often experienced of integrating his figures, based on drawings executed *in situ*, into the background, which was conceived retrospectively, by generalising the background and focusing his attention on the movement of the figures.[20] The four principal players, in alternate jerseys, span the composition like a frieze. Limb or hurley connects each player pictorially to the next, emphasising the dramatic movement from right to left that is so indicative of one of the world's fastest, and oldest, field sports. BR

20 See S.B. Kennedy 1991, p.183.

20. The Ball Alley

Jack B. Yeats

A love for sporting events and the sense of occasion that surrounded them was a constant source of inspiration for Jack B. Yeats throughout his career. As a young man in London he worked as a sports reporter for a number of journals, including *Paddock Life* and *Sporting Sketches*,[21] illustrating with remarkable skill dramatic moments in football matches and swimming races or the decisive blow in a boxing match. From about 1895, he began to look towards the west of Ireland for subject matter, which, predictably, included events such as horse racing and hurling. His first *Sketches of Life in the West of Ireland*, primarily watercolours, were exhibited in London and Dublin in 1899. Though his work was to depart dramatically from its graphic origins, Yeats consistently revisited and re-examined sporting subjects and later in life often returned to sketches he had made many years before, appropriating them to his more mature thematic concerns.

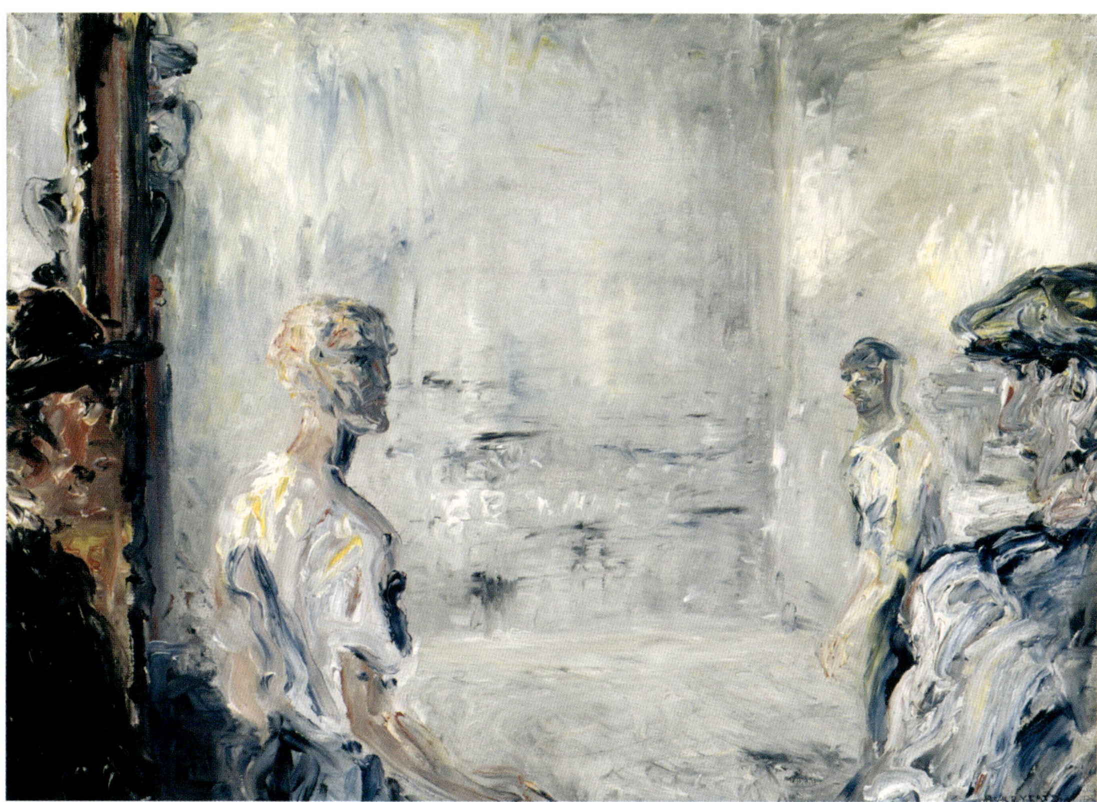

Jack B. Yeats (1871-1957)
20. The Ball Alley
c.1927
Oil on canvas
46 x 61 cm
Dublin City Gallery The Hugh Lane

In 1905, Yeats was invited by J.M. Synge to accompany him on a month-long tour of the west of Ireland.[22] Together they travelled throughout Connemara and Mayo, Synge recording his experiences in writing and Yeats his in sketches. While passing through Swinford, West Mayo, Yeats made a sketch of a handball alley, which he painted in watercolour the following year. The watercolour, which depicted four boys playing handball and has been described by Hilary Pyle as a study in movement, light and open space,[23] features the same pale palette as *The Ball Alley*, painted some twenty years later.

An unusual composition, *The Ball Alley*, unlike the earlier watercolour, does not represent the action of the game, but rather depicts either the beginning of a game or a pause during one. One of the competitors turns to confront a spectator, producing a psychological interplay between the figures similar to that identifiable in Yeats's more lyrical work. Much of the canvas is dedicated to the minimal structure of the ball alley, and its pale colour, enlivened with touches of green and blue, emphasises this moment of tension between the figures and lends the work an almost surreal atmosphere.

Yeats was particularly attracted to the achievements and endeavours of the individual competitor and in his sporting images bestowed upon his figures, whether boxers or jockeys, a heroic status among the people. In *The Ball Alley*, the more prominent of the two players clearly personifies Yeats's romantic vision of the sporting hero. His athletic build and tousled hair invite mythological associations and qualify an image that may have its origins in the folk myths and popular adventure fiction that Yeats loved to read.[24] Interestingly, handball was a game that allowed its competitors to attain an almost iconic status.[25] Unlike team sports, such as football and hurling, it was not embraced with a pronounced sense of local allegiance by communities or parishes, but rather produced individual champions. Players were acclaimed for their technical ability, singular characteristics or even amiable eccentricities, and treated as heroes among fans of the game.[26] Before the establishment of organised competitions by the GAA, great players were known to travel the country in search of opponents. Drifting between fairs and markets, they challenged local players for purses and in doing so captured the imagination of the public.[27]

Due to its simple rules and requirements, handball was also a game of the people and has been played in Ireland for centuries, with equal enthusiasm, by various sections of society. If one did not have access to a ball alley, house gables and church ruins were easily adaptable and as the sport did not require any specific dress, it was not uncommon to see priests in robes or officers of the Royal Irish Constabulary on the court.[28] The game was even known to be enjoyed by the aristocracy, and landlords often supported players in their area when they competed against those in other rival districts. Some landlords were even known to give free sites and materials for the construction of ball alleys on their land. Lord Edward Fitzgerald constructed a number of ball alleys in Kildare, which in the years prior to the 1798 Rebellion became meeting areas for the United Irishmen.

Perhaps by coincidence rather than design, Yeats painted *The Ball Alley* during a period of great change in the sport of handball. The early twenties saw the sport fall under the control of the GAA and in 1923 the first official handball competition was organised. The formation of the Irish Handball Council in 1924 led to the standardisation of court sizes and, more controversially, to the abandonment of the hard ball in favour of a softer rubber ball. Under new rules, the sport was played by amateurs, and the matchmakers and stake holders who had been very much part of the old game disappeared.[29] Yeats's picture, with its swirling strokes of paint, is a tribute to or vision of the sport's more romantic past. The golden-haired figure, reminiscent of the charismatic players who once dominated the game, appears to challenge all around him, including spectators. DM

---

21 Tinney 1998, p.50.
22 Synge's tour of the west of Ireland was prompted by a suggestion made by John Masefield, who was working for the *Manchester Guardian*, that Synge should write articles on the Aran Islands for the paper. Synge decided instead to investigate the life of the people in Connemara and West Mayo. See Pyle 1970, p.87.
23 Pyle 1993b, p.150.
24 Mayes and Murphy 1993, p.84.
25 In 1784 the legendary Buck Whaley was said to have left his home on St Stephen's Green to win a purse of 100 sovereigns by playing handball against the walls of Jerusalem.
26 McElligott c.1984, p.9.
27 *bid*, p.23.
28 *ibid*, p.9.
29 Today the game is played outside Ireland, with a healthy following in Canada and the United States.

21. Bowling Match at Castlemary, Cloyne

Daniel MacDonald

Daniel MacDonald, the son of a caricaturist James MacDaniel, was a native of Cork. His oeuvre features an unusually broad range of picture and subject types, from highly finished still-life paintings to animal portraits, melodramatic narratives like *The Rebel* (private collection) and *The Discovery of the Potato Blight in Ireland* (Delargy Centre for Irish Folklore, UCD), enigmatic compositions such as *Figures by a Coffin* (NGI),[30] and local, documentary pictures including the *Bowling Match*.

Bowling (pronounced 'boweling'), also known as bullets, bowl playing or road bowls, is a game played only in Ireland, and even then in a highly localised fashion, limited now to Cork and Armagh and small parts of Limerick and Waterford. [31] It is understood, however, to have been played more widely in the eighteenth and nineteenth centuries and in the early decades of the twentieth century. A number of theories exist regarding the origins of the sport. One is that it was introduced by Dutch soldiers of William of Orange on their arrival in 1689. An alternative theory, preferred by current followers, proposes that the sport was introduced by weavers from Yorkshire and West Lancashire employed in the linen industry that was particularly strong in Armagh and Cork.[32]

The game involves two competitors attempting to throw a 28 ounce solid iron ball or bullet (possibly originally a cannonball) from the beginning of a road course to the end in as few throws as possible. It is an intensely physical sport, but also requires considerable skill, as players spin the ball around corners and over undulations on the course. Endurance is also an important element, as courses generally measure between four and five kilometres. The courses are basically stretches of public highway, but to the bowling fraternity they 'comprise a specific course distance with virtually every hill and bend precisely named'.[33] Betting remains a regular and popular sideline activity.

The rather awkward pose of the main figure in MacDonald's painting, fundamentally different from any studies from the antique the artist might previously have undertaken, is in fact consistent with the technique adopted by bowlers as they attempt to generate maximum momentum for their throw. The figure appears to be adopting the technique traditionally favoured in Cork, which involves rotating the arm a full 360° before releasing the bullet. It is a dramatic and extremely physical method, by which bowlers appear to launch themselves into the air, and one with which MacDonald was evidently familiar.

The artist appears to have taken some artistic licence in the orientation of the crowd of spectators, however, perhaps in order to make his image more immediately legible. As well as behind the bowler, followers of the sport stand ahead on the course as it allows them to follow the trajectory of the ball more closely and to find it when it comes to rest. Indeed, the manner in which the crowd breaches to make way for the bullet is one of the game's most distinctive images.

This is one of a number of scenes of local sport, recreation and parochialism chosen by MacDonald, from dancing and hunting to faction fighting. Indeed, it is a celebration of the everyday life that was soon to be cruelly and dramatically interrupted by the Great Famine. While the Famine did not arrest all forms of communal entertainment and leisure, Cork was among the counties worst affected by its ravages. MacDonald soon turned his attention to graver matters with his seminal *The Discovery of the Potato Blight in Ireland*, a poignant, albeit theatrical, reflection on the plight of the rural poor, and painted in so-called Black '47, the worst year of the Famine.

When *Bowling Match at Castlemary, Cloyne* was shown at an exhibition organised by the Cork Art Union in September 1842, the *Cork Examiner* declared that though it 'demands our attention' the scenery and colouring were 'too fine for its subject'.[34] Their reporter also looked past the immediate subject to note the 'the squire, or well-dressed young farmer, leaning forward, less to mark the chances of the bowl, than to put his 'commether' on the coquettish little peasant girls before him'.[35] He saw perhaps, more sport in the picture than its audience would immediately have recognised.

As Peter Murray has noted, MacDonald avoids 'excessive sentimentalising or idealising' in his description of the assembled crowd and focuses instead on the competition at hand.[36] Admittedly, while the spectators represent a cross-section of the local community, the competitors belong to the more elevated ranks of County Cork society. It seems that bowling, like hurling and handball, was patronised by the gentry for much of its early history, but their active involvement as late as the 1840s does seem rather unusual, as by then the sport enjoyed an essentially plebian following.

The man 'lofting' the bowl is Abraham Morris, a wealthy Cork merchant and yachtsman of Dunkettle.

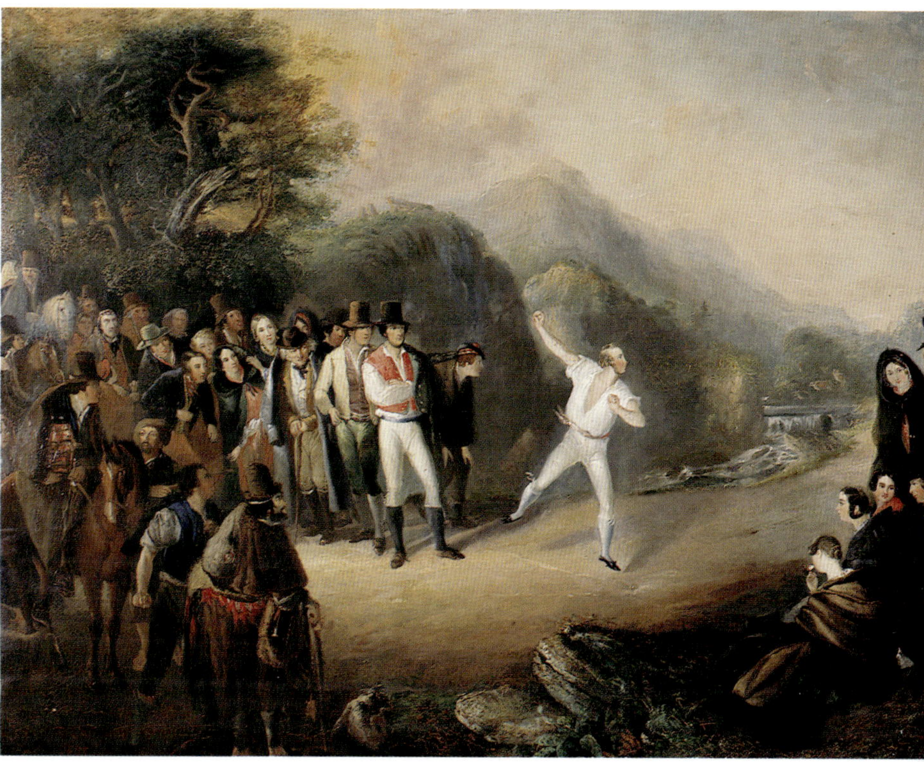

Daniel MacDonald (1821-53)
21. Bowling Match at Castlemary, Cloyne
1842
Oil on canvas
102.8 x 130.8 cm
Crawford Municipal Art Gallery, Cork

His opponent is Montifort Longfield of Castlemary, Cloyne (just a dozen miles from Dunkettle). Both men were prominent Orangemen and politically Tory.[37] A range of Irish types and social groups are represented, albeit disproportionately, in the crowd. Recognisable by the quality and design of their clothes, these include the gentlemen competitors and their immediate friends and associates, local labourers and a wandering beggar or *bacach*.[38] The gentlemen bowlers are curiously conservative and old-fashioned in their dress, while many of the women in attendance wear variations of the Irish cloak that remained popular into the twentieth century and appears in a number of the works in this exhibition.[39] A humorous cameo is provided by the young woman sitting in the foreground, who holds Morris's hat and coat but appears more interested in the scent of a rose than in the competition.

The standing stone, the only obvious suggestion of topographical specificity, refers to the dolmen that was to be found on the Castlemary estate. Otherwise, as Peter Murray has commented, 'neither the hills nor the picturesque river exist in anything other than the painter's imagination'.[40] BR

30 For information on this picture, see Le Harivel 1983, p.27.
31 Another form, Moors Bowling, is still practised in the Netherlands.
32 Toal 1996, p.7. See also Murray 1997, p.18, and Dunlevy

and Ó Gráda 2003.
33 Toal 1996, pp.1-2.
34 *Cork Examiner*, 3 October 1842.
35 *ibid*.
36 Murray 1997, p.18.
37 Dunlevy and Ó Gráda 2003, p.226.
38 *ibid*, pp.225-26.
39 For a detailed analysis of the dress MacDonald's painting, see Dunlevy and Ó Gráda 2003, pp.225-26.
40 Murray 1997, p.18.

Gabriel Hayes (1909-78)
22. The Cork Bowler
Oil on panel
124.5 x 94 cm
Eddie Jordan

22. The Cork Bowler

Gabriel Hayes

Though they draw on the same subject matter, this painting and MacDonald's depiction of a bowling match of a century earlier (cat.21) differ radically in composition and execution. Hayes has subordinated the social nature of the event, so central to MacDonald's picture, to the physicality of the sport. The crowds that attend the match in MacDonald's representation are here reduced to just one spectator, an everyman figure deeply absorbed in the activity. His presence, however, serves as much as a dynamic adjunct to the bowler as an acknowledgement of the sport's local following. His specific posture seems integrally linked with the bowler's immediate endeavour. Like the abruptly cropped, stocky tree behind him, which as a continuation of the bowler's leg creates an emphatic diagonal across the composition, he leans forward and looks keenly ahead, anticipating the delivery of the bullet. The picture preempts later sports photography, as the bowler enters the shot vigorously and his shoe cuts the bottom corner of the frame.

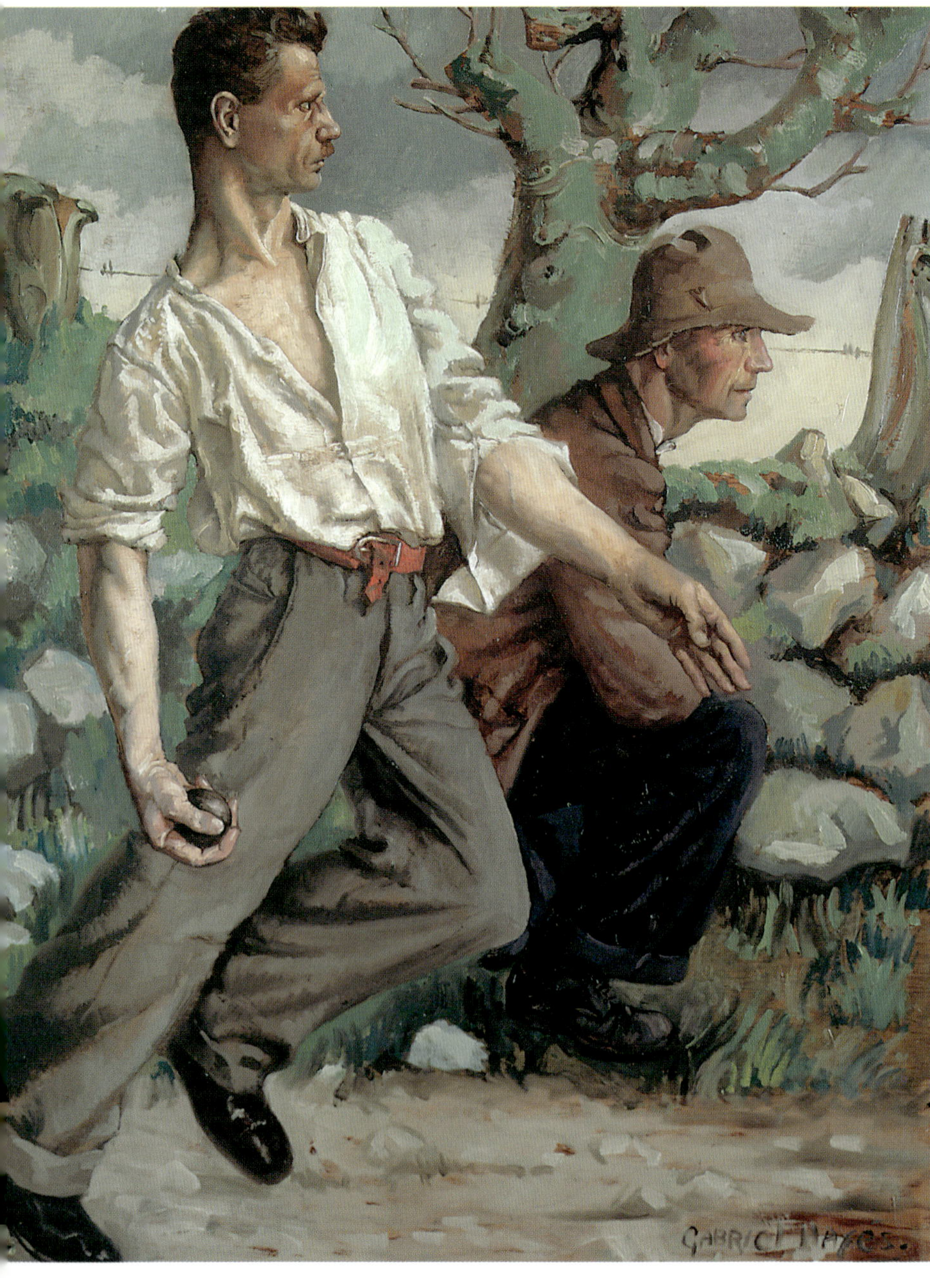

Born in Monasterevin, the Kildare town recorded in Letitia Hamilton's *Donkeys* (cat. 78), Gabriel Hayes is best known for her design of the decimal Irish halfpenny, penny, and two pence coins.[41] She was principally a sculptor, and the figures in this painting possess a strength of form and monumentality that is redolent of her work in stone, a typical example of which is her representation of the *Three Graces* (1941) on the façade of the DIT, Cathal Brugha Street in Dublin. This painting, in composition and technique, also calls to mind the monumental studies of Irish types by Sean Keating, such as *Men of Aran, Men of the South* and *Men of the West*, though the political subtext of those pictures, the sense of immanence identified by Ciarán MacGonigal,[42] is here conspicuously absent. While Keating's *Men of the South* look stoically into the future, Hayes's characters fix their eyes steadfastly along the course of their bowling match.

Hayes's picture represents another example of the fundamental difference in approach to similar subjects between nineteenth and twentieth-century artists. Just as Elizabeth Rivers was drawn to the formal, pictorial potential of a scene at a local dance (cat. 14), while Howard Helmick focused on narrative (cat. 6), Hayes here explores the dramatic, compositional possibilities of a bowling scene while MacDonald had emphasised its social quality. In doing so, however, Hayes drew on similarly keen skills of observation, capturing the distinctive, exaggerated posture of the bowler. BR

41 These coins were first struck in 1969, but all early strikings bore the date 1971.
42 Ciarán MacGonigal, 'Men of Aran- An Trá, Inis Oírr', sales catalogue James Adam & Son, 23 March 2005.

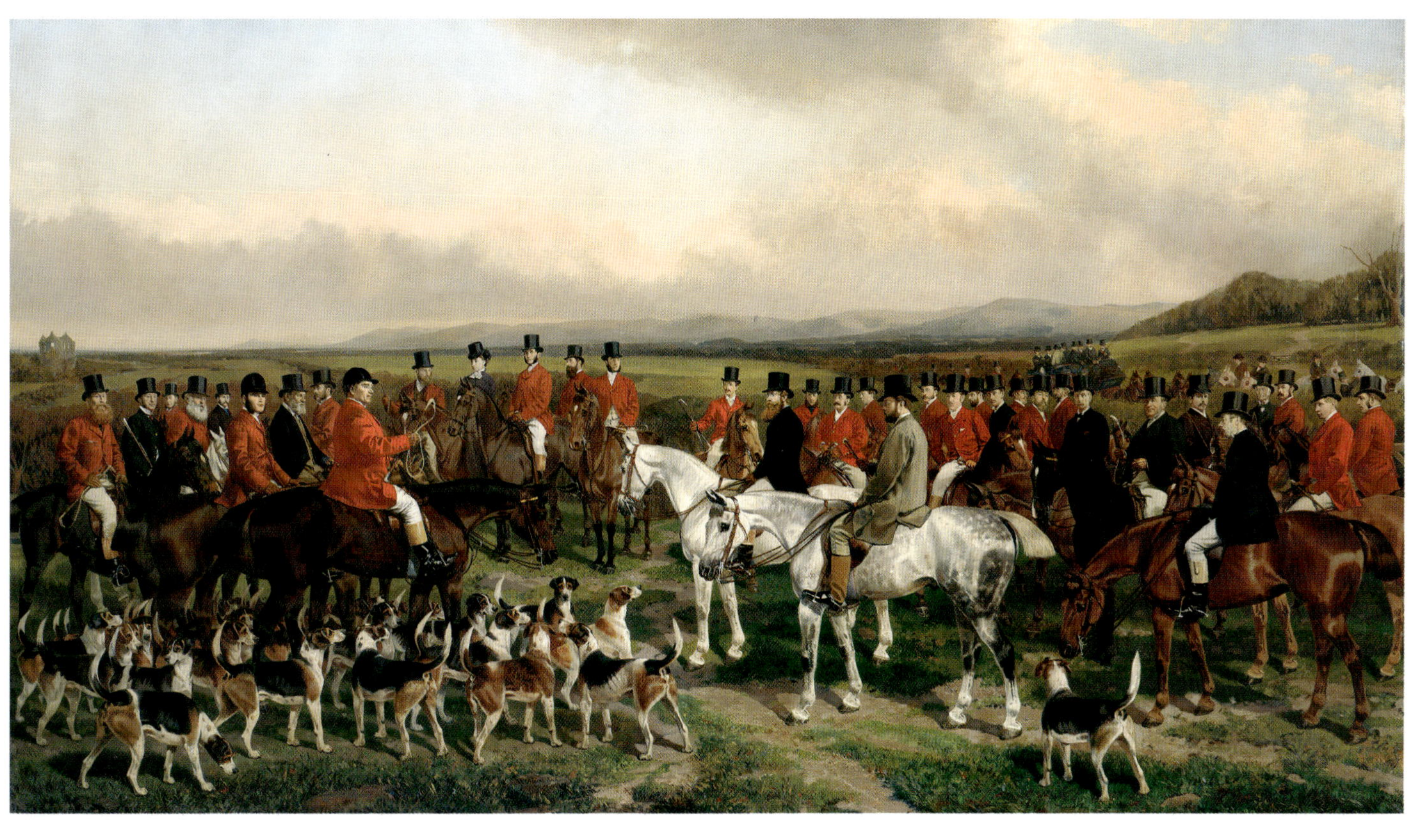

William Osborne (1823-1901)
23. The Ward Union Hunt
1873
Oil on canvas
109 x 184 cm
National Gallery of Ireland

23. The Ward Union Hunt

William Osborne

> *Oh! the Harrier makes music that's sweet to the ear,*
> *And the note of the foxhound rings home to the brain,*
> *But the sport we love best is a spin with the deer,*
> *O'er the pick of the pasture, the pride of the plain...*[43]

From the 1870s to the mid-1890s,[44] when Irish hunting enjoyed particular popularity, the Ward Union Stag Hounds was one of the most prestigious hunting clubs in Ireland. Established in 1854, its hunting grounds covered much of north County Dublin and Meath and since 1864, its kennels have been located in Asbourne. Though the fox had become the quarry of choice for most Irish hunting clubs from the late eighteenth century, the Ward Union was one of the few Irish packs that continued to hunt stag. Though the area in which they hunted was predominately flat, open terrain used for grazing cattle, it also featured numerous ditches and fences for big jumping and it was not uncommon for the first fence to unseat quite a few riders. Nevertheless, the Ward was renowned throughout Ireland and Britain for the pace at which its members rode cross-country,[45] and inspired the poet George John Whyte-Melville to proclaim in his *Songs and Verses* that 'the tail of a comet's, a joke to the Ward'.[46]

Hunting on horseback had always been a decidedly upper-class recreation in Ireland. In the seventeenth and early eighteenth century most hunting packs belonged to wealthy individuals and permission to accompany the hunt was by invitation only. Edmund Burke used an example from hunting to illustrate the divide between classes and denominations, suggesting that one of the rare occasions that a Protestant landowner would ever converse with a Catholic was to ask directions when lost hunting.[47] While the foundation of subscription packs in the mid-eighteenth century led to the demise of many private packs, the subscription fees and other expenses meant that only those with ample funds could afford membership.[48] Due largely to its proximity to the capital, the Ward Union attracted a large number of subscriptions from men and women from Dublin and its environs, including wealthy businessmen and government officials. In fact, it was known to attract the biggest numbers of any Irish pack, with hunting fields often numbering up to 250 riders. Special trains were chartered from the Midland and Great Western Railway Company to convey members and their mounts to the twice weekly meets, on Wednesdays and Saturdays during the season.[49] Though hunting's popularity was illustrated through the numerous subscription packs that emerged in the mid-to-late nineteenth century, its progress was not without disruption. During the Land War, a great deal of agrarian tension in Ireland was directed against hunting. Mounted hunts, viewed by many as the embodiment of landlordism, were sometimes sabotaged as they passed.[50]

Despite its passion for the horse, Ireland produced relatively few specialist painters of hunting and racing. Robert Healy, George Nairn, Michael Angelo Hayes, Samuel Spode and William Osborne are among a select few.[51] Admittedly, hunting featured in various guises in the work of landscape painters, including Joseph Tudor, Thomas Roberts and, even earlier, in a naïve landscape of Kilruddery, County Wicklow (private collection), but sporting painters, as these hunting specialists are known collectively, were scarce.

Osborne attended the Royal Hibernian Academy schools in 1845 and from 1851 onwards devoted himself almost entirely to painting animals. Concentrating primarily on horses and dogs, he displayed an impressive knowledge of the anatomy, behaviour and idiosyncrasies of his subjects. His work attracted many admirers among hunting enthusiasts and Osborne became a popular choice for those commissioning individual or group portraits of huntsmen and women with their prize animals. It seems likely, when considering the scale of the painting, that *The Ward Union Hunt* was commissioned by either the club or one of its wealthy members. The painting was presented to the National Gallery of Ireland in 1934 by William Jameson, a member of the Ward Union who appears second from right in the painting. His family, the Jamesons of whiskey distilling fame, had both an interest and involvement in the pictorial arts. William married Flora Mitchell, and Magdalen, daughter of John Jameson, married the painter Nathaniel Hone in 1872. William's presence in the painting may suggest that he was involved in commissioning the work.

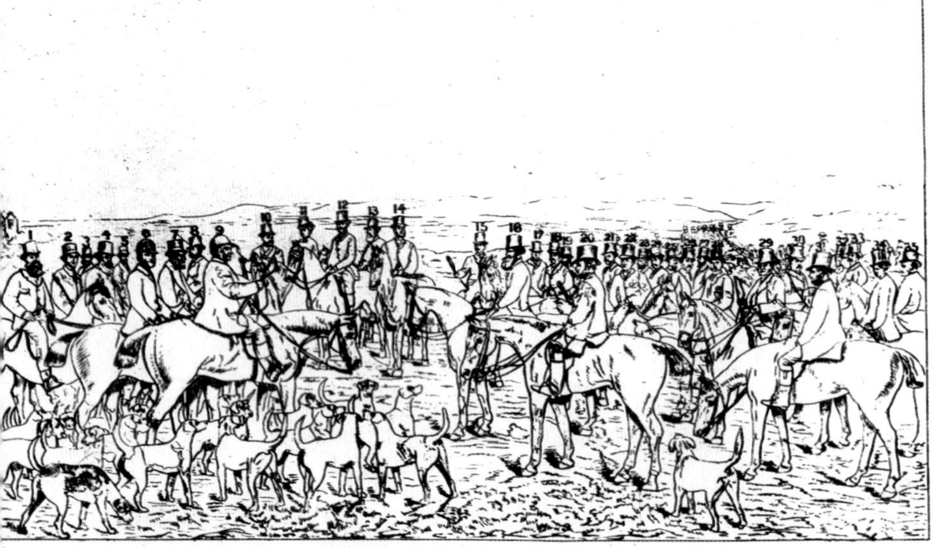

Fig.24. Key to William Osborne, *The Ward Union Hunt*

The painting, which depicts thirty-five members, their mounts and attendant pack of hounds against a flat landscape, is a *tour-de-force* for the artist. Osborne seized the opportunity afforded by such a large composition to exhibit his skills, and some of the studies of horses and dogs are of exceptional quality. Osborne portrays each animal individually and naturalistically, animating an otherwise formal arrangement, but also increasing the overall complexity of the composition.

The depiction of the riders in their red hunting jackets, the presence of the hounds, and the inclusion of other details, such as an open-top carriage obstructed by plain-clothed riders, suggest that the picture depicts the gathering of the pack at the beginning of a hunt. It has been suggested that Osborne's work was based on a photograph,[52] and a print after the painting, accompanied by a key, was produced for sale. Huntsman and Master of the Hounds, Charles Brindley, appears in the foreground, surrounded by his well-trained pack. To the left is his 'whip-in' and son Jem, who later inherited his father's position. The tallest figure in the background is Leonard Morrogh, one of the most respected huntsmen in Ireland.[53] In 1866 he replaced (the late) Capt. Montgomery (first from left) as Field Master and led the Ward through one of its most successful periods. Next to Morrogh is his wife, who was also a formidable rider. When the Empress of Austria, a great fan of the hunt, made her Irish debut with the Ward, she rode Mrs Morrogh's brown thoroughbred hunter Domino.

After the hunt, Morrogh was so impressed by the Empress's ability that he offered his wife's horse to her as a gift.[54] Although Mrs Morrogh is the only woman included in the painting, it was not unusual for women to hunt with packs and by 1900, though handicapped by skirts dangerously weighed down with lead, women were becoming Master of the Hounds.[55] The Viceregal Court was also connected with the Ward, most notably during the time of lords Spencer (wearing black in the centre of the picture), Londonderry, Houghton and Zetland, who were known to invite large parties from England to join them on the hunt.[56]

Cleverly, Osborne has positioned the viewer in line with the riders, creating the illusion that we too are mounted on horseback. The work is a portrait at three levels, those of huntsmen, horses and hounds. Unsurprisingly, considering Osborne's expertise, the animals are executed with far greater sensitivity than the hunters, who are, by comparison, 'doll-like and wooden'.[57] The animals lend a sense of energy to the work, appropriate to the beginning of a hunt, and certain details, such as the intimate interaction between the white horses and hounds is an obvious, if sentimental reference to Osborne's more popular works. DM

---

43 "The Ward', dedicated by permission to Mrs J.L. Morrogh', in Whyte-Melville 1872, p.98.
44 Norton 1991, p.28.
45 Bowen 1955, p.176.
46 Corballis 1891, p.18.
47 Everett 1994, p.96.
48 A subscription pack is one that is financed partly through members' subscriptions and organised events, such as point-to-point, whilst the master foots the remainder of the bill.
49 Bowen 1955, p.180.
50 C.A. Lewis 1975, p.57.
51 Wynne 1983, p.36.
52 Crookshank and Glin 2002, p.201.
53 Corballis 1891, p.77.
54 Norton 1991, p.28.
55 Pakenham 2000, p.126.
56 Bowen 1955, p.179.
57 Crookshank and Glin 2002, p.201.

24. The Barbour Cup, The Westmeath Point-to-Point

Letitia Hamilton

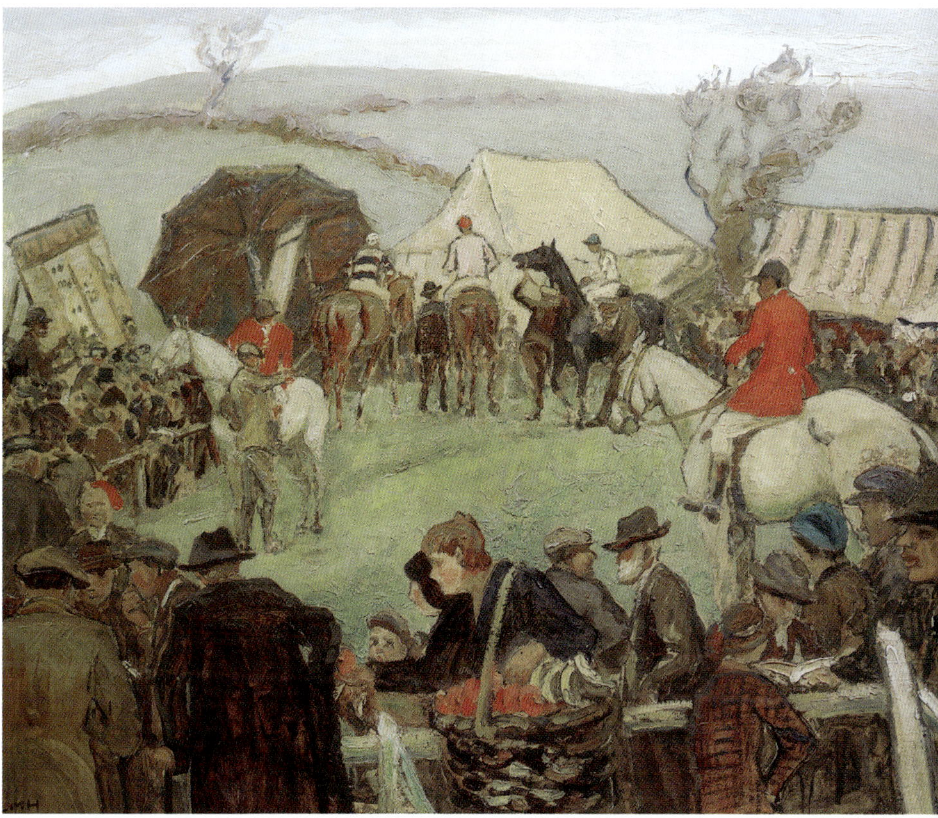

Letitia Hamilton (1878-1964)
24. The Barbour Cup, The Westmeath Point-to-Point
Oil on canvas
62.5 x 65 cm
Private collection

Once known as the Redcoat Races, point-to-point meetings have always been associated with hunting. It is believed they originated in the eighteenth century, when members of one of Ireland's most famous hunts, the Duhallow in Cork, raced from Ballyclogh Church steeple to its equivalent in Doneraile. The event gave rise to the term steeple chase.[58] Traditionally, a point-to-point is raced across a three-mile stretch of open country. Courses are unmarked and usually include a variety of uncompromising obstacles such as walls, ditches and banks. With the establishment in the mid-eighteenth century of subscription hunts, [59] point-to-points became a popular method of raising money to help finance hunting clubs.[60] Usually held around March, at the end of the hunting season, they also provided clubs, which invariably drew their membership from the more affluent sections of society, with the opportunity to interact with local communities. Clubs relied heavily on the support of local farmers, whose land they used throughout the season, and point-to-points provided a broader section of the community with a day's entertainment.

'A horse Protestant', according to her younger contemporary Anne Yeats, Letitia grew up at Hamwood House in County Meath with a devotion to country pursuits, sharing the family's 'love of horses, though in the Hamilton family it was [her] two brothers who were always in the saddle.'[61] In her painting *The Barbour Cup*, she has depicted the main event of the annual point-to-point meeting of the Westmeath Hunt. Named after Frank Barbour (1908-1912), the Master of the Hunt, who inaugurated the event in 1910, the race was a type of Grand National for point-to-point horses.[62] The facility with which Hamilton has captured the atmosphere of the day suggests that she attended the race meeting and, in accordance with her practice, that her painting was derived from sketches produced on the spot.

Point-to-point meetings often drew huge crowds,[63] and in some areas represented major social events. Bookies, tick-tack men (who relayed the odds) and various side shows were present and local businesses, pubs and even schools often closed to allow people to attend.[64] In 1928 John William Seigne noted:

> *...point-to-point races, arranged by the various hunts had grown wonderfully in popular favour during recent years and it is extraordinary what a number of country people turn up to see them, every hill or other point of vantage is crowded and some of the best horses and cross country riders take part in them.*[65]

In Hamilton's painting, a large crowd has gathered tightly around the parade ring, which has become the focal point for the spectators' attention over what appear to be the last minutes before the off. The figures in the foreground are particularly well-defined, while the bulk of the crowd is represented as a random pattern of shapes and forms, punctuated by an occasional discernible figure.

Hamilton has included a number of charming details, which lend character to individuals among the crowd and demonstrate the artist's acute eye for local detail. One individual among a group of men on the left, for example, holds his hand to his mouth as bets are discussed. Another leans in to hear the conversation, while a fruit-seller proffers an apple from her basket. Meanwhile, on the right, a man and woman read through the race programme. Arranged around the ring are large tents and the bookies' pitches, at which they display their odds on large boards. Within the ring the jockeys, already in the saddle, make final preparations. One speaks to a trainer, while others are led out for the start of the race.

As Hamilton did not date her work it is often difficult to ascertain when specific pictures were executed. *The Barbour Cup*, however, features many details typical of her early work, such as the simplification of forms and the use of a limited palette. Touches of red, provided by the hunters' jackets and the fruit, enliven areas of the canvas, but the work is painted predominately in muted tones of green and brown appropriate to the rural, outdoor nature of the scene. The painting is composed around the circular motif of the parade ring, viewed from above. The detail and activity of the scene is confined to the area immediately around the ring, leaving an empty green space at its centre. Though the view extends into the distance, the sky is represented merely by a thin banner of blue, and the hills in the distance by a simple pattern of green forms. The figures in the foreground, some of which appear in profile, seem like flat cut-out shapes, and the tent canvases filled in simply in off-white. This interest in the reduction of shapes was strongly influenced by the work of Paul Henry, who was, like Hamilton, a founder member of the Dublin Painter's Society. Point-to-point races and hunting were subjects Hamilton explored throughout her career. In a much later painting, *The Meath Hunt Point-to-Point* (private collection), she depicts a similar scene, but in a much looser hand. [66] DM

---

58 C.A. Lewis 1975, p.120.
59 As the name implies, a subscription pack is one that is financed partly through members' subscriptions and organised events, such as point-to-point.
60 C.A. Lewis 1975, p.57.
61 Pyle 1997a, p.123.
62 Bowen 1955, p.198.
63 The large attendance at meetings was influenced somewhat by a rule laid down by the INHS Committee in 1900, which stipulated that no money was to be taken at any gate, stand or enclosure at point-to-point races. Watson 1969, p.131.
64 Clarke 1995, p.3.
65 Seigne 1928, p.124.
66 Hamilton was awarded a bronze medal for the painting at the Olympic Arts Competition in London in 1948.

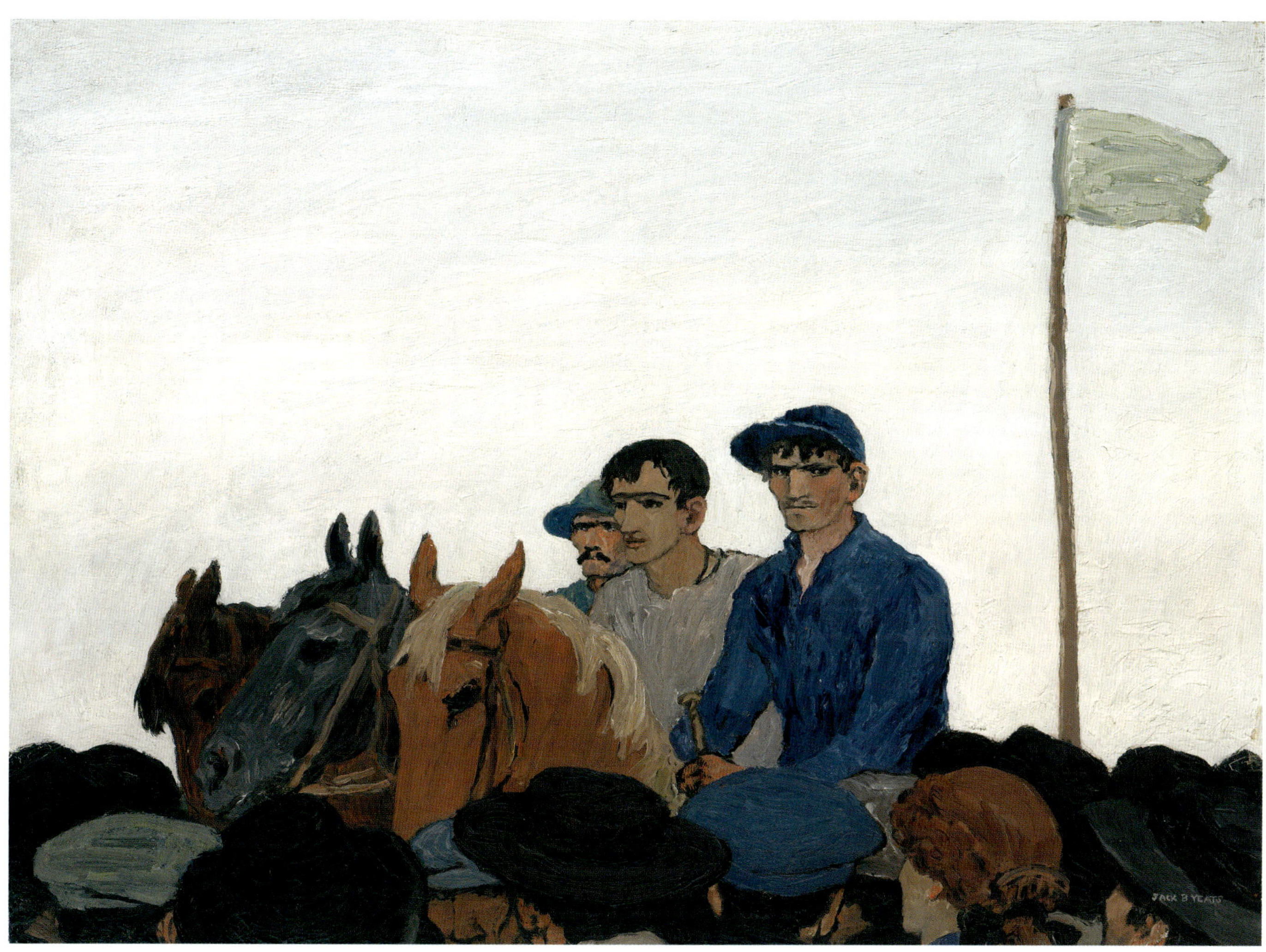

Jack B. Yeats (1871-1957)
25. *Before the Start*
1915
Oil on canvas
46 x 61 cm
National Gallery of Ireland

25. Before the Start

Jack B. Yeats

Jack B. Yeats had a great love of horse racing, and the drama and narratives it produced was a consistent source of inspiration for him throughout his career. Many of the images he produced while earning a living as a sports reporter for London journals were of jockeys in the saddle, and around 1895, when he began to turn his attention to the west of Ireland, Yeats was predictably drawn to Irish racing. He was particularly attracted to strand races, which not only provided the subject for his first exhibited work at the RHA but also became a key theme in his *Sketches of Life in the West of Ireland.* [67] These small images, predominately painted in watercolour, demonstrated Yeats's tremendous ability to capture both the power of the animals and the excitement of the occasion. Racing was a subject that incorporated two of his great passions, sporting events and horses, and when he began to paint in oil around 1910, it remained a common theme of his work.

Race meetings have been a hugely popular form of sporting entertainment across Ireland for centuries and a day at the races was considered as much a day's holiday as any other annual celebration. The expansion of the country's railway system in the mid-to-late nineteenth century and the subsequent arrival of cars greatly increased the accessibility of horse racing as a spectator sport. Large numbers of people could attend even the most local meetings and, as one would expect, those courses closest to railway stations enjoyed the biggest crowds.[68] Writing of the Galway races in *Rambles in Ireland* (a publication for which Yeats provided a number of illustrations) Robert Lynd recalled that 'thinner and thinner became the population of the town as holiday makers with excited eyes' made their way to the race course and that the air was 'full of the murmur of holiday' as bookmakers, fruit-sellers, showmen and Aunt Sallies set up their stalls.[69]

Yeats captured vividly on many occasions the atmosphere of a day at the races. However, in this small oil painting of three jockeys on their mounts, the artist has focused his attention on a specific moment, recording the acute tension and high emotion that attended the start of a race. Hilary Pyle has noted that the three jockeys exude, respectively, determination, nervousness and aggression. [70] The figure in green appears focused on the task ahead while his fellow competitor in blue, lips pressed together, returns unflinchingly the gaze of the viewer. The jockey in the centre, his eyes wide, seems distinctly nervous by comparison.

The sense of tension in this work is emphasised further by the gathering of a tightly packed crowd around the horses, the manner in which the jockeys are silhouetted against a large pale sky, and the stark isolation of the flag flapping in the wind. This very deliberate arrangement of space exhibits Yeats's growing understanding of the potential of composition as a way of conveying meaning in his work. Another painting of 1915, *The Orator (private collection)*, features a very similar composition, in which a low horizon and empty sky elevate the figure of a public speaker above a crowd. In *Before the Start*, Yeats extends the respect that a public speaker might be said to expect to humble jockeys with whom it was not perhaps so readily associated. By placing them against this empty sky, Yeats affords his jockeys a heroic position among the people.

In *Before the Start*, like *The Orator*, the viewer shares the level of the crowd. This was to become a regular feature of Yeats's depictions of public events and an effective method of implying the artist's presence and of creating the impression that the viewer too is among the crowd. This interaction between the viewer and the subject is exemplified by the way in which a single figure within the crowd turns towards the viewer, his face, with dark eyes, rough complexion and suspicious expression, interrupting the line of hats and heads and introducing character to an otherwise anonymous assembly.[71]

Before the Start is a fine example of Yeats's growing confidence in the use of oil paint. Though his style was to change radically during the 1920s, the work of this period shows a definite development in the application of paint and use of line. Areas of thick impasto and broad brush work display Yeats's conviction in handling the medium and in the description of texture. The use of heavy black outlines, a characteristic of his earlier work and relic of his work as an illustrator, is still present in the rendering of the crowd, but his brush now strays, albeit cautiously, over the lines. DM

67 *The Strand Races, West of Ireland*, was exhibited at the RHA in 1895.
68 Lalor 2003, p.502.
69 Lynd 1912, pp.32-34.
70 Pyle 1997b, p.202.
71 Pyle 1986b p. 40.

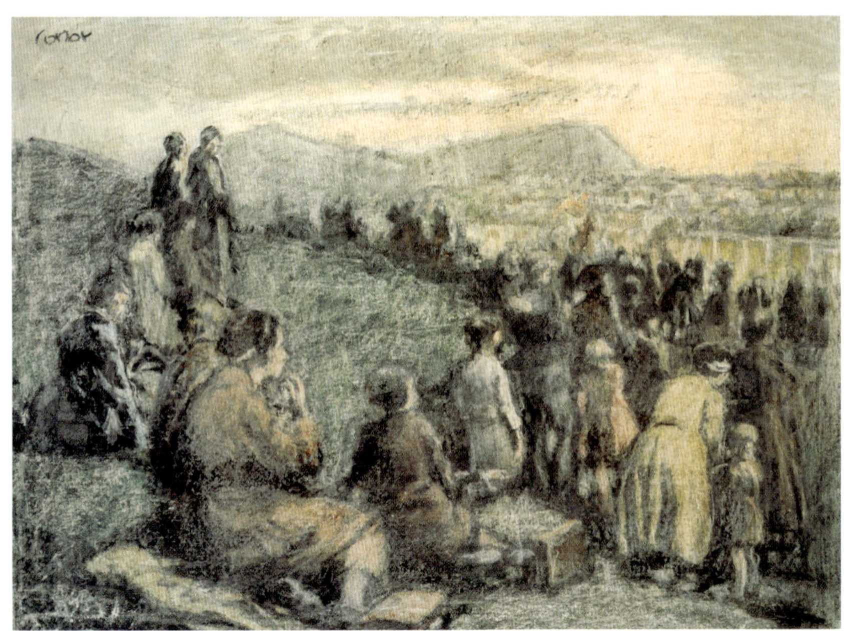

William Conor (1881-1968)
26. At the Races
Wax crayon on paper
46 x 58 cm
Frank & Fern Ó'Lorcáin

26. At the Races

William Conor

This picture stands as another testament to William Conor's artistic preoccupation with the lives of ordinary people. Ostensibly a painting of a race meeting, the picture records the collective activity of spectators rather than the horse racing itself, as a large and essentially anonymous crowd takes precedence over the horses and jockeys that are partly obscured in the middle distance.

Though his focus here is principally on human activity, it is worth noting that Conor was very accomplished at painting and drawing horses and donkeys. Indeed, equestrian subjects recur throughout his oeuvre, from polo players and their mounts to humble nags, draught horses and numerous images of race meetings, such as *Approaching the Starting Gate* (Royal Ulster Academy). In reviewing the annual exhibition at the RHA in 1949, the *Irish Times* picked out for comment the 'vigorous, lively figurative compositions for which [Conor] is celebrated including 'Going to the Races".[72] Conor's sketchbooks feature numerous studies in pencil of horses and riders, which demonstrate the artist's unusual facility in depicting action and movement and suggest a genuine familiarity with his subject.

The setting for Conor's drawing is uncertain, but the rather exaggerated hills in the background suggest that it may be Down Royal, one of Ireland's oldest courses. The Down Royal Corporation of Horsebreeders, established by charter in 1685, established a course in Downpatrick, but in the early years of the eighteenth century moved to its current location at the Maze, Lisburn. A course remained at Downpatrick and hosts the Ulster National, one of the most significant events in the racing calendar.

Conor's focus on the crowd in this depiction of a race meeting, an inclination often shared by Jack B. Yeats, represents a significant shift away from the concentration on the riders, stable hands and horses that had characterised sporting pictures in Ireland in the eighteenth and nineteenth centuries. Indeed, the genre was surprisingly poorly represented in Ireland in the 1700s, a period during which racing and other equestrian sports enjoyed remarkable popularity among a broad section of the population.[73] The nineteenth century witnessed an increase in the number of specialist sporting and animal painters in Ireland, but their style tended to mimic formal and conservative sporting art in England, and consequently to neglect the social aspect of racing and hunting and the key role played by local communities in their survival and success.
BR

72 *Irish Times*, 25 April 1949.
73 See, for example, Figgis and Rooney 2001, pp.401-05.

27. Blighted Hopes

George Collie

In Collie's diminutive study, an old man sits dejected, holding his greyhound loosely on a lead. One assumes that the dog's bid for racing glory has failed, and with it the fortunes of its elderly owner, whose disconsolate air contrasts with the levity that attends most of the other recreational pursuits shown in this exhibition. S.B. Kennedy's description of this picture as 'a study in character' is accurate, if rather understated, and consistent with what else is known of Collie's oeuvre.[74] Monaghan-born Collie displayed a prodigious talent, exhibiting at the RHA for the first time at the age of eighteen. He trained at the Dublin Metropolitan School of Art but pursued further studies in London and Paris before returning to teach at his Dublin *alma mater* and ultimately establishing his own studio.[75] Impressively, Collie exhibited at every Royal Hibernian Academy exhibition between 1930 and 1975.

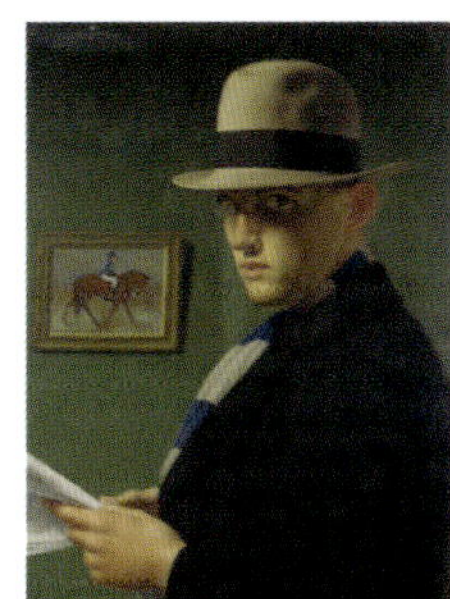

Fig.25. **John Luke**, *The Tipster*, 1928, Ulster Museum

Collie's hapless character is the antithesis to John Luke's *The Tipster* (fig.25), painted just a few years earlier and also in the collection of the Ulster Museum. Luke's gambler (a self-portrait) is as calculating and confident as Collie's figure is obvious and dejected.[76] Even the tipster's fedora, shading the eyes in a manner redolent of Sir Joshua Reynolds' enigmatic self-portraits, sits squarely on the young man's head, while the old man's hat in Collie's painting is awry, perhaps as a result of repeated and anxious mopping of the brow or scratching of the head. Collie certainly had an appetite for misfortune and hardship in his work, expressed clearly in his Taylor Prize-winning painting of 1927, the *Midday Meal* (private collection), which depicts inmates eating soup in the frugal surroundings of the Dublin Union and calls to mind the academic social realism of Hubert von Herkomer. Indeed, it is regrettable that

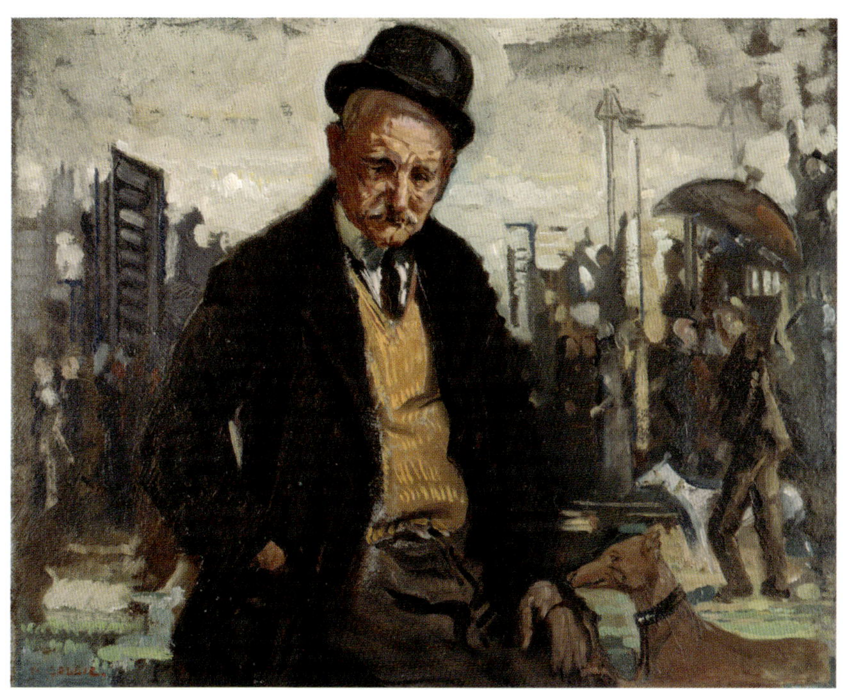

George Collie (1904-75)
27. Blighted Hopes
c.1933
Oil on board
34 x 41.8 cm
Collection Ulster Museum, Belfast

Collie did not produce more genre works of this kind, as he appears to have had a notable, if rather old-fashioned, capacity to imbue his subjects with pathos. His numerous formal portraits, such as *The First Three Trustees of the Haverty Bequest* (Dublin City Gallery The Hugh Lane) are, by comparison, competent but unremarkable, and his ecclesiastical works conservative.

The first greyhound race with a mechanical lure, an American development, was staged at Celtic Park, Belfast, on 18 April 1927. Just a few weeks later, Shelbourne Park in Dublin (which remains the principal greyhound racing centre in the city) was opened. BR

74 S.B. Kennedy 1991, p.182.
75 In Ireland, Collie trained under Tuohy, Sleator and Keating.

28. The Liffey Swim

Jack B. Yeats

In *The Liffey Swim* Jack B. Yeats captures the atmosphere and thrill of an event that has been part of Dublin's annual sporting calendar since 1920. Yeats moved to Dublin in 1917 and it was not long before he became the quintessential Dubliner. As Bruce Arnold has reflected, 'the city was the centre of his universe and its people were the heroes and heroines of much of his art'.[77] His depiction of the occasion also represents a return to the sporting themes that had inspired much of his early work, but which he had abandoned for a time to concentrate on quieter, less dramatic subjects during the early 1920s.[78]

Jack B. Yeats (1871-1957)
28. *The Liffey Swim*
1923
Oil on canvas
61 x 91 cm
National Gallery of Ireland
See Foldout opposite page 57

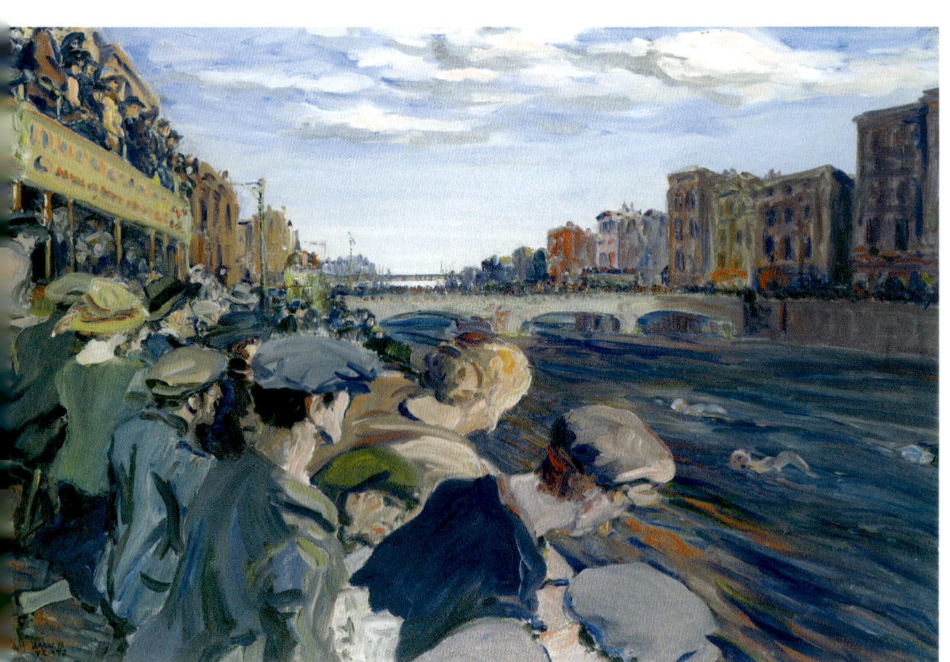

The swim, held between late July and early August, was promoted in 1923 as 'the biggest free spectacle of the year in Dublin'.[79] It was organised by the Leinster Branch of the Irish Amateur Swimming Association (IASA), [80] and was initially conceived by three of its members: Ben Fagan, Gus Cullen and Harry Brennan. While crossing the Liffey after leaving the AGM of the IASA at the Clarence Hotel, the three men agreed that the river would be a great place to hold a race. Notwithstanding initial concerns regarding the quality of the water, Fagan, who had some knowledge of public health, decided that the river would be safe enough to swim in at high tide. Twenty-seven competitors took part in the first race in 1920, and by 1923 thirty-four of the fifty men who had enrolled faced the starter.[81] After undressing at Messrs Guinness' premises, which were made available for the occasion, the competitors entered the water at Victoria Quay from a Guinness barge, which was drawn across the river. The race finished a mile and a half down river, before Butt Bridge, where prizes were awarded to the first six home. The nearby Tara Street Baths were made available for washing.

The implication in Yeats's painting that the event became extremely popular with the people of Dublin in these early years is confirmed by an *Irish Independent* report on the swim of the period:

an enormous crowd of spectators, expectant, good humored, hilarious, joking and laughing heartily at its own discomfort gladly born for the purpose of witnessing the great swim, lined the quays and manned the bridges spanning the river from Messrs Guinness Wharf, Victoria quay, Knightsbridge to Butt Bridge.[82]

In the uncertain atmosphere of Dublin in the early 1920s, the Liffey Swim was a celebratory event, in which citizens, regardless of age or class, could participate in either a competitive or supportive capacity. All of the competitors were assigned a time handicap; the strongest in 1923 entering the water a full nine minutes after the starting gun had been fired. It was not unusual for fathers to finish before their sons. Distinguished guests, some of whom were afforded privileged access to the starting barge, attended the early races, which were also scheduled to take place in the evening to allow people to attend after work.

In his painting, Yeats invites his audience to engage with the event by cleverly placing them among the people. The crowd leans forward, drawing the viewer's eye to the swimmers, who have reached a key point in the race and surge towards the finish line. However, Yeats is not concerned exclusively with the competitors in the water. By distorting the perspective, he allows his picture to encompass the entire occasion. In the foreground, spectators of all ages jostle for position. Similarly, people on the trams travelling along the quays do not miss the opportunity to catch a glimpse of the race. [83] It is likely that the character in the brown fedora is the artist himself,[84] and the woman wearing the elaborate yellow hat his wife Cottie, who was such a central figure in his life.[85] By placing himself within the crowd, Yeats asserts his identity as observer of, and part of, Dublin life. Curiously, however, he also elevates and thus detaches himself slightly from it, reinforcing his role as artist.

While it has been assumed that Yeats's painting records the 1923 swim, contemporary evidence suggests otherwise. The *Irish Independent* reported that 'it rained now and then, but like a deluge during the concluding stages of the race' and that 'a canopy of umbrellas ten deep lined the river'.[86] Yeats, in contrast, depicts a relatively clear sky on a warm evening when not a single umbrella is required. Rather than recording a specific occasion, therefore, *The Liffey Swim* seems the product of Yeats's memories of the event and his own artistic expression.[87] It is an optimistic image, in which a city's people have come together to partake in a local event.

The composition is divided diagonally into two sections, the right of the canvas showing the action in the water and the location, and the left capturing the activity on the quay. From a vantage point on Bachelors Walk, one can identify Aston Quay on the other side of the river and in the middle ground O'Connell Bridge, spanning the river and marking the swimmers' proximity to the finish line. Further back is the horizontal form of the Loopline Rail Bridge,[88] which cuts across the distinctive profile of the Custom House, its missing cupola a faint reminder of the destruction caused during recent events.[89]

From the early 1920s onwards, Yeats's style developed dramatically and *The Liffey Swim* marked his growing interest in Expressionism and an abandonment of his familiar use of strong line and flat colour. The painting is rendered in broad, loosely applied brush strokes, which suggest rapidity of execution and convey a sense of energy in keeping with the atmosphere of the occasion. Yeats's increasing use of emotive colour is also evident. The vibrant reds in the water, for example, are echoed throughout the composition, connecting the crowds with the competitors and emphasising the excitement that attended the event.

Yeats was awarded a silver medal for his portrayal of this unique sporting event at the 1924 Olympic Arts Competition in Paris (Fig.26). The following year he exhibited the painting at the RHA, where it was priced £300, a considerable amount for him at this time.[90] The picture was well-received, one critic commenting that 'his painting of the quayside buildings is arresting, but the charm of the picture is in the people, those men and women of ordinary life which Mr Yeats gives life to on canvas'.[91] DM

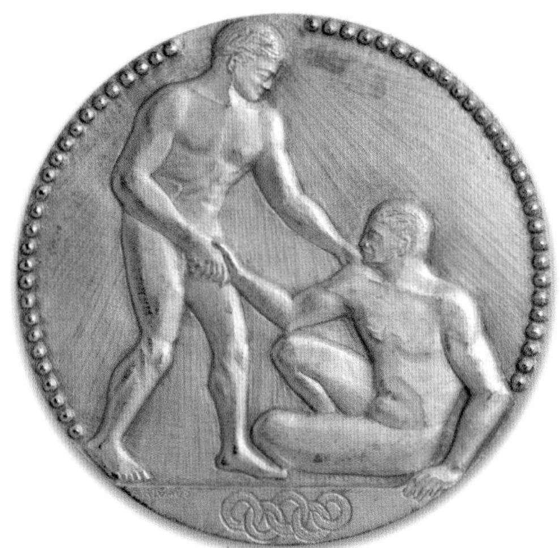

Fig.26. Jack B. Yeats's Olympic silver medal, 1924

77 Arnold 1998, p.202.
78 Pyle 1997b, p.212.
79 *Irish Independent*, 30 July 1923.
80 The Leinster Branch of the IASA took over the organisation of the event and only clubs affiliated with the Leinster Branch were eligible to compete.
81 *Irish Independent*, 20 August 1923. It was not until 1991 that female competitors took-part in the event.
82 *ibid*.
83 Having been first introduced into the city in 1872, the tram network expanded rapidly, was electrified in 1899 and by 1915 could boast twenty-one separate routes on the basically radial system.
84 Pyle 1986b, p.50.
85 Arnold 1998, p.203.
86 *Irish Independent*, 20 August 1923.
87 See Pyle 1997b, p.15.
88 The Loopline Rail Bridge was constructed to general opposition in 1891.
89 The cupola was destroyed by fire during the Civil War (1922-23).
90 Pyle 1986b, p.50.
91 *Irish Times*, 6 April 1925.

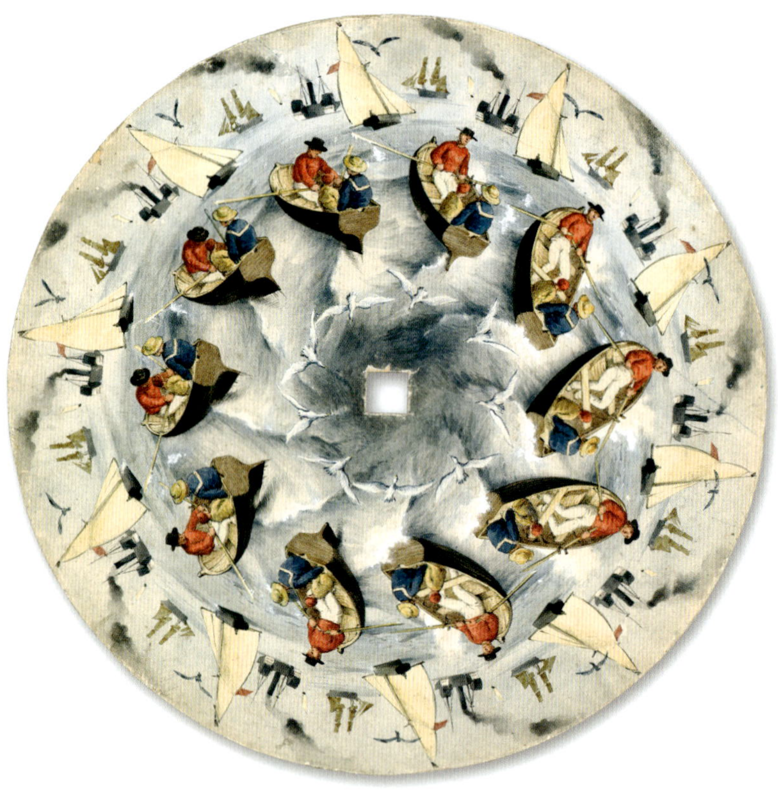

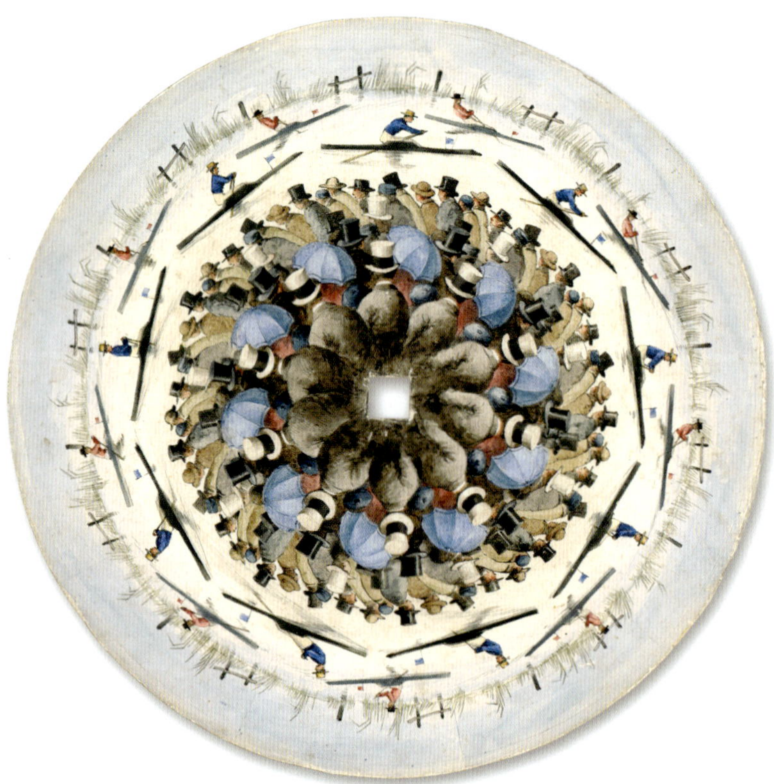

29. Rowers on the sea

Michael Angelo Hayes

30. Regatta

Michael Angelo Hayes

Though Michael Angelo Hayes is best known as an equestrian watercolourist, specialising in military subjects, and for his studies of the Bianconi cars,[92] these phenakistoscope disks are best appreciated in the context of the artist's fascination with anatomy, locomotion and photography.[93] Hayes was one of the founder members of the Dublin Photographic Society, established in November 1854, just a year after the inception of an equivalent body in London.[94] The society was founded by a number of committed amateur photographers who had been meeting informally for some time previously at the apothecary shop of William Allen in Henry Street.[95] The council subsequently met monthly at the Royal Dublin Society's headquarters in Leinster House, where they would discuss experience and technique and listen to short papers delivered by fellow members.[96] Hayes was not the only professional artist on the council, as the sculptor Joseph Kirk had occupied a seat since its foundation, and the painters George Mulvany, James S. Mulvany, Bernard Mulrenin, William Brocas and George Sharpe were also early members. Sir John Joscelyn Coghill, first president of the society, was also an accomplished amateur painter.

Hayes exhibited regularly in England, where he lived for six years, and in Ireland, and was generally well-received by the press. He also provided illustrations for a number of publications, including five drawings for *The Ballad of Savourneen Deelish* (1846).[97] A bound key to his final exhibit at the Royal Hibernian Academy, *H.R.H. the Prince of Wales Installed as a Knight of the Most Noble Order of St Patrick in St Patrick's Cathedral, Dublin* was published in 1874.[98]

In November 1876, Hayes delivered a paper to the Royal Dublin Society entitled 'On the Pictorial Delineation of Animals in Rapid Motion'. With this paper, and a subsequent pamphlet published the following year under the same title, Hayes attempted to describe accurately the action of a galloping horse.[99] This phenomenon, which Hayes also illustrated diagrammatically in his pamphlet, had confounded artists for centuries. Its solution has been attributed to Eadweard Muybridge, who demonstrated the sequence through the use of photography, but Hayes came very close to beating Muybridge to it, producing his pamphlet the year before photographs from Muybridge's seminal series of attitudes of humans and horses in motion were published in *The Scientific American* and *La Nature*. It appears that these two pioneers, though working at the same time, were unaware of each other's studies.

Significantly, having employed magic lantern slides to illustrate his findings, Hayes concluded the presentation to the Royal Dublin Society by inviting members to view a phenakistoscope, an invention he felt sure was familiar to his audience. He reflected that it was 'generally pronounced to be a faithful and accurate representation of the action of a living animal in full gallop'.[100]

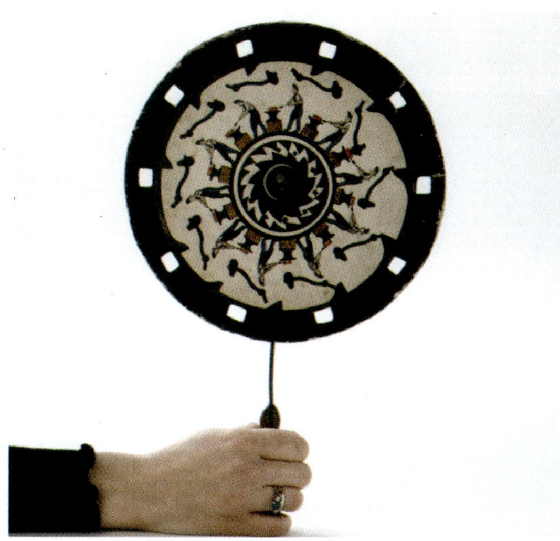

Fig.27. Phenakistoscope, Belgian, 1833

The phenakistoscope was invented simultaneously in 1833 by the Belgian physicist Joseph Plateau and the Austrian Simon Stampfer. A development of Faraday's Wheel, the device, employed principally as a toy, animated sequential images through the use of one or two rotating disks. When two disks were used, the outer disk featured slots, the inner disk drawings of successive action. These were mounted on a single axis, and spun in the same direction, so that when the inner was viewed through the slots on the outer, the images appeared to move. The version with one disk operated on the same principle, and featured both slots and drawings, but needed to be viewed in a mirror. The phenakistoscope, which became known by a number of other names, including phantasmascope and fantoscope, remained popular until the introduction of the zoetrope, which did not require a mirror and could be viewed by more than one person at a time. The abovementioned Eadweard Muybridge used the zoetrope and a subsequent development, the zoopraxiscope, to display his photographic sequences.

These are two phenakistoscopes from a collection of fourteen extant disks by Hayes, which animate a variety of subjects from birds on a pond to dancers, hunters and a revolving globe. They are the only works of their kind by Hayes known to exist and are particularly significant in the context of his research and interests, as none of his photographs is known to survive. Many of the growing number of painters in Ireland who had developed an interest in photography in the second half of the nineteenth century used photographs as reference points for their canvases. Hayes's direct involvement in the promotion of photography appears to have been relatively short-lived (confined to the 1850s) and did not distract him from his painting. Having been elected an associate of the RHA in 1853 and a full member the following year, he was appointed secretary in 1856, though he resigned after a year as a result of differences with other academicians over Academy finances. He was reinstated as member in 1860, as secretary in 1861 and retired in 1870.[101]

Rowing in Ireland became increasingly ordered and controlled during the nineteenth century. The Pembroke Club was founded in 1836 in an attempt to organise better and more formally a sport in which students of Trinity College had taken part for some time, and had premises on the Dodder at Ringsend.[102] Shortly afterwards, the Kingstown Boat Club was established (which later evolved into the Royal St George Yacht Club) and within a short period both were competing with several other new Irish clubs, such as the Liffey, Dublin and Waterford clubs, as well as invitees from Britain, at events such as the Dublin River, Kingstown and Malahide regattas. As the decades passed, regattas became annual rather than one-off affairs, and the clubs continued to hold in-house competitions for their members.

The recovery of rowing following a difficult decade in the wake of the Famine resulted in the inauguration of numerous rowing regattas in the 1860s, and the sport featured regularly in the *Irish Sporting Times* and other journals.[103] Many regattas were hosted by yacht clubs and a lively and at times antagonistic relationship between these and their rowing counterparts, borne of technical differences, persisted for many years. In 1865 alone, some ten regattas were recorded from Belfast to Cork.

Rowing was, of course, principally the preserve of the privileged, and drew its participants from the

Opposite Page:
Michael Angelo Hayes
(1820-77)
29. Rowers on the sea
1870s
Watercolour on paper
(phenakistoscope disk)
36.5 x 36.5 cm
Private collection

Opposite Page:
Michael Angelo Hayes
(1820-77)
30. Regatta
1870s
Watercolour on paper
(phenakistoscope disk)
36.5 x 36.5 cm
Private collection

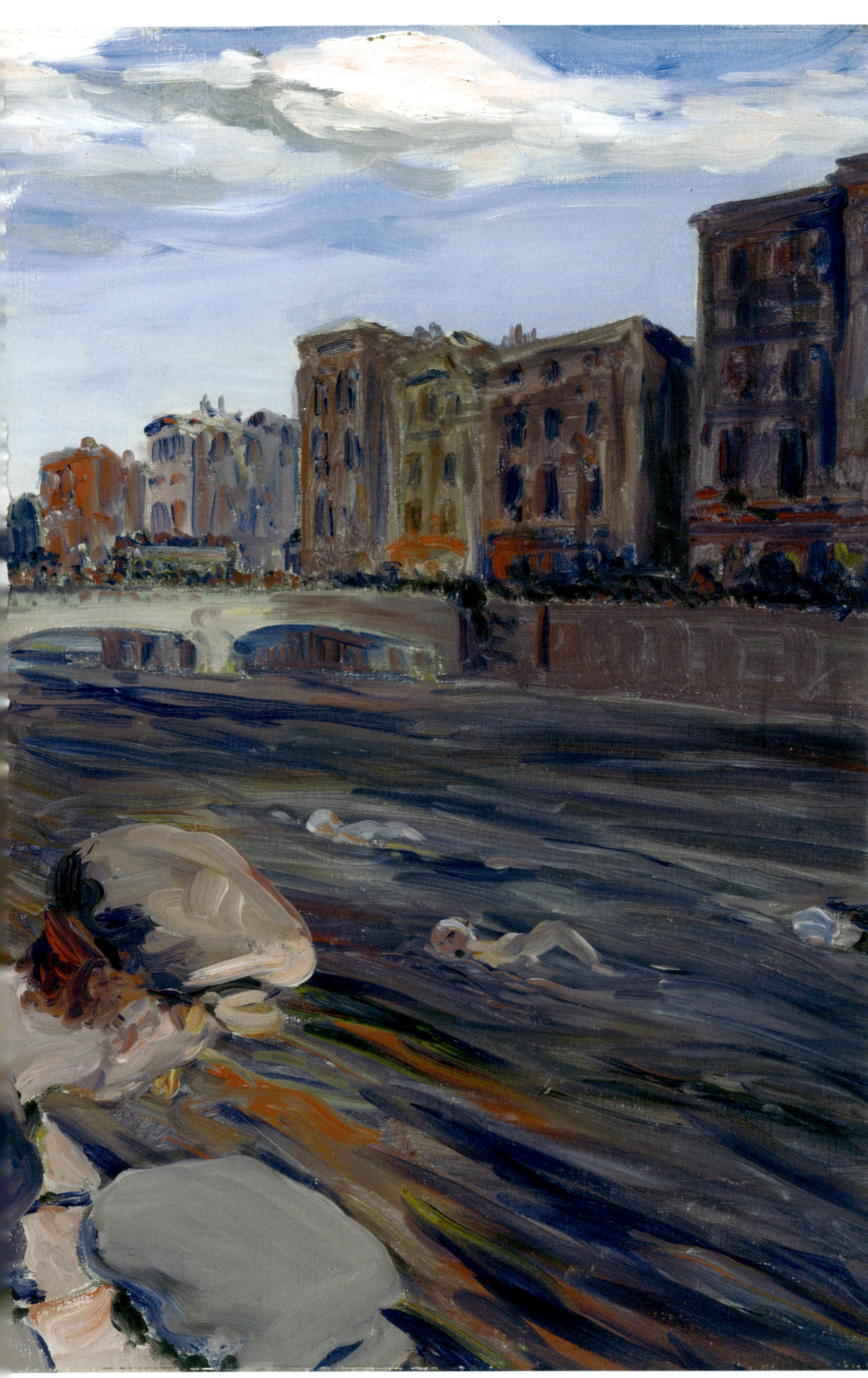

Jack B. Yeats (1871-1957)
28. *The Liffey Swim*
1923
Oil on canvas
61 x 91 cm
National Gallery of Ireland
See page 65

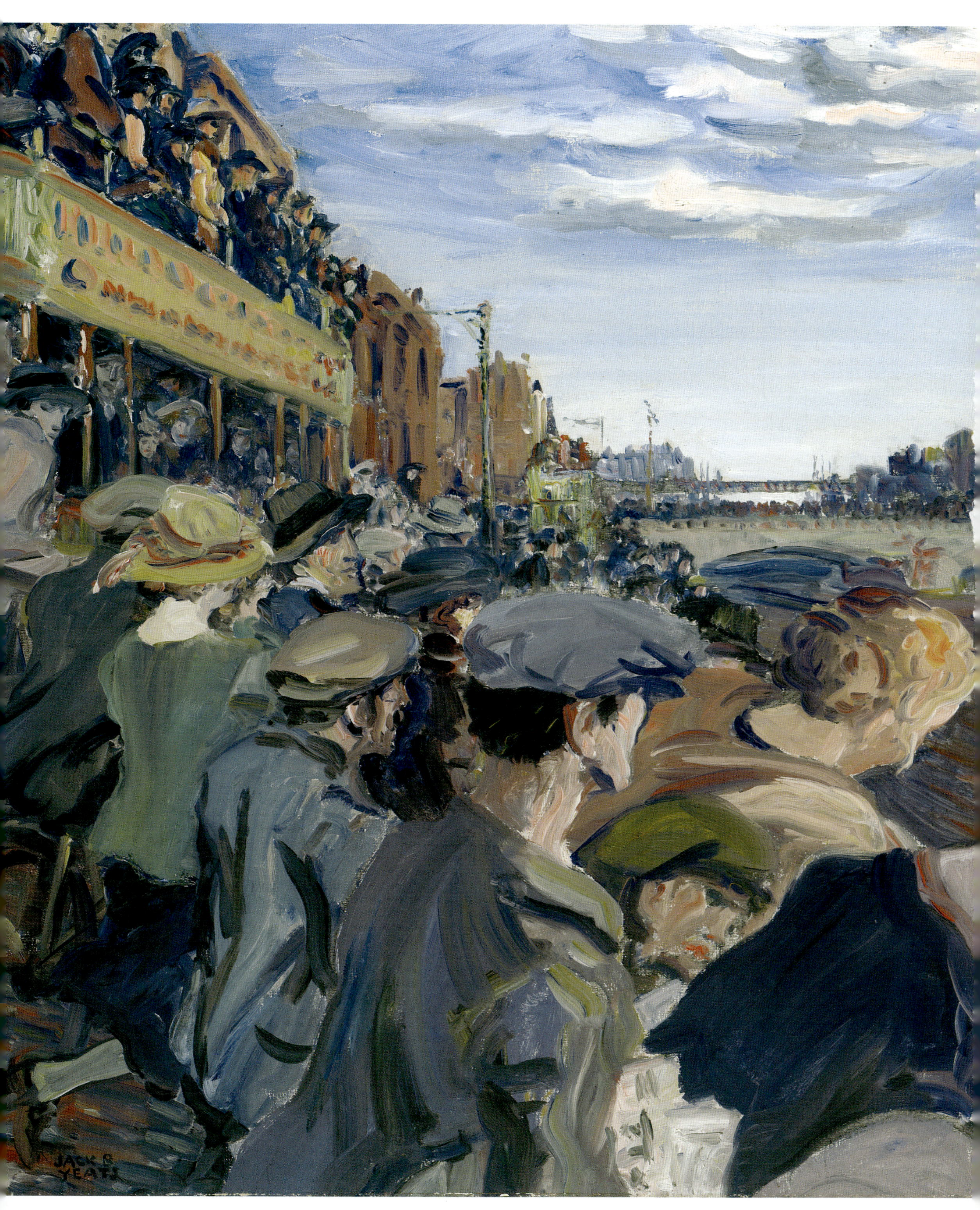
JACK B
YEATS

educated, professional classes. Towards the end of the malaise of the 1850s, one veteran lamented the competition of years past 'when a grandstand used to be erected at Ringsend point, and fair ladies and gallant gentlemen bestowed their fairest smiles and well-merited plaudits upon the doings of the stalwart oarsmen'.[104] *Bell's Life* reported that the large attendance at a race held on the 11 October 1862 at Ringsend for the Dublin University Rowing Club Challenge Cups was 'composed almost exclusively [of members of the club and their friends]; for, though there was a large attendance, it was composed almost exclusively of such- 'the public,' strange to say, not showing in force'.[105] Hayes's painting suggests an atmosphere more akin to that conjured up by the *Irish Times* in its review of the Dublin University Boat Club's regatta at Ringsend in summer 1866, when 'the Pidgeon House road from Ringsend to the Fort was lined with spectators in a manner which gave the appearance of a racecourse. Every available spot that presented a good view of the portion of the river marked out for racing... was taken advantage of, and a lively interest was expressed in each event'.[106] Late nineteenth-century photographs, and Jack B. Yeats's painting of 1925 (NGI) record that crowds assembled along the banks of the Liffey at Islandbridge to watch the Trinity Regatta.

The race depicted here by Hayes is between single sculls. The boats appear to feature outrigging, a technical development first introduced in the 1840s, which allowed the oars to be suspended away from the side of the boat, thus increasing its stability and affording the oarsman greater leverage. The open umbrellas testify to the inclement weather with which rowers frequently had to contend, and which often interfered with competitions. A ball court, designed for the playing of fives, was erected for the Pembroke Club in 1845 to provide some alternative activity when the weather made rowing impossible.[107]

Cyril Barrett maintained that the novelty of Hayes's investigations of animals in motion lay in the fact that with them the artist was not appealing to 'some independent source, such as a camera' but rather 'to observation'.[108] These phenakistoscopes testify to Hayes's scientific application to the task of understanding movement, but also draw on the artist's exceptional skill in the use of paint. They have been painstakingly finished so that they function not just as illustrative pictorial sequences but also represent accomplished works of art and animation in their own right. BR

---

92 See Le Harivel and Wynne 1984, pp.81-83.

93 Born in Waterford, Hayes was the son of the talented portrait painter Edward Hayes, who also specialised in watercolour. In 1842, in recognition of his skill at painting horses, Michael Angelo was appointed painter-in-ordinary to the lord lieutenant.

94 Hayes appears with his colleagues in a group photograph of the council of 1856.

95 Chandler 2001, p.65.

96 The society's journal, *The Dublin Photographic Journal*, first appeared in January 1855.

97 See Delia Millar, 'Michael Angelo Hayes' in *DNB* 2004, vol.26, pp.36-37.

98 The installation took place on the 18 April 1868. An edition of the key is in the Centre for the Study of Irish Art at the NGI.

99 Hayes first delivered this paper to the Royal Dublin Society in November 1876.

100 Quoted in Barrett 1973, p.42.

101 This was not Hayes's only brush with controversy. While serving as a Dublin city marshal, a position he had taken up first in 1867, he was also involved in a libel action for caricaturing the former lord mayor, Sir W. Carroll.

102 Blake 1991, p.4. The club's early membership did not consist entirely of Trinity undergraduates, but rather also included numerous Dublin gentlemen. A rival body, the University Rowing Club, was established in 1843 with which the Pembroke Club amalgamated to form the Dublin University Rowing Club in 1847.

103 Blake 1991, p17.

104 Quoted in Blake 1991, p. 17.

105 *ibid*, p.19.

106 *ibid*, p.23.

107 *ibid*, p.8.

108 *ibid*, p.8.

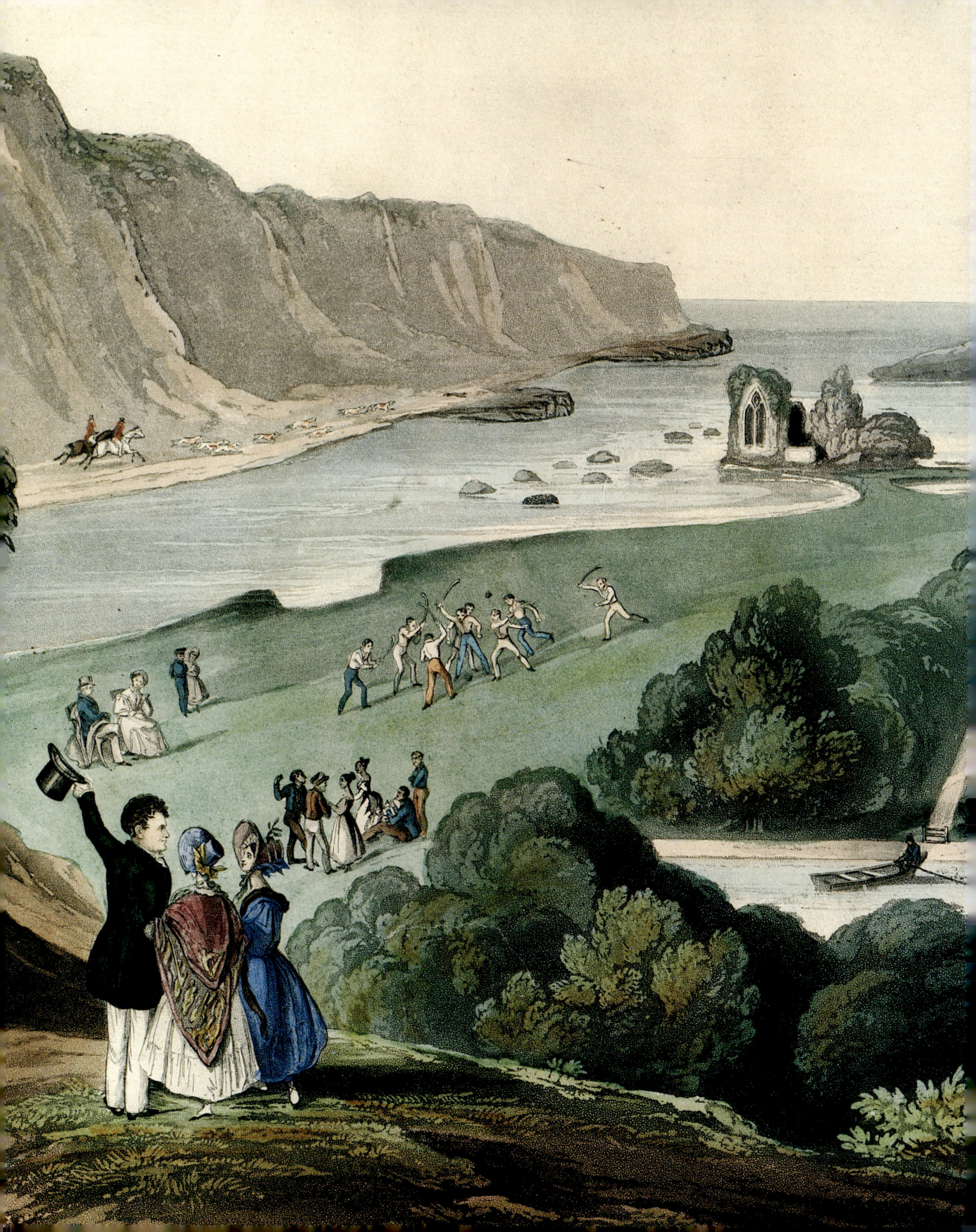

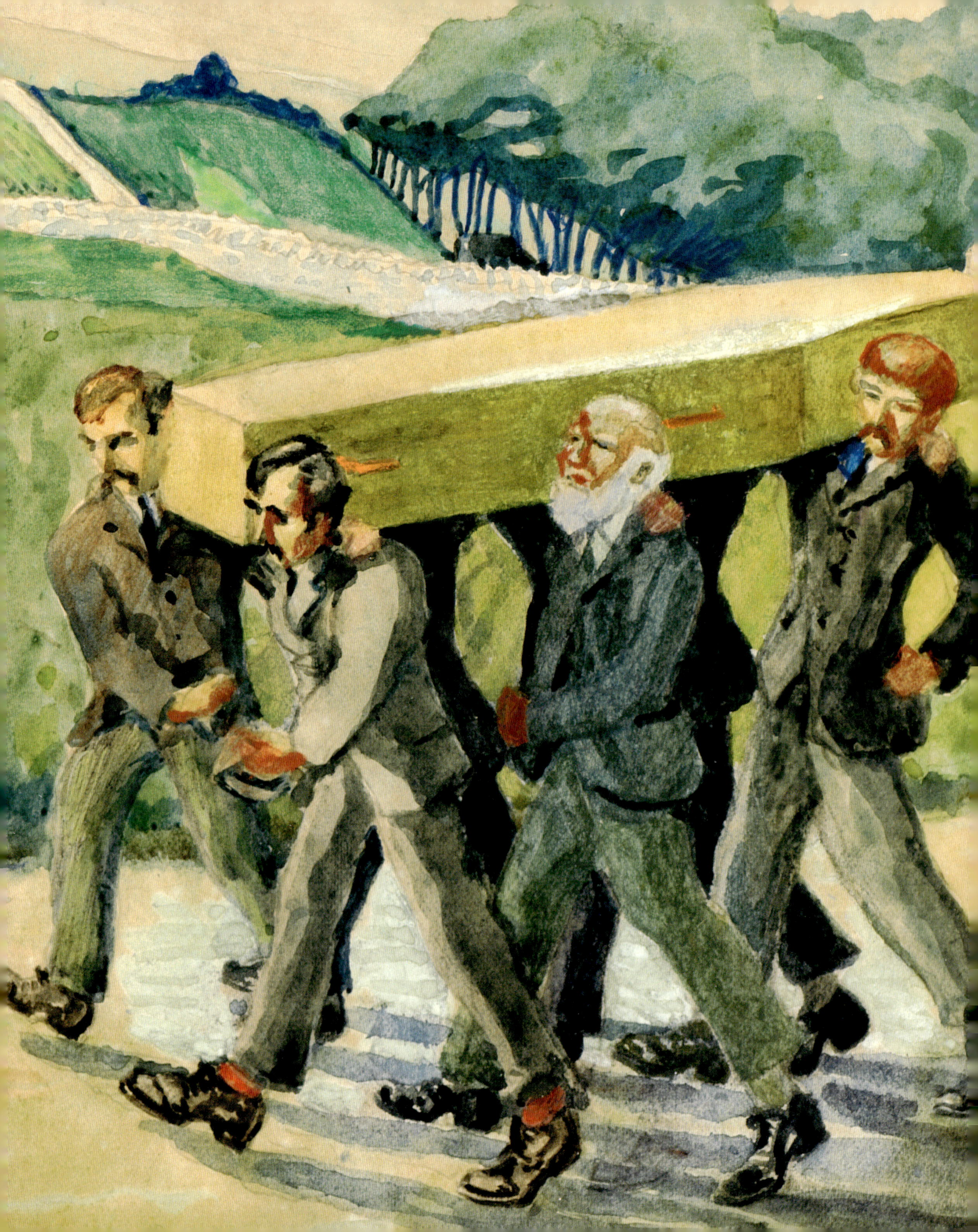

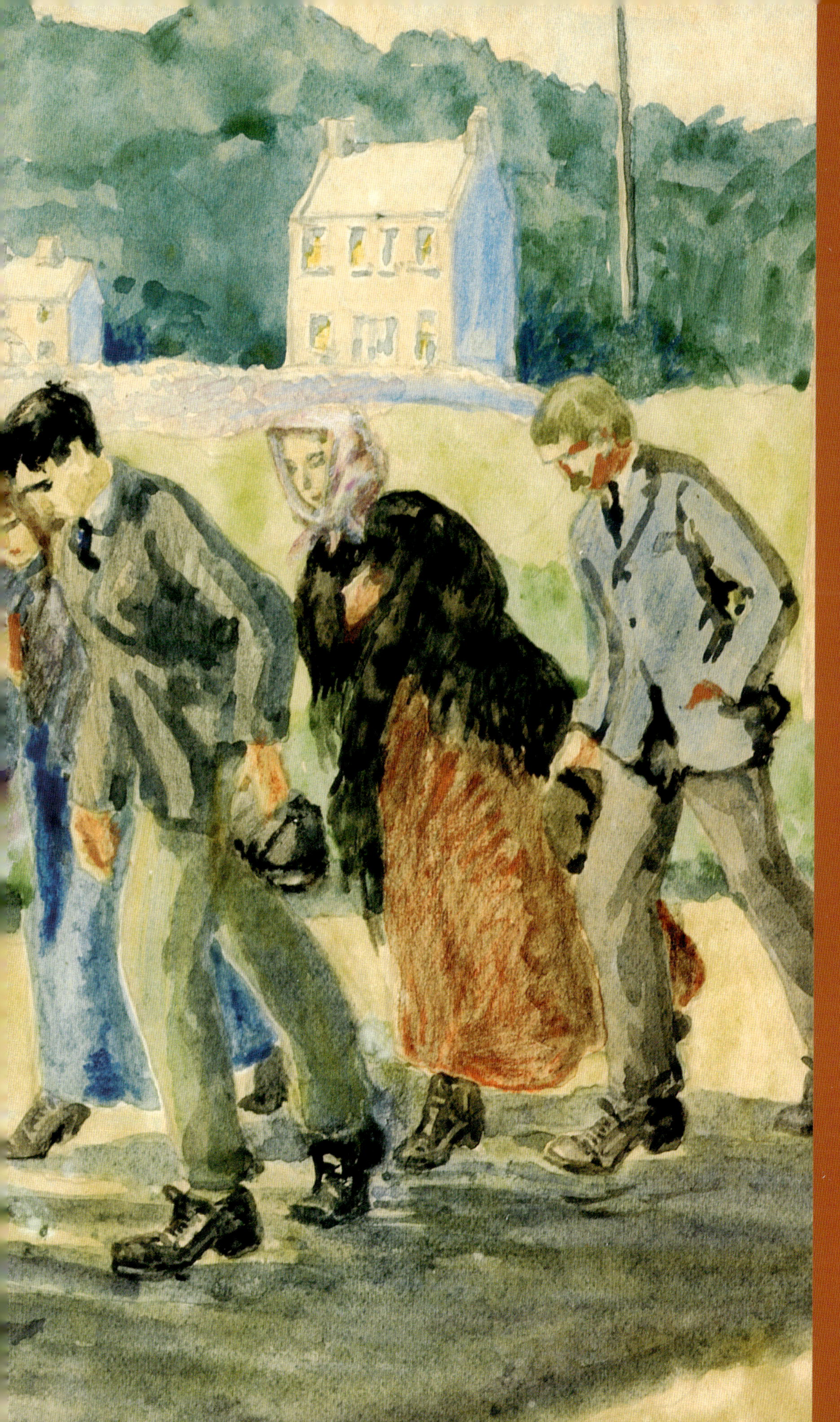

Ritual & Religion

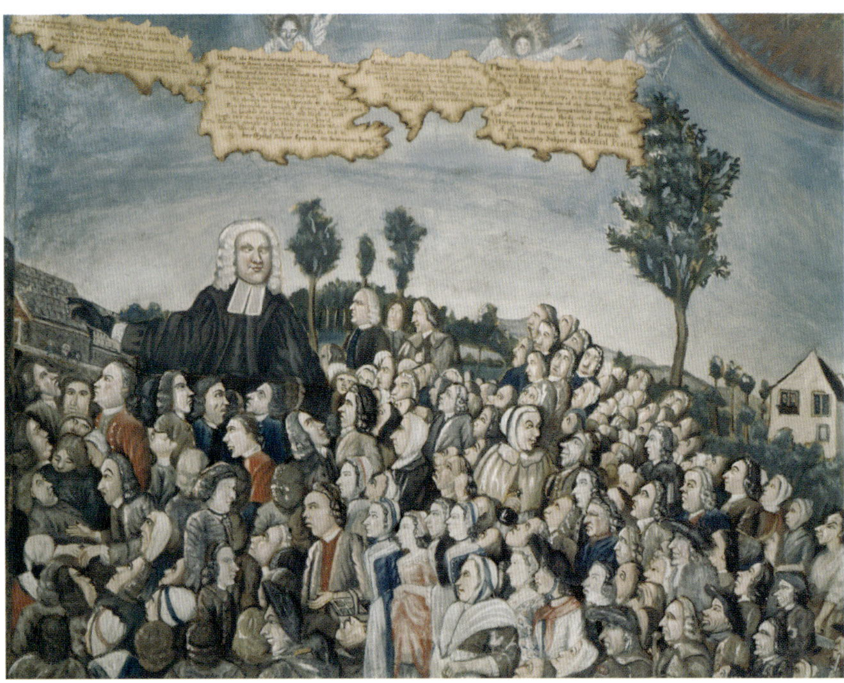

William Miller (d.1779)
31. Rev. George Whitefield (1714-70) Preaching in the Timber Yard at Lurgan, 12 July 1751
Gouache on paper
33 x 43.5 cm
Collection Ulster Museum, Belfast

31. Rev. George Whitefield Preaching in the Timber Yard at Lurgan, 12 July 1751

William Miller

William Miller was a cambric manufacturer whose 'remarkable mechanical and inventive powers' evidently extended to drawing.[1] Lurgan-born, he was a man for whom this subject was socially significant, artistically interesting and historic,[2] and what makes this picture particularly noteworthy is the documentary quality it shares with many of the more sophisticated works included in this exhibition. Like Maria Spilsbury Taylor's image of John Wesley preaching in Rosanna (cat. 32), Miller's work includes 'likenesses of the Lurgan people of the day' including 'a well-known idiot woman' who William Jackson Pigott maintained 'is easily distinguished'.[3] It seems that Miller made a habit of executing portraits, and was known to paint on glass 'likenesses of himself and his wife and friends'.[4] Through both the artist's sense of whimsy and perhaps limited technical ability, the picture departs markedly from naturalism, resembling more closely stylised book illustration. Miller's application to creative pursuits is borne out by the fact that this picture is, in fact, a collage consisting of individual portraits that would have been time consuming to produce.

The visit of the Rev. George Whitefield (pronounced Whitfield) to Lurgan was an event of considerable importance. The Oxford-educated Presbyterian minister was a skilled and animated orator, whose firebrand sermons from the pulpit were renowned. His ministry had taken him to North America, where he preached to congregations of poor colonists and proselytised to Native American communities throughout the south and east. He believed that redemption came through good intentions and deeds and stressed the need for rebirth in his teachings. Appropriately, he appears in Miller's picture in voluminous convocation dress, towering physically and morally above his congregation. Preaching was his lifeblood, and he delivered thousands of sermons, many from his portable pulpit. Having finished the previous year exhausted and confined to bed due to an attritional schedule of preaching and travel he declared that 'the pulpit is my cure'.[5] Indeed, within a short number of months of his visit to Lurgan, Whitefield was back in America. A vainglorious figure, he inspired intense feelings among champions and detractors alike, and from the 1740s was the target of much satirical invective, earning the appellation Squintum on account of the pronounced squint in the left eye that he had had since childhood.

Lest one should equate this image too closely with other views of social gatherings displayed in this exhibition, however, it is worth noting that Whitefield regularly denounced the public amusements that many of these pictures represent, from musical performances, dances and card games to the theatre.[6] This is all the more interesting when one considers Whitefield's own theatrical acumen. His sermons were characterised by humour, anecdotes, fearsome tirades and often tears.

Significantly, Whitefield was not the only celebrated preacher with whom Miller came into contact. In April 1762, John Wesley, during a visit to Lurgan, fulfilled his long-held desire of meeting the artist. Four years earlier, he had seen in Lurgan a talking wooden statue, 'unique and almost unparalleled in the world',[7] designed by Miller, and was curious about its creator.[8] The invention, which is understood to have announced the hour- 'Past twelve o'clock- O how the time runs on!'- but had difficulty when pronouncing the letter 'r',[9] obviously captured Wesley's imagination and on yet another visit in June 1773, he inquired of Miller if the artist had any plans to perfect his statue and was amazed to hear that 'no man of fortune' appeared willing to patronise the enterprise.[10] Whitefield and Wesley were deeply divided theologically, particularly on the question of predestination. Though Wesley, in accordance with Whitfield's wishes, delivered the sermon at his funeral, their differences had never been reconciled.

Sadly, Miller died prematurely, leaving a young family. He appears to have been a remarkable, compulsively creative individual. One of his daughters, who was just seven years of age when her father died, remembered watching him painting a picture of flowers on glass despite his failing health. BR

1 Strickland 1913, vol. II, p.115.
2 Around 1760, Miller married Sarah Hoope, who was herself from Lurgan.
3 Piggott 1906, p.142.
4 *ibid.*
5 Whitefield 1771-72, vol. II, p.345.
6 Boyd Stanley Schlenther, 'George Whitefield', *DNB* 2004, vol.58, p.646.
7 Stuart 1819, p.501.
8 Allingham 1906, p.47.
9 Stuart 1819, p.501.
10 Wesley understood that Miller intended to build two statues which would 'sing hymns alternately with an articulate voice'. Allingham 1906, p.47.

32. John Wesley Preaching in Ireland

Maria Spilsbury Taylor

Maria Spilsbury Taylor was confirmed into the Established Church in England, having been, like her mother, excluded from the Moravian Church of which her father was a member. She maintained, however, strong connections with independent and evangelical clerics.[11] Her artistic oeuvre, which includes many religious and missionary subjects, such as *Christ Feeding the Multitude, the Second Miracle of the Loaves and Fishes* (1804) and *The Return of the Spies from the Promised Land* (1805), reflects this pronounced religiosity. *John Wesley Preaching in Ireland*, which draws on the artist's social circle and personal experience, boasts a duality absent from these evangelical works.

In 1814, Maria and her husband John Taylor, a man whose religious fervour exceeded her own, accepted Sarah Tighe's invitation to move to Ireland with their two children. Their motives were both financial and evangelical, but the genuineness evident in *John Wesley Preaching in Ireland* is consistent with their experience there.

This picture, therefore, is best considered in the context of the zealous proselytising and preaching that fell firmly within the Taylors' own immediate social and religious frame of reference, and that of the modest but close-knit Methodist population of Wicklow. The painting shows Wesley on his final visit to Ireland in 1789 preaching to an attentive audience under a Spanish chestnut tree in the grounds of Willybank (or Willowbank), a cottage on the 300-acre Rosanna estate (which is also represented in *Wedding Dance at Rosanna* (cat. 33). The house in the background may be the building in which

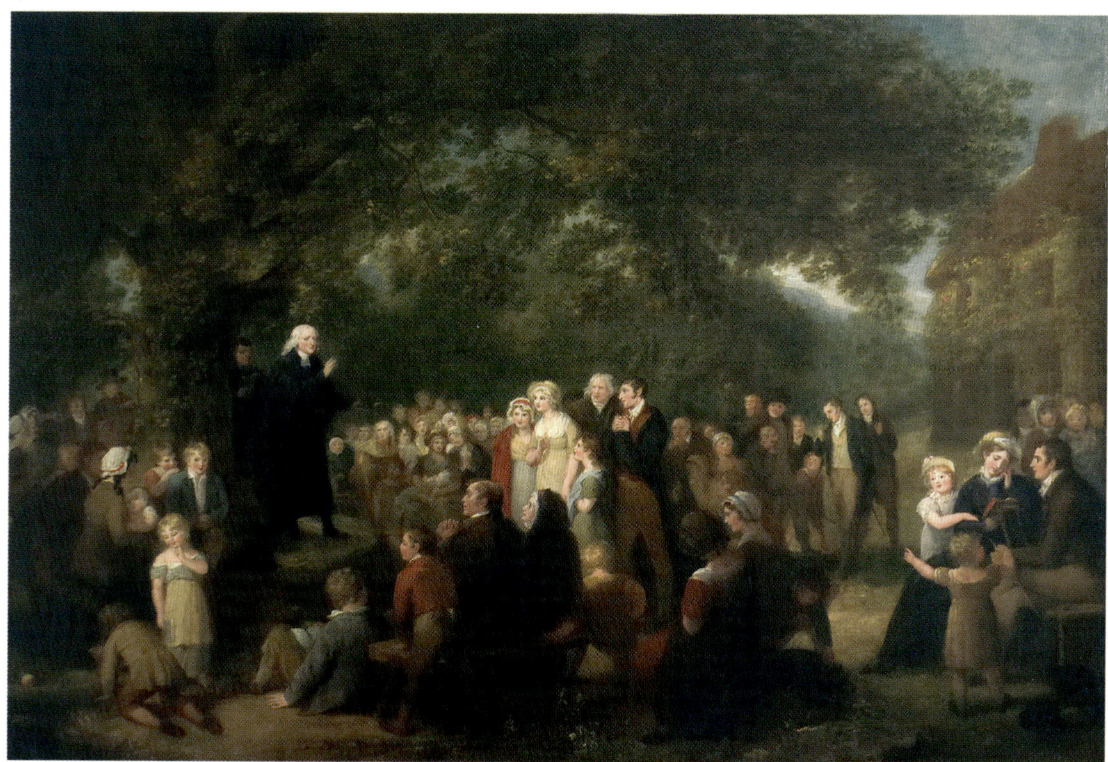

Maria Spilsbury Taylor (1776-1820)
32. John Wesley Preaching in Ireland
c.1815
Oil on canvas
74.5 x 102.7 cm
John Wesley's House & the Museum of Methodism, London

religious assemblies took place. Completed in July 1815, the painting is nostalgic, as Wesley had died some twenty-four years earlier. However, Taylor went to considerable lengths to ensure that the scene appeared authentic, populating it, as William Miller had done in his image of the Rev. Whitefield (cat. 31), with familiar local characters, among them Mrs Tighe's brewer, the Rosanna postboy, Molly Handcock, who was in service to the Tighes, a centenarian called Mrs Bryant, an elderly man who had been converted by John Taylor, and a woodranger by the name of Murphy. She also included, again impossibly, her husband John and her children, including six-month-old Sarah Ann Rosanna.[12] The presence of the family attests to their devoutness but also establishes them firmly as members of this local congregation. The figure of Wesley was based upon a portrait by George Romney commissioned by Mary Tighe, which was in Rosanna and had been engraved by Taylor's own father, Jonathan Spilsbury.

Wesley, who did not enjoy universal popularity among more conventional clerics, travelled to Ireland for the first time in 1747 and returned on some twenty occasions. As became his ministry, he travelled widely, preaching outdoors, encouraging the formation of local societies and enlisting the help of lay preachers 'to spread his message of justification by faith and Christian perfection'.[13] One of the notable characteristics of evangelicalism in Ireland in the second half of the eighteenth century was its lack of homogeneity and the relative success of the different denominations and doctrines in particular areas. The Arminian Methodism associated with John Wesley, for example, fared less well in Ulster than Whitefield's Calvinistic Methodism.[14] The close association between Wesley and Rosanna was demonstrated by the installation of an organ in the long room specifically for him by the Tighe family.[15] BR

11 Yeldham 2005, p.190.

12 Taylor had three children at the time, Jonathan (b.1809), Susanna Maria (b.1812) and Sarah Ann (b.1815). She subsequently had two more, Henry Atwood (b.1817) and John William Augustus (1818). See Yeldham 2005, p.195.

13 Myrtle Hill, 'Methodist Church', in Lalor 2003, p.721.

14 Hempton and Hill 1992, p.15.

15 Yeldham 2005, p.196.

33. Wedding Dance at Rosanna, Co. Wicklow

Maria Spilsbury Taylor

Maria Spilsbury Taylor's close attention to portraiture as well as her penchant for genre, depicting all walks of life, is clear from her surviving Irish sketchbooks, which show the people who lived and worked on the Tighe family estate at Rosanna, Ashford, County Wicklow. Taylor's *Pattern at Glendalough* (cat. 81) shows the gentry and peasantry in close proximity, emphasising their positive mutual dependence in the buying, selling and recreation that accompanied such religious gatherings. Taylor's father, an engraver, spent time as a drawing teacher at Rosanna, where Maria also subsequently worked as a governess.[16] This painting shows the outside of that house, with its high windows, rouched curtains, and fashionably-dressed people at the window. Indeed, comparison with her watercolours and sketches of the interior of the house demonstrates that this is probably the drawing room, where curtains of the same distinctive orangey-red hue hung from a Venetian window. The house was built of Dutch brick, and this view of the front corner of its façade accords visually with John Hayward's watercolour of the house of 1805, Taylor's own sketch (fig.28), and the contemporary description of it being 'adorned by the richest woods in the country'.[17]

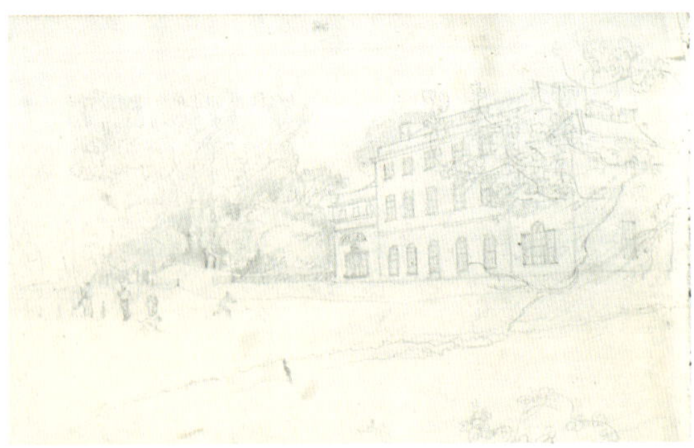

Fig.28. **Maria Spilsbury Taylor,** Sketch of *figures playing cricket on the lawn in front of Rosanna*, 1815, pencil on paper, NGI.

In her compelling analysis of Irish weddings, Linda May Ballard explains how uninvited guests were usually made welcome at wedding parties just as, traditionally, they were at wakes. Sometimes these guests turned up in disguise, dressed in special costumes made out of straw, which cunningly concealed their faces. Similarly, Christmas 'rhymers' wore straw outfits, but Taylor's scene cannot be set in winter as the trees are in leaf. Furthermore, though Taylor's pencil study of the same subject is not dated, the next drawing in the relevant sketchbook is inscribed '11 August 1815'.[18] Wedding 'strawboys' were best known in the south of

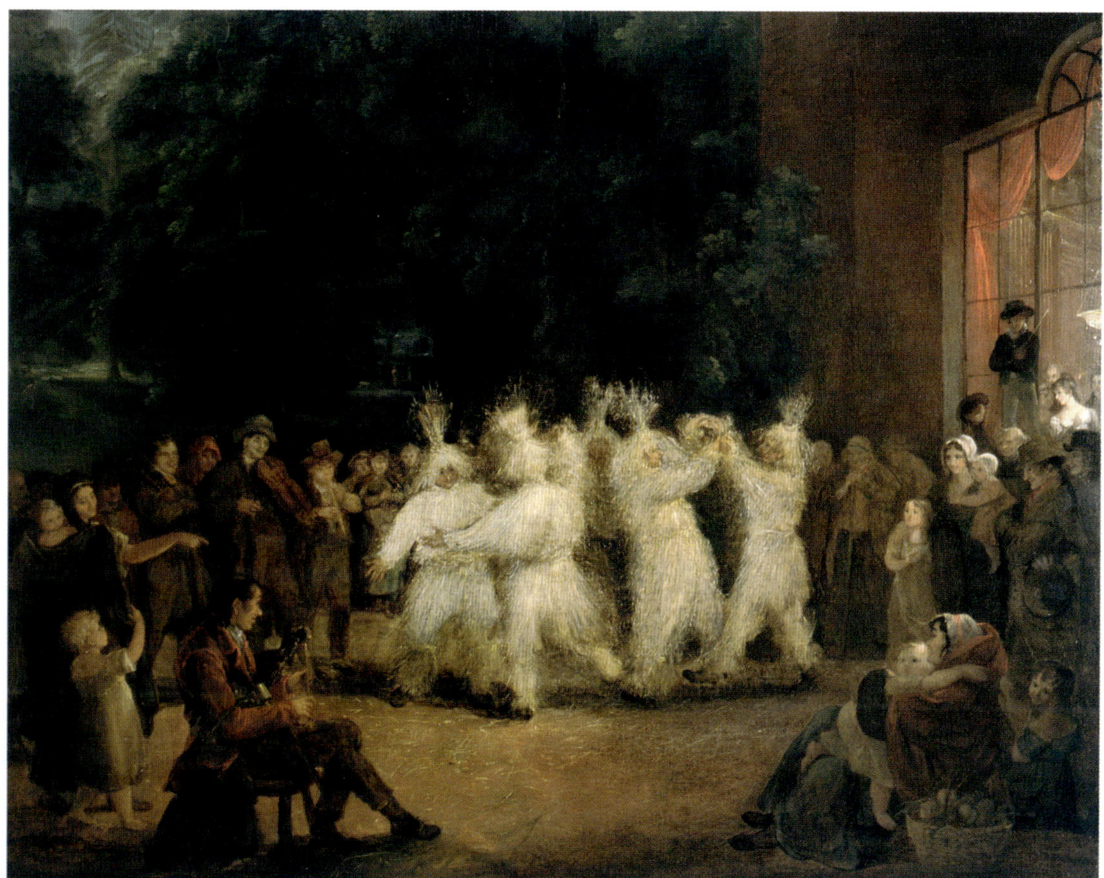

Maria Spilsbury Taylor
(1776-1820)
33. Wedding Dance at Rosanna, Co. Wicklow
1815
Oil on canvas
63.5 x 76.5 cm
W. Galen Weston &
Hilary M. Weston

Ireland, where in some places their customary visits prevailed until the 1960s. They expected to be given something to drink, and sometimes their leader, or captain, would request a dance with the bride.[19] Their behaviour varied regionally and according to each group or circumstance. Ballard analyses how 'sometimes the leader danced with the bride, the rest with bridesmaids and no doubt other young girls as well, depending on the size of the group... all wasn't necessarily sweetness and light...On the other hand, if the Tighe family were model landlords, it makes very good sense... that the tenantry would want to wish them well in the traditional way at a wedding...'.[20]

To be unwelcoming or turn away such boisterous, disguised visitors courted trouble, and if they felt hard done by, the strawboys might remove their straw costumes on departure and throw them up into the trees, where conspicuous traces would linger ominously. One account from Newry where 'they generally stayed outside' recalls how they 'reached a briar through the window...catching the bride by the hair of her head.'[21] Elsewhere disgruntled strawboys blocked peoples' chimneys, leaving rooms full of smoke, and high spirits degenerated into acts of malice and jealousy.

Conversely, the strawboys' visits could herald good luck for the newlyweds, and after drinking, dancing and singing sometimes until the small hours, they unmasked and made a bonfire of their costumes in the yard'.[22] Taylor's scene seems to include the boys in a positive mood, with dancing that symbolised the integration of the couple in the community. She shows them unmasked, suggesting the end of their visit, when if they had felt welcome, they would usually have removed their disguises as a prelude to burning the straw outside the house. These strawboys dance to the fiddle, uilleann pipes and whistle, admired by a circle of families, with barefoot women carrying their children and pointing to the ritual.[23] One of the smartly dressed boys from the big house looks down from outside the window, while just inside a young woman, who must be the bride in her fashionably low-cut white dress, looks out. The atmosphere is convivial and light-hearted, the dancers illuminated by light gleaming from indoors. Taylor used the large windows of Rosanna deliberately on a number of occasions to illuminate her interior scenes. Mary Blanchford, a relative of the Tighe family, referred in 1789 to 'the gaiety which reigns there, which inclines everyone to eat, and to drink and to rise up to play to make the pleasures at the present moment their ruling passion'.[24] Valerie Pakenham describes the Tighe family as 'model landlords', and although little historical evidence has yet emerged describing strawboys at aristocratic weddings elsewhere, such celebratory communality seems highly plausible.[25]CK

16 Kinmonth 2006, pp.245-46.

17 Wright 1820, pp.57-58. Quoted by Charlotte Yeldham in Laffan 2006, pp.231-33, figs 162-63. For further discussion of sketches of the interior of Rosanna see Yeldham 2005, p.198, fig.8.

18 See NGI 19433.

19 Ballard 1998, p.122. The author is especially grateful to Linda Ballard for her analysis of the painting and the folklore surrounding the subject of strawboys and weddings.

20 Linda Ballard. Correspondence with the author, 2006.

21 See Ballard 1998, p.122.

22 *ibid.*

23 The piper's fingering, using the first joints of the fingers, would still be considered standard practice.

24 Quoted in Yeldham 2005, p.190.

25 Packenham 2000, p.140.

34. Mass in a Connemara Cabin

Aloysius O'Kelly

A contemporary novelist's appraisal of this painting, when it was exhibited at London's Royal Academy in 1883, betrays her preference for sentimentality:

Here there is some warmth and colour, and we see that the kneeling figures are faithfully taken from life. A certain hardness and clean sweptness, and a severe determination not to idealise or even notice the grace that often lurks about the rugged truth, forbid us to love the picture, but it gives evidence of power, and the artist, Mr Aloysius O'Kelly, ought yet to do excellent service to his country after time has somewhat mellowed his method and softened his dealings with positive fact.[26]

It is O'Kelly's straightforward approach to his subject matter that enhances its value as an historical document. The painting may be interpreted as a rare view of the widespread practice of holding mass and

Aloysius O'Kelly (1853-1941)
34. Mass in a Connemara Cabin
Exh. 1889
Oil on canvas
134.5 x 180 cm
On loan to the NGI from the people of St Patrick's, Edinburgh and the Trustees of the Archdiocese of St Andrew's and Edinburgh

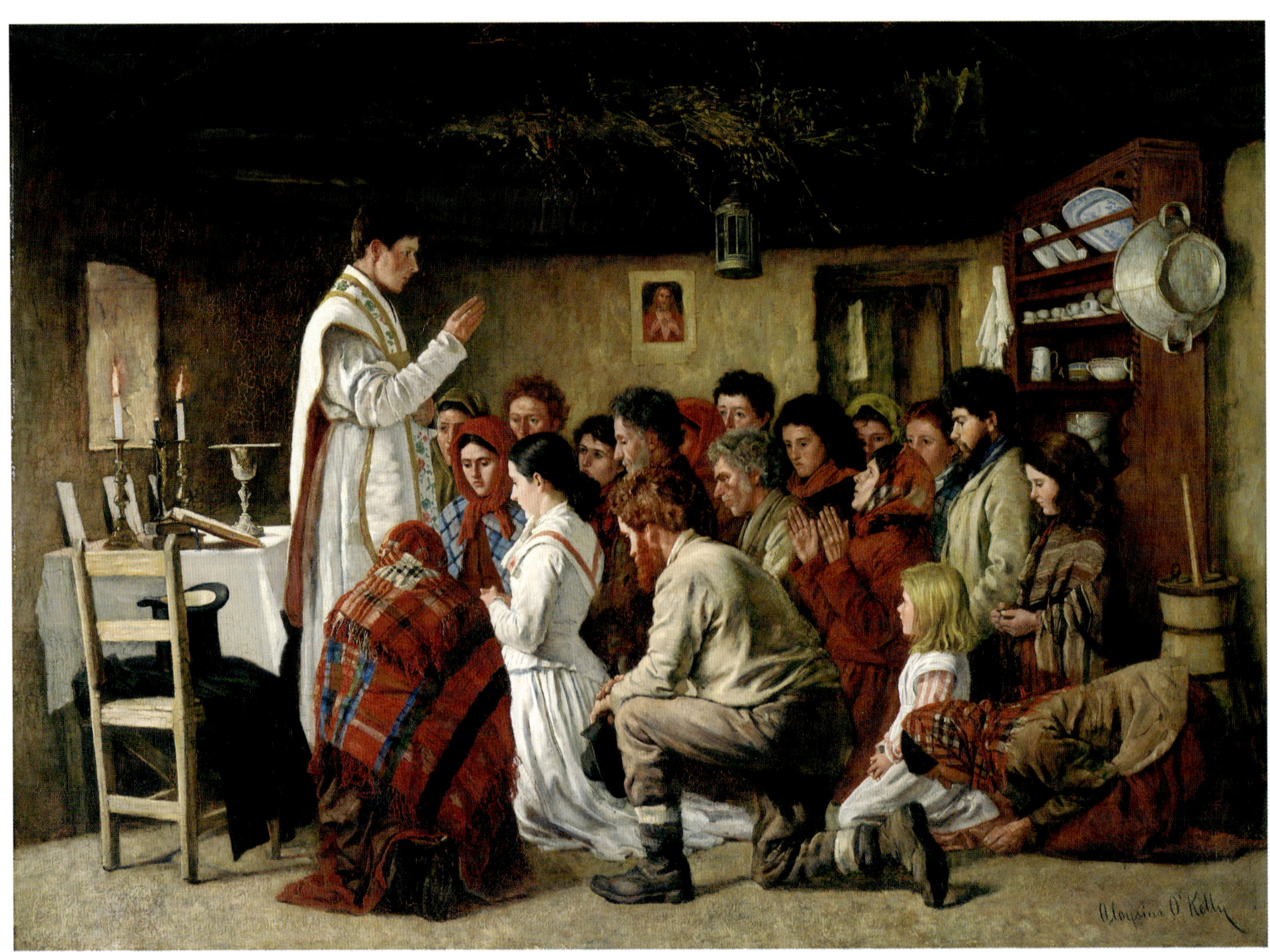

then confession in a private farmhouse. This custom was known as 'The Stations', and still survives in some rural areas. It originated as a way of enabling Roman Catholics to practise their religion during times of oppression when they were forced to meet in secrecy. By the eighteenth century it had become widespread, but the church authorities in Rome were actively discouraging it by the nineteenth century. Priests gained considerable income from their duties at such events- in fact, their fees were often higher than for the equivalent work in church- and by the 1880s, a period of insurgence, this type of service was perceived as closing the gap between the priest and his people. Religious gatherings were by that time often followed by political meetings. The way the young priest stands facing his flock and amongst them might have been read as controversial at a time when the Land League was gaining political momentum.[27] Alternatively, O'Kelly may be depicting an Ordination Mass, an occasion when a new priest returned to his home place to hold a first mass among his neighbours and family, and traditionally was dressed in white for such an occasion. This reading is reinforced by the priest's youthful appearance.

O'Kelly's serious documentary approach to this subject contrasts with the humour of popular novelist William Carleton, and J. Wrightson, whose illustration of Carleton's short story 'Phaddy Entertaining the Priests' focuses on the copious food and drink being laid out, as was customary at Station masses. [28] The empty vessels tossed aside, and the woman carrying in trays to replace them while children fall asleep by the fire, suggest protracted conviviality. Various written descriptions dwell lightheartedly on the priest's special breakfast, which originally preceded the religious ceremonies, and subsequently evolved to become the evening feast, which survives as the social highlight of these events to this day. The event was the catalyst for clearing and cleaning, even involving the cutting of the children's hair and, when possible, the visit of a tailor to make new clothes, 'along with the lustration which every fixture within the house was obliged to undergo'.[29]

In preparation for the Stations and the unusual influx of visitors, people cleaned, scrubbed and reappraised their furniture, so that the home could be seen in its best light. The flurry of excitement preceding this social day is described further by Carleton:

Every preparation was accordingly entered into...the dresser, chairs, tables, pots, and pans, all underwent a rigour of discipline, as if some remarkable event was about to occur: nothing less, it must be supposed, than a complete domestic revolution, and a new state of things.[30]

In most households The Stations was the catalyst for repainting all the furniture and woodwork, and the thick layers of over-painting on surviving country furniture results largely from this ritual.[31] Depending upon the size of the parish, the cycle of households which hosted the occasion might recur as often as twice per decade. O'Kelly's dresser is carved with rope moulding, as was typical of the west (and coastal areas in the southeast), and has the red paint which was fashionable for its resemblance to the mahogany furniture of 'the big house'. Beside it the utilitarian objects of the farm kitchen, such as the strainer and the dash churn for making butter, take their place near the best plates reserved for display or occasional use. The unframed print of the Sacred Heart beneath the half-loft was also typical of such Catholic homes, where economy dictated that decorative items earned their keep by fulfilling a practical role.

The most common layout of the western farm kitchen positioned the fireplace opposite the parlour, or 'west room', which usually doubled as a bedroom and can be seen here through the doorway to the right. The dresser was often placed like this to impress visitors coming through the front door, which in O'Kelly's picture also provides the main source of light on the far left hand side. The kitchen table was nearly always positioned beneath the front window, where anyone preparing food would have sight of people approaching the house, and light for their work. Its scrubbed top has been dressed with the altar cloth, candles and chalice, as was customary. Indeed, improvised tables are still arranged for such events in West Cork. The young priest has laid aside his Chesterfield coat and silk top hat, which he evidently wore for his journey to the house. The company are dressed in their best clothes, the girls in white, the women in their homespun shawls and red petticoats. O'Kelly presents those in attendance as individuals, not ciphers, and lavishes attention on every detail of the accoutrements associated with their daily lives, which have been carefully prepared to look their best for the event. Despite the ordinary setting, the painting is emotionally charged.[32] CK

---

26 Mullholland 1889, p.484. Quoted in O'Sullivan 2000, p.16. Scholars had known this composition from watercolours and sketches, but the painting only recently came to light in Scotland.

27 Kinmonth 2006, pp.181-85.

28 See Carleton 1911 (edition illustrated by J. Wrightson).

29 Carleton 1990, pp.155-56.

30 Carleton 1911, vol.II, pp.286-87.

31 Kinmonth 1993, pp.22-27.

32 O'Sullivan 2002. See also O'Sullivan 1999 and Kinmonth 2006, fig. 182.

James Humbert Craig
(1878-1944)
35. Going to Mass
c.1935
Oil on board
37.7 x 50.5 cm
Crawford Municipal Art Gallery, Cork

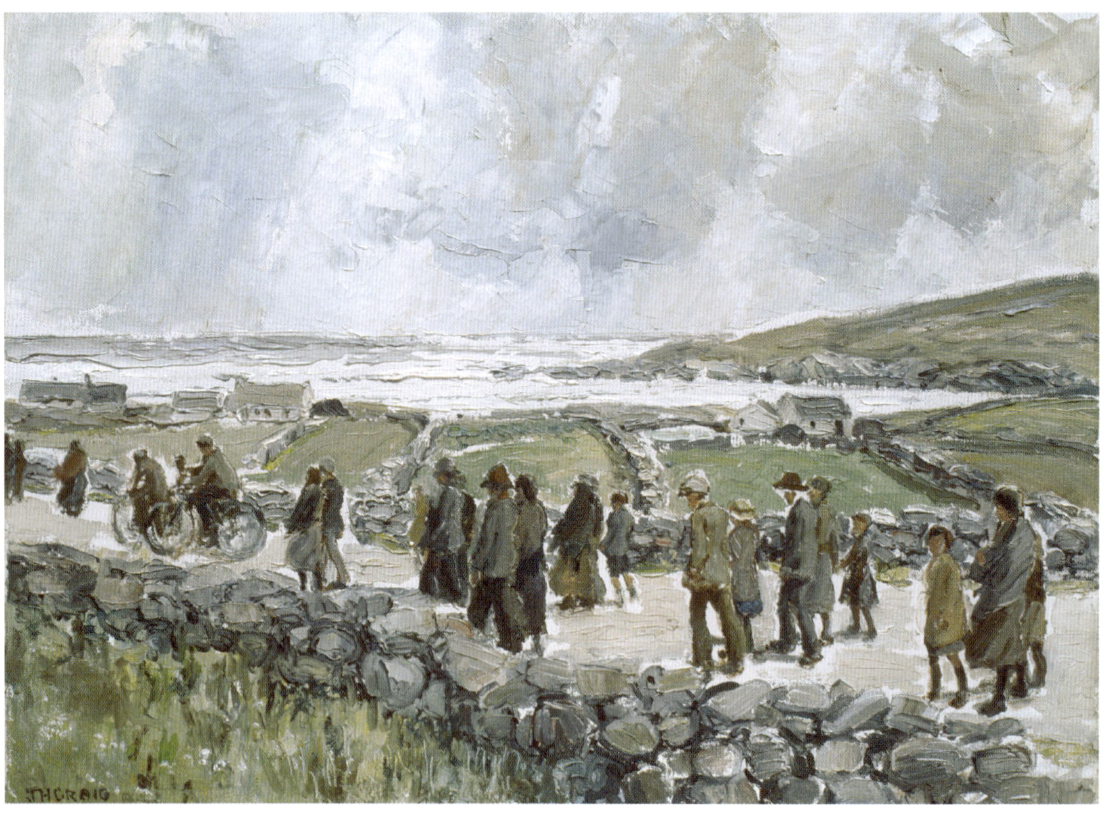

35. Going to Mass

James Humbert Craig

James Humbert Craig was one of a number of Belfast-born artists, including Paul Henry and Gerard Dillon, who were drawn to rural Ireland, and particularly Connemara, in the early decades of the twentieth century. Like the figures in Henry's *Old People Watching a Dance* (cat. 9), whose earthy solidity suggests the world they inhabit, the people in Craig's picture seem integrally linked with the wild, rugged landscape through which they walk. The sombre greys and browns of their Sunday best complement the stone walls, slate roofs around them and the Atlantic sky above. The people's slow progress, driven by piety or duty, is emphatically communal, as all ages are represented among their number. Their silent purpose is remarkable, interrupted only by the sudden awareness of the young girl on the right of the presence of an observer. She turns her head directly towards the viewer but curiously remains at a distance due to the invisibility of her features. This enigmatic detail alone arguably makes more of Craig than the mere raconteur of the landscape that he has been described as.[33]

Curiously, this picture's cachet seems rooted in its ordinariness. It is a picture of any Sunday or holy day. Craig has generalised the weather conditions so that the season is of no marked importance. Equally, the lack of any notable landmarks means that one can take the picture to represent almost anywhere on the Connemara coast. Meanwhile, Craig's deliberate omission of the church to which the crowd makes its way evinces the fact that the custom and discipline of walking and arriving together, as much as attending mass itself, was a fundamental part of religious observance and community activity.

Craig was essentially a landscape painter and it is interesting to see the way in which his figures are incorporated technically into the overall composition. One can see clearly that he conceived the painting, including the figures, as an integral whole. The areas between the figures are filled in sketchily, while the figures themselves are summarily detailed. This suggests an instinctive, unfussy approach to painting that is consistent with the fact that Craig was largely self-taught.[34] His subordination of the figures to the landscape is exemplified by the expanse of the sky, which occupies almost half of the composition. Craig's choppy use of a palette knife in the rendering of the sky cleverly implies the blustery wind that one can see elsewhere blowing the women's shawls into their backs. His technique became increasingly loose in the last years of his life,

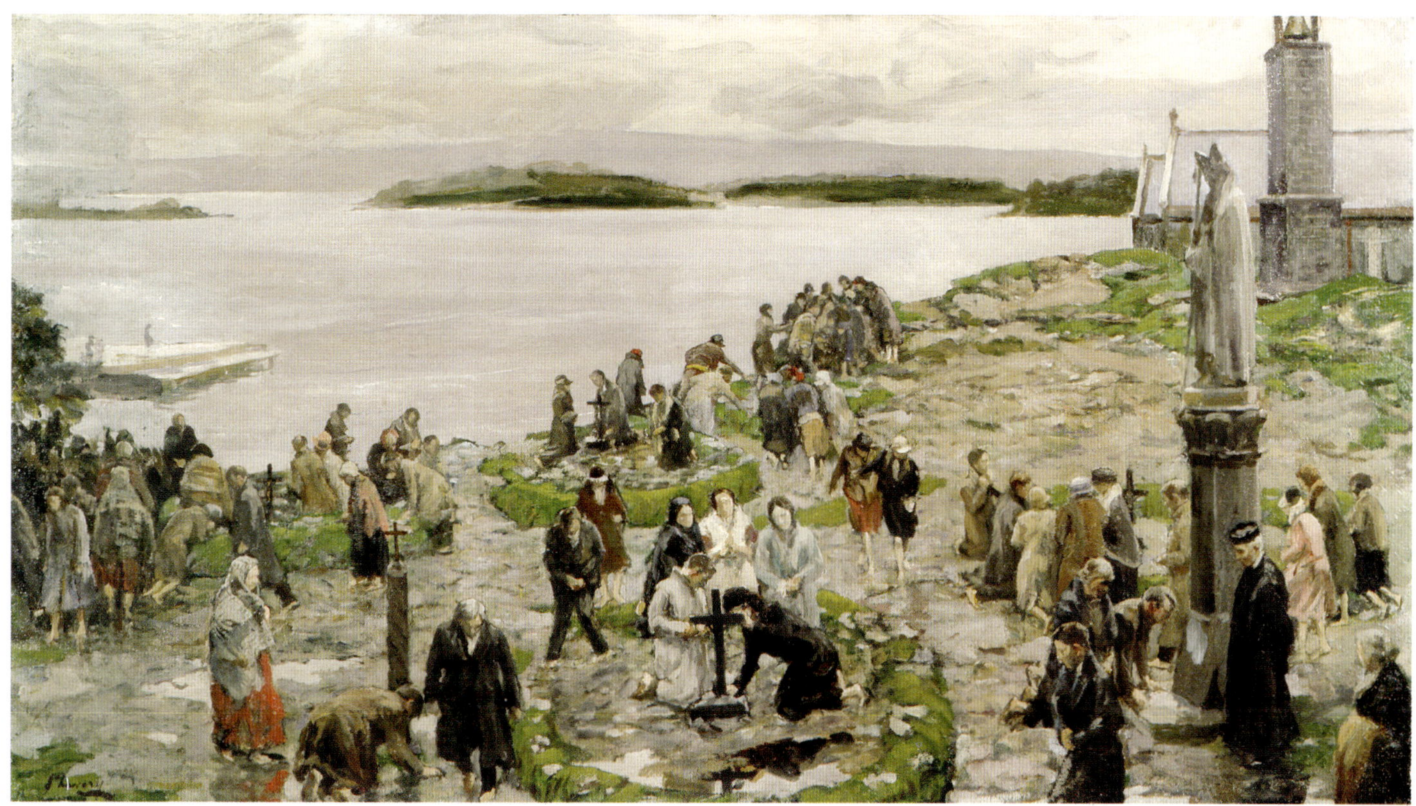

and his palette more intense and colourful (see, for example, *Early Summer, Glendun* (private collection)), but it retained the tonal contrasts that lent a richness and textural quality to his landscapes. This painting is the product of a creative spirit of more substance than the 'tweedy' Humbert Craig described by John Hewitt, who merely 'painted billowy clouds and sunlit bogs'.[35]

Though he did, as here, include figures on occasion in his pictures, Craig was less concerned with human types than with the formal and atmospheric qualities of the landscape. Enthralled by the countryside, whether in Donegal, the Glens of Antrim or Connemara, he did not possess the almost anthropological curiosity about its inhabitants that was shared by a number of his close contemporaries, such as Lamb and Keating. However, this did not diminish the painting's appeal, and its resonance among the Irish public was demonstrated by the popularity it enjoyed in printed form after the artist's death.[36] BR

35 S.B. Kennedy 1989-90, p.51.

36 Craig did attend the Belfast College of Art, but failed to complete a single term.

37 John Hewitt, 'Conor's Art', in Wilson 1977, p.108.

38 Murray 1997, p.54.

36. St Patrick's Purgatory

Sir John Lavery

According to tradition, Oileán na Naomh (or Station Island), on Lough Derg, County Donegal, was the scene of St Patrick's purgatory, a period of forty days during which he fasted and saw visions of heaven and hell. Since the Middle Ages, the island has attracted pilgrims, emulating St Patrick's experience through fasting, penitence, collective prayer and sleep deprivation.[37]

This pilgrimage, with its notoriously austere conditions, may seem an unorthodox form of recreation. However, such activity remained popular through the nineteenth and twentieth centuries and was recorded by a number of notable writers. Indeed, much of its attraction might be said to have been attributable to the aura that surrounded the site rather than the practicalities of the pilgrimage itself. William Carleton, who wrote at length of St Patrick's Purgatory, as the site itself had become known, remembered that as a consequence of the legends he had heard from his father he felt his 'imagination fired with a romantic curiosity to perform a station at that celebrated place'.[38] The reality proved for him rather different, however, and he subsequently dismissed himself merely as 'one of the millions of fools that have, century after century, degraded their understandings by coming hither'.[39]

John Lavery (1856-1941)
36. St Patrick's Purgatory
1929-30
Oil on canvas
258.5 x 106.5 cm
Dublin City Gallery The Hugh Lane

Though impressed by the discipline that was central to the Lough Derg pilgrimage, and humbled by the pilgrims' piety, John Lavery, for his part, looked on his visit to the island in 1929 as a fundamentally artistic undertaking, though not without its professional hardships. Enlivened by the primary colours of peasant dress in Connemara, he was disappointed by the 'everyday types' he encountered on the island, likening them to anyone one might see on the streets of Dublin or Belfast.[40] Nevertheless, his visit and the asceticism that attended it inspired a number of significant works. The barrenness and remoteness of the island, so fundamental to the pilgrimage, appear to have compensated for the lack of colour Lavery remarked upon. Indeed, these qualities must have presented a substantially new challenge to an artist and bon viveur instinctively drawn to, among other delights, the flounce of contemporary fashion, the opulence of Edwardian interiors and the colour and light of the Mediterranean. It was a challenge that he appears to have been eager to embrace and he expressed concern and frustration in a letter to Thomas Bodkin that the benign weather that prevailed during his visit might make his pictures of Lough Derg 'look like a crowded summer resort making Purgatory a thing to long for'.[41] The resulting 'uncoordinated' compositions, *St Patrick's Purgatory* in particular, reflect the rather unexpected, disorientating experience to which Lavery alludes in his autobiography.[42] With its mixture of city and rural folk, austerity and fine weather, Lough Derg was for Lavery, like religion, at once impressive and confounding. His artistic pilgrimage certainly did not fulfill his expectations as North Africa had done.

Purgatory was, in any case, an experience for which Lavery certainly had no appetite. In fact, he justified his disinclination to take his head 'out of the paint-pot for a moment' to think of things other than painting by maintaining that he had 'a purgatory of my own, and that to get mixed up with another one would be more than I could bear'.[43] One can only assume that this remark was tongue-in-cheek, however, as he completed *The Walnut Tree, St Patrick's Purgatory, Lough Derg* (Dublin City Gallery The Hugh Lane), based on sketches produced on the island, in the rather less than purgatorial surroundings of the Hôtel Beau-Site in Cannes the following year.[44] BR

37 Pilgrims are permitted to sleep on the second night, but are restricted to eating bread and drinking tea.

38 Carleton 1843, p.xvi.

39 *ibid*, p.239.

40 Lavery 1940, p.204.

41 Letter from Lavery to Thomas Bodkin, 10 August 1929, (no. 551), Trinity College Library, Dublin. Quoted in McConkey 1993, p.166.

42 *ibid*.

43 Lavery 1940, p.206.

44 See Hunt Museum 2005, p.7.

37. An Island Funeral

Jack B. Yeats

Yeats's painting of a small boat carrying a coffin and mourners across a choppy sea is a sombre and intimate study of human emotion, tradition and community. It has been suggested by Hilary Pyle that the painting probably depicts a funeral party making its way from The Great Blasket, off the coast of Kerry, to the mainland, where the body is to be buried.[45] This custom was necessary due to the absence of a church or graveyard on the island.

The Blaskets, the most westerly part of Ireland, comprise a number of islands, the largest of which supported a small community on its eastern side until 1953, when the population was officially evacuated.[46] Many of the islanders were originally from mainland villages, but evicted by Lord Ventry during the first half of the nineteenth century, moved to the Blaskets in hope of a better life. The absence of services and constant travelling across the three-mile stretch between island and mainland, however, made life on the island a constant struggle.[47]

Death was treated with great respect by the island people and old superstitions regarding the dead were faithfully observed. In her letters to her friend George Chambers, Eibhlis Ní Shuilleabháin wrote that 'when there is a dead man on the Blaskets everybody is frightened'.[48] As a result, every aspect of the funeral, from the collection of the coffin to the preparation of the body, had to be carried out according to tradition. Following the wake, the coffin was carried on the shoulders of four men along the 'Boreen na marbh' (Road of the Dead) and loaded onto a boat. It was then brought to the mainland, where it could be buried in the village of Dun Chaoin or the small town of Ventry, depending usually on where the family plot was located.[49]

Although Yeats may never have visited the Blasket Islands or possibly even the remote areas beyond Dingle, he did visit West Kerry in 1921. Among his sketches are views of the Blasket Islands from Cahirsiveen and a study of a woman wearing a type of black shawl that was typical of West Kerry and features in *An Island Funeral*. Yeats's visit to that part of the country and his interest in the Blaskets may have been inspired by the writings of his friend and

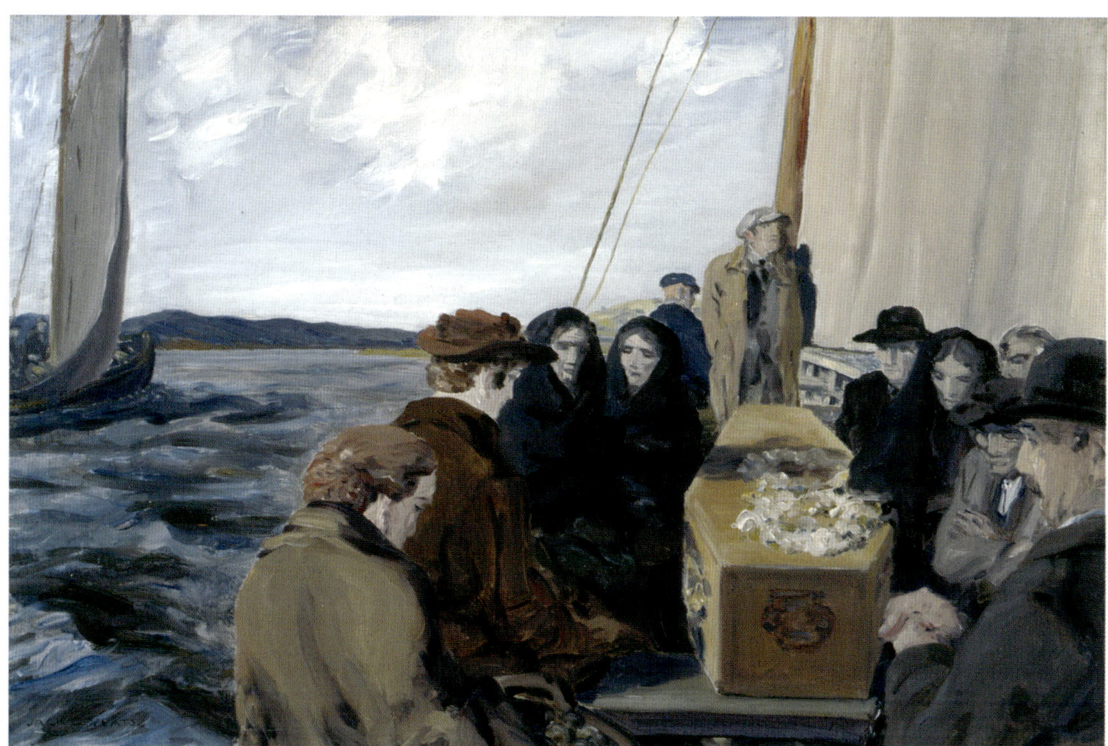

Jack B. Yeats (1871-1957)
37. *An Island Funeral*
1923
Oil on canvas
61 x 91.5 cm
Sligo Municipal Collection, The Model Arts & Niland Gallery, Sligo

erstwhile travelling companion J. M. Synge, described as 'the first famous visitor' to the island in 1905.[50] Although it has been suggested that Yeats painted only what he had seen, it is unlikely that he witnessed a funeral from the Blasket Islands as intimately as his picture implies.[51] Furthermore, inaccuracies in the work suggest that his knowledge of the custom was acquired from secondary sources, possibly including Synge.[52] Most notably the boat appears to be much larger than the *naomhogs* used by the Blasket Island fishermen. These light canoes, which could take a small sail, did not hold many more than the four men required to carry the coffin, and women had to travel in other boats. [53]

It seems that Yeats was principally concerned with creating a dramatic composition and consequently presents a general interpretation of the island custom. The local men and women aboard the boat represent the various members of the community who would participate in the funeral. The three women wearing black shawls, one of them perhaps the mother or wife of the deceased, display various stages of grief. Another woman, who wears a flowered hat, is possibly a relation who has returned to the island to attend the funeral. The detachment from the mourners of the men positioned at opposite ends of the coffin suggests that they are perhaps undertakers. Assembled tightly around the coffin, the figures obscure the structure of the boat. Apart from the mast and a section of the bow, the fabric of the boat is hardly visible, implying that the people, as much as the boat in which they travel, bear the coffin to its final destination. This sense of community and camaraderie is emphasised by the inclusion of a second boat, which enters the picture from the left. Although positioned inaccurately ahead of the boat carrying the coffin, this escort provides a visual connection to the larger community, reminding us that the boat (and the body) does not make the journey alone.

Yeats began to refer to death in his paintings from 1915 onwards. [54] Indeed, the subject of a funeral procession had already featured in his 1918 painting *The Funeral* (Walters Art Gallery, Baltimore). Based on a sketch made while travelling in Connemara with Synge, that painting closely resembles *An Island Funeral* thematically. It features a similar focus on community, custom and the specific method by which the coffin is carried (in this case the jaunting car, another iconic mode of transport). The earlier work, however, does not boast the vibrant and expressionistic manner that Yeats began to develop in the early twenties. As regards execution, the *An Island Funeral* can more readily be compared to *The Liffey Swim* (cat. 28) also of 1923.[55] *The Island Funeral* displays a similar abandonment of line and flat colour in favour of an expressive style characterised by fluid brush work. As part of this expressive use of colour, Yeats has applied dramatic dark touches to the surface of the water between the two boats. Reflecting the atmosphere of the occasion, this evocative use of paint and colour establishes a connection between the people and their environment.

DM

45 Pyle 1992, p.182.

46 Lalor 2003, p. 97.

47 Ua Maoileoin n.d., p. 7

48 Ní Shuilleabháin 1992, p.38. Ní Shuilleabháin was married to Seán Criomhthain – a son of Tomás Criomthain, An tOileanach (The Islandman). The letters chart the last twenty years of human occupation of the island

49 Ní Shuilleabhain 1992, p. 39 and Ó Guithín 1982, p. 109. In her autobiography, Peig Sayers recalls that the body of her son, who had fallen from a cliff, was brought to Ventry graveyard to be buried.

50 Ua Maoileoin n.d., p. 30. Synge's account of his days spent among the island people, *In Wicklow West Kerry and Connemara,* for which Yeats provided the illustrations, was published posthumously in 1911.

51 Tinney 1998, p.28.

52 In his account of his stay on the Blasket Islands Synge mentions discussing the death of a local fisherman with his host. Synge 1911, p. 89.

53 The author is grateful to Daithí de Mórdha of the Blasket Island Heritage Centre for his observations on this painting.

54 Tinney 1998, p.28.

55 *An Island Funeral* and *The Liffey Swim* were painted on identically-sized canvas.

38. A Funeral in Mayo

Harry Kernoff

Harry Kernoff's preference for depicting the colour and activities of urban life was in evidence throughout his career, as he captured the city of Dublin and its varied inhabitants. While many of these citizens were friends and acquaintances of the artist, observed in their regular haunts, most were random people. Portraying them at work or socialising in the shops, bars, parks, back alleys and beaches of the city, Kernoff provided a wonderful record of Dublin during his life time. He also looked beyond the capital for inspiration, however, and from about 1934 onwards made regular painting trips to Kerry and the west of Ireland. Attracted by Mayo in particular, he visited Castlebar and the coastal town of Westport on a number of occasions.[56]

The setting for Kernoff's painting *A Funeral in Mayo* is easily identifiable by the ridge formation and triangular profile of Croagh Patrick in the background. Famous as a site of pilgrimage, in the course of which thousands of people climb to its summit each year, the mountain slopes steeply into Clew Bay, just south of Westport. In the foreground

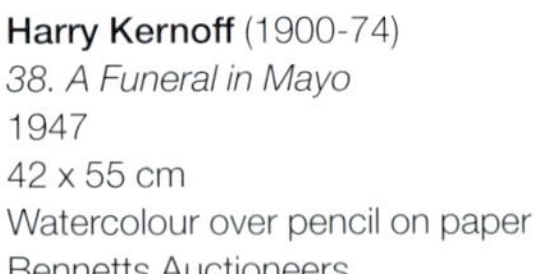
Harry Kernoff (1900-74)
38. A Funeral in Mayo
1947
42 x 55 cm
Watercolour over pencil on paper
Bennetts Auctioneers

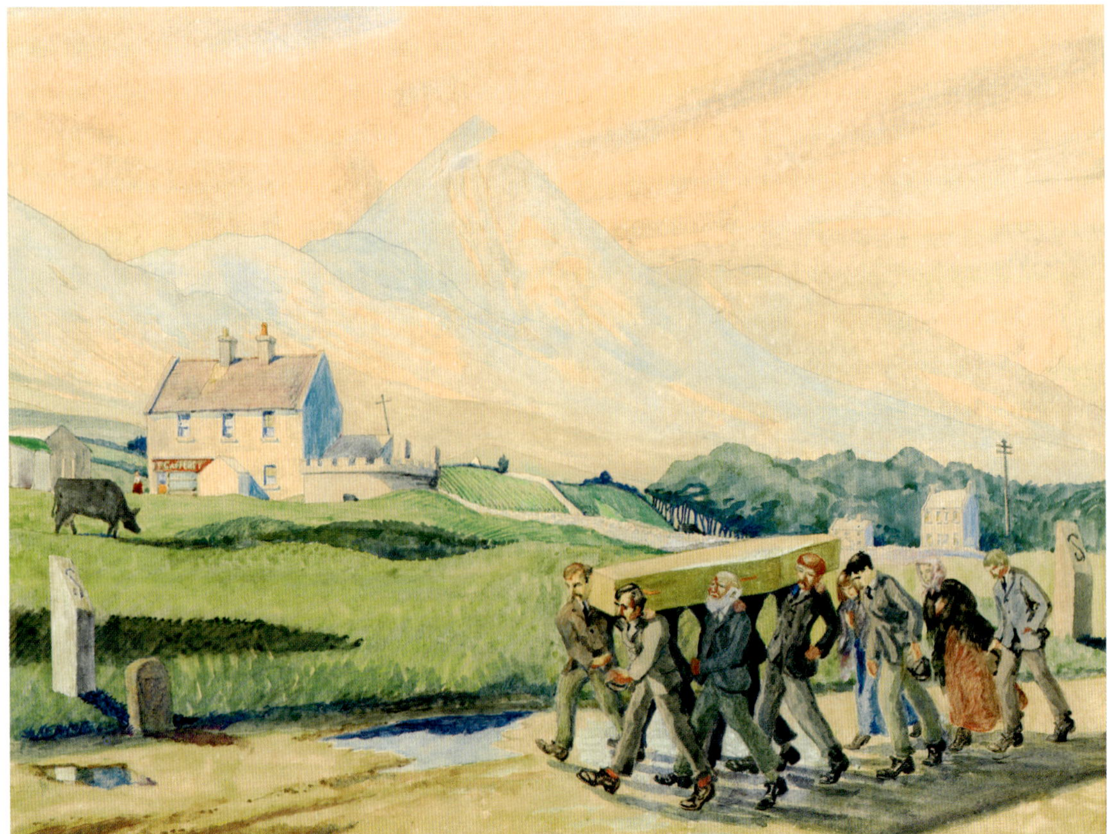

of Kernoff's painting a funeral party makes its way along an uneven road. The coffin, borne on the shoulders of six men, is accompanied by just a small gathering of people, suggesting the remote and relatively sparsely populated area in which the funeral takes place. The prominence of a pub or shop in the middle ground - one can make out the name of the proprietor on a sign above the door - is appropriate to both the social and commercial importance of such premises in rural areas. Shops of this kind, found throughout Ireland, were known to host numerous businesses including drapers, general stores, grocers, butchers, and even, in more isolated areas, undertaking.[57] Under the Coroners Act of 1846, a coroner could direct that a dead body be brought to the nearest 'tavern, public house or house licensed for the sale of spirits' and require the owner or occupier of such a place to allow the body to be kept there until an inquest had taken place.[58] Before the age of the motorised ambulance and hearse, this provision made good sense as publicans usually had cool store rooms in which bodies could be kept from decomposing.

Kernoff counters the looming presence of the mountain and tempers the maudlin subject through the use of bright colour and the slightly caricatured portrayal of the figures in the foreground. He attended the Metropolitan School of Art during a period that promoted an academic tradition to which figurative drawing was central, and was, an accomplished draughtsman.[59] His naïve and often awkward depiction of the figure, therefore, was a deliberate subversion of this academic tradition. It has been observed that Kernoff's compassionate and personal approach 'reflected his own gentle consideration for his subject'.[60] His work was admired and when he began to exhibit at the RHA his paintings of Mayo, the settings for which were vastly different from those of his Dublin scenes, it would appear they were received equally well, one critic making the astute observation that:

> *Harry Kernoff has gone west and brought with him the vivid eye and quaint technique that enabled him to record the subtle moods of the Dublin scene. In his paintings of the Mayo mountains he has given a new twist to the Irish Landscape.*[61]

The painting, executed in watercolour, reminds one of Kernoff's graphic wood-cuts, which were executed in a clear, linear style and were often theatrical in nature. This graphic style accommodated the attention to detail that Kernoff displayed but was neglected by many of his contemporaries in favour of painterly effects and atmosphere. Details such as the name above a shop, merchandise on sale, individual bottles on the shelf of a bar, or the fruit and vegetables of a roadside grocer characterised his work in various media. Essential but banal, such details were always of interest to Kernoff and afforded his work a notably local quality.

This interest in the minutiae of his subjects may be attributable to Kernoff's work in theatre set design, a practice that also seems to have informed the narrative and dramatic quality of his work. In *A Funeral in Mayo*, the figures appear to stumble in from 'right of stage' and the landscape in the background, thinly painted, serves as a scenic backdrop. The grazing cow, meanwhile, presented in profile and painted in flat colour, seems more like a stage prop than a living animal. Kernoff was a member of a dynamic social group that included artistic, literary and theatrical figures. He drew and painted many of them and designed sets and costumes for theatrical productions, including some at the Gate Theatre, where he worked alongside Martin Murphy, a figure who appears in his *In Davy's Parlour Snug* (cat. 72).[62] DM

---

56 Kernoff exhibited a number of his paintings of Castlebar and Westport at the RHA between, 1945 and 1955.

57 Kearns 1996, p.53.

58 This legal provision was not removed until 1962.

59 He studied under Harry Clarke, Patrick Tuohy and Sean Keating.

60 McAuley 2003, p.11.

61 *Irish Independent*, 25 April 1949.

62 MacGonigal 1976, p.4.

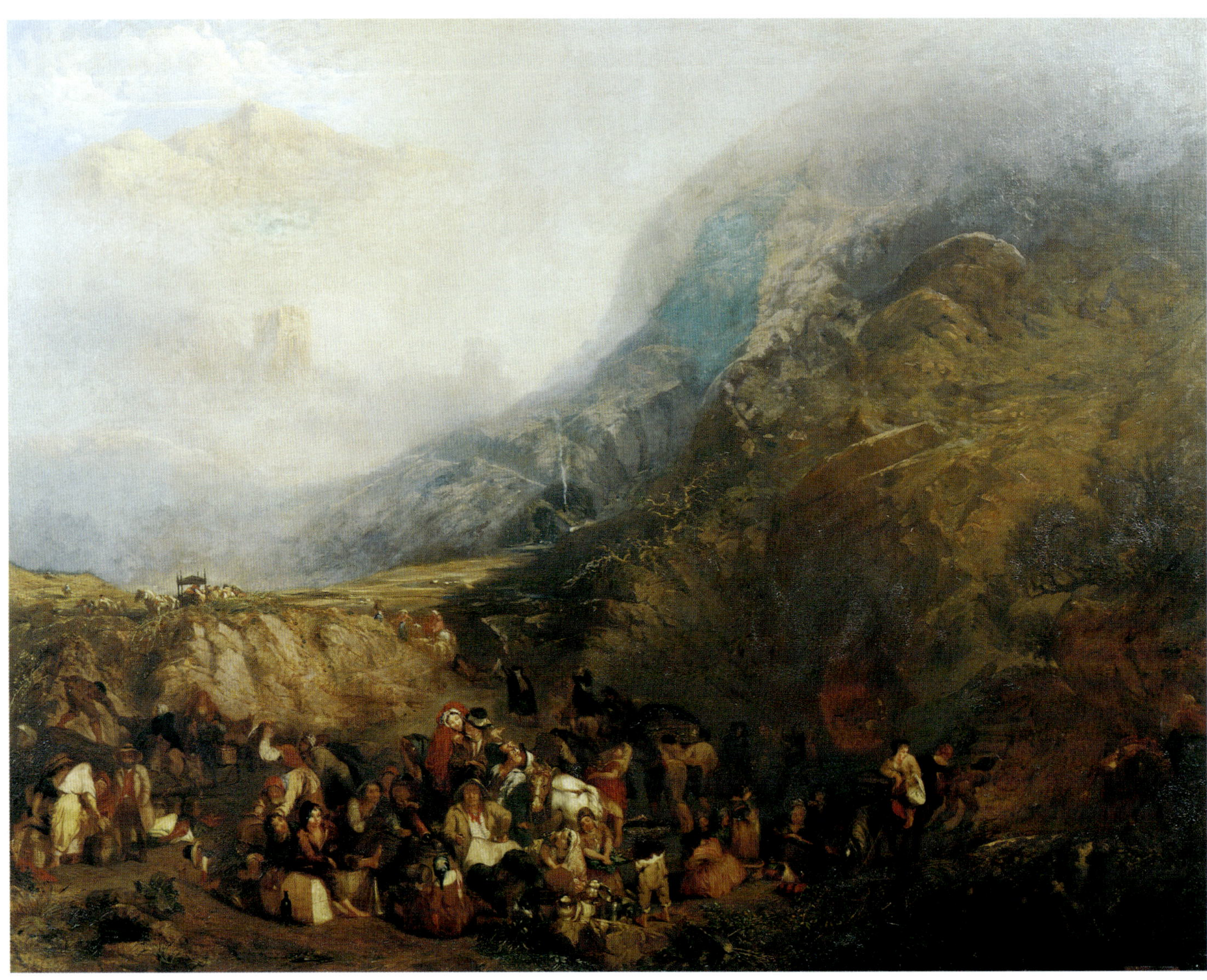

William Willes (c.1780-1851)
39. The Mock Funeral
1851
Oil on canvas
102 x 127 cm
Private collection

39. The Mock Funeral

William Willes

Mock Funerals, also known as American Wakes, were held to mourn the emigration of friends and relatives on the assumption that it was highly unlikely that they would ever return; for many families this was a final goodbye. The custom, which seems to have originated in Ulster, was initially practised in both the Catholic and Protestant communities, but from the 1830s, when the necessity for emigration fell hardest on the peasantry of the west, it became specifically associated with Irish-speaking areas. Those leaving would invite their friends and family to a wake on the night before their departure and, as with wakes commemorating the dead, stories were told, keening was heard and poitín consumed. Willes was working on his picture in 1849, the last year of the Great Famine, and it is an unusually direct response to issues of land, dispossession and emigration.

Towards the centre of the composition figures symbolically carry an empty coffin, while a horse-drawn hearse progresses out of the picture to the left. This illustrates the ritual known as the convoy. Those emigrating were accompanied part of the way by those they were leaving behind. The distance that those emigrating overseas must travel (incomprehensible to those who had rarely been far from their native fields) is suggested by the figure peering through a telescope. It has been suggested that the French flag at lower left conveys a political message. The February Revolution of 1848 had seen the establishment of the Second Republic; the Young Irelanders had attempted an abortive uprising and it was to France that James Stephens had fled in that year.[63] Few Irish artists of the nineteenth century addressed so directly the issue of emigration in their work. The more usual artistic approach may be illustrated by the poignant sentimentality of Edwin Hayes's *An Emigrant Ship, Dublin Bay, Sunset* of a few years later (NGI). The fact that the artist's brother, Sir James Shaw Willes, was Justice of the Common Pleas in England makes the social comment implicit in the picture even more surprising.

William Willes was a Cork artist who initially studied medicine before taking lessons from Nathaniel Grogan, whose influence is apparent here. However, Willes gives a very specific twist to the tradition of Grogan, updating his master's famous picture *The Wake* (private collection) to give it contemporary relevance. Works such as *Goalers – Playing Hurley* (National Library) and *Round Tower, Scattery Island*, which he exhibited at the Royal Academy in 1848, demonstrate a consistent interest in Irish customs and antiquities. Willes has risen to the challenge of his subject, painting a more ambitious and compositionally complex work than usual. Completed shortly before his death, it was exhibited posthumously in Cork in 1852 and, according to Strickland, '"The Mock Funeral" was accounted his best picture.'[64]

Willes's recorded exhibits include Irish landscapes along with more ambitious history pictures such as *The Scene from the Palace of Aegisthus*, from the *Electra of Sophocles*, his first Royal Academy work. In *The Mock Funeral* he takes inspiration from a tragedy closer to home and more recent in date. However, while the brooding mountain setting adds a sense of foreboding to the scene, the atmosphere among the figures is resigned rather than despondent. Certainly it lacks the melodramatic intensity of grief communicated in Frederic William Burton's *The Aran Fisherman's Drowned Child* (NGI). Instead, the foreground shares many of the characteristics of fair or market scenes by artists from Francis Wheatley to Erskine Nicol. Along a diagonal in the central group of figures, a courting couple, a man knocking back a drink and two children intent on their chores, suggest that life carries on even in circumstances of parting and loss. Celebration as well as grief, and merry-making as much as mourning were always part of the ritual of wakes for both the dead and the living.

It might be noted that Willes does not portray the worst effects of the Famine. His figures are generally plump and, despite the odd barefoot child, well-clothed. However, it was a sad fact that it was often the relatively better off, those who could afford the fare to America, who were able to flee the Famine. Willes may also be deliberately editing and softening the scene for public consumption; the picture was intended for exhibition – and sale. The viewing public were attuned, in exhibition pieces at least, to only a palatable version of rural poverty rather the extremes of its actuality. True conditions perhaps intrude in the fact that the wake is being held in the outdoors rather than, as was almost universally the case, in the home of one of those about to depart. This suggests that here homelessness through eviction may have been one of the motivating facts in the decision to emigrate.

One jarring note to the picture is more difficult to explain. The landscape is typically, if slightly exaggeratedly, Irish; the scene could well be set in the Kerry mountains. Smoke rises from the chimney of a cottage in the valley beyond. Puzzlingly though, in the mist behind looms what seems to be an enormous gothic cathedral, quite unlike anything in Ireland. This 'ethereal element' recalls the work of German artists such as Friedrich's *Cross in the Mountains* (Staatliche Kunstsammlungen Dresden) and, as has been recently suggested, may represent 'the heavenly Jerusalem or perhaps the New World that awaits the emigrants'.[65] This otherworldly apparition, a universal sign in the midst of the specific and humdrum, invites us to feel that we witness a wake not merely for an individual – as in the work of Grogan or Burton – but for a people.

Willes seems to have been unique among nineteenth-century artists in depicting a mock funeral in oils. Certainly it was a challenging subject for a picture intended for exhibition. The tradition, however, continued in literature, being playfully alluded to by Joyce in *Finnegan's Wake* (1939), while a Kerry source, quoted by Dolan, shows both the continuity of folk memory and the absolute alteration in economic circumstances: 'times have changed from when there would be an American wake: people are flying over for the weekend now'.[66] WL

---

63 See Christie's *Irish Sale*, 20 May 1999, p.126.

64 Strickland 1913, vol. 2, pp.531-32.

65 Rooney 2004b, p.39

66 Dolan 1999, p.283.

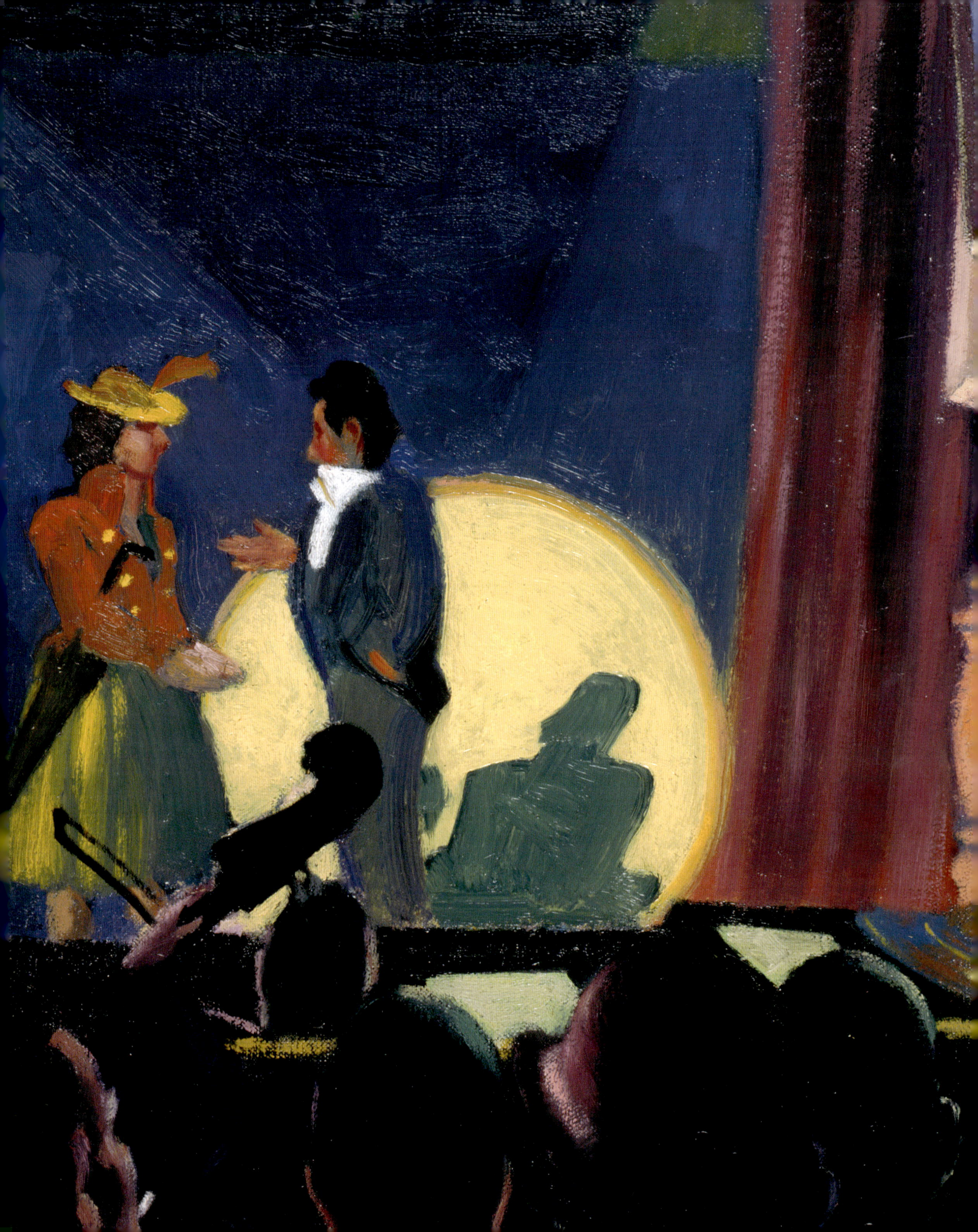

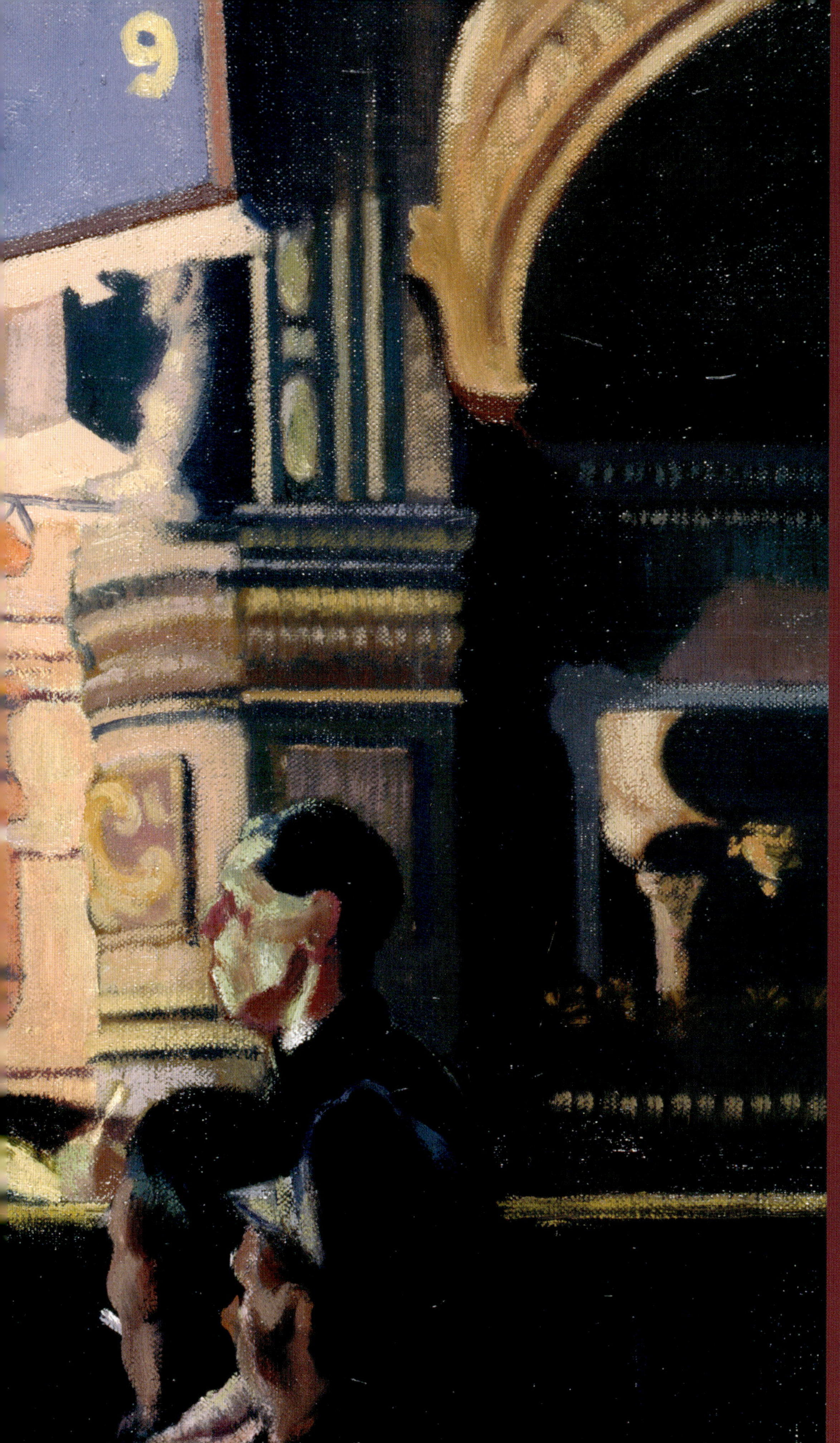

Light Entertainment

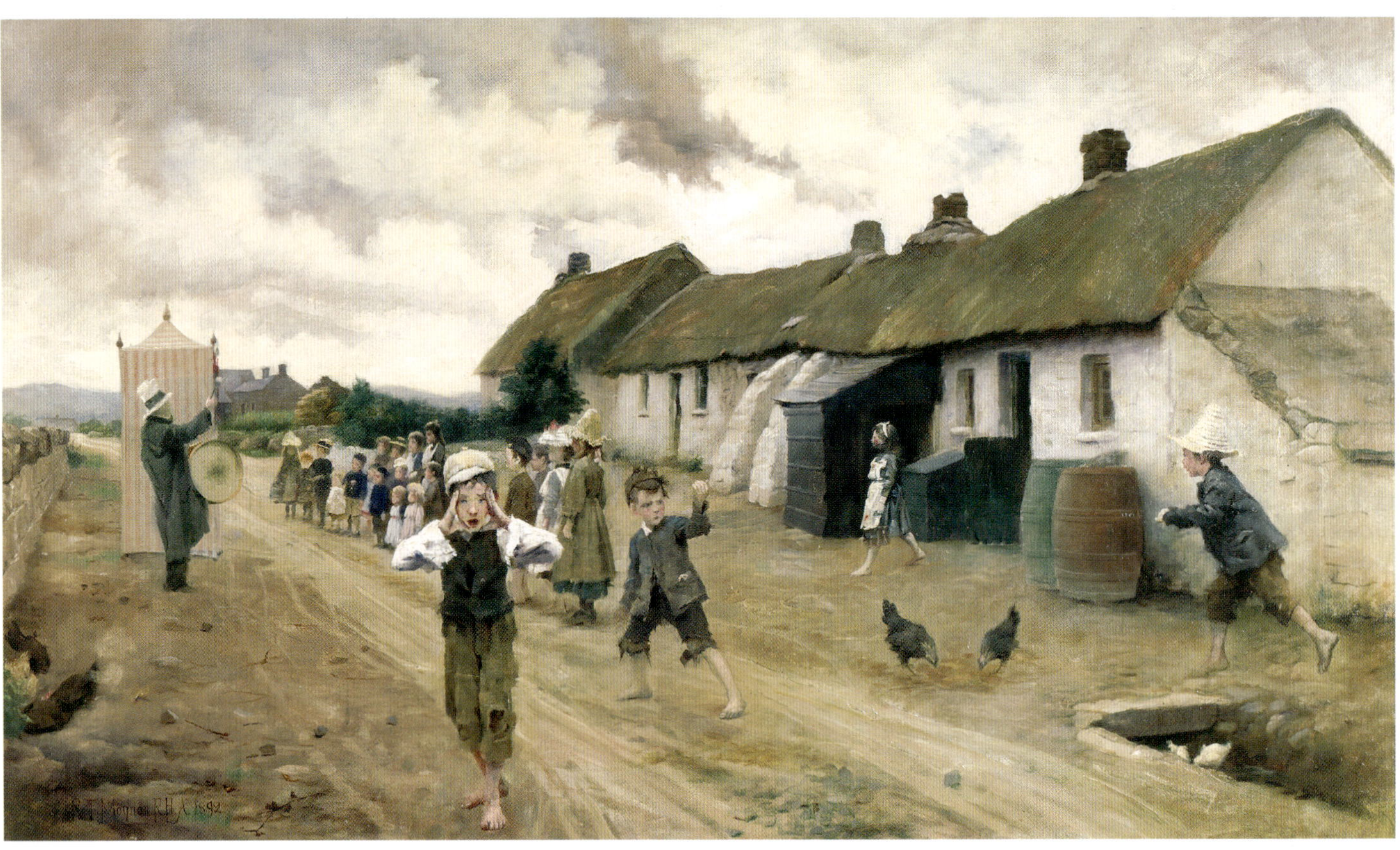

Richard Thomas Moynan
(1856-1906)
40. A Travelling Show
1892
Oil on canvas
61 x 101.5 cm
Private collection courtesy of Karen Reihill Fine Art

40. A Travelling Show

Richard Thomas Moynan

Richard Thomas Moynan was particularly adept at painting children, portraying them not only as animated, mischievous or contemplative but also, in keeping with an increasing awareness across Europe of the plight of indigent children, as sometimes disconsolate and anguished. His portraits of flower sellers, news boys and match girls are both topical and poignant, and echo the work of his compatriot Walter Osborne, Continental predecessors such as Bastien-Lepage[1] and Marie Bashkirtseff, and documentary photographs like those of Thomas Barnardo. His talents in this area were acknowledged by the contemporary press in Ireland, though often the pictures' perceived sentimentality rather than their poignancy was stressed. However, while the *Irish Times* suggested in 1896 that Moynan was 'rapidly becoming the waif's artist',[2] the rather more prescient *Freeman's Journal* declared him three years later 'a devoted and almost incomparably able interpreter of child life in art'.[3]

For *A Travelling Show*, Moynan combined this ability with the more general and audacious skill in depicting the figure he had demonstrated while a student at the Académie Royale des Beaux Arts in Antwerp. There he became the first Irish artist to be awarded first place in painting from the living model at the annual *concours*.[4]

A Travelling Show is particularly interesting as a record of recreation in that, like William Conor's *Queue for the Picture House* (cat. 42), it is much less a study of the performance than a record of the excitement and energy that attended it. Cleverly, Moynan has placed the puppeteer's booth at right angles to the viewer so that the anticipation of the show is communicated through the activity of the children who assemble in front of it or rush and summon their friends to it. The bottler announcing with a drum the imminent start of the show and the young boy in the foreground, calling out emphatically to stragglers, increase the narrative tension of the scene.

Punch and Judy shows enjoyed considerable popularity, particularly in parks and on beaches in the nineteenth and early twentieth centuries in Britain and Ireland. The origin of the principal characters, first known in Britain as 'Punch' and 'Joan', is uncertain, though the genre certainly developed from Commedia dell'Arte, a form of improvised popular comedy in Italy from the sixteenth to the eighteenth century, and Punch specifically from the character of Pulcinella.[5] An Irishman featured among the *dramatis personae* of Punch and Judy shows at one time, but played a negligible part in the narrative.

Puppet shows had been popular in Britain long before the advent of the Punch and Judy show and are mentioned frequently in Tudor and Stuart literature. Various writers, from the diarist Samuel Pepys to Charles Dickens mention open-air puppetry.[6] Public concerns about the violence and lack of respectability of such shows persisted through its history. In *Tom Jones*, Henry Fielding introduces a reformed puppet showman who claims that in contrast to audiences of 'such idle trumpery' as Punch and Judy shows, people 'rise as much improved from my little drama as they do from the great'.[7]

Jonathan Swift's lengthy description of a Punch performance in *A Dialogue between Mad Mullinix and Timothy* is thought to refer to the Dublin puppeteer Stritch. In 1730, the Irish Master of the Revels threatened to impose an exorbitant levy on Stritch's show, but was dissuaded from doing so following public demonstration through the streets of Dublin in support of the puppeteer.[8] Swift captures some of the anticipation evident in Moynan's painting of over a century and a half later:

Observe, the audience is in pain,
While Punch is hid behind the scene
But when they hear his rusty voice,
With what impatience they rejoice!

Traditionally, the Punch and Judy show 'with its wife-murder, its hanging and its devil' appealed to rather macabre sensibilities that found even darker expression among the large crowds that habitually attended public executions in the eighteenth and nineteenth centuries in England and Ireland.[9] Despite the fact that the Punch and Judy audience was principally made up of children by the end of the nineteenth century, the stories themselves were 'nowhere as innocuous as nursery literature implies'.[10] Indeed, the burlesque anarchy of the show appealed to a younger audience.[11] The speed and physicality that were inherent in hand puppetry were also attractive to children, certainly when compared with the refinement and gentility associated with more adult-oriented marionettes and the like. Though the quality of this 'alfresco vagabond entertainment' was variable,[12] the lawlessness and chaos that was so much part of the Punch and Judy conceit represented a stark, and at times subversive counterpoint to the strict religions that exercised, both directly and indirectly, control over the peasant and working classes.

By placing the brightly striped booth of the bottler rather starkly by the roadside, opposite a row of modest cottages, Moynan communicates the impromptu nature of this form of entertainment. While Punchmen could not guarantee sizeable audiences, they were versatile and mobile, and theirs could prove a lucrative business at fairs, races and markets. However, Moynan's performers look rather incongruous in this relatively barren, rural and impoverished environment. It certainly seems far removed from the crowded beaches and fairs with which Punch and Judy shows are more readily associated.

The figure by the puppeteer's box playing the drum, called the bottler or 'drum-and-pipes man', was a standard feature of the show. Indeed, the bottler's presence can be traced through numerous pictorial sources. His or her role was to attract the attention of surrounding crowds (as is the case in Moynan's painting), to provide dramatic musical accompaniment to the performance itself and on occasion to introduce to the audience new characters as they appear. The bottler often played instruments as well as the drum, very often pan pipes, but also trumpet or horn.

Punch and Judy shows, were a regular attraction at carnivals and fairs. Indeed, one writer in *Fraser's Magazine*, discussing the popularity of the Punch and Judy show at fairs, referred to Judy 'chattering and fighting in the booths of mountebanks at Donnybrook or St Bartholomew's fair'.[13]

Moynan was not alone among easel painters of the second half of the nineteenth century in choosing Punch and Judy as a specific theme or incorporating the subject into a larger composition. Others included Arthur Boyd Houghton, Thomas Smythe and William Powell Frith, whose painting *Ramsgate Sands, 'Life at the Seaside'* (Royal Collection) of 1852-54 features a Punch and Judy booth. The subject was very unusual, however, in Irish painting. William Conor, a doyen of child subjects, exhibited a watercolour entitled *Funny Mister Punch* at the RHA in 1956. It seems possible that Moynan sourced his child models from the Masonic Orphan Schools with which he was closely associated through membership of the Dublin Lodge of St Cecilia.[14] The school's headmaster was a fellow mason, and Moynan produced drawings of school activities for the Masonic magazine.[15] BR

---

1 See, for example, Bastien-Lepage's *A London Boot Black* (1882).

2 *Irish Times*, 2 March 1896.

3 *Freeman's Journal*, 6 March 1899.
4 O'Regan 2004b, pp.60-61.
5 Punch's wife did not become known as Judy until the early nineteenth century.
6 Pepys recorded that stopping to watch a puppeteer perform made him late for an appointment with the king, while Dickens referred to a puppeteer in *The Old Curiosity Shop*.
7 Fielding 1985, p.567.
8 Leach 1985, pp.23-24.
9 *ibid*, pp.30-32.
10 *ibid*, p.100.
11 Even Punch's distinct, rasping voice, traditionally made with the use of swazzle, appealed to a young audience.
12 Leach 1985, p.15.
13 *Fraser's Magazine*, vol. III, no. xv, April 1831, pp.351, 354. Quoted in Leach 1985, p.64. Bartholomew Fair was a carnival held for centuries on St Bartholomew's day (24 August) in West Smithfield in London
14 Moynan was honoured with a special dinner by his fellow lodge members for his charitable involvement with the schools.
15 O'Regan 2004a, p.24. President of the Royal Hibernian Academy, Thomas Alfred Jones, was also a fellow member of the Masonic lodge.

41. The Olympia, Dublin

Maurice MacGonigal

Under the influence of impresarios like Dan Lowrey, Arthur Lloyd and the Gunn brothers, Dublin theatre in the nineteenth century followed a London model, promoting music-hall and variety productions. In 1879, Lowrey opened the vast Star of Erin Theatre of Varieties on Dame Street, which later became known as the Empire Palace Theatre and subsequently as the Olympia.[16] Like the Gaiety, which had opened in November 1871, the Olympia took its place among a number of prestigious theatres built in Ireland in the second half of the nineteenth century, including the Athenaeum (later the Opera House) in Cork, opened in 1866, and the magnificent Grand Opera House in Belfast, constructed in 1895.

Dan Lowrey also managed the Grafton Theatre in Dublin and the Alhambra Theatre of Varieties in Belfast. While the Grafton (later known as the Bijou and then the Savoy) closed in 1884, and the Alhambra was forced to close after a fire in 1959, the Olympia remains one of Dublin's most popular theatres. As well as staging live entertainment of

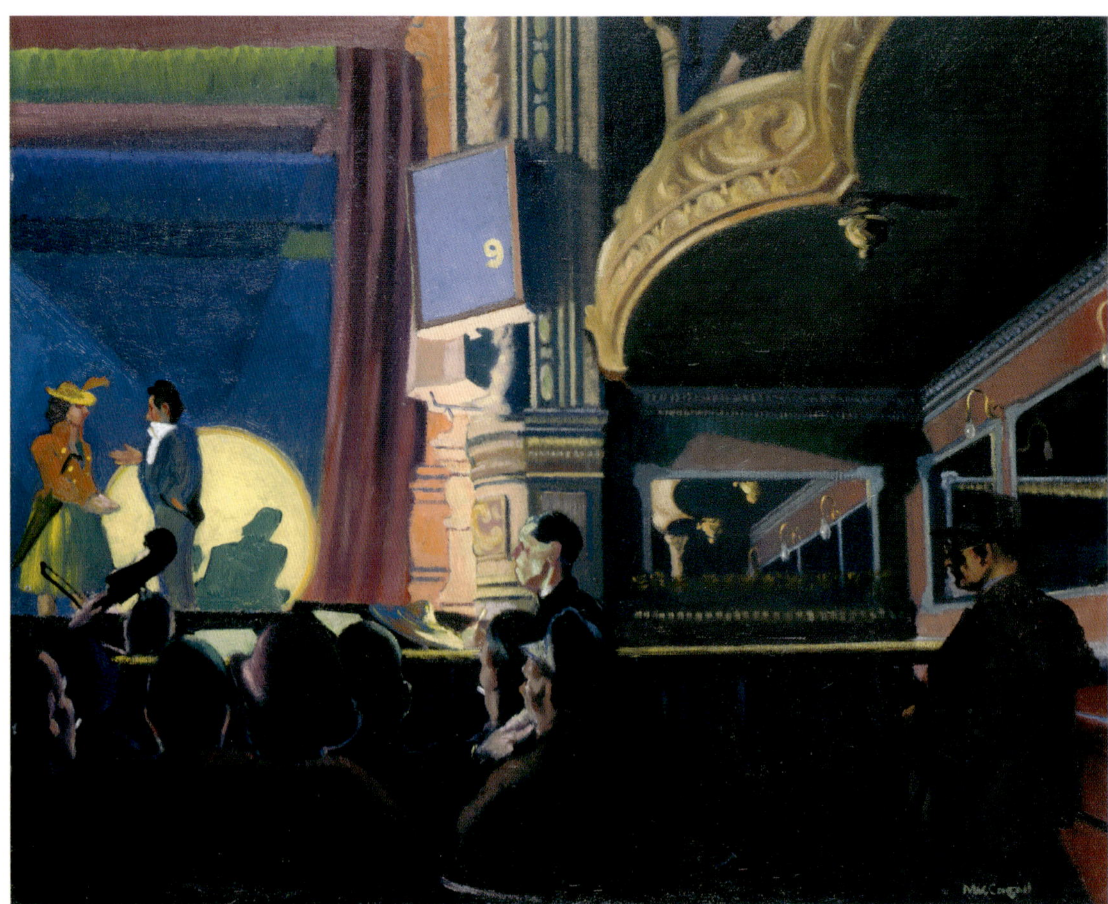

Maurice MacGonigal (1900-79)
41. *The Olympia, Dublin*
c.1935/6
Oil on canvas
63.6 x 76.5 cm
Collection Ulster Museum, Belfast

various genres, the Olympia was also the venue for the first public cinema screening in Ireland on the 20 April 1896, just four months after the world's first screenings in Paris and two months after their equivalent in London.[17] By the 1920s, so close was the connection between theatre and cinema that film stars including Charlie Chaplin and Tom Mix made guest appearances at the Gaiety.

This scene from the auditorium of the Olympia is a *tour-de-force* of linear composition for MacGonigal, an artist associated more immediately with freer outdoor character studies and landscapes in the west of Ireland. The painting has a distinctly abstract quality that contrasts with its ostensibly orthodox theme. The pattern of strong vertical, horizontal and diagonal lines conspire with MacGonigal's more familiar, liberal use of vibrant colour and dramatic tonal contrasts to create a picture that is, as John Losito and James Steward have said, 'inherently theatrical'.[18] As Gerard Dillon did in *Yellow Bungalow* (cat. 15), albeit to different effect, MacGonigal manipulates and distorts the interior space to enhance his composition. False space, represented by the reflections in the mirrors to the right, conjoins with distorted space (the distended boxes overlooking the stage), and real space to present an image that is at once familiar and disorientating. Nor were these incidental or impulsive modifications, as MacGonigal developed the painting from a large number of pencil sketches he executed on the spot over a protracted period. Moreover, the fragmentation of the picture plane that this style of composition involved was not dissimilar to the methods with which MacGonigal would have been familiar from his early work in stained glass.

Standing in shadow on the right hand side of the painting and easily recognisable by his distinctive hat is Harry Kernoff, one of MacGonigal's close friends.[19] Retrospectively, Kernoff might be said to represent here not just himself, but all those artists who patronised the theatre, knew its protagonists (both on and backstage) and in some cases produced artwork for it. In the later part of his career, MacGonigal designed sets and posters for productions at the Abbey Theatre, Dublin while Kernoff also produced set and costume designs for the theatre. Kernoff often accompanied MacGonigal to the theatre, and it is interesting that MacGonigal should have acknowledged his artist friend so openly in this urban subject, as he preferred to isolate himself from such contemporaries and friends, who included Charles Lamb, on his frequent and productive visits to the west.[20] This painting coincides with a lengthy period of busy occupation for MacGonigal in Dublin, though he appears to have found time to make occasional trips to Connemara and Achill.

If, as has been suggested, this painting depicts a rehearsal rather than a performance proper, it implies an even closer association between the art and theatrical milieus in Dublin in the 1930s, as Kernoff's shadowy but prominent presence would attest to the fact that he enjoyed privileged access to the theatre, as too, by implication, did MacGonigal.

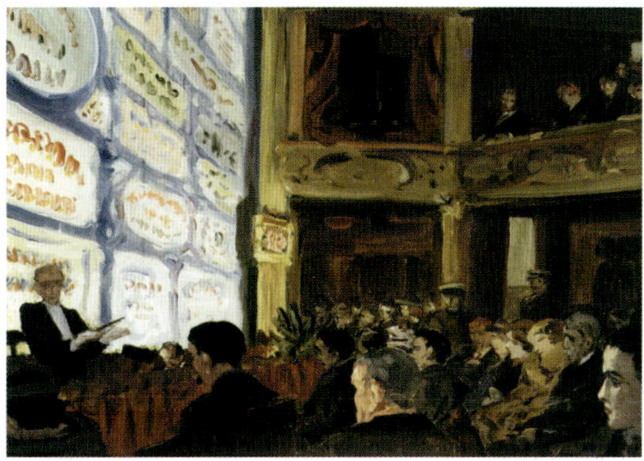

Fig. 29. **Jack B. Yeats,** *Patriotic Airs*, c.1923, oil on canvas, Brian P. Burns Collection.

Surprisingly perhaps, MacGonigal, an artist with well-documented nationalist affiliations in his youth,[21] and Jack B. Yeats, a keen observer of Irish political flux in the early decades of the twentieth century, painted notable images of the Olympia and Gaiety (fig. 29) theatres respectively, but neglected to paint equivalent pictures of the Abbey Theatre, which was much more closely identified with political and cultural radicalism. Indeed, the association of art with the Abbey tends to concern portraits of its patrons and pioneers, such as Jack B. Yeats's own brother W.B. Yeats, Lady Gregory and John Millington Synge, rather than records of the fabric of the building. Yeats did paint a watercolour of a performance at the Mechanics' Theatre,[22] which subsequently became the Abbey, but conceded to Lady Gregory in 1909 that he rarely sketched there.[23] BR

16 The music-hall was built on the site of what had been the Connell's Monster Saloon in 1855.

17 Rockett et al 1987, p.3.

18 Berkeley Art Museum 1998, p.188.

19 MacGonigal also places Kernoff prominently in his *Studio at the Dublin School of Art* of c.1935 (Limerick City Gallery of Art).

20 See Crofts 1997, p.140.

21 Having joined Na Fianna Éireann in 1917, MacGonigal was interned first in Kilmainham Jail and then Ballykinlar Camp, Co. Down.

22 See Fitz-Simon 2003, p.50.

23 Pyle 1992, p.xlv.

William Conor (1881-1968)
42. *Queue for the Picture House (Shankill Road, Belfast)*
1930-34
Oil on canvas
90 x 70 cm
Ulster Folk & Transport Museum

42. Queue for the Picture House (Shankill Road, Belfast)

William Conor

In 1927, after a trip to Philadelphia and short periods in London, during which he had befriended John Lavery and Augustus John, William Conor returned to his native Belfast. In the city, which had suffered during the Great Depression, penury and poor living conditions were very much a part of daily life. Unlike many of his contemporaries, however, Conor consistently found the modest lives of ordinary people more interesting than those of the better off, and Belfast's streets and its people became the principal subject of his work. Rather than focusing on the plight of the working-class, Conor demonstrated in his art an ability to derive harmony and joy from the most mundane themes. He dedicated his career to interpreting life in and on

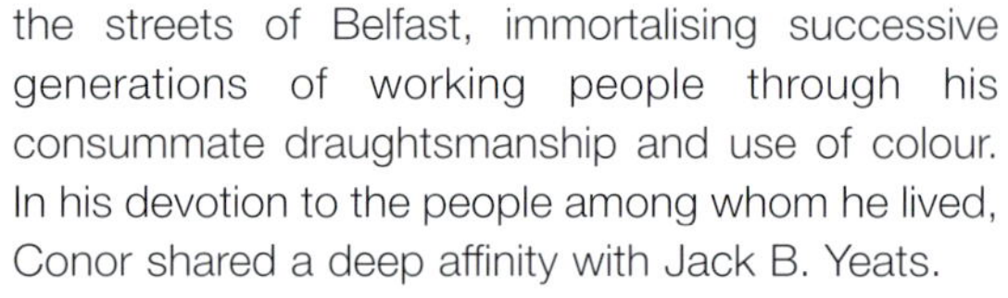

the streets of Belfast, immortalising successive generations of working people through his consummate draughtsmanship and use of colour. In his devotion to the people among whom he lived, Conor shared a deep affinity with Jack B. Yeats.

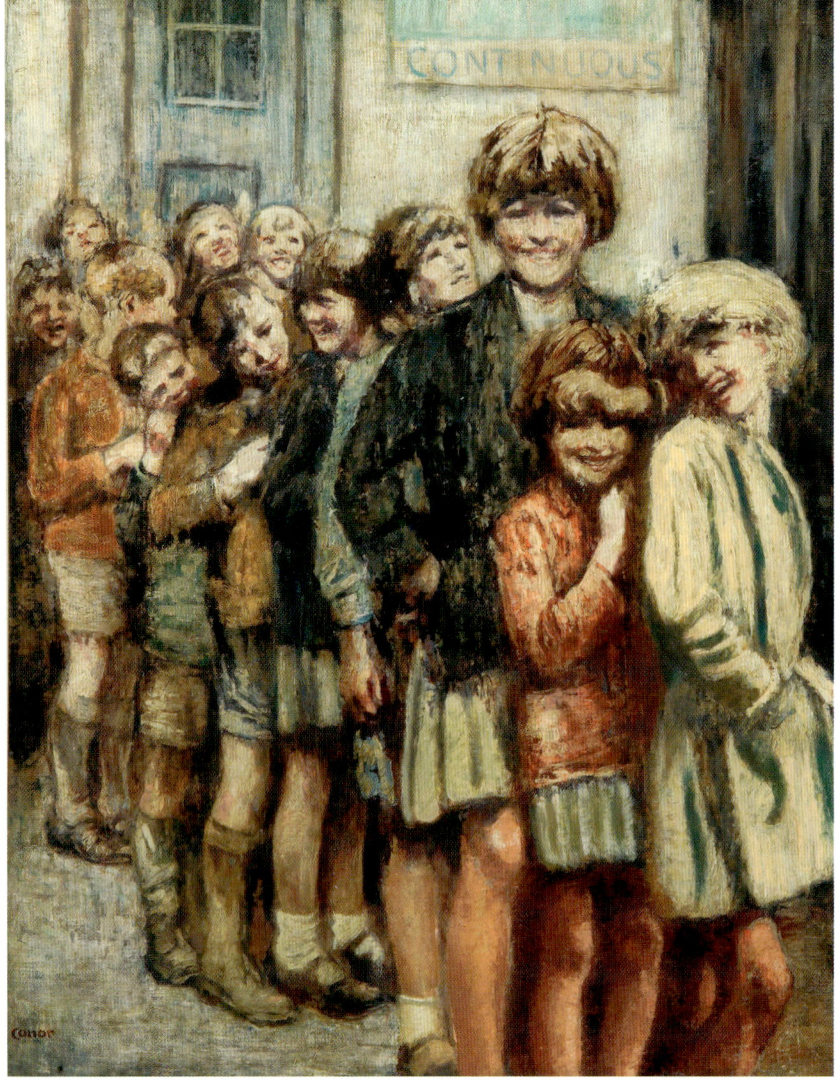

Following the first film screenings in Belfast at the Alhambra and Empire theatres in 1896, cinema enjoyed a rapid rise in popularity and in 1910 alone five cinemas opened in the city.[24] The boom in cinema-going in the 1930s, which followed the arrival of 'Talkies' in the 1920s, was reflected by the substantial increase in the number of auditoria constructed throughout Ireland. The particular popularity of cinema in Belfast was attributed largely to the zeal and foresight of Michael Curran, a cinema proprietor, and J. McBride Neill, a Belfast architect, who erected some of the finest cinemas in Ireland.[25] *Queue for the Picture House* can be read as a general record of the burgeoning popularity of cinema. Typically, however, Conor focuses on the most humble of its manifestations, a group of children queuing outside a cinema theatre on the Shankill Road.

Children appeared regularly in Conor's work and are often depicted embracing the simple activities that provided a welcome respite from the chores of the day. In *Queue for the Picture House*, the artist communicates with great skill the anticipation of a line of children, tumbling over each other while attempting to hold position in the line. They are most likely queuing for a weekday or Saturday matinée, the performance by which many children were introduced to the world of cinema and which typically consisted of a number of films. Although the type of films shown at a children's matinée varied over time, the arrangement usually remained the same. A show in the 1930s would typically include a cartoon and a comedy, starring a well-known figure such as Charlie Chaplin, followed by a feature film and the weekly serial.[26]

Conor's picture is most probably set outside the Shankill Picturedrome, owned by Joe McKibben, which opened its doors to the public on the 19 December 1910. Michael Open has noted that although it opened the same day as the larger Kelvin Cinema in Belfast city centre, the event attracted considerable attention from the press. The theatre became well-known and loved by local residents, who referred to it affectionately as the 'Wee Shankill' or 'Little Joe McKibben'.[27]

Conor has chosen to exclude from his painting the more glamorous characteristics of a theatre building, most notably the billboard and theatre entrance, though one can see the bottom of a poster. Instead, he focuses on a queue of ordinary children gathered outside and skillfully communicates through their expressions the magic of a trip to the cinema. One can sense their excitement as they await entry: some chatter and laugh among themselves, while others gaze upwards, perhaps at the name of the film they are waiting to see.

Similar records of children queuing outside the cinema feature in photography and newsreels of the time. It was common practice for cinema managers to commission films on local subjects, including crowds outside their cinema, which they would then show in the theatre itself, and such works may well have influenced Conor's picture.[28] Though Conor is known to have often sketched furtively, the three girls at the front of the queue in this picture are certainly aware they are being recorded. The tallest of the three looks directly at the viewer, while the two younger girls appear nervously excited by the attention they are receiving.

Though painted in oils, the painting displays a similar surface quality and handling to the oil pastels that were among Conor's favourite media. The palette is also typical of many of the artist's pictures and the strong, earthy colours and blues and greens, offset by dark shadows, evoke a strong sense of the built environment. In the naturalistic depiction of the children, and Conor's textural technique, the image is somewhat, and appropriately, reminiscent of old photographs in which finer details have blurred and deteriorated. There is a sense of nostalgia about the image, which in its simplicity has captured a particular moment in time. This is appropriate, perhaps, as the Shankill Picturedrome was one of the first of many Belfast cinemas to decline in the face of competition from grander and more comfortable theatres. It eventually closed in 1958.[29] DM

24 Morash 2002, p.156

25 Lalor 2003, p.199.

26 Open 1985, pp.91-92.

27 *ibid*, p. 150.

28 One of the earliest examples of this, *Children's Matinée* (1914) shows a crowd of children waiting outside the Vaudeville Cinema in Colchester, to see the children's matinée performance on Saturday, 3 October 1914.

29 Open 1985, p.77.

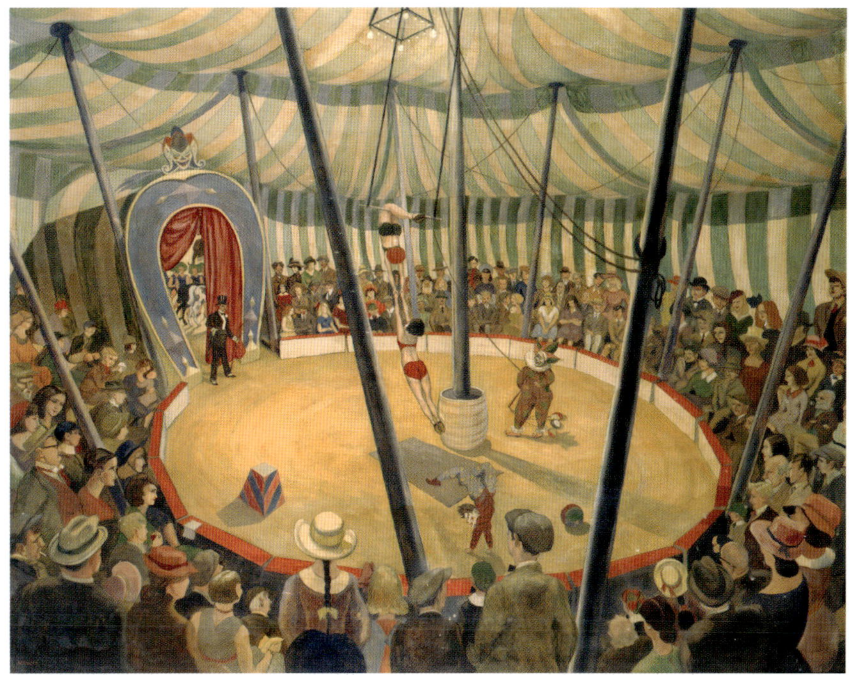

43. Country Circus

Harry Kernoff

Harry Kernoff (1900-74)
43. *Country Circus*
Exh. 1938
Oil on board
120 x 150 cm
Jonathan Clague
See Foldout opposite page 95

Kernoff delighted in depicting everyday life, and both his work and what is known of his sensibilities suggest that he was particularly attracted by the notion of collective activity. As Eamonn Carr has recently noted, while Kernoff's elaborate depiction of fishermen drawing their currachs on to a western shore is thematically redolent of the work of such fellow artists as Keating, Henry and MacGonigal, it is also consistent with Kernoff's positive response to the endeavours of the Association of Revolutionary Artists (AKhRR), to whom he spoke in Russia as a member of the delegation from the Friends of the Soviet Union in 1930.[30] His appreciation of the AKhRR's commitment to the elevation of the ordinary worker was explicitly manifest in his pictures *We Want Work* (National Library of Ireland) and the dramatic *A Labour Meeting* (private collection), in which a leader of the labour movement delivers a speech from a rostrum to an eager crowd, but is more subtly evident throughout his oeuvre.[31] Many of Kernoff's larger compositions are populated by disparate characters, who though engaged in a variety of activities seem somehow connected by common purpose, be it industrial, social, or recreational. Kernoff was also extremely gifted at capturing and enlivening the physical environment in which this human activity took place. From Winetavern Street to Portabello, from Galway to Killarney, and from the

Dublin Mountains to Dalkey, Kernoff's settings are emphatically 'living' places. Among the devices he employed to communicate this was to twist, exaggerate and distort space and the built environment so that they become animated elements of the composition, as various as the people who walk among them. In the context of this awareness of social connection and individual distinctiveness, Kernoff's enthusiasm for the theatre seems entirely fitting, and his fascination for the circus equally so. Here, the tall splayed polls of the big-top and the billowing canvas they support create an arresting, irregular pattern within which the performance takes place.

The circus was a particularly popular form of entertainment throughout Ireland in the late nineteenth and early twentieth centuries, when European circuses included Ireland in their itineraries.[32] The Irish circus profession was predominantly associated with families, such as those of John Duffy and Edward Fosset, who toured towns and villages in Ireland and concentrated on equestrian acts and performing clowns and jugglers.[33] Such themes attracted many Irish artists, including Yeats and Jellett, who were inspired by the colour and spectacle of performances under the big-top.

In *Country Circus*, one of Kernoff's largest works, the artist displays a keen interest in costume, apparently revelling in the description of both the audience's and the performers' dress. Indeed, such is the variety and colour of the clothing worn by the spectators that the trapeze artists, tumbler, clown and ringmaster, in their more elaborate and exotic dress, seem almost to get lost among the throng. On closer inspection, the clown's costume calls to mind Kernoff's own theatre costume designs, of which he produced a large number. Appropriately, Kernoff held an exhibition of his work, including a series of costume designs, at the Civic Theatre in the Town Hall, Dun Laoghaire in 1929. A collection of stage and costume designs, most dated either 1928 or 1929, were donated to the National Gallery of Ireland by the artist's sister in 1975.[34] With works like *Country Circus*, Kernoff developed what Ciarán MacGonigal has succinctly described as 'a visual dictionary of Irish types'.[35] Though many distinguished, famous, and in some cases now legendary figures feature among his portrait sitters, it was to the character of his subjects, rather than their celebrity, that Kernoff was principally drawn. BR

30 Eamon Carr, 'Currachs, Connemara', sales catalogue, Whyte's (26 April 2005), p.56.

31 *A Labour Meeting* was one of seven pictures by Kernoff illustrated in *Isskusto Massie* (Art of the Masses), the journal of the AKhRR.

32 Lalor 2003, p.200.

33 Duffy's Circus, established in 1775, was one of the first family circuses in Ireland and remains one of the largest, along with Fosset's, which was established in 1888.

34 See NGI 3167-3184.

35 MacGonigal 1976.

Sidney Smith (1912-82)
44. *From the Flies*
1943-44
Oil on canvas
45.7 x 71.1 cm
Collection Ulster Museum, Belfast

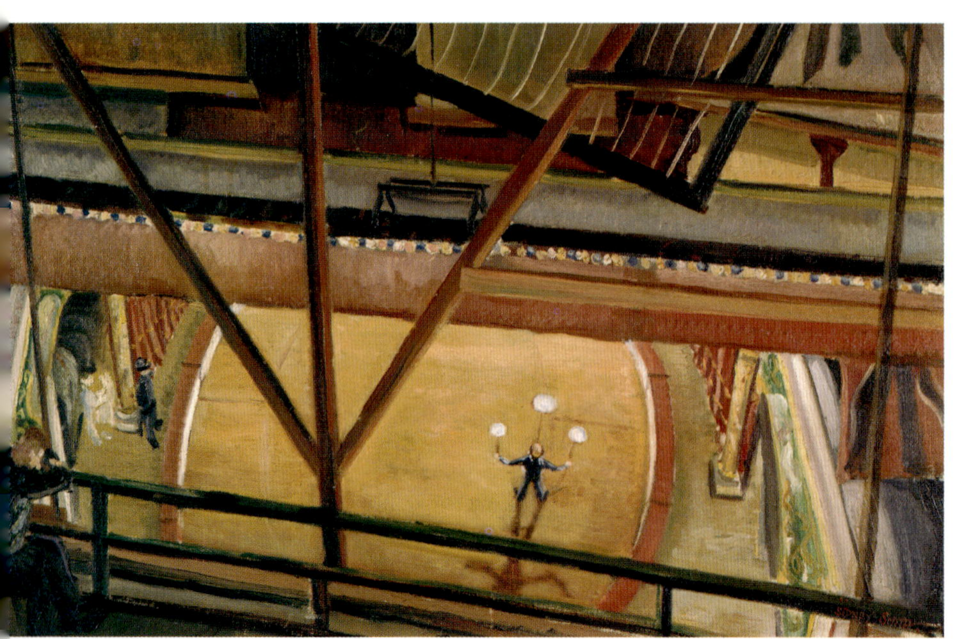

44. From the Flies

Sidney Smith

Described by the poet John Hewitt as one of the outstanding Northern Irish painters of the mid-twentieth century, [36] Sidney Smith is perhaps best known for the large murals he produced for restaurants, cafés and as part of private and public commissions during the fifties and sixties. However, before painting his first mural in 1944 (and moving subsequently to London in 1948), [37] Smith had made a name for himself as an emerging artist of note in his native Belfast.

Born in 1912 to parents of Jewish origin, Smith was raised in the Protestant, Shankill area of the Crumlin Road. In his early twenties he attended evening classes at the Belfast College of Art and also received private tuition from R. Boyd Morrison, a Belfast artist who stressed the importance of drawing.[38] In 1940, assisted by his parents, Smith moved into a studio on the top floor of 20 Howard Street, where he appears to have become more prolific, exhibiting at each RHA annual exhibition until 1944.[39] Also featuring in local Belfast galleries and at the Ulster Academy of Arts, his work of this period consisted predominantly of portraits and local landscapes.

Though the subject of *From the Flies* might appear at first glance to be an unusual choice for Smith, it does in fact reflect his keen interest in performing arts. An enthusiastic guitarist, he also enjoyed theatre and the circus, and when the Ballet Rambert visited Belfast in 1947, Marie Rambert, who found his work charming, allowed him to sketch her dancers backstage.[40] Using watercolour and pastel, Smith produced a body of work that demonstrated his strong draughtsmanship and displayed the influence of Degas. *From the Flies* is viewed from a position of privileged access, the dizzying heights of the theatre flies. In the picture, one peers through various structural elements towards the stage below, which is occupied by the lone figure of a plate spinner, who appears to balance one pole and plate tentatively on his chin, and two more on outstretched hands. The glare of the powerful stage lights cast his shadow on an otherwise empty surface.

Smith's fascination with the circus was shared by his fellow Belfast artist and close friend Tom Carr, with whom he regularly painted. Smith and Carr often shared models in the former's studio, including on occasion clowns and acrobats from Dr Richard 'Dick' Hunter's circus, and when Duffy's Circus came to Belfast the two artists worked together drawing the performers.[41] Not all circuses were travelling shows like that represented in Kernoff's *Country Circus* (cat. 43). Instead, some were attached to theatres, such as the circus at the Royal Hippodrome, Great Victoria Street, Belfast, which is likely to have provided the setting for Smith's picture. That circus, operated by G.L. Birch, Jack Delino and Dick Hunter, performed various acts on the stage of the theatre. Hunter was a charismatic figure, well known in Belfast not only as a circus ringmaster but also as a respected anatomist and embryologist.

While *From the Flies* may not evoke the sense of excitement and colour that one might automatically associate with the circus, and is communicated in Kernoff's *Country Circus*, it does provide an interesting view of a popular form of entertainment from an unusual perspective. By removing the viewer from the main area of the theatre, the circus and the performance become almost incidental elements of an unorthodox picture, which cleverly balances subject and composition. Smith has allocated a considerable amount of space to the area of the flies, and obscures the view of the stage. An elaborate framework and the thick curtain, which extends across the picture, divides the canvas into a pattern of vertical, horizontal and diagonal lines, which together with the flat circular shape of the stage, lend the work an distinctly abstract quality. DM

36 Chabanais and Goldberg 1994, p.235.
37 *ibid.*
38 Snoddy 2002, p.618.
39 Smith had exhibited there for the first time in 1938.
40 Chabanais and Goldberg 1994, p.239.
41 *ibid.*

Francis Robert West
(c.1749-1809)
45. *Miss Mathew, Lady Knapton and Miss Piggott playing Cards*
Crayon on paper
44.2 x 53 cm
Private collection

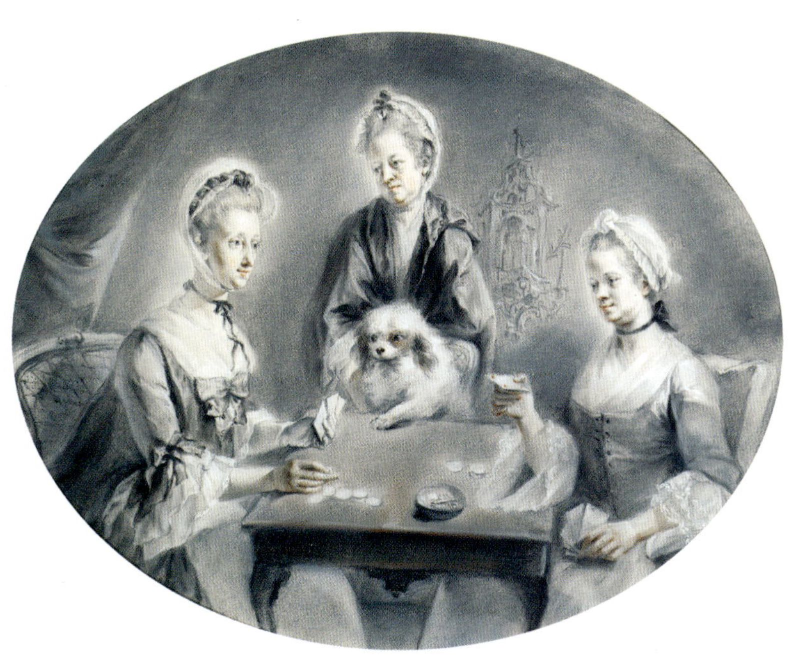

45. Miss Mathew, Lady Knapton and Miss Piggott playing Cards

Francis Robert West

46. Two boys playing a game of Goose

Francis Robert West

These are two of a series of nine oval sketches by West of fashionable families engaged in recreational and social activities ranging from sewing and picking flowers to taking tea.[42] Cards remained a recreational activity for both men and women among the gentry and aristocracy into the nineteenth century.[43] Gambling, though frowned

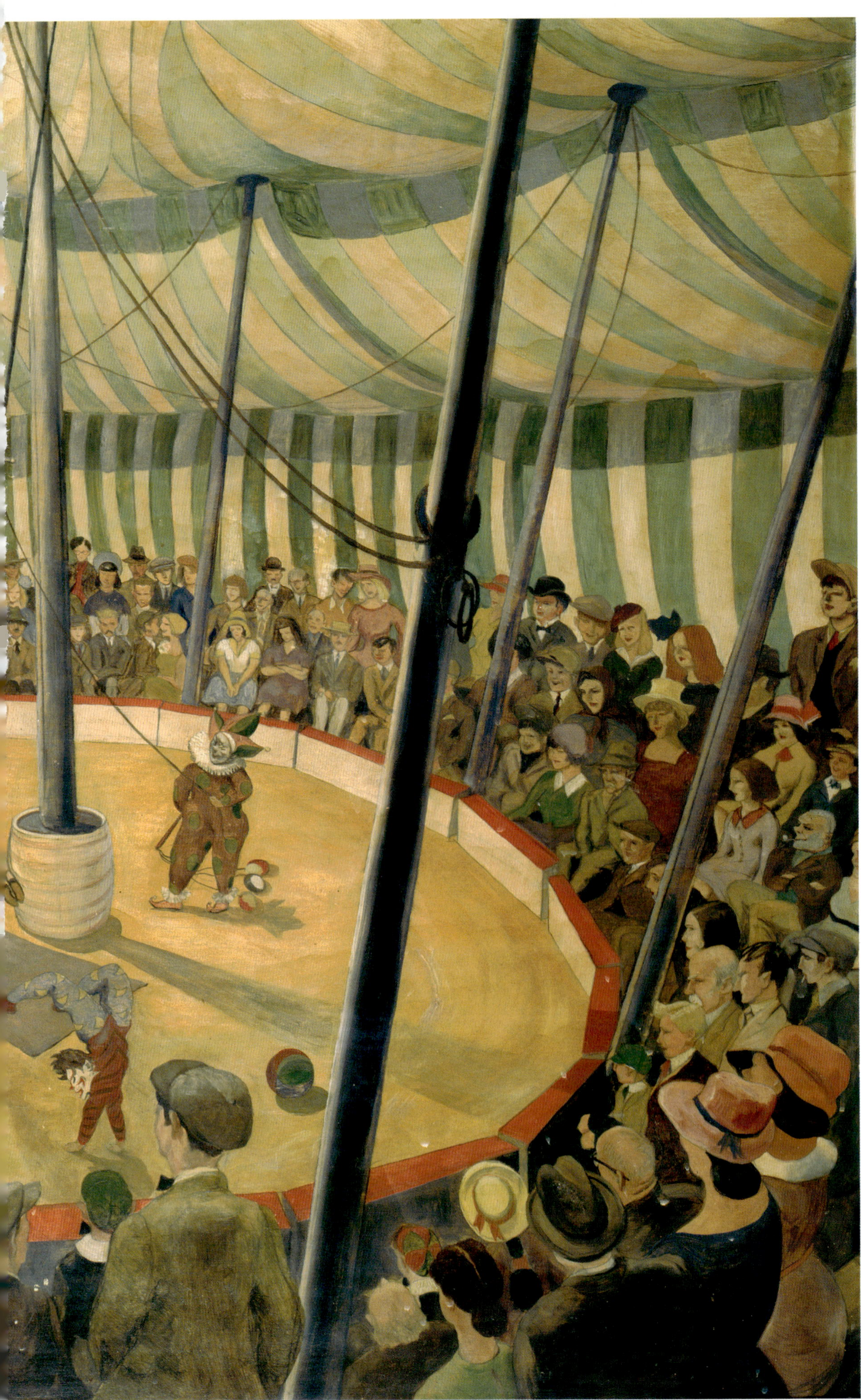

Harry Kernoff (1900-74)
43. *Country Circus*
Exh. 1938
Oil on board
120 x 150 cm
Jonathan Clague
See Page 94

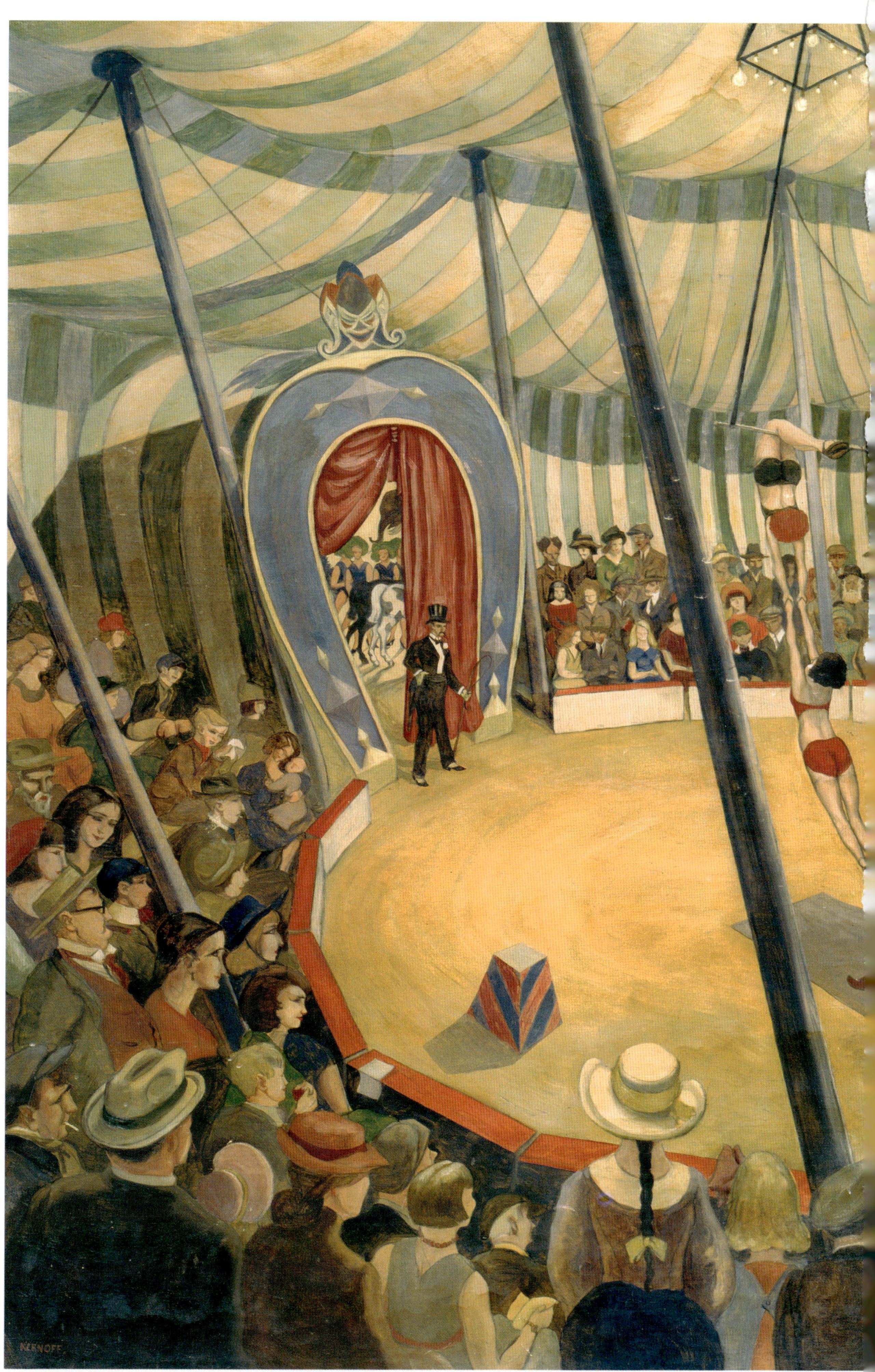

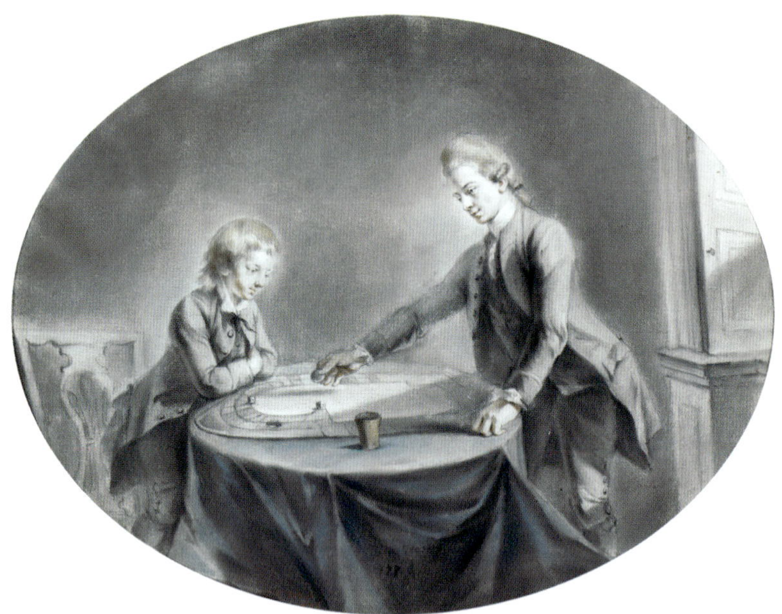

Francis Robert West
(c.1749-1809)
46. *Two Boys playing a Game of Goose*
Crayon on paper
44.2 x 53 cm
Private collection

upon by the conservative and prudish, was popular, although there was a considerable contrast in attitudes towards games in which large amounts were wagered and those involving nominal sums.[44] Many were aware or alarmed by the addictive nature of gambling and equated it with moral misdemeanours. Sir Edward O'Brien, for example, claimed that attending to his horses protected him from cards, dice and prostitutes.[45] Ultimately, however, even those who might have had religious and moral scruples about betting - the folly of staking on chance - do not seem in practice to have been inhibited from playing. Mrs Conolly even went to the lengths of running a casino at Castletown.[46] Wealthy families frequently invested in 'playing tables' specifically designed to accommodate the likes of chess, backgammon and dice.

Basset was among the now obsolete card games enjoyed in the eighteenth century. Mrs Delany remembers the duke and duchess of Dorset retiring to the 'basset table' for an hour after the dancing had finished at a grand ball at Dublin Castle.[47] A card game to which gambling was central, it enjoyed particular popularity among the upper classes, *The Compleat Gamester* declaring it 'the most courtly' and 'only fit for kings and queens, great princes, noblemen, &c'.[48] This particular game was also favoured by those of high rank largely because they were among the few to be able to facilitate the substantial gains and accommodate the commensurate losses that were an integral part of the game.

The finesse of West's drawings is appropriate to the gentility of the sitters, if not the subjects, and consistent with the artist's reputation. In 1777, West's proficiency and status saw him succeed his father Robert as Master of the Figure School at the Dublin Society Schools and in these studies and others, one sees the artist attempt to emulate such accomplished exponents of dry media as Hugh Douglas Hamilton, Robert Healy, and his own father. This tradition was continued by West's own son, Robert Lucius, whose subsequent lengthy tenure as Master of the Figure School from 1809 to 1845 meant that 'virtually every Irish artist for over a century' was educated by a member of the West family.[49]

The drawings possess a relaxed charm that suggests that their execution provided West with respite from formal portraiture. One is particularly struck by the fluffy lap dog in the drawing of the ladies playing cards, who with one paw on the table observes proceedings like a kind of canine croupier. The betting chips on the table, the rather grave expression on Lady Knapton's face and the furtive way in which Miss Piggott protects her hand from view, however, indicate that this ostensibly informal game had a competitive edge.

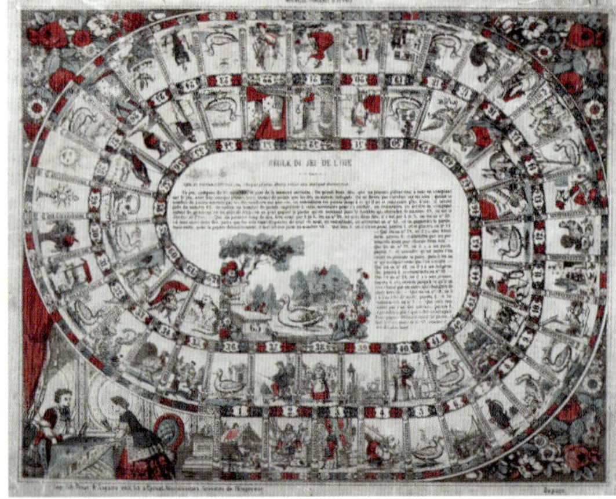

Fig.30. Goose board, Pinot & Sagaire, French, c1860.

Goose, the board game of Italian origin that features in the second drawing, was registered with the Stationer's Hall in London as early as 1597. It could be a curiously moralistic game, the aim of which was to reach heaven, the seat of happiness, at the centre of the board.[50] The path to this target was measured out in spaces, more than half of which were illustrated with virtues and vices. In a similar manner to the rather more secular Snakes and Ladders, landing on a virtue allowed a player to move forward, while landing on a vice forced him or her backwards, often all the way back to the start. As recorded in West's picture, children in particular were encouraged to play the game as it encouraged good sportsmanship and a competitive spirit but also impressed upon them the benefits of good and moral judgement. One particular set of unambiguous instructions for the game read as follows:

WHOEVER possesses PIETY, HONESTY, TEMPERANCE, GRATITUDE, PRUDENCE, TRUTH, CHASTITY, SINCERITY, is entitled to Advance six numbers toward the Mansion of Happiness. WHOEVER gets into a PASSION must be taken to the water and have a ducking to cool him. WHOEVER possesses AUDACITY, CRUELTY, IMMODESTY, or INGRATITUDE must return to his former situation till his turn comes to spin again, and not even think of HAPPINESS, much less partake of it.

The young boys, gentlemen in miniature, wear the fine, formal attire of their elders, but their expressions at least point to more childlike preoccupation. Contentedly absorbed in the game, they seem unaware that they are being observed.
BR

---

42 Other sitters in this series include Viscountess Northland and the hon. Lady Staples.

43 A sketch by Mrs Wingfield of a game of cards involving men and women at Adare Manor in 1844 is in the collection of the Irish Architectural Archive. See Packenham 2000, p.104

44 The author is grateful to Dr Toby Barnard for his assistance in cataloguing this work.

45 Barnard 2004, p.233. O'Brien also included hunting with hounds among these vices.

46 *ibid*, p.17.

47 Llanover 1861, vol. I, p.337.

48 *The Compleat Gamester* (1721), pp.23-24. Quoted in Barnard 2004, p.75.

49 See Crookshank and Glin 2002, pp.90-91.

50 There were many secular versions of the game.

47. Gambling for a Goose

Joseph Malachy Kavanagh

Joseph Malachy Kavanagh is a confounding and frustratingly uneven painter, albeit one capable of producing works of technical quality and originality. Among these are his sophisticated Continental etchings, images of Irish peasants at work (such as his well-known *Carting Seaweed on Sutton Sands* (NGI)), and his distinctive, crepuscular landscapes and winter scenes. At the same time, however, Kavanagh executed many staid religious portraits, uninspiring pastoral scenes, and melodramatic biblical subjects. A critic writing for *The Studio* in 1902 acknowledged that Kavanagh had 'at least the virtue of individuality', but predicated this somewhat by deeming the artist's painting style as 'little more than pleasant caprice'.[51]

The present work is all the more interesting when considered in the context of Kavanagh's unpredictability. He painted few interiors or genre scenes, and one wonders why he turned his hand in this instance to such a specific genre subject. It seems unlikely that it records a particular episode,

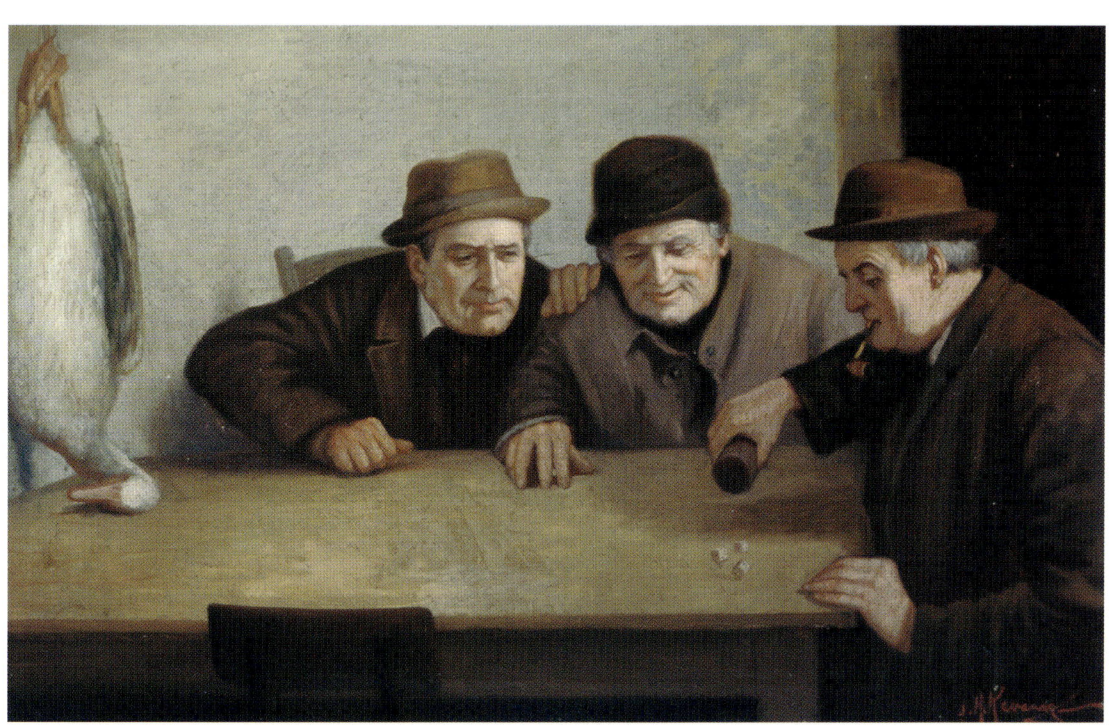

Joseph Malachy Kavanagh
(1858-1918)
47. *Gambling for a Goose*
Oil on canvas
51 x 76 cm
Private collection courtesy of Whyte's Auctioneers, Dublin

but may represent a familiar occurrence in Dublin life that he found inherently attractive pictorially. Kavanagh favoured outdoor subjects, particularly landscapes, later in his career. However, *Gambling for a Goose* shares its origins with his landscapes and street scenes. The muted palette, replete with browns and ochres, and even tonality of the picture, for example, also mark much of his landscape work, and stem from his study with Walter Osborne and Nathaniel Hill under Charles Verlat in the 'Natur' class at the Académie Royale des Beaux-Arts in Antwerp in the early 1880s. The scale of the figures is unusual for Kavanagh, however, differing greatly from better known works like *Cockle Pickers, Dublin Bay* (private collection) in which, as Ethna Waldron bluntly states, 'the figures are far enough away for us not to notice any weakness in drawing'.[52]

A corollary of this limited palette is that some of Kavanagh's paintings, particularly his figurative work, including *Gambling for a Goose*, appear rather flat. Kavanagh utilised a restricted colour range throughout his oeuvre with varying degrees of success (see for example, his *Old Dublin-Marrowbone Lane* (private collection), a picture of poor urban dwellers making their way along a snow-covered street). In this case, the planarity is offset by strong verticals and horizontals and by the necessarily compact nature of the setting. Like so many of the artists represented in this exhibition, Kavanagh has employed the theatrical conceit of placing his figures unevenly at just two sides of the table, so that they can all be seen clearly by the viewer. The table also seems to tilt outward slightly, like the rake of a stage.

The subject is specific and straightforward. Three elderly men throw dice for the prize of a goose, which hangs limply from the wall beside them. The setting, however, is rather ambiguous. While the fact that the men are wearing their outdoor hats and coats might suggest that the game takes place in a public house, no other detail in the interior corroborates this. Conversely, the men's tense but fond interaction suggests that they are friends and might conceivably be meeting in the home of one of their number to play the game, but again, Kavanagh has omitted any domestic detail to confirm this. Their sport and the tense anticipation that attends it are, in any case, of greater importance.

Following his return from the Continent, Kavanagh settled in Clontarf and focused on subjects from north County Dublin. Rather than scenes of everyday life, however, he was drawn increasingly to landscape, producing and exhibiting picturesque and dramatic views of places nearby such as Portmarnock, Portrane, Swords and Sutton. In 1910 he was appointed Keeper of the Royal Hibernian Academy, a position that afforded him residence in the Academy's premises on Abbey Street in Dublin. He was fortunate to escape the building when it was destroyed by shelling during the Easter Rising in 1916, but lost many of his paintings in the fire and never fully recovered from the experience. BR

51 *The Studio*, vol. XXV (1902), p.210.

52 Waldron 1968, p.326.

48. Recreation

Fr Jack P. Hanlon

Though studies for the priesthood might not always have been compatible with art training, Fr Jack P. Hanlon's art practice was not an incidental occupation, but rather the product of considerable training, erudition and innate talent. He studied in Belgium, Spain and, on the advice of Mainie Jellett, his tutor in Dublin, under André Lhote in Paris. Hanlon had a thorough knowledge of Old Masters and was equally *au fait* with Modernism. Far from a peripheral figure, he challenged in his own work artistic orthodoxy, particularly in his approach to religious subjects, and drew on his familiarity with both Cubism (which was attributable to Lhote) and Fauvism.[53] Lest one should doubt Hanlon's *bona fides* as a Modernist on account of his unorthodox occupation (for an artist, at any rate), one should remember that he sat on the committee of the Irish Exhibition of Living Art inaugurated in 1943, alongside the likes of Mainie Jellett, Evie Hone, Sybil and Louis le Brocquy, Margaret Clarke and Norah McGuinness. While Jack B. Yeats declined to join them on the committee, he did exhibit with them. Hanlon was also a keen and judicious art collector, who purchased works by such Continental artists as Poliakoff, Vlaminck and Lhote. At his death, he also left works by Irish artists, among them Norah McGuinness, Jack B. Yeats, Patrick Scott, Barrie Cooke and Camille Souter. His friends in Ireland included Letitia and Eva Hamilton and he exhibited throughout the world, from Dublin and London to Paris, Brussels and even the Venezuelan city of Maracaibo.[54] Hanlon also received a number of awards.

The setting for this painting itself would have been very much to Hanlon's liking. He inherited a passion for flowers from his mother and retained an interest in gardening throughout his life, winning the novice section of the Horticulture Society's spring gardens competition in 1960.[55] Indeed, this love

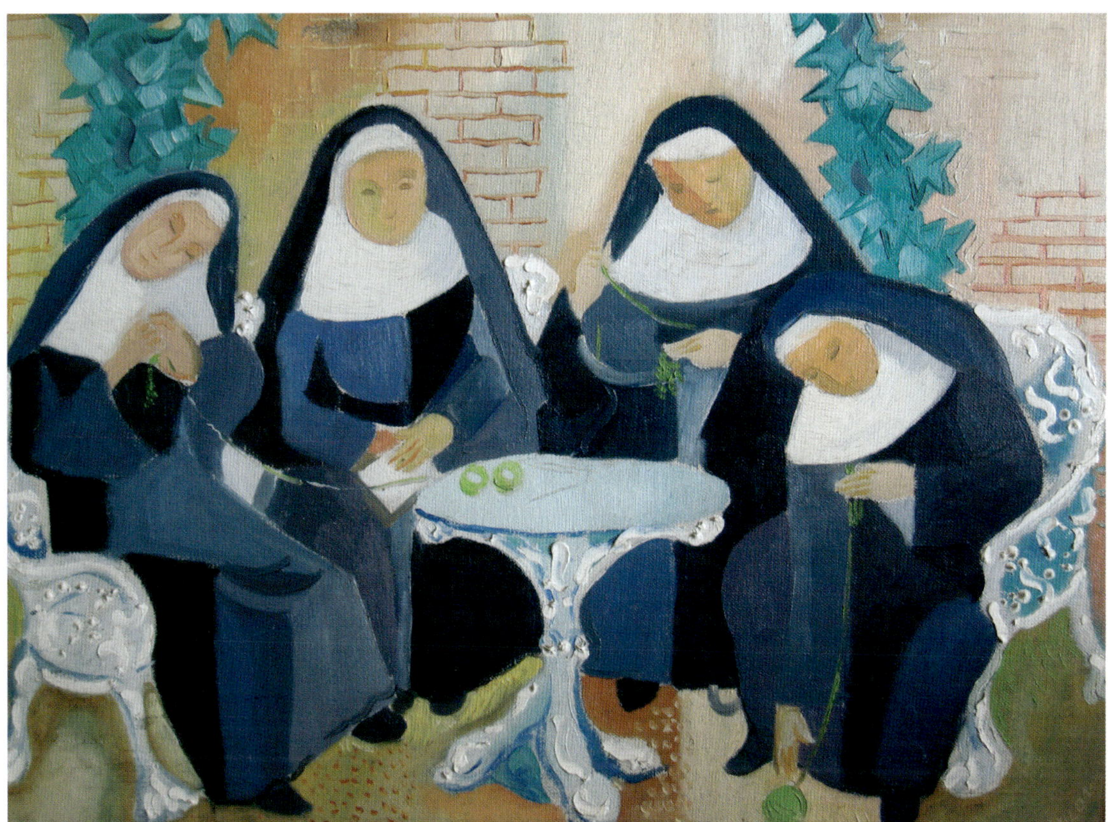

Fr Jack P. Hanlon (1913-68)
48. *Recreation*
1950
Oil on canvas
45 x 55 cm
Crawford Municipal Art Gallery, Cork

for nature might reasonably be assumed to have inspired the colourful but subtle palette that characterised both his oil paintings and watercolours. Admittedly, his palette also points more to his Continental training than to the example of his Irish contemporaries and recent predecessors.[56] In the context of this exhibition, it is interesting to note that Hanlon claimed in an interview of 1960 that he found Connemara and Donegal, such inspirational locations for colourists like Dillon, MacGonigal and Solomons, 'too sad and desolate' and was drawn more instinctively to the colour and light of the Mediterranean.[57]

Recreation is a lighthearted but respectful reflection on life within a religious order. It also challenges common perceptions of religious communities (implied here by the tall brick wall against which the women sit) as ascetic and reclusive. Hanlon, who was ordained to the priesthood by the Auxiliary Archbishop of Dublin in 1939, would have been sensitive to such views and well-positioned to redress them. The picture represents a departure from the more austere religious themes he painted and the ecclesiastical commissions he was to undertake a few years later.[58] *Recreation* is a highly stylised and contrived composition, in which the nuns sit theatrically round just one side of a table, framed by a proscenium arch of ivy or clematus and apparently unaware of their observer. The characters appear to be sitting in silence, but their quietly social application to their task, and gentle interaction counters the austerity implied by their religious garb.[59] BR

53 Hanlon studied in Belgium, Spain and under André Lhote in Paris, exhibited in New York, Paris, Brussels and regularly in Dublin.
54 Jn Coleman 1988, p.224.
55 *ibid*, p.222.
56 *ibid*, p.224.
57 Michael O'Reilly, 'The Priest Painter', *Ave Maria* (Notre Dame Indiana), vol.103, (5 February 1960), pp.8-10. Quoted in Jn Coleman 1988, p.224.
58 Hanlon executed works for churches in Cork, Donegal, Limerick and on the Isle of Wight.
59 A work by Hanlon with the complementary title *Priests in a Garden* featured in a sale at James Adam & Son in 1992.

Jack B. Yeats (1871-1957)
49. *At the Zoo*
1902
Pencil and watercolour on paper
12.8 x 9 cm
National Gallery of Ireland

Jack B. Yeats (1871-1957
50. *Eating Biscuits*
1902
Pencil and watercolour on paper
12.8 x 9 cm
National Gallery of Ireland

Jack B. Yeats (1871-1957
51. *The New Giraffe at Dublin Zoo*
1902
Pencil and watercolour on paper
12.8 x 9 cm
National Gallery of Ireland

Jack B. Yeats (1871-1957)
52. *The Giraffe's Attendant*
1902
Pencil and watercolour on paper
12.8 x 9 cm
National Gallery of Ireland

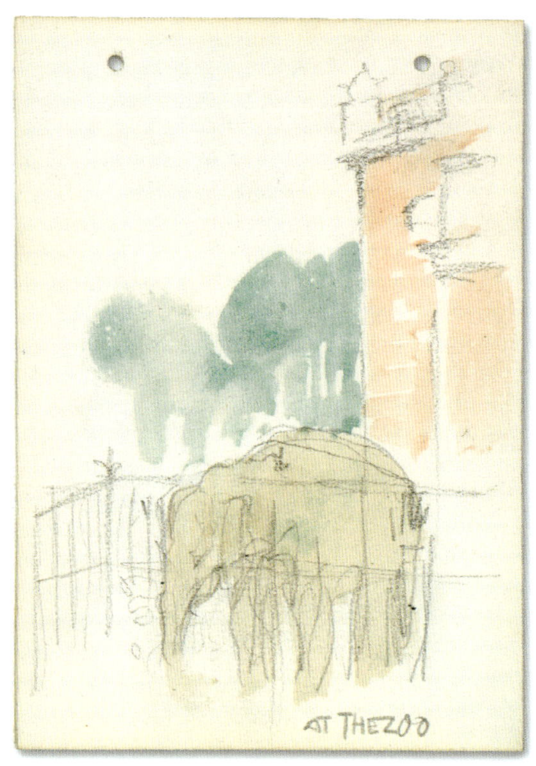

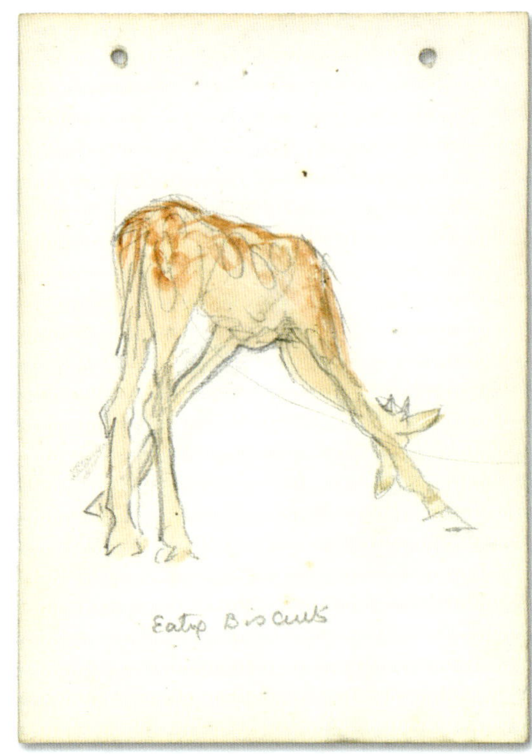

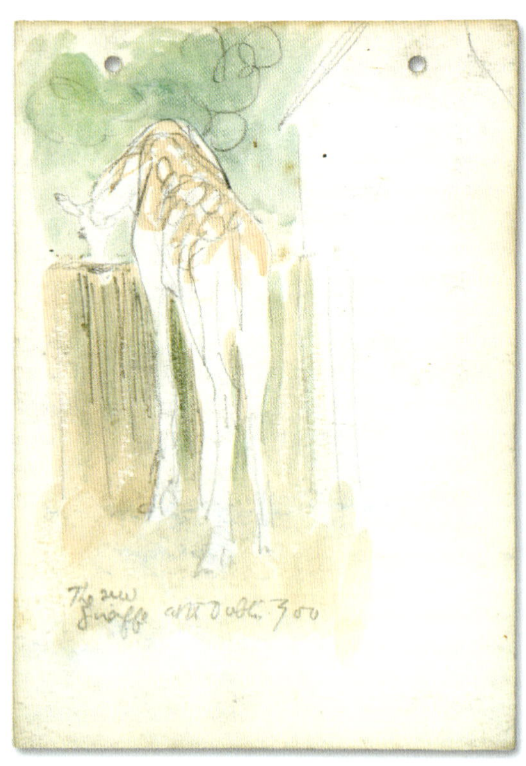

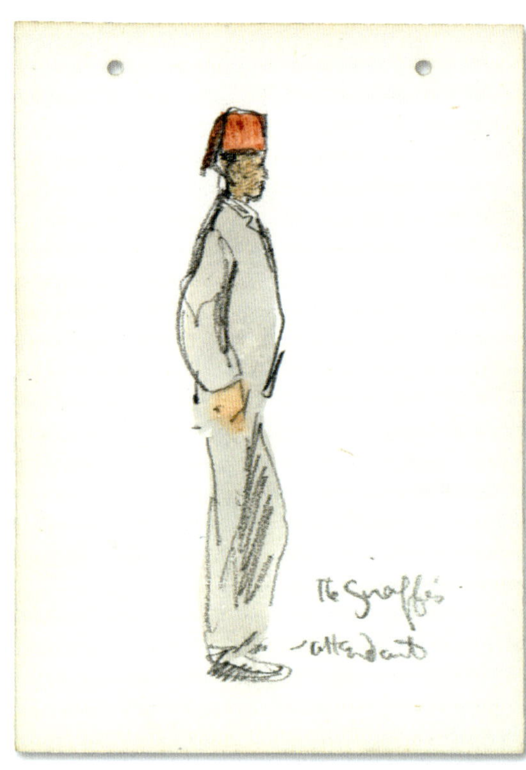

49. At the Zoo

Jack B. Yeats

50. Eating Biscuits

Jack B. Yeats

51. The New Giraffe at Dublin Zoo

Jack B. Yeats

52. The Giraffe's Attendant

Jack B. Yeats

Having first opened its doors to the public on 1 September 1831, the Zoological Gardens (or Dublin Zoo as they are now known) currently attract some 750,000 visitors per annum. Though the zoo's profile, practices, function and size have all changed radically over the generations, its advantageous and picturesque location in the Phoenix Park has remained unchanged.[60] The establishment of the zoo was directed by the Zoological Society of Ireland, itself established just over a year earlier, on 10 May 1830.[61] The first animal inhabitant of the zoo, a wild boar, was soon joined by more of various species, including Canadian wapiti, a sambar deer, emus, ostriches, a leopard, a hyena and a wolf. Some of these came from London Zoo, while others were presented by King William IV.[62] By the Society's first general meeting in 1832, the zoo's collection included some 123 species of animal: 'forty-seven mammals, seventy two birds, and four reptiles'.[63] The first giraffe arrived at Dublin Zoo as early as 1844 and the first lions in 1885.

The zoo originally covered a mere 2.2 hectares and boasted just a small number of buildings. Others were added as the decades passed, including the thatched cottage which used to be the entrance lodge (1833) and the Director's Residence (1866). While a number of the first permanent enclosures still stand, each has been redeveloped and adapted to suit better the needs of its animals. The Roberts House, for example, originally erected in 1902 to accommodate lions, was comprehensively redesigned and now serves as a walk-through aviary.

Predictably, the zoo has been visited by many artists, amateur and professional, interested in studying animals from life. Among the most notable were William and Walter Osborne, both of whom exhibited at the Royal Hibernian Academy studies that they had executed at the zoo. William Osborne, a specialist and extremely accomplished animal painter, exhibited a number of studies produced during a lengthy period, including *Lion's Head* (1858) and *Study of a Royal Bengal Tiger, from specimen in the Royal Zoological Gardens, Phoenix Park* (1864). In 1880, father and son exhibited together, William with *Lioness and Cubs-in the Zoo, Phoenix Park*, and Walter with *Study of a Tiger's Head from Life*. *In the Jungle*, the title assigned to a painting William showed at the RHA in 1900, suggests that he might have incorporated some of these studies into larger scale fanciful works. In 1957, Letitia Hamilton exhibited a painting entitled *Flamingoes at the Zoological Gardens, Phoenix Park* at the RHA. Yeats obviously enjoyed and exploited the zoo for similar artistic reasons, and he produced numerous sketches of different details in the sketchbooks that he kept with him at all times. This selection of sketches exemplifies the facility for rapidly recording subjects on the spot that Yeats demonstrated throughout his sketchbooks.[65] BR

---

60 Dublin Zoo is now 'a conservation and education institution' involved in a large number of breeding-programmes. Peter Wilson, 'Zoological Gardens Dublin', in Lalor 2003, p.1163.

61 In 1838 the society changed its name to the Royal Zoological Society of Ireland when Queen Victoria was invited to become its patron on her coronation.

62 MacGowan n.d., p.15.

63 Peter Wilson, 'Zoological Gardens Dublin', in Lalor 2003, p.1162.

64 The importance of the zoo as a resource was affirmed when William showed his African Lion, Zoological Gardens, Phoenix Park at the RHA in 1900.

65 These sketches all feature in Sketchbook 14 in the Yeats Archive in the NGI.

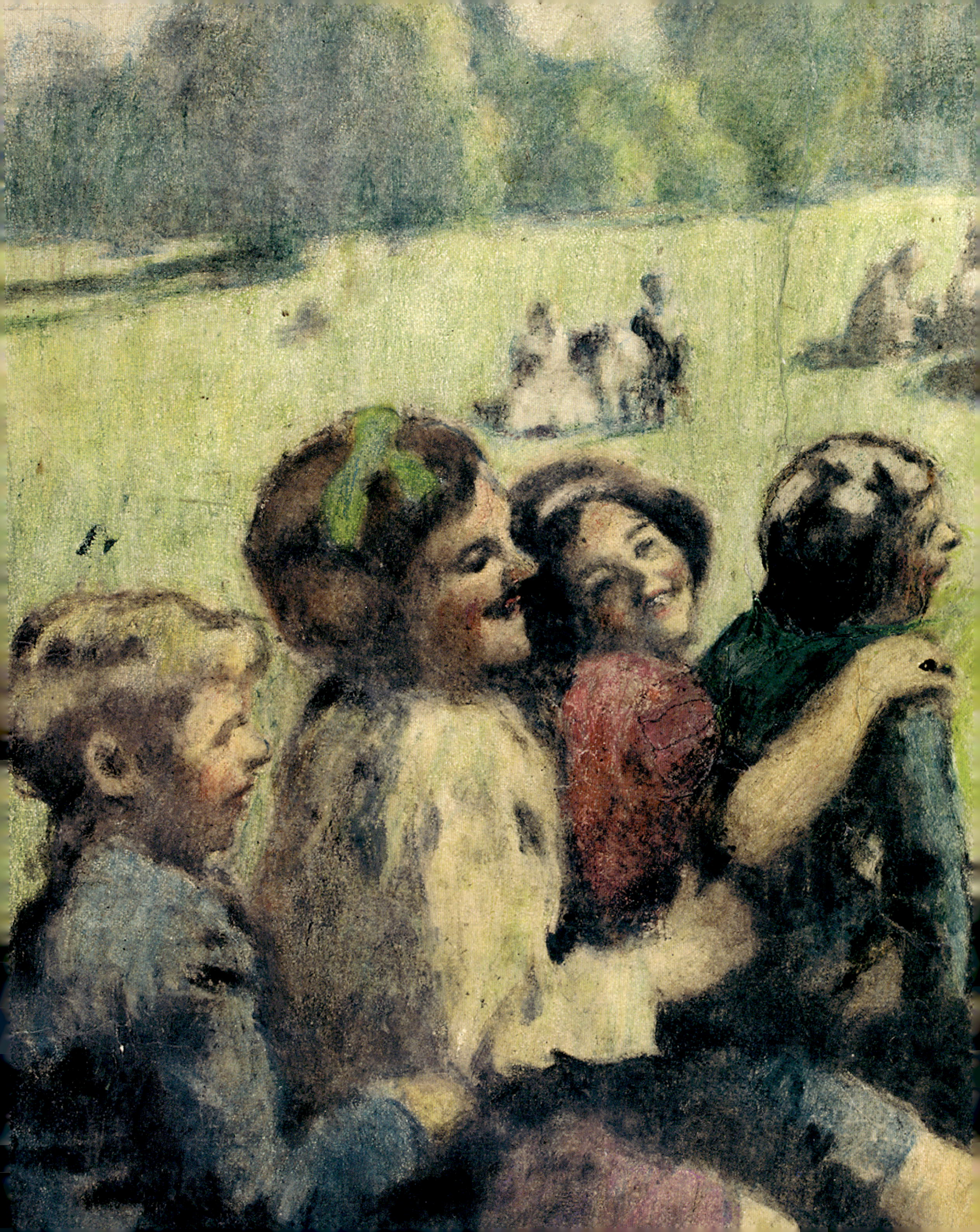

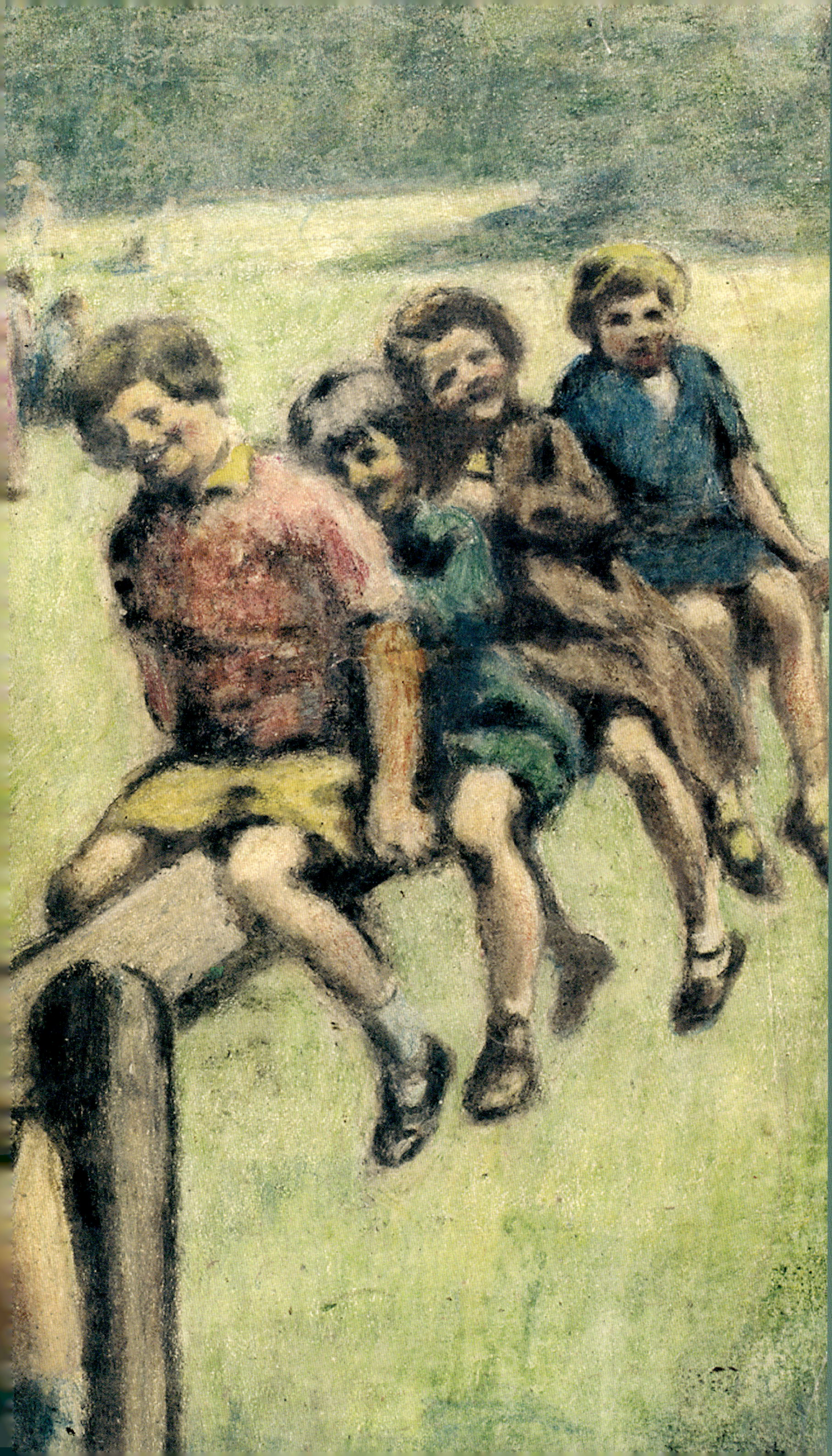

Sun, Sea & Symbolism

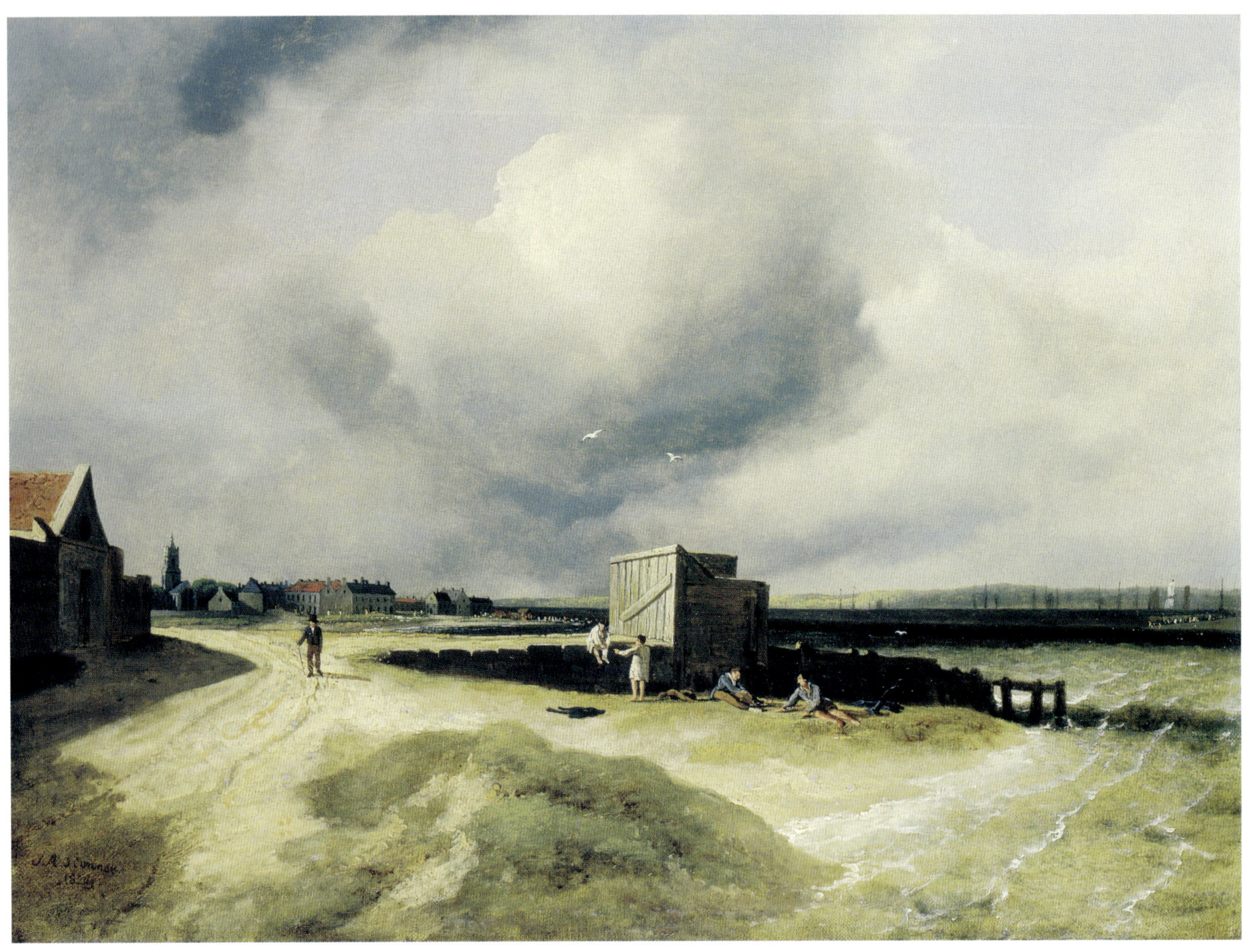

James Arthur O'Connor
(1792-1841)
53. View of Irishtown from Sandymount
Oil on canvas
35 x 45 cm
Private collection

53. View of Irishtown from Sandymount

James Arthur O'Connor

Dublin Bay was widely admired by writers and celebrated similarly by artists, who worked in a variety of media and produced both panoramic views and scenes of specific locations on the north and south shores.[1]

O'Connor was both accomplished and adaptable in his practice, producing a wide range of picture types, from topographical pictures to picturesque rural scenes, dramatic seascapes, romantic landscapes, and hybrid curiosities.[2] He was also competent in etching, and in the use of pencil and watercolour. Subjects such as this view of Irishtown, however, demonstrate more empirical sensibilities. Diminutive but exacting, such pictures seem the product of more random, but similarly keen observation. Similarly unorthodox landscapes by O'Connor include his *Bay Scene, Seapoint* (private collection), and *A View on the Coast near Brighton* (private collection). Neither the composition nor detail provides a clear or immediate indication of the subject of this picture. Irishtown, its ostensible focus, appears in the distance, framed by two contrasting structures in the middleground, and it is in the prosaic juxtaposition of these that much of the interest of O'Connor's painting lies. The gabled-end on the left belongs to Cranfield's baths while the wooden fishermen's hut on the right provides shelter for a group of opportunist swimmers.[3] Established shortly after 1797 by the carver Richard Cranfield (1731-1809) and using the supposedly efficacious water of Dublin Bay, the baths were private, self-contained and effectively inaccessible to the local impoverished population. This was just one of a number of similar baths established in Dublin in the eighteenth century to take advantage of the widely-held faith in the benefits of bathing in sea water. As early as 1747, Richard Mathew stated that 'The Cittizens of Dublin have as I hinted sometimes passd taken an Humour (I cant tell how long it will hold) To Vissite Irishtowne, and for this Season, all the little Cabbins are hired by Lodgers, to have the Advantage of Bathing in Salt Watter…'.[4] Other bathing huts, marked on Roe's map, and John Roque's seminal map of 1756, as being 'for women', could be found immediately adjacent to the village of Irishtown.

From his viewpoint on Scald Hill, near Sandymount, O'Connor incorporates the coastal village of Irishtown (and details such as St Matthew's Church),[5] the South Wall (a recently completed and remarkable feat of engineering above which the masts of tallships appear),[6] and the low hills of Clontarf and Raheny on the north side of the bay. To these topographical details, O'Connor has introduced human interest that illuminates our understanding of everyday life in Dublin in the early years of the nineteenth century. This is not extemporary detail. A pen and ink drawing by O'Connor, of exactly the same subject, which one can reasonably assume to be preparatory sketch, indicates that he experimented with both the composition and the figures. The swimmers occupying the middle ground in the oil painting supplant a group of labourers pausing from their work in the drawing.

In the finished oil, the characters, two in their undershirts, who rest and talk in the shade of the fishermen's hut, are probably local. Their clothes do not indicate affluence, and their behaviour is at odds with prevailing etiquette among the higher echelons of society. Admittedly, women were more subject to social constraint, but the activity of the men in this picture is particularly casual and public. Indeed, these figures contrast with the static figure on the path to the left of the composition. Such figures, anticipating the staring characters who stand stock-still in early photographs, feature throughout O'Connor's oeuvre.

The easy recreation of the bathers belies what is likely to have been their daily experience. Though recorded as prosperous at the beginning of the eighteenth century, both Ringsend and Irishtown were far from affluent by the early 1800s. Barbara Verschoyle, Lord Fitzwilliam's agent, observed with alarming vitriol in 1801 that the people of Irishtown were 'wretchedly poor - & ever must be so while they are so idle - I had no idea they were half so bad - until I went through their Cabins…'.[7] She then vowed to replace any evicted defaulters with 'improving tenants'.[8] One did not have to travel far to encounter the type of society she had in mind. A short distance away lived the artist William Ashford, for whom Gandon had designed a villa in Sandymount in the late 1780s. Verschoyle's jaundiced view was corroborated just a few years before O'Connor painted this scene by Warburton, Whitelaw and Walsh, who referred to the 'wretched village of Ringsend, consisting of a few ruinous houses'.[9]

As John Hutchinson has pointed out, pictures such as this appealed to the middle classes.[10] Occupying a category between genre painting and topographical landscape, they record prosaic activity among Dublin's visitors and inhabitants but, typically, do not provide any indication of the quotidian hardship endured by the city's poor. Despite this hardship, the citizens of Dublin came to Ringsend and Irishtown for occasional horse racing and, as illustrated in O'Connor's picture, bathing.[11] Of particular interest on the right of the composition is a sloping gangway on the South Wall, along which a line of passengers queues for a ferry to the mainland or to an eastbound ship at anchor. From the seventeenth to the nineteenth century (before the development of the harbours of Howth and Kingstown), Ringsend, a short distance beyond Irishtown, was the 'chief point of embarkation and disembarkation for passenger traffic'.[12] BR

---

1 Among the other artists to paint the bay were Francis Place, William Jones, William Ashford, John Henry Campbell, Thomas Sautelle Roberts and William Sadler.

2 For an account of O'Connor's life and an overview of his work, see Hutchinson 1985.

3 For a more detailed analysis of this picture, see Brendan Rooney, 'James Arthur O'Connor', in Laffan, 2001, pp.148-177.

4 Letter from Richard Mathew to Lord Fitzwilliam, Dublin, 27 August 1747, Pembroke Correspondences, National Archives, Dublin, 97/46/1/2/5/46.

5 'Part of the Estate of the Rt Honble the Earl of Pembroke & Montgomery/ Surveyed by John Roe/ Revised by A. Neville Jun. 14 York Street 1826'. National Archives, Dublin, 97/46/4/17

6 Though by the middle of the eighteenth century the main construction of the north and south walls was virtually complete, development continued into the nineteenth century. See Gilligan 1988.

7 Letter from Barbara Verschoyle to Lord Fitzwilliam, 5 April 1801, Pembroke Estate Letter Book, vol. I, National Archives, Dublin.

8 *ibid.*

9 Warburton et al 1818, vol. II, p. 441.

10 Hutchinson 1985, p. 120.

11 Ringsend and Irishtown were also renowned for good pickings of cockles and shrimp.

12 Ball 1903, vol. II, p. 35.

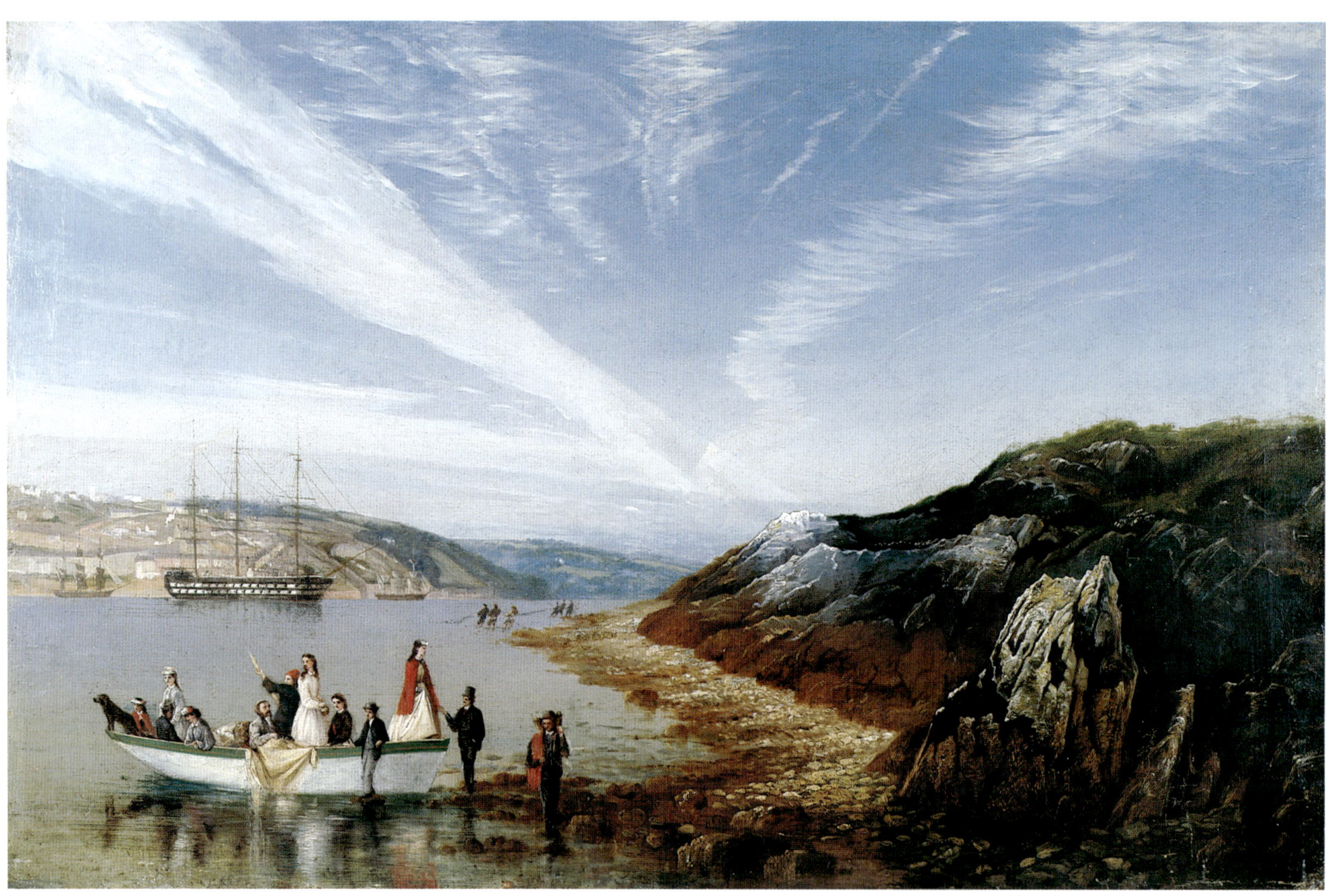

George Mounsey Wheatley Atkinson (1806-84)
54. A Boating Party in Cork Harbour
1840
Oil on canvas
60.9 x 91.4 cm
Crawford Municipal Art Gallery, Cork

54. A Boating Party in Cork Harbour

George Mounsey Wheatley Atkinson

In this painting an affluent boating-party lands on Spike Island in the middle of Cork Harbour, presumably to enjoy a picnic in the picturesque, albeit militarised surroundings it provided. Their small vessel transports day-trippers where before it might have carried contraband. In the eighteenth century, the island had a reputation for providing refuge for smugglers, though the incidence of smuggling at the time was so common that it was probably no more popular there than on any other islands and secluded coves along the coast. In any case, the final decades of the eighteenth century saw the island 'transformed from a smuggler's den, and an uninhabited island, into a fortified place'.[13] A star-shaped fort, built by the architect Michael Shanahan under the direction of Colonel Charles Vallencey in the 1790s, was designed to defend the harbour against French invasion as part of a larger naval complex comprising barracks and a military hospital, which developed over subsequent decades.

In 1847, in response to growing resistance (both local and Antipodean) to the practice of transportation, the island was selected as the site for a 'male convict depot'[14] and by 1850 accommodated two and half thousand prisoners, although their number subsequently declined dramatically.[15] A number of the leaders of the 1848 rebellion, including William Smith O'Brien and John Mitchel, were held on the island prior to transportation. The American visitor Asenath Nicholson recalled that on her visit to Spike Island in 1848 her party found 'convicts from every part of Ireland, who were deemed worthy of an exile from home for the space of seven years… Some of these young men and boys had thrown a stone into a bread shop, some had stolen a turnip, and some a sheep; but every one was induced by extreme hunger to do the deed'.[16] The last convicts of the nineteenth century left the island in the mid-1880s.

As was common among specialist marine painters, including William Brydges Beechey and Edwin Hayes, Atkinson enjoyed depicting the sea's various moods and aspects and the multifarious vessels that sailed upon it. At the Cork Art Union exhibition of 1845, John

F. Maguire praised Atkinson as having 'beheld the sea in all its phases, in its terrible grandeur as in its placid beauty; to his mind every craft that floats upon the waters is familiar - he is conversant with the rig of the largest frigate, as of the smallest pilot boat, and knows every block and rope and spar that form that beautifully yet intricate symmetry so puzzling to the eye of a landsman'.[17]

In this case, Atkinson captures the bay's 'perfectly smooth' waters as described by Samuel Lewis in his *Topographical Dictionary of Ireland* published just five years previously.[18] Mirror-like, these waters hide the dangers between the island and the mainland, and give no indication of the 'much agitated' conditions that prevailed on the seaward side.[19] Resting at anchor in the background is an impressive two-deck ship of the line (that is, a warship large and powerful enough to occupy a place in the battle line).[20] Its imposing presence does not, however, disturb the overall calmness of the scene. Indeed, the painting does little else to suggest that Cork harbour, with its regular commercial, military and emigrant traffic, was among the busiest ports in the world at the time. It is novel to think that many middle-class families who owed their fortunes to the city's mercantile status and success could observe the comings and goings of vessels from their handsome residences around the harbour.

The activity represented in this picture also has the distinction of being one of which the artist himself, an experienced seaman, would have wholeheartedly approved. Furthermore, the leisure of the boating-party, which seems to extend to the casual action of their staff, is emphasised by the labour of the fishermen dragging their nets ashore in the background. Atkinson affirmed his close association with both Cobh and the sea by holding an exhibition of his work in a specially built pavilion in the town to coincide with the visit of Queen Victoria and Prince Albert to the harbour in 1849. BR

13 Js Coleman 1893, p.2.
14 *ibid,* p.5.
15 Having served as a so-called Treaty Port during the First World War, Spike Island's fortifications were eventually taken over by the Irish Government in 1938 and renamed Fort Mitchel.
16 Nicholson 1851, p.249.
17 Quoted in Murray 2005, p.90.
18 S. Lewis 1837, vol. II, p.572.
19 *ibid.*
20 Murray 2005, p.90.

55. The Royal Mail Packet 'Leinster' outside Kingstown Harbour

Richard Brydges Beechey

Maritime art is replete with paintings recording the moods, potency and picturesque qualities of the sea

Richard Brydges Beechey
(1808-95)
55. The Royal Mail Packet 'Leinster' outside Kingstown Harbour
1868
Oil on canvas
77.5 x 110 cm
Private collection
See Foldout opposite page 115

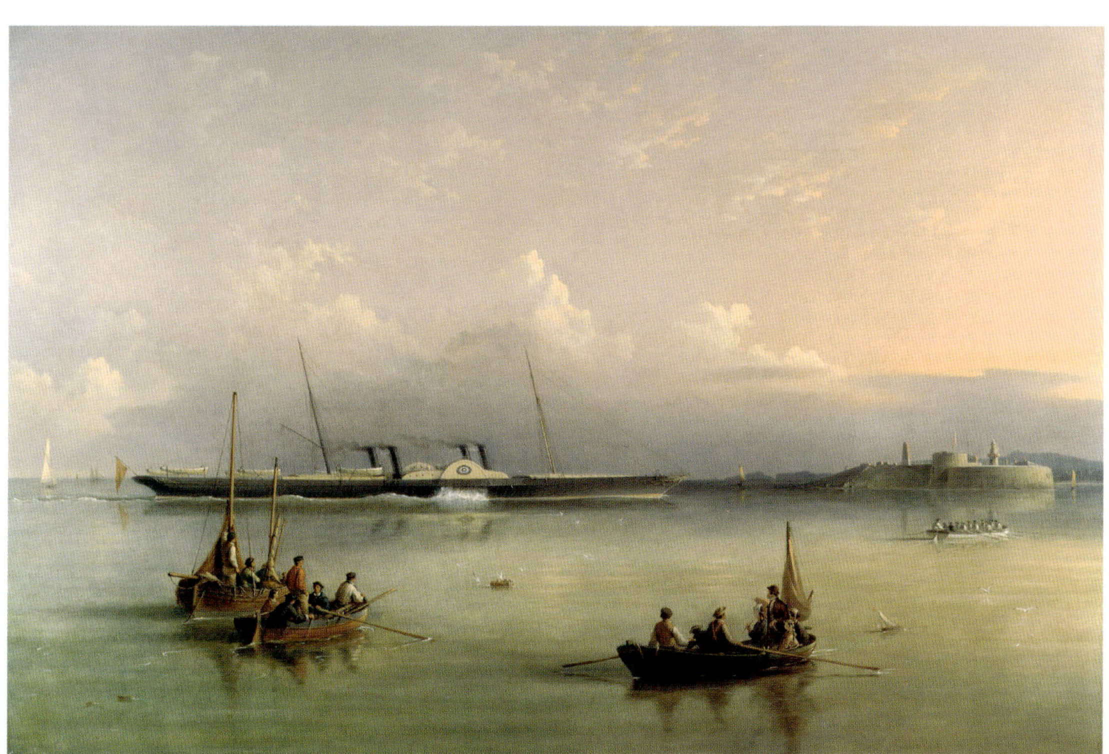

and with empirical records of the finely engineered vessels that sailed upon it. This painting adheres to the former tradition, presenting Kingstown (now Dun Laoghaire) harbour on a particulary mild evening, and introduces a novel, human element to the latter. A seaman by profession, Beechey understood both vessels and the sea.[21] As the paddle steamer *Leinster* glides in to port, creating the slightest of wakes, fishermen and a party of pleasure-boaters pause to admire it. By juxtaposing a recreational boat, fishing boat, the packet steamer and other vessels, Beechey illustrates the variety of ways in which the sea was exploited. The still waters in the picture, however, belie Dublin Bay's fearsome reputation. The diminutive sailboat that a child pulls by a string behind his own vessel complements the scene's benign atmosphere but also serves as a counterpoint to the impressive scale of the *Leinster.*

This depiction is consistent with the reputation of the *Leinster,* which was widely admired for its speed, reliability and sophisticated engineering. In 1860, the City of Dublin Steam Packet Company introduced into service a quartet of steamers, *Connaught, Leinster, Munster* and *Ulster,* which subsequently made the Holyhead to Kingstown mail and passenger service 'a model to the world'.[22] The *Leinster,* engined like the *Connaught* by Ravenhill, Salkeld & Company, was the first of the four to be completed.[23] The 'Four Provinces', as they were known collectively, raised the average speed for the crossing from 11.7 to 14.5 knots and yet more in the 1880s when their engines were replaced.[24] They were remarkably advanced for their time and in their thirty-seven years in service 'never lost a passenger, crew member or mail bag, and in their last eleven years never missed a single passage'.[25] By comparison, the packet ship that carried John Wesley on his first visit to Dublin in August 1747 took twenty-six hours to make the journey from Holyhead to Ringsend.[26] The quartet were ultimately replaced in 1897 by four new 'Provinces', which were considerably larger and faster. The *Leinster* featured among the fleet of twelve vessels that was made available by the City of Dublin Steamship Company to passengers wishing to attend the O'Connell Centenary celebrations in Dublin in August 1875 (cat. 79). *The Times* reported that an estimated 10,000 persons would wish to travel from all across England to those events in Dublin.[27]

In Beechey's painting, one can clearly make out the turtle-back covering the foredeck that was added to allow the vessel to negotiate heavy seas under power.[28] The construction of this cover proved weaker than was the case with the other vessels and was badly damaged in a storm of February 1861. Overall, however, the City of Dublin Steam Packet Company's quartet of ships was sturdy, quick and reliable and helped to provide a service that gave 'the utmost satisfaction to the travelling public and to those who depended on the speedy delivery of the mail'.[29] BR

---

21 The Leinster is accurately depicted. Alterations made to the vessel in 1885 removed the two aft funnels.
22 Ireland 1986, p.246.
23 Smyth 1984, p.49. The Ulster and Munster were engined by James Watt of Birmingham.
24 Ireland 1986, p.246.
25 *ibid,* p.247.
26 Smyth 1984, p.32.
27 The Times, 30 July 1875.
28 *ibid,* p.49.
29 *ibid,* p.50.

56. On the Beach

George Russell (AE)

57. The Skipping Rope

George Russell (AE)

George Russell was a painter, poet, writer, playwright, journalist, critic, economist and political observer, but was also a mystic and Theosophist.[30] He worked with Sir Horace Plunkett on the staff of the Irish Agricultural Organisation Society and served as editor of *The Irish Homestead* and its successor *The Irish Statesman,* but also published prose and poetry (with titles like *The Candle of Vision, The Avatars* and *Imaginations and Reveries)* and produced pictures inspired by his mystical musings. His art itself echoes the duality in his makeup, often fantastical in concept but orthodox in execution.

Russell's visionary and pragmatic inclinations were manifest, perhaps unexpectedly, in his attempts to establish a school of Irish painting that would complement the Literary Revival in which he had also played a prominent role. To this end, he organised an exhibition in 1899 of modern Continental paintings in Dublin, hoping that the work of such artists as Daumier, Degas, Manet, Monet and Whistler would inspire his compatriots and provide a gauge against which they could judge themselves. It proved an altruistic, albeit not entirely successful, enterprise.

The complexity of Russell's character is undoubtedly compounded by the fact that he is known more generally as 'AE', a pseudonym derived from the Gnostic term Aeon, which a printer had mistakenly shortened but to which Russell himself evidently took a liking. The occasionally impenetrable quality of his pictures is strengthened by the artist's disinclination to assign titles to his work, a tendency

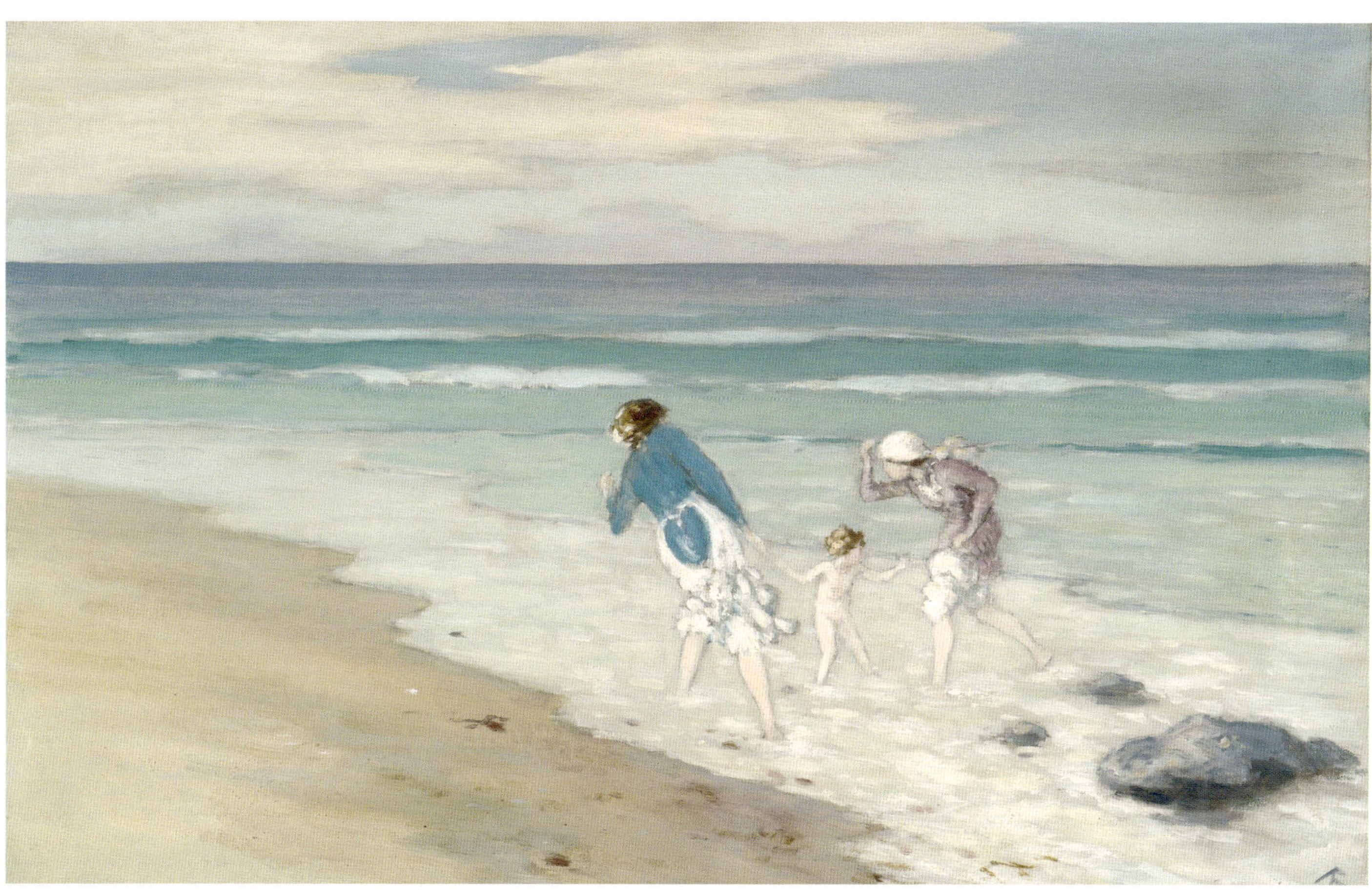

George Russell (AE)
(1867-1935)
56. On the Beach
Oil on canvas
53.4 x 81.4 cm
Collection Armagh County Museum

that has prompted auction houses and galleries over the decades to adopt lines from his poetry in their stead. Though this may seem successful at first glance, it often affords the paintings a singularity at odds with the intense, exploratory process of which they were a product.

Despite Russell's mystical associations and inspiration, *On the Beach* and *The Skipping Rope*, which are typical of a large proportion of the artist's work, seem as rooted in personal experience as they are visionary. Russell, like Estella Solomons, was captivated by the formal and atmospheric qualities of the Donegal landscape. From the early years of the twentieth century, he adopted the custom of travelling annually to Sheephaven in Donegal, an area that he regarded as the spiritual centre of Ireland.[31] He normally stayed in a cottage at Breaghy, near Dunfanaghy, but sometimes removed to the so-called 'Fairy House', a tiny building in the woods on Marble Hill, overlooking Sheephaven Bay and its sandy beach. Painting was for Russell an avocation which he indulged fitfully, but it is significant that he was most prolific during these creative summer sojourns on the north-west coast. He is understood to have returned to Dublin from Donegal with piles of canvases, some of which he would continue to work on at weekends.

Admittedly, pictures like *On the Beach* and *The Skipping Rope* are evocations of atmosphere rather than topographical representations of recognisable places or detailed depictions of human activity, but they are relatively conventional and owe a debt to Russell's observation in Donegal. One might even argue that these paintings, executed as if conjured up through hazy memory, have more resonance and impact than the artist's numerous fairy pictures, which Dorothy Walker dismissed with uncompromising candour as 'deeply silly'.[32] Russell, convinced by the veracity of his expression, would undoubtedly have been vexed by such criticism.

Certainly, it is in compositions such as these, which owe a debt to personal experience but boast more esoteric purpose, that realism and symbolism converge. Nor are they as far removed from the work of other Irish artists as one might imagine. As S.B. Kennedy has contended, Irish artists of this period were drawn to Symbolism, an art form that could not only 'arouse national and patriotic

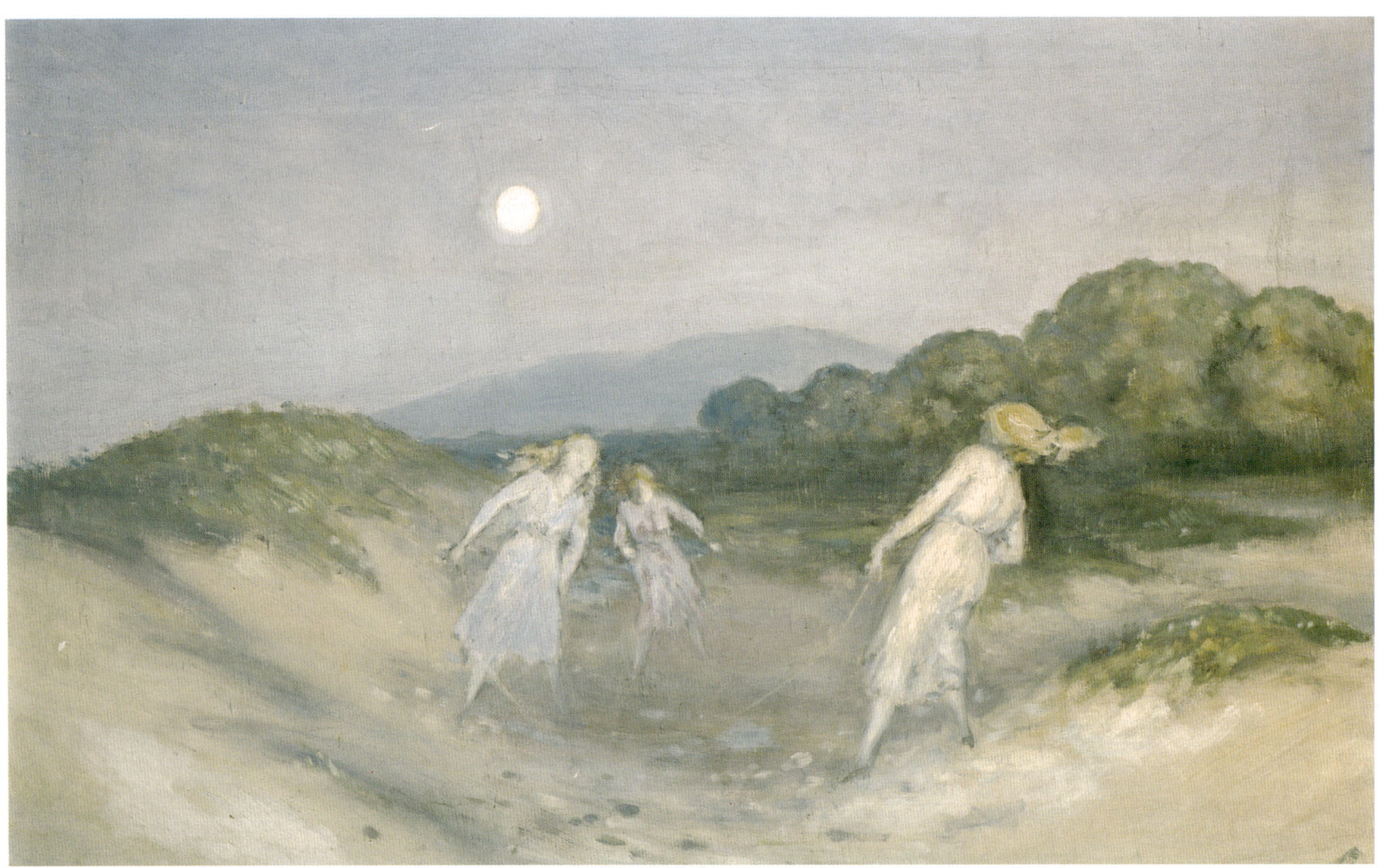

George Russell (AE)
(1867-1935)
57. The Skipping Rope
Oil on canvas
53.6 x 81.4 cm
Collection Ulster Museum, Belfast

sentiment' but also define it.[33] There are also echoes of W.B. Yeats's spiritual and idealised drama in Russell's paintings. Russell was among the painters with whom Paul Henry exhibited for the first time in Dublin in October 1911,[34] and though one might imagine that their work hung rather incongruously together, it is interesting to note that Henry reflected in an interview with the *Irish Times* in 1941 that he had always been conscious of the 'other worldliness' and the 'sense of mystery' in the Irish landscape.[35] William Conor, for his part, also sought to capture the intangible in his paintings, claiming that his ambition was to 'reveal the Spiritual character of [Belfast] people in all [its] vigour, in all its passion, humanity and humour'.[36]

The prominence of children in Russell's pictures is far from incidental. Their blithe energy and imagination point to a freedom of spirit consistent with the visions Russell had developed from Theosophy, Irish mythology, memory and waking dreams. In articles in the *Irish Statesman*, Russell lamented the stagnation that he observed in rural Ireland, brought about by a lack of amenities and emigration, but saw promise in young people. Indeed, theirs were qualities to which the artist himself seems to have aspired, the countess of Fingall describing Russell as 'having the young heart that never grows old'.[37] It seems that for Russell young women and children conveyed the notion of the spirit world as much as the woodland nymphs, fairies and other supernatural beings that recur throughout his oeuvre and more effectively than the weathered peasants who inhabit his paintings less frequently.

In the context of this exhibition, it is interesting to note that Russell maintained that the demise of rural communities was attributable to the fact that there was often 'no village Hall, no library, no gymnasium, no village choir, no place to dance except the roadside' and that there was also a dearth of book shops.[38] However, as Terence Brown has pointed out, Russell, the teetotaller, seemed reluctant to concede that the public house played a key role in the creative life of the Irish.[39]

Russell produced abstracted landscapes that went some way towards capturing the ethereal qualities of Ireland and its people. The unevenness in the technical quality of these works is partly attributable to the fact that they were the product of short periods of intense activity by the artist. However, Russell's prolific output itself is a testament to the zeal with which he approached his work. He painted, as he wrote, 'with dangerous facility'.[40] Indeed, his technique was not universally popular. It has even been suggested that James Humbert Craig, when admonished by Russell for his deficient technique, put on his fellow artist's spectacles and announced that the difference in the appearance of their pictures must have been attributable to Russell's shortsightedness.[41] Champion of the French style, George Moore, for his part, having changed his mind about Russell's artistic abilities, referred to him as 'the Donegal Dauber'. BR

30 The artist was born George William Russell in Lurgan. Russell joined the Theosophical Society in Dublin in 1890 but resigned eight years later as his own theories had developed beyond its confines.
31 Hutchinson 1983.
32 Walker 1997, p.17.
33 S.B. Kennedy 1989-90, p.48.
34 The other painters exhibiting at the Leinster Hall on that occasion were Grace Henry, Count Markievicz and Frances Baker.
35 Morrow 1941.
36 Wilson 1981, p.105.
37 Fingall 1991, p.241.
38 AE, 'Rural Clubs and National Life', *Irish Statesman*, 12 January 1924, quoted in McConkey 1990, p.63.
39 Brown 1990, p.42.
40 Kennelly 1967.
41 Nulty 1978, p.3.

58. Peace

Mainie Jellett

Though profoundly different at first glace, the ordered composition of this early painting anticipates the strict construction of Jellett's later work, and specifically the technique of *Translation* and *Rotation* for which she is much better known. Indeed, preparatory sketches for this work, featuring thorough over-drawing in one case and a matrix in another, as well as individual figure studies in oil survive to evince the artist's schematic, almost mechanical method. The painting was well-received, however, and won for Jellett the Taylor Prize from the Royal Dublin Society in 1920.

More significant, though, in the context of this exhibition is the subject of the painting. Begun at Fintragh House, Donegal, in the summer of 1919, and finished in Dublin in the autumn or winter of that year, the picture typifies the halcyon holidays spent by Jellett and her sisters in Killybegs.[42] These idyllic days, as can be seen from Bay Jellett's diary, were marked by such relaxed activity as bathing in the sea, picnics, fishing, tennis, tea on the beach and cycling (for which Mainie cared little).43 Bruce Arnold has described aptly these holidays on the north-west coast, which lasted many weeks, as 'occasions of untrammelled pleasure'.[44] Predictably, the other recreational activity in which Mainie in particular indulged was sketching. While doing so, she was frequently joined by her friend Judith Weir, who lived with her mother nearby.

Though depicting a part of the country that Mainie loved, this painting evokes more the lazy, relaxed atmosphere of a summer's day than it does the specifics of the local Donegal landscape. Moreover, the painting and its very title eschew the tense political state in which the country found itself at the time and in which Jellett's own family was caught up. The painting features the artist's sisters Babbin and Betty, their cousin Letitia Stokes, and another unidentified sitter.[45] The Jelletts were avid readers and Mainie produced several studies of members of the family absorbed in books.

Significantly, Jellett did apply the Cubist-inspired techniques that she had developed in France (under the influence of Albert Gleizes in particular) to more traditional subjects later in her career. Having spent many years working predominantly on so-called paintings-without-subject, Jellett was commissioned by the Irish Government to paint murals for the Irish Pavilion at the Glasgow Industrial Exhibition in 1938 and New York the following year. Her designs were again evocative rather than empirical, but included such traditional subjects as *Turf-cutting, Fishing from Currach, Spinning Wheels and Spinneries and Horses Grazing,* and drew on the artist's affection for the west of Ireland as well as her deep spirituality.[46] BR

Mainie Jellett (1897-1944)
58. Peace
1919
Oil on canvas
61.5 x 81.5 cm
Hubert S. O'Connor

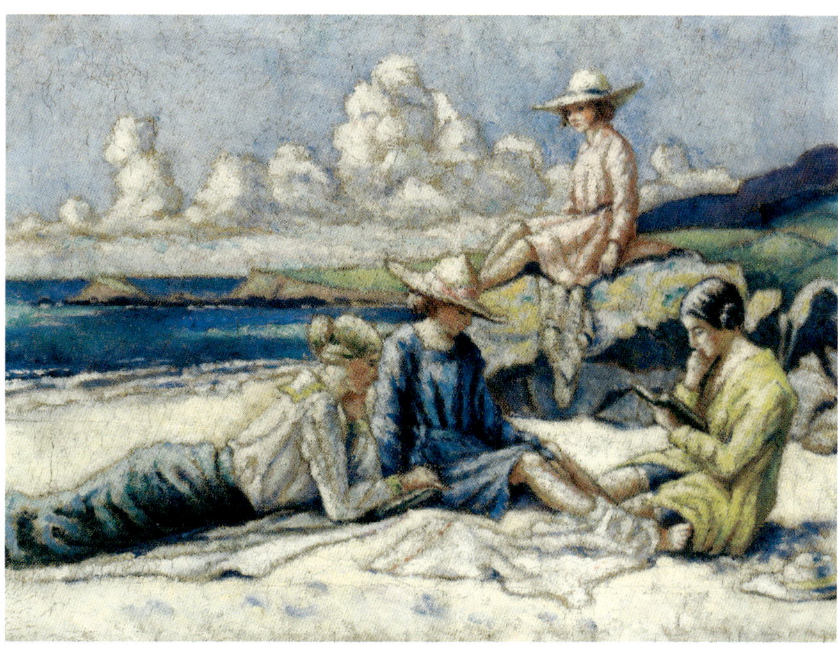

42 Arnold 1991, pp.32-33.
43 The painting coincides with William Jellett's success in the general election of July 1919, when he was elected as a Unionist to one of the Trinity College seats.
44 Arnold 1991, p.32.
45 IMMA 1991, p.55.
46 See MacCarvill 1958, pp.19-20.

59. In the People's Gardens, Phoenix Park

Mainie Jellett

In the Edwardian Dublin in which Jellett grew up, outdoor activities offered a relaxed contrast to the formality of home life. As the child of wealthy parents, Jellett played tennis, and took part in skating and cycling around her Dublin home, while her sister Bay's diary portrays holidays in Killibegs as an idyllic round of swimming, fishing and long picnics. Throughout her life, her correspondence makes frequent mention of the weather, of the warmth of the sea and her response to the outdoors. This side of Jellett's character rather balances the impression of her as a cerebral artist, relentlessly engaged in the intellectual manipulation of form. Like her teacher Orpen a few years before at Howth, Jellett enjoyed painting members of her family in relaxed poses in Dublin's outdoor spaces, a particularly charming example being a study of Bay reading in the gardens of Fitzwilliam Square close to the family home (private collection). Here, in a decoratively Impressionist technique, she swiftly notates three young women, no doubt also members of her family, sitting on the grass of the Phoenix Park.

Mainie Jellett (1897-1944)
59. In the People's Gardens, Phoenix Park
1919
Oil on canvas
61.5 x 81.5 cm
Hubert S. O'Connor
Private collection courtesy of Milmo-Penny Fine Art

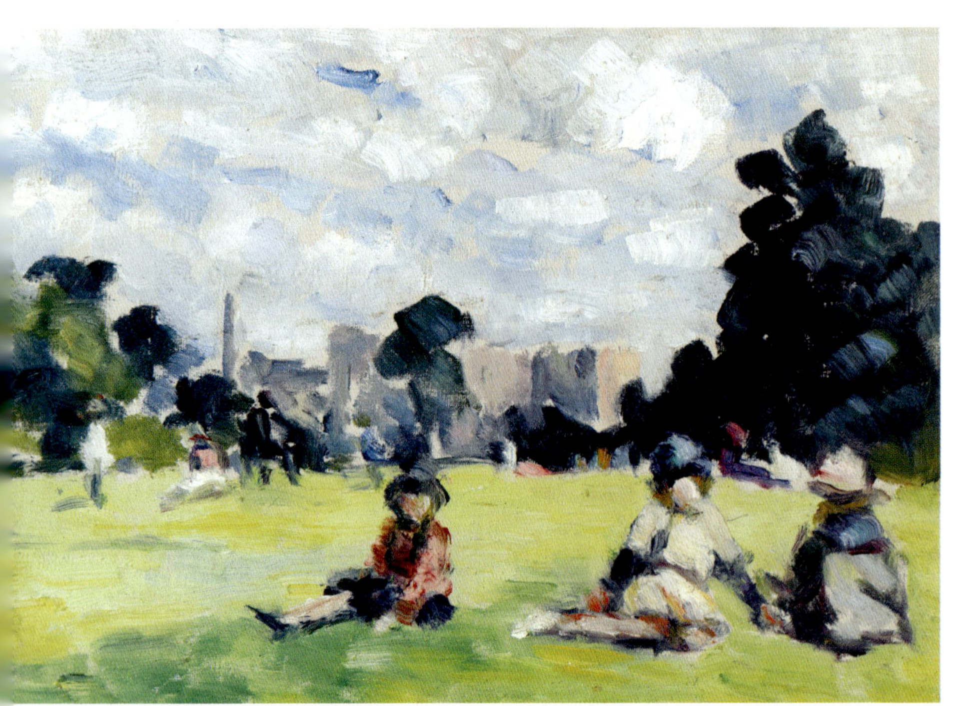

The picture can be dated to 1920 or possibly a year earlier. In this year, crucial to Jellett's artistic development, Ireland was in the middle of the ravages of the War of Independence. Very early the following year Jellett followed Evie Hone to Paris and, in February, began her period of study of André Lhote. Paintings such as this and the ironically entitled *Peace* (cat.58) of 1919 avoid the political events which beset the county, events in which the artist's family were actively involved. At this very moment the artist's father William, a hard-line Unionist, was actively engaged in opposing Home Rule, despite the fact that it had been passed through the Westminster parliament. In April 1920 Jellett herself had attended the annual meeting of the City of Dublin Unionists. The overwhelming victory of Sinn Féin in the 1918 general election had threatened everything that the family stood for politically, and with it the carefree existence of privilege which several of Jellett's early works conjure up. That works such as this were painted as a deliberate antidote to the violence and uncertainty that engulfed the country was clearly recognised at the time. In the autumn of 1920 her joint exhibition with Lilian Lucy Davidson was reviewed favourably by the *Irish Times:* 'It is gratifying to find art joyously disporting itself in Dublin in these troublesome times, and a visit to this exhibition is a tonic which can be safely recommended to worried citizens'.[47]

In these times of heightened tension, depictions of certain places inevitably took on a political charge. This would have been all too apparent to as articulate an observer as Jellett. The Phoenix Park, home of the Lord Lieutenant, site of the Magazine Fort and scene of the murder of Chief Secretary, Lord Frederick Cavendish by the Invincibles in 1882 was symbolic both of the continuity, and the contestation, of the Union. This is rather emphasised by the Wellington Monument looming in the background. Jellett was an intelligent and articulate observer who would have been aware of these political resonances. Indeed at this very moment in her career, she was producing rather more heavy-handed, political allegory in support of her family's position of die-hard Unionism, designing the cover for a pamphlet to be published by the Irish Unionist Alliance.[48] In this context the 'joyful note in Miss Jellett's pictures', which the *Irish Times* noted and which rings out from this delightful sketch, can be seen either as a poignant feeling of imminent loss, an enjoyment of the last days of summer, or a deliberate retreat into art, ignoring wider issues of society and nation. WL

47 Quoted in Arnold 1991, p.44.
48 *ibid*, p.42.

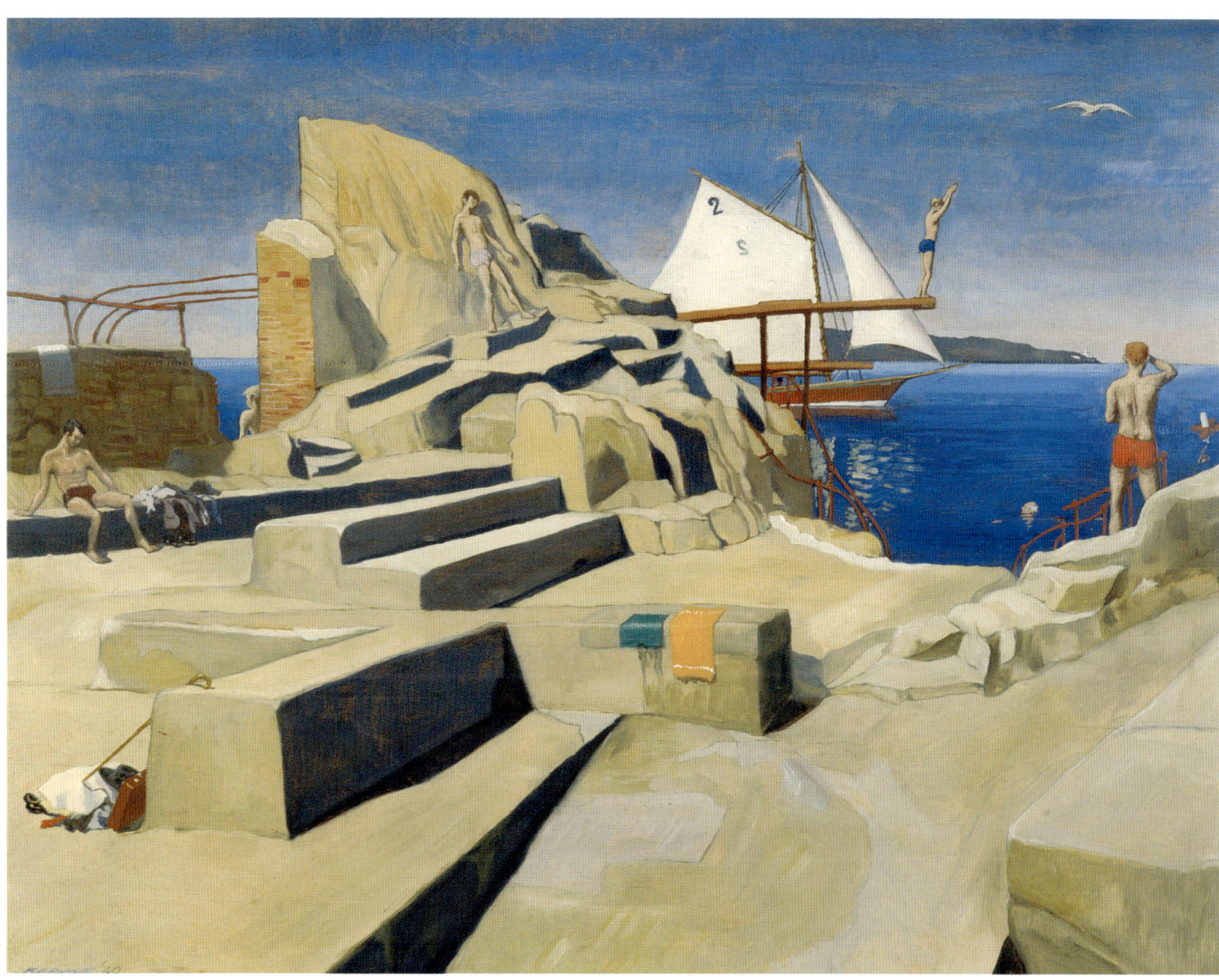

Harry Kernoff (1900-74)
60. The Forty Foot, Sandycove
1940
Oil on board
61.5 x 75.5 cm
AIB Art Collection

60. The Forty Foot, Sandycove

Harry Kernoff

61. Bank Holiday, Killiney, Co. Dublin

Harry Kernoff

Though not a native Dubliner, Harry Kernoff took the city to his heart and portrayed the rhythm of its daily life with great sympathy and often humour. This affinity for the city was noted as early as 1936 by the critic John Dowling. 'Kernoff is not only a Dubliner' he observed, 'but he is a convinced "towny". Shapes are what interest him, such as the mass of a building against the sky or a pattern of roofs and chimney pots, and his feeling for the city with its jumble of houses and shops and quays, its bridges and ships and machinery is emphasised by a difference between his handling of these subjects and his more pastoral themes'.[49] Between the town and country, the urban and pastoral, the outdoor spaces of south Dublin's bathing spots provided Kernoff with inspiration for a group of pictures of the early 1940s; *Bathers– Naylors Cove, Bray* exhibited at the RHA in 1940, and the two works included here, *The Forty Foot, Sandycove and Bank Holiday, Killiney*, exhibited in 1941 and 1942 respectively.

Bathers had featured occasionally in Irish landscape art from the mid-eighteenth century, with the motif appearing in the work of William van der Hagen, George Mullins and Thomas Roberts. These and later portrayals of bathing can be seen to reflect different social attitudes to the activity and, in more formal terms, questions of decorum and genre, of the classical or classicised against the more humble or everyday. Francis Wheatley's graceful nymphs

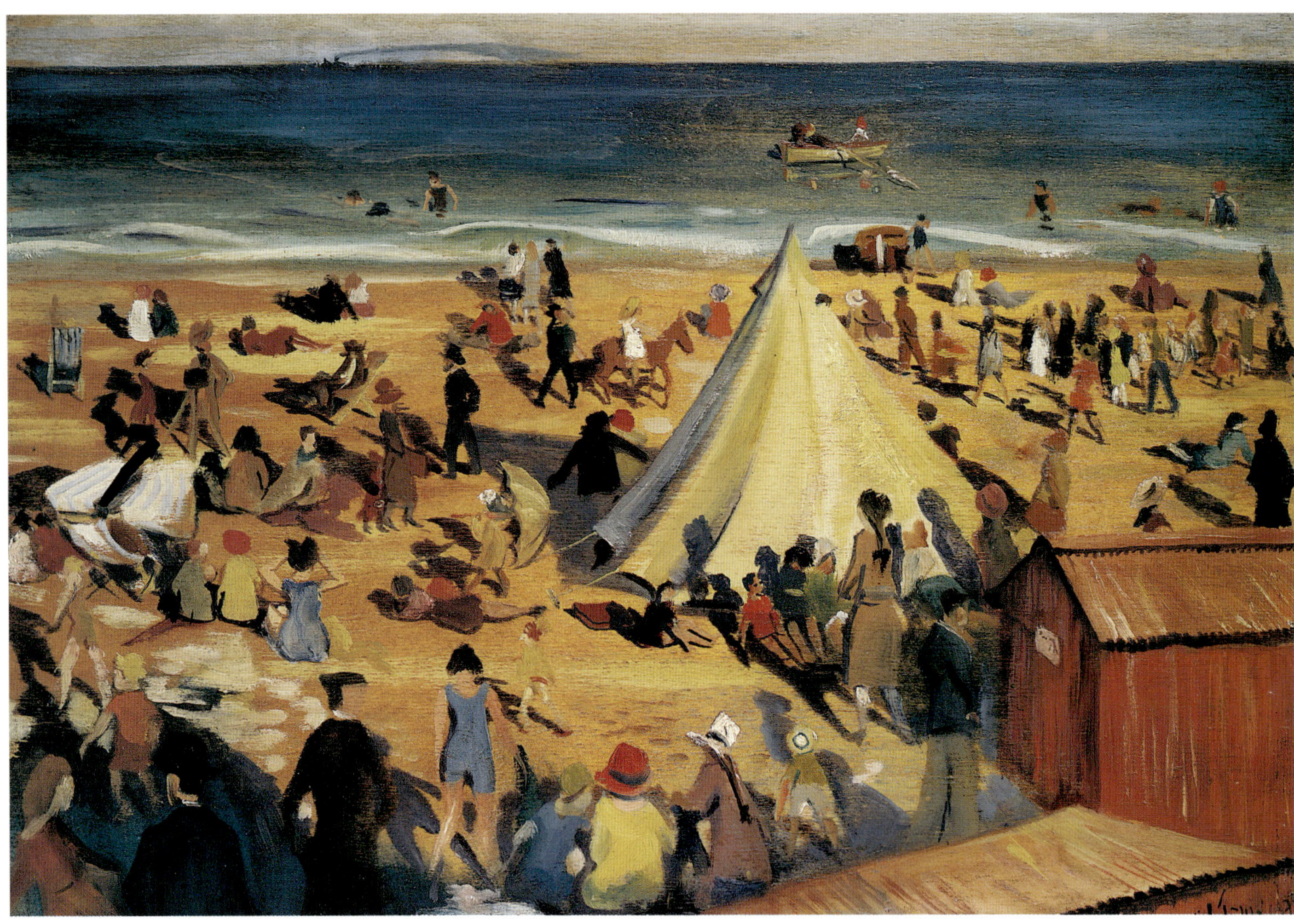

Harry Kernoff (1900-74)
61. Bank Holiday, Killiney, Co. Dublin
Exh. 1842
Oil on panel
36 x 46 cm
Private collection

disporting themselves at Leixlip (Paul Mellon Centre, Yale) are derived from the world of art, from François Boucher and more specifically Domenichino's *Diana Hunting* (Museo Borghese, Rome). James Arthur O'Connor's views of bathers at Ballsbridge (private collection) and Irishtown (cat. 53) begin the move towards a more realistic or empirical view of the subject. These changes were not chronological alone. William Mulready, for example, reinvests his bathing figures with a classical dignity quite at odds with the earlier and more prosaic example of O'Connor.

Likewise, beach scenes became popular in the Victorian and Edwardian periods, from Robert Ponsonby Staples to, most famously, William Orpen. One earlier example which can be compared directly with Kernoff's work, as it also depicts the beach at Killiney, is an oil by Richard Thomas Moynan of 1894 (AIB Art Collection). Unlike the bank holiday crowd in Kernoff's picture, strolling, swimming and boating, Moynan shows an emptier beach, with rather more decorous figures. Moynan's oil is very much a landscape with figures, with the focus on Bray Head in the distance. Kernoff by contrast, eschews the beautiful scenery of the Wicklow hills; his view is out to sea, with the emphasis squarely on the crowd scene. Reflecting the relaxed subject matter, it is a joyous picture of families enjoying their leisure time. This rather belies the fact that it was painted during the austerity, and uncertainty, of the Emergency. *Bank Holiday, Killiney* is a particularly attractive example of Kernoff's rhythmic, somewhat abbreviated, style. He deliberately leaves areas of the panel unpainted so that the golden brown of the unprimed wood, with the grain running from left to right, effectively represents the sand of the beach and gives a rippling effect to the whole work.

In contrast to the quickly painted and spontaneous *Bank Holiday, Killiney, The Forty Foot, Sandycove* is a more considered work. The sharp and curiously even light that floods the scene, contrasting with the elongated shadows along the lines of perspective, gives a feeling of other worldliness to what is otherwise a carefully observed scene. In this it echoes both the contemporary work of John Luke and the example of Georgio de Chirico, an artist whom Kernoff is known to have admired. The feeling of stillness and anticipation (again a contrast to the implied noise of *Bank Holiday, Killiney*) is shortly to be broken as the bather on the diving board plunges into the sea.

It seems that sea swimming was slower to become popular here than in England. While of course swimming was a popular activity for children living near the sea at all periods, as an organised activity, until at least the mid-nineteenth century, it was largely the preserve of the privileged. In the 1760s, for example, the duchess of Leinster bought a bathing lodge for her children by the sea at Blackrock before having the rock blasted away to form a pool. The opening of the Kingstown to Dublin railway made Blackrock, Seapoint and Sandycove accessible to Dubliners in search of sea swimming. The earliest evidence of swimming at Sandycove dates from 1849. Some time later, engineers from the Ballast Board and the Commissioners of Kingstown Harbour (who held the land in lease from the Carysfort family) cut into the rock to form two bathing places on either side of the Battery adjacent to the Martello Tower.[50] Sandycove Swimming Club was founded in 1882 and is still in existence today.

Although the figures in Kernoff's picture are all decorously clad, the wearing of costumes at the then all-male bathing was the source of at times furious debate; they were obligatory after 9am. In a bitter legal dispute, after the Commissioners' lease had expired, much rested on the matter of wearing costumes. At issue was whether the Forty Foot was subject to the jurisdiction of the Kingstown local authorities: Mervyn Wall, author of a 1960s pamphlet on the bathing place, recalled:

The case excited great indignation among regular Forty Foot swimmers as it was seen as an attempt by the local authority to restrict their immemorial right to bathe without costume whenever the urge took them…the present writer remembers being told by a Catholic clergyman that his father was prepared to go to prison in defence of this right. 'My poor father', the priest said 'always maintained that bathing costumes were unhealthy and that he defied the entire British Empire to get him into one.[51]

At the time the Forty Foot was very much a gentlemen's domain; indeed the same author noted that among the reasons for its popularity was the fact 'that women are strictly debarred from entry'[52] Certainly this all-male ethos is reflected in Kernoff's picture and again offers a different view of Dublin's leisure activities to the family day out on Killiney Beach.

The origins of the Forty Foot's name are unclear; certainly the water is not of the stated depth at this point. Nor, however, is the alternative derivation from the Forty Second Foot Regiment conclusive. Although stationed in Dublin for much of the nineteenth century, they were normally billeted at Richmond Barracks and it does not seem to have been shown that they also occupied the Sandycove Martello Tower. Surprisingly, given his interest in Joyce, Kernoff does not allude to the many literary and artistic associations of Sandycove and the Forty Foot. He excludes from view the Martello tower from which, in the opening section of *Ulysees*, Buck Mulligan proceeds to bathe. Mulligan's inspiration, Oliver St John Gogarty, recalled swimming at the Forty Foot with Arthur Griffith (and rescuing him on a return swim to Bullock Harbour), and also described bringing a most unwilling W.B. Yeats to swim at the Forty Foot. A little earlier William Orpen recalls seeing Richard Piggot, forger of Parnell's letters, swimming there.

County Dublin beach scenes continued to feature in post-war Irish art. Letitia Hamilton's *Portmarnock Beach* (private collection) rather echoes Killiney in its exuberant rhythm, while Rush and its bathers was one of the main subjects of Patrick Leonard's oeuvre. WL

---

49 Quoted in Snoddy 1996, p.235.
50 Wall 1962, p.13.
51 *ibid*, p.17.
52 *ibid*, p.19.

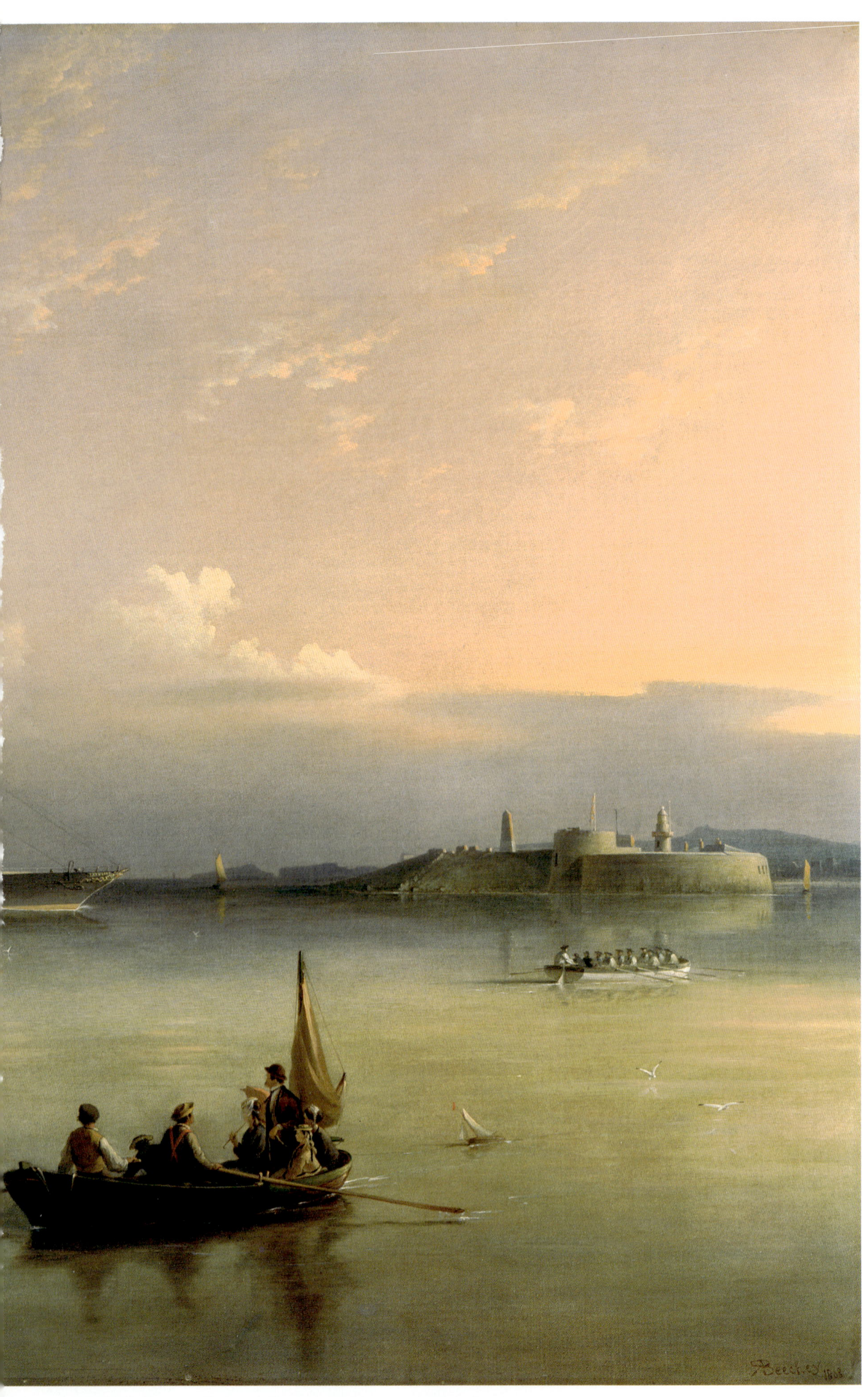

Richard Brydges Beechey
(1808-95)
55. The Royal Mail Packet 'Leinster' outside Kingstown Harbour
1868
Oil on canvas
77.5 x 110 cm
Private collection
See page 108

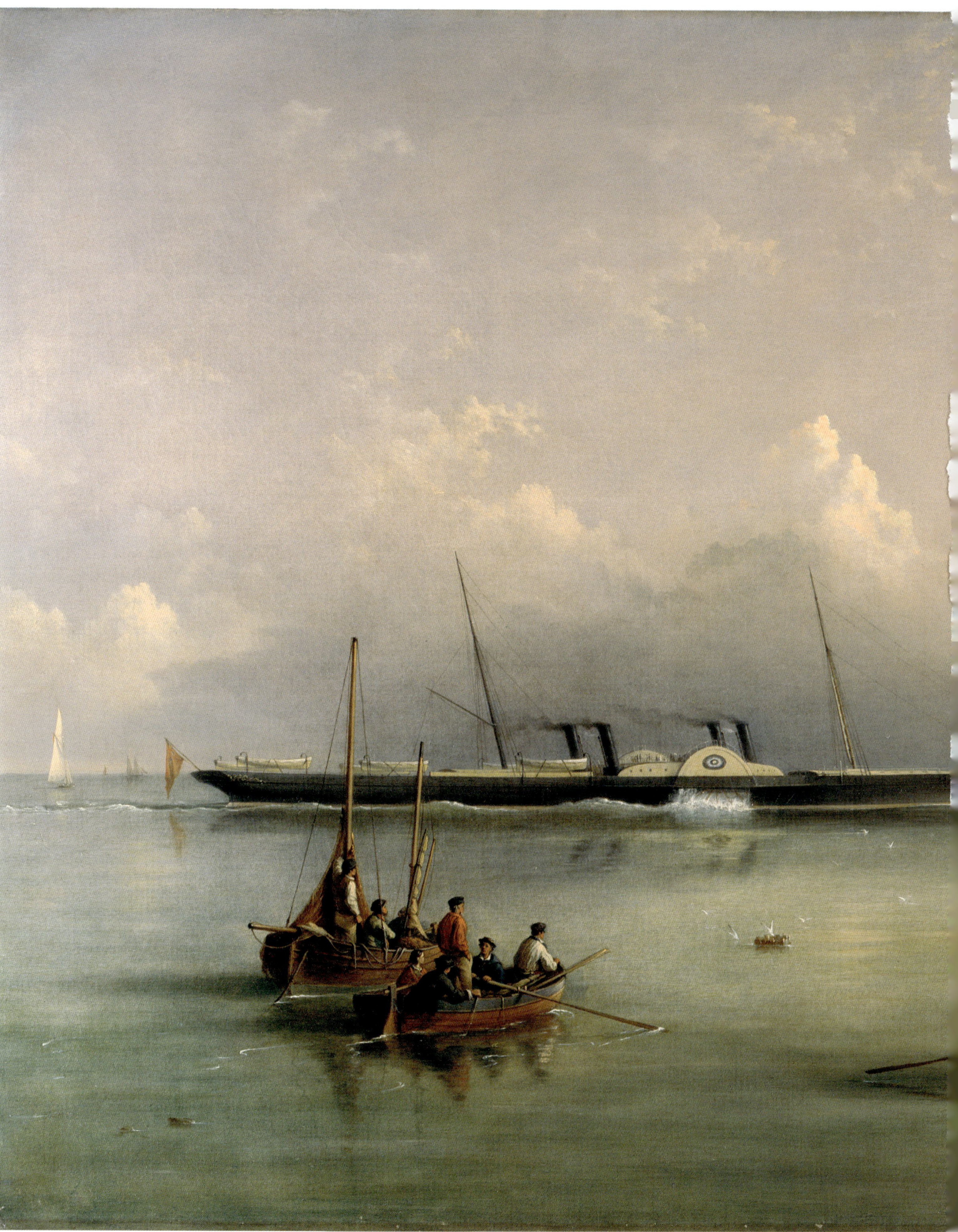

Louis le Brocquy (b.1916)
62. A Picnic
1940
Wax-resin medium on mounted canvas
40 x 40 cm
Irish Museum of Modern Art

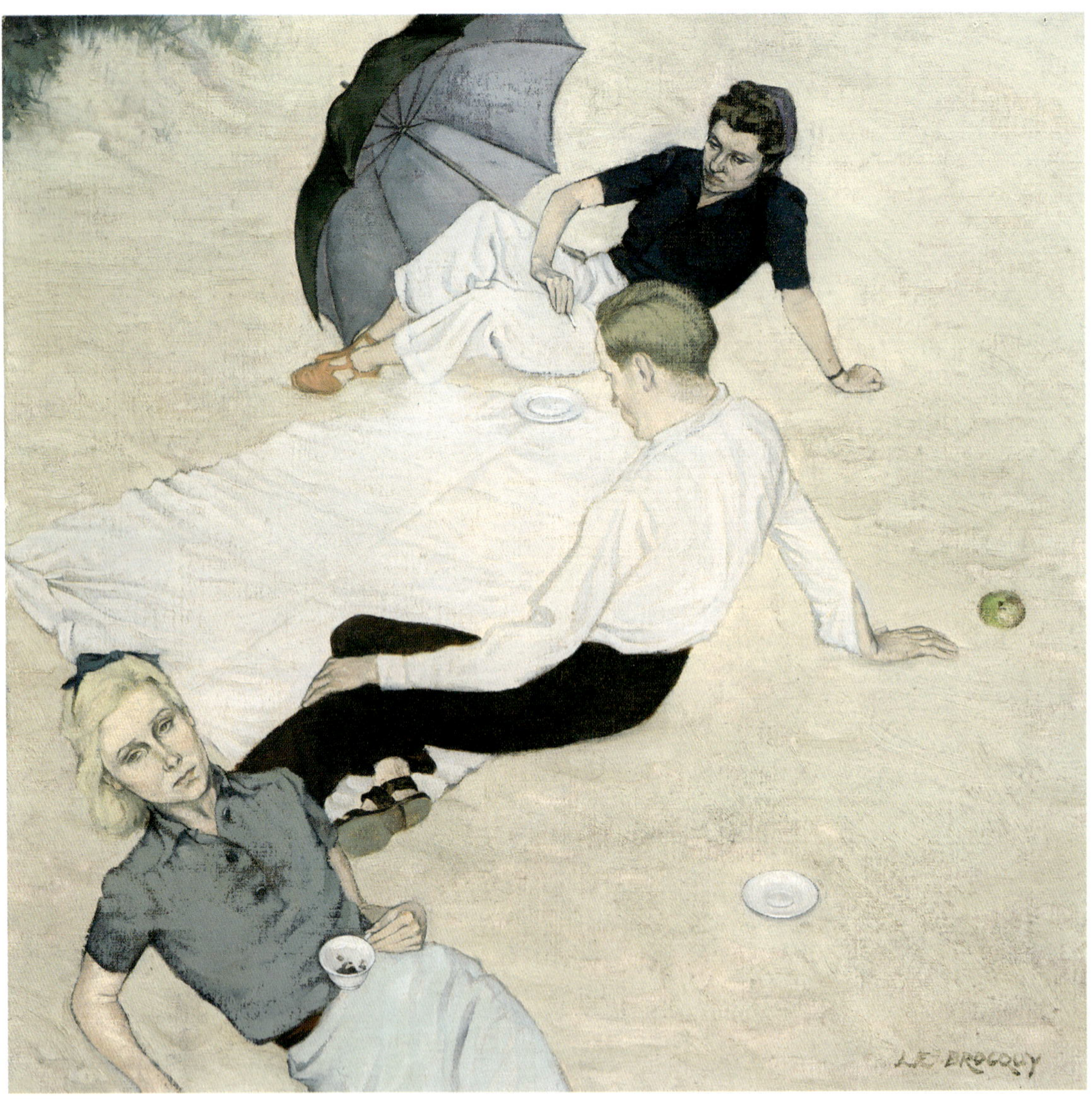

62. A Picnic

Louis le Brocquy

Though Louis le Brocquy is identified closely with ethereal images of the human head, which feature a distinctive palette with subtle dashes of colour, much of his early work displays an eclectic variety of artistic styles. Between 1938 and 1945, seeking an individual form of expression, he produced a body of work that ranged from the academic to the Modernist but was always confidently executed.[53] This method of artistic development may be attributable to the fact that le Brocquy did not receive a conventional artistic education. It was not until the age of twenty-two, when he left the family business, that he made the decision to pursue a career as an artist.[54] Encouraged by his mother, he travelled across Europe, visiting the great collections of London, Paris and Geneva and undertook the 'oldest method of learning', studying from Old Masters. [55] Indeed, his exposure to Spanish, Venetian and Impressionist painting was reflected in his early work. Two early pictures *A Girl in Grey* (Art Gallery, Kingston-upon-Hull) and *Southern Window* (Dublin City Gallery The Hugh Lane), both painted in 1939, show the influence of Manet, while his intriguing composition *A Picnic,* painted on his return to Ireland, was inspired by Degas's *On the Beach* (fig.31).

The sense of intimacy between the woman and girl and the more general social interaction conveyed in Degas's painting is conspicuously absent from le Brocquy's work, which he painted in his studio on the top floor of 16 Fitzwilliam Street, Dublin. Le Brocquy arranges his three figures, a man and two women, around a white cloth on a sandy beach, but eschews the social occasion in which they participate.[56] The cloth laid out before them is strikingly bare and appears to serve little purpose. Interestingly, each figure has been assigned an object with which one might associate social interaction: a cigarette, a cup of tea and an item of food. Disinterested, however, they gaze in different directions and connect solely as integral elements of the composition.

Despite its ostensibly simple subject, *A Picnic* is fundamentally an exercise in painting and bold composition. This is exemplified by the bird's-eye view of the subject, which flattens the painting and presents figurative elements as abstracted shapes, carefully arranged across the picture plane. This flattening of the surface represents an obvious reference to Degas, and demonstrates the interest in Japanese print-making that le Brocquy shared with the French painter. The elimination of shadows by the saturation of the scene with light emphasises further this planar effect.

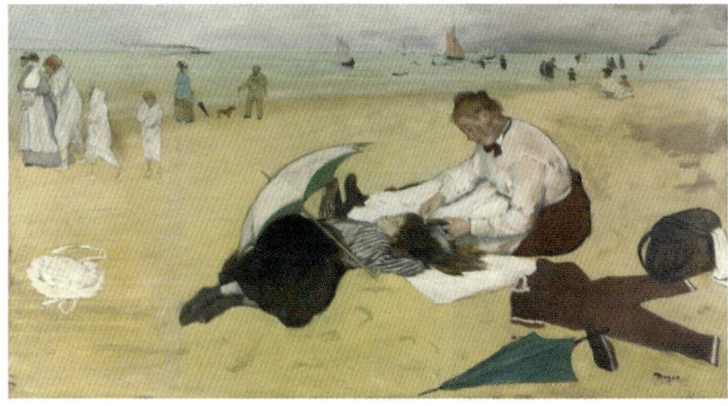

Fig: 31. **Edgar Degas,** *On the Beach,* 1876-77, Sir Hugh Lane Bequest

While Degas's scene extends to the horizon and includes a number of other figures as well as sailing boats in the water, *A Picnic* provides little sense of the world beyond the space inhabited by its three figures. Produced in accordance with le Brocquy's expressed interest in 'the art of painting',[57] the work demonstrates the artist's rigorous consideration of pattern and surface. Strong lines and a palette of neutral tones (inspired perhaps by Whistler) dominate the picture, and reflect the inertia of the figures. Although the surface of the sand is rendered with broad brush strokes, its pale yellow colour and the wax-resin medium create a virtually indefinable surface. Its contrived, abstract quality is interrupted only by the clump of grass in the top left and the small mound of sand created by the woman's red shoe. This shoe, the most strongly coloured element of the painting, anchors the surface to reality as it pushes sand over the cloth.

The three reclining figures, essentially separate life studies, demonstrate le Brocquy's superb draughtsmanship and keen eye for detail. There is, however, a distinct and deliberate awkwardness in their juxtaposition, particularly that of the woman in the foreground, who appears to slide off the bottom of the painting, with the two figures above. Le Brocquy has reflected that he was still learning to paint while working on *A Picnic*, and the lack of cohesion suggests a greater concern for pictorial arrangement than realistic rendering of space. Though the figures are socially isolated, they are compositionally connected. The central figure of the man bridges the gap between the two women and completes a continuous pattern that extends across the picture plane and terminates with the open umbrella. The umbrella, another direct reference to Degas, is composed of tonal sections and provides a strong contrast to the white rectangular cloth that occupies a large area in the centre of the canvas. The male figure's arm, meanwhile, and an apple and saucer, punctuate the large empty space to the right just as a discarded bonnet does in Degas's work.

Alistair Smith has opined that *A Picnic* allows us to witness the various concerns of the mature artist-to-be and hints at a number of thoughts that were to become major themes in le Brocquy's later work. [58] The isolation of the individual was a central issue in his series of paintings of travelling people and later in depictions of children, even those in a family setting.[59] Similarly, the human figure has remained a constant presence in le Brocquy's work, and the consideration of spatial abstraction and pattern in evidence here anticipates perhaps the metaphysical images that were to characterise le Brocquy's work.
DM

---

53 His early achievements were recognised by the RHA and from 1937-41 he was represented annually at the RHA until his painting *Spanish Shawl* was rejected, an event which partly led to the initiation of the Irish Exhibition of Living Art.

54 From 1934 to 1938, le Brocquy studied chemistry at Trinity College, Dublin and worked in his family's business, Greenmount Oil Company.

55 Crookshank 1966, p.8.

56 Le Brocquy's models were Sedra Osborne, Arthur Osborne and Patsy Stoney, sister of le Brocquy's first wife Jean Stoney.

57 Le Brocquy 1996, p.14.

58 Glennie et al 1996, p.20.

59 Walker 1997, p.38.

William Conor (1881-1968)
63. Coortin'
c.1922
Oil on canvas
75.6 x 50.2 cm
Collection Ulster Museum, Belfast

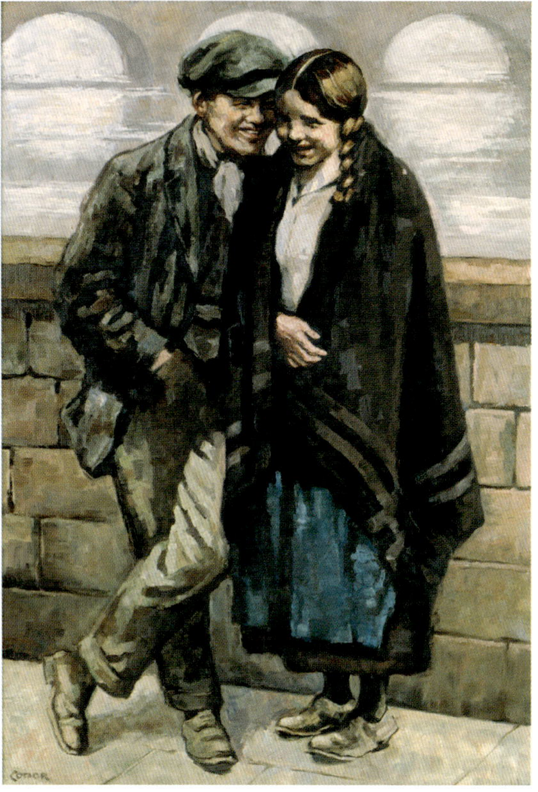

63. Coortin'

William Conor

A large proportion of Conor's pictures, despite their often austere setting, is characterised by the sheer good humour of the people who populate them. Courting, like singing, playing and competing in sport, provided welcome respite from the hardship of the working day.

As John Hewitt has noted, Conor struggled with anatomical accuracy in this picture, as elsewhere, particularly in the detail of the young man's crossed legs.[60] It is otherwise, however, a harmonious and unfussy composition that typifies Conor's approach to such themes. He was most successful, it is true, with what Hewitt has called the 'simplest arrangements',[61] and tended to avoid abstraction in his work. This clarity must be attributable to a large extent to his work as an illustrator, which was by its nature rigorous and measured. The deliberate manner in which Conor outlined his figures and arranged them frontally, visible in many of the examples included in this exhibition, may equally be traceable to the artist's practice as an apprentice poster designer in his early twenties.[62] A graphic quality certainly pervades his work, whether in oil or dry media. Conor also received important commissions for mural and costume designs for which he would have been able to draw on his considerable experience in producing graphic works.

It is interesting to note that John Lavery, whose approach to his work might be described as more painterly, greatly admired Conor. Lavery had been first introduced to him in London in the 1920s, and a short number of years later presented Conor's *At the Pump*, which he had purchased at an exhibition of Conor's work in New York, to the Brooklyn Museum.

With strong verticals and horizontals, this is a self-contained but deceptively complex work. Conor avoided expansive settings and compositions, preferring instead to focus his audience's attention on small groups and couples. Nowhere is this inclination more evident than in this picture, in which the young couple is presented in the shallow space between the viewer and the wall against which they lean. Cleverly framing their tilted heads is one of the arches of the bridge in the background. However, despite this controlled organisation of space, Conor has managed, typically, to communicate the essentially human nature of the scene. No extraneous details threaten to distract the viewer from the simultaneously intimate and universal narrative. With a modicum of detail Conor manages to imbue the figures with character, the young woman seeming as bashful as her suitor is mischievous.

This is yet another snapshot of everyday life in Belfast in which Conor specialised and excelled. Here the young couple wear simple, functional attire of a kind typical throughout the cities of Ireland and Britain. He sought to immortalise the mundane in his work, believing that it was in ordinary episodes and details that the true identity of local communities resided. His characters ranged from the mill worker, the 'shawlie' and the child playing, to the seanchaí and the musician, and his unusual ability to understand the city and represent the fabric of its life has been widely acknowledged. BR

60 John Hewitt, 'Conor's Art', in Wilson 1981, p.116.
61 *ibid*, p.118.
62 Conor worked for the lithography firm of David Allen & Sons Ltd for about five years.

64. The See-saw

William Conor

Jonathan Bell has quoted William Conor's close friend and fellow artist Mercy Hunter as having said presciently that Conor was 'a happy man and he painted things happily. And even if he was painting

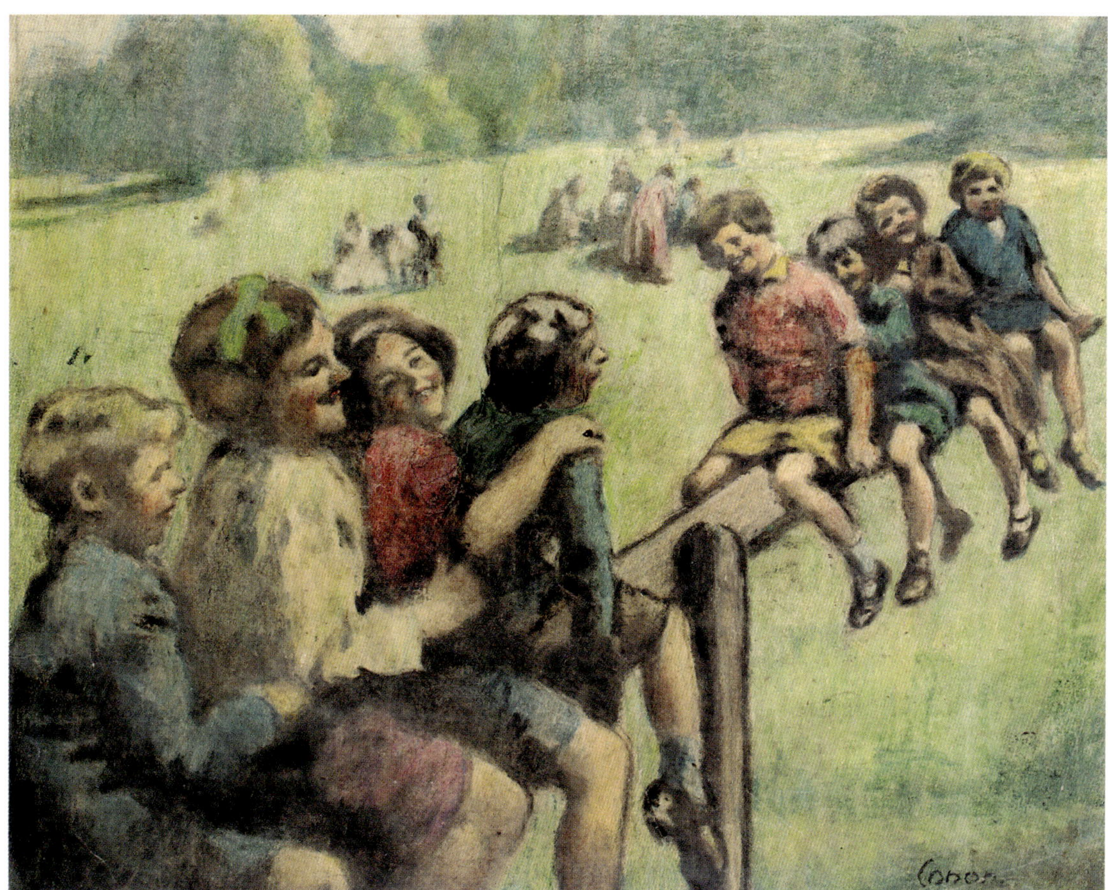

William Conor (1881-1968)
64. The See-saw
Wax crayon on paper
49.5 x 60 cm
Private Collection

poverty, it was a sort of happy poverty'.[63] It is true that images of the bleaker, desolate side of urban and rural life are conspicuously outnumbered in Conor's oeuvre. Conor did delve into the darker sides of life but it was in recording mirth, often in the face of austerity, that he excelled. His images of everyday life fall short of being celebrations of the triumph of community over adversity as they provide scant evidence of the true hardship endured by the socially disadvantaged. However, he cannot be said to have abrogated moral or social responsibility in avoiding the grimmer side of life in his art. His body of work was selective rather than obfuscating. It was, as Brian Kennedy has observed, fundamentally 'optimistic'.[64] Conor was neither by admission nor demonstrably a political or polemical artist.

The carefree, excited play of children on a see-saw on a bright summer's day can be seen as a kind of pictorial antidote to some of the harsher realities - illness, physical hardship, penury and unemployment - of life in working-class Belfast in the 1920s and 1930s, and a counterpoint to the daily toils of artisans and the lower middle-class. Significantly, and notwithstanding the complexity of Conor's identity, these pictures, including those of children at play, transcend the sectarianism that had crept with increasing virulence into Belfast from the late nineteenth century onwards.[65] Conor delighted in depicting recreational activities, from music and games to singing, dancing, visits to the beach, theatre and even polo. Other works, including *Lamp-post Swinging* (Ulster Folk and Transport Museum) and *Queue for the Picture House* (cat. 42) echo the cheeriness communicated in *The See-saw*, and reflect the artist's fascination with the collective nature of children's recreation. His ability to communicate glee and good-humour was unsurpassed. Nor was it one-dimensional. He could capture with equal alacrity the jovial confidence of an army recruit, the celebratory air of a wedding party, or the giddiness of a dancing couple. BR

63 Bell 2002, p.14.
64 B. Kennedy 1993, p.33.
65 This is not to say that the city's communities were represented equally but rather that Conor's paintings in essence record common, human experiences.

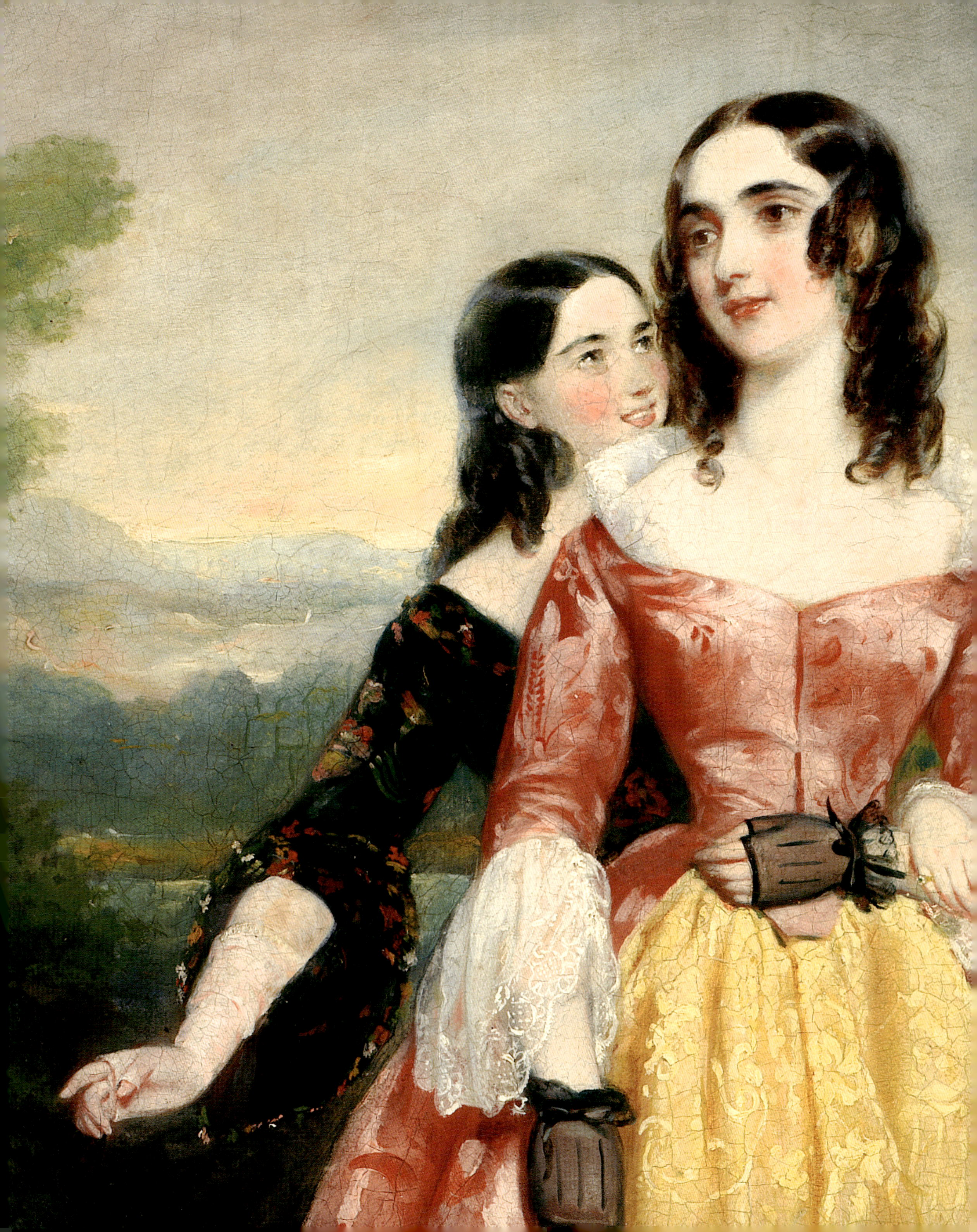

Clubs, Pubs & Parties

James Worsdale (c.1692-1767)
65. *The Limerick Hell Fire Club*
c.1740
102.2 x 77 cm
Oil on canvas
National Gallery of Ireland

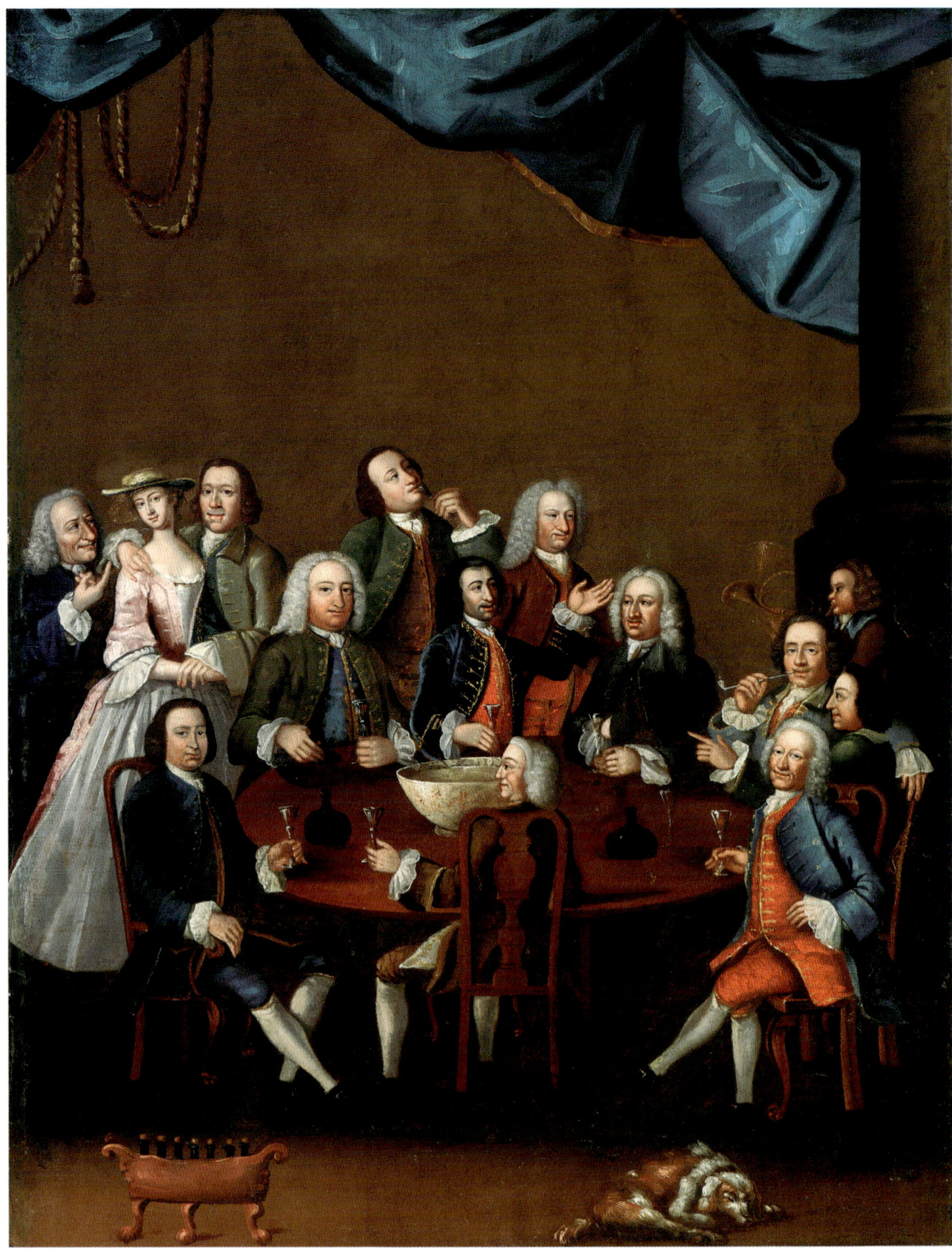

65. The Limerick Hell Fire Club

James Worsdale

The relative absence of the conversation piece as a genre in eighteenth-century Irish art has been commented on; this is particularly surprising given the informal conviviality for which Irish society of the period was noted.[1] James Worsdale's portrayal of the Limerick Hell Fire Club can be counted as one of the earliest surviving examples of this type of informal group portrait set in an interior. At the same time it gives a rare visual perspective into a specific group of provincial gentry society. As if posing for a photograph, eight members of the club sit around the large table, glasses in hand, other members striking poses behind. The column and drapery give an ironic monumentality to the scene of revelry, although this is rather undercut by the conveniently placed wine cooler and sleeping dog in the foreground.

The various Hell Fire Clubs were the most famous of the many, often interconnected, clubs, drinking societies and Masonic lodges that arose in the course of the eighteenth century. The original London club was founded around 1716 by the duke of Wharton and survived various attempts to suppress it until 1730. The artist of the present work, James Worsdale, together with the 1st earl of Rosse, founded a Dublin club in 1735. The members of the Dublin club were painted by Wordsale in a work commissioned by the 1st Baron Santry (NGI).[2]

Worsdale, a pupil of Godfrey Kneller, was resident in Ireland for about a decade from 1735. Of modest talent, he still met with ready success, though largely for his disreputable if entertaining character, which drew the condemnation of Swift. 'We thank your Good City [London] for the Present it sent us of a Brace of Monsters called Blasters or Blasphemers or Bachanalians (as they are called here in Print) where of Worsdale and Lints [Bernard Lens] (a painter too, as I hear) are the leaders'.[3] Two notes ring out in Swift's comments. The idea of sexual impropriety as being an English import– though he makes no mention of the Irish peers, lords Rosse and Blarney who were equally instrumental in the creation of the Dublin club– and the transgressive position of the painter, of uncertain social position in a society such as eighteenth-century Ireland both hidebound by social stratification and, at times, surprisingly fluid in the movement of men of talent between classes.

The sexual libidinous world of 1730s Ireland clearly attracted Worsdale. He is was one of the band of 'adventurers of the brush' who clearly found the frontier aspect of early eighteenth-century Ireland congenial with its at times relaxed morality and opportunities for adventure and advancement. According to some verses published in Dublin in 1740 he used his art as a tool of seduction; he would 'frequent, as Painter, his employer's house, and thence [delude] his mistress or his spouse'.[4] Others were even more direct in their criticism. 'A little cringing creature' wrote George Vertue 'we have known this painter – & have detected his barefaced mountebank lyes'.[5] However, given the paucity of portrait painters working in Ireland in the 1730s and 40s he won some prestigious commissions, painting, for example, the Lord Lieutenant, the duke of Devonshire. Also involved in the theatre, he was appointed Deputy Master of the Revels in 1741 by Luke Gardiner.

The Limerick Hell Fire Club met at Askeaton Castle under the stewardship of Edward Croker of Ballynagarde, who commissioned this group portrait. The club was unusual in including one female member, Mrs Blennerhasset. The poet Daniel Hayes gives a good impression of its riotous activities:

But if in endless Drinking you delight
Croker will ply you till you sink outright,
Croker for swilling Floods of Wine renowned
Whose matchless Board with various plenty crowned
Eternal scenes of Riot, Mirth and Noise
With all the thunder of the Nenagh boys
We laugh, we roar, the ceaseless Bumpers fly
Till the sun purple's o'er the Morning sky
And if unruly Passions chance to rise
A willing Wench the Firgrove still supplies.[6]

A plaque formerly attached to the picture plausibly identifies eight of the fourteen sitters, including Croker himself and his son John; Windham Quinn of Adare (the father of the 1st earl of Dunraven); John Bayly of Debsborough; Pierse Creagh of Dangan, and Henry Prittie (later 1st Baron Dunalley). A further member was Richard FitzGerald, 22nd Knight of Glin. Mrs Blennerhasset can be identified as the solitary woman in the picture, the man embracing her is presumably her husband, Arthur of Riddleston, while it has been suggested that the man on the far left who beckons to her suggestively may be Daniel Hayes, whose verses, quoted above, come from his poem *To Mrs Blenerhasset*.[7] As might be expected, membership of the club followed the close ties of friendship and family along which the squirearchy of Limerick operated – Henry Prittie, for example was the brother in-law of Edward Croker and very shortly after the picture was painted married the widow of his fellow club member John Bayly. Clubs such as this, the emergent Masonic movement, and indeed less obvious social gatherings such as hunts, manifested – and cemented – informal networks of political and economic power in remote rural areas to create a feeling of group identity.

The fundamentally social nature of these clubs was illustrated by their predilection for meeting in inns and taverns. Such focal points in Dublin included the Eagle Tavern in Cork Hill, near Dublin Castle, the King's Tavern in Fowne's Street and the Eagle in Eustace Street. Ultimately, however, all clubs became subject to some extent to the politicisation that increasingly characterised eighteenth and nineteenth-century Ireland. Many politicians themselves were members of more than one club, and sometimes of British as well as Irish clubs. The simultaneously social and political nature of these clubs has been described by Martyn J. Powell: 'the consumption that went on within Irish clubs was just as important as the consumption of political culture that came with joining a society'.[8] He has further observed that 'one's ability to carouse into the early hours of the morning could be an important asset to any aspiring politician'.[9] Certainly, Worsdale's portrait captures the 'lubricious atmosphere' of this segment of County Limerick society.[10]

Sometimes the indulgence of these clubs prompted admonishment, even from the likes of as notoriously excessive a figure as Lord Chancellor Fitzgibbon. He described the Dublin Whig Club as nothing but a 'porter club', while Alexander Haliday deemed the members of his own Belfast Whig Club as 'our northern guzzlers'.[11] The ascendant classes in Ireland were no strangers to bawdy behaviour. Nor was it restricted to private clubs. For instance, Kutu-kutu, a peculiarly Irish activity that involved squatting and hopping about with one's hands behind one's knees, was common throughout the country.

Although unusual in Ireland, the genre of portraits of gentlemen merry making had several contemporary English equivalents. Very close in date is Philip Mercier's *Sir Thomas Samwell and his Friends* (Beaverbrook Foundation, New Brunswick) while slightly later are George Knapton's portraits of members of the Society of Dilettanti. Mercier's image shows a Northamptonshire squire 'who obviously took great pride in his capacity to indulge in the delights of drunken bonhomie'. Solkin sees in it and specifically also in the Limerick picture 'the country interest's antipathy to cultural refinement, indeed its long-standing distrust of modernity in general.'[12] Here, although smartly dressed, the club members are clearly defined as provincial squires rather than Dublin sophisticates. Worsdale's clumsily naïve style accords rather well with the good-hearted revelry of these country gentlemen who, however much they may have affected to offend the pieties of Limerick society with their solemn oaths and initiation rites, were really nothing more sinister than a group of thirsty squires at play.[13] WL

1 Crookshank 1992, p.16.
2 For the commission see Strickland 1913, vol. 2, pp.536, 565.
3 Williams 1963-65, vol. 5, p.97.
4 Strickland 1913, vol.2, p.564.
5 British Library, Addit. Ms 23076 f.37.
6 Quoted in Crookshank and Glin 2002, pp.47-48.
7 Crookshank and Glin 1969, p.41. For further discussion of the identification of the sitters see NGI 1988 p.70.
8 Powell 2005, p.87.
9 *ibid*, p.151.
10 Barnard 1998, p.49.
11 Quoted in Powell 2005, p.87.
12 Solkin 1993, p.102.
13 For a discussion of rather playful aspects of Hell Fire Club imagery see, W. Laffan, 'From Paper to Pillar, *Miscelanea Structura Curiosa* and the Cumberland Column', in Laffan 2005, pp.18-21.

66. The Adelphi Club, Belfast

Joseph Wilson

Somewhat later than in the rest of the country, Belfast saw the rise of a series of private clubs and societies in the 1780s. This coincided with a period of rapid expansion in the town. The Chamber of Commerce was established in 1783, the White Linen Hall in 1784 and the Ballast Board a year later.[14] Dating from 1783, Joseph Wilson's group portrait of the Adelphi Club is a rare visual document of this moment in Belfast's societal life. Members of the club are shown in the private room of a tavern, seated around a circular table on which are shown glasses, two 'tapered-mallet' carafes of wine or brandy and a stone-ware jug of beer. A few books scattered on the table suggest the literary pursuits of the clubs members. On the wall behind hang two of the sitters' hats while small portraits decorate the room.

The Adelphi Club, consisting of the 'literati of Belfast', was centred on the colourful figure of Amyas Griffith.[15] It was one of several such institutions, with overlapping membership, that for the first time gave the town an incipient artistic and literary scene. Griffith and his friends were also members of the Philharmonic Society and the more politically focused Constitution Club.

The picture was commissioned by Griffith and, from the left, shows the actor Andrew Cherry, with an unidentified figure standing next to him; next comes Michael Atkins, owner and manager of the Belfast theatre, then Griffith himself holding a foaming tankard of ale; James Pilkington sits facing him, followed by the actor Richard Cox Rowe. Rowe is followed by Mr Haslett and Thomas Gibson, both merchants, the artist Joseph Wilson holding his palette and finally John Bernard, another actor. As

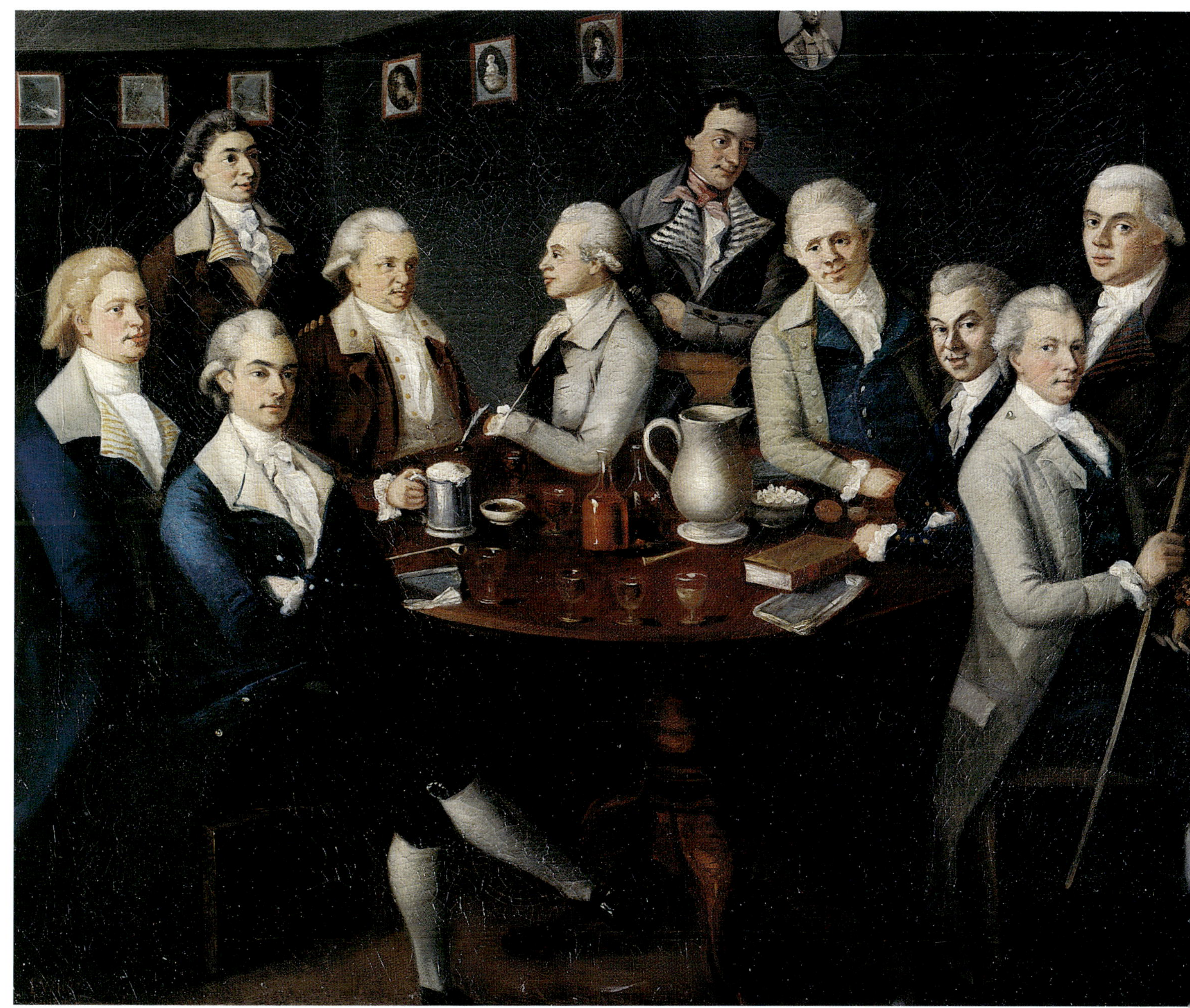

well as providing convivial society the club clearly served a networking function for its members. Cherry and Atkins were business partners and Atkins offered John Bernard a position as manager of his new theatre.

Griffith, founder of the Adelphi Club, was a difficult and controversial figure. Born in Roscrea, by the age of twenty-seven he was described as having an 'insatiable love of fame'.[16] He lived in Belfast between 1780 and 1785, serving as Surveyor of Excise until his dismissal from this position for his support of Waddell Cunningham in a contested by-election and for printing political pamphlets on his private press. John Barnard gives a memorable pen portrait of Griffith in his memoirs:

Though not eminent as a singer he was the leading talker of the evening: he had an original stock of ideas, and great fluency in delivering them. Unhappily he was deformed both in his back and legs, which procured from many the title of the modern Aesop. One thing, however, distinguished him more than his bodily peculiarities – a complacency of mind, which could not only tolerate his defects being alluded to, but permit him to laugh at them himself.[17]

Joseph Wilson (fl. 1766-93)
66. *The Adelphi Club, Belfast*
1783
Oil on canvas
61 x 74 cm
Private collection

The artist Joseph Wilson, a fellow member of the Adelphi Club, was closely connected with its founder. The *Belfast Mercury* for 13 January 1786 advertised an 'excellent likeness' of Griffith by 'Joseph Wilson of Belfast, portrait painter'. This was later engraved as the frontispiece to Griffith's *Miscellaneous Tracts*. Around the time that he painted the picture, Wilson joined the influential Masonic Lodge 257 of which Griffith was Past-Master and Captain General. Lodge 257 was itself intimately connected with the Volunteer movement. The seventeenth toast of the lodge, as recorded in Laurence Dermott's handbook, *Ahiman Rezon,* which in rather unmasonic fashion gives a full account of its practices and membership, makes explicit the links between Freemasonry and the Volunteer Movement. 'May the gallant VOLUNTEERS OF IRELAND inevitably unite in Brotherly ties and be as faithful to each other as Free-Masons have ever been found to be.'[18] Several of Wilson's portraits depict prominent Volunteers in uniform, including Lieutenant Hugh Hyndman (Ulster Museum) and John Bateman FitzGerald, Knight of Glin (private collection). Despite his rather limited talent as a portrait painter, he even attracted the patronage of the earl of Antrim, a member of both Lodge 257 and a leading Volunteer. Indeed, it seems very likely that by 1781, Wilson was himself a member of the 3rd Division of the Belfast First Volunteer Company.[19]

Little is recorded of the activities of the Adelphi Club. However, given the connection between the two organisations and the overlap of membership, the atmosphere of its meetings can perhaps be best captured by some verses composed for Lodge 257 and recorded in *Ahiman Rezon*:

In the social Amusements of Life let us live,
Prove every Delight Love and Friendship can give,
Where easy Good-nature gives converse a Zest,
And Sense in the bright Robes of Humour is dress'd
Where Wisdom & Strength and sweet Beauty combine,
Our Souls to improve and sweet Tempers refine.[20]

This self-improving, rather worthy, tone accords well with the sober, decorous manner in which the Adelphi Club chooses to present itself in Wilson's picture. They are neatly and appropriately dressed and only Griffith is shown holding a drink. This itself may have had patriotic connotations, rather than being mere refreshment. In his role as Surveyor of Excise, Griffith had imposed the 'Lagan Duty' on English beer being sold in Belfast. This earned him the gratitude of local brewers who in 1782, the year before the picture was painted, presented him with a silver club– presumably the one he holds so prominently here. When he fell on hard times in Dublin he bitterly recalled having to sell both the Adelphi Club picture and the silver cup, suggesting they were amongst his most prized possessions.[21]

Given the paucity of conversation pieces in eighteenth-century Irish art, a comparison with James Worsdale's *The Limerick Hell Fire Club* (cat. 65) is inevitable. This, however only highlights differences between County Limerick in the 1730s and Belfast in the 1780s, between country gentry and a developing urban middle class. Nevertheless, the two pictures are valuable – and rare – evidence of how different groups of Irish men chose to be presented at moments of informal leisure. As Powell has noted, 'clubs and societies provided largely homosocial enclaves of conviviality, sociability and social discipline that, among their many manifest and latent functions, endowed their members with greater social and political authority than they would get on their own'.[22] The actors of the Adelphi Club employed each other's services while the overlapping membership of the club, Lodge 257 and the Volunteer Movement, as noted above, gave Wilson many of his sitters. Indeed, although the theatrical resonances of the name Adelphi are clearly appropriate to the professional affiliations of several members of the club, this sense of the word was only just becoming current at the time the picture was painted (deriving from the Adams brothers' building by the Thames in London). The primary Greek meaning – brothers – with its Masonic overtones, recalling the subtitle of *Ahiman Rezon* – 'Help to a Brother' – is rather more apposite, suggesting the fraternal links of friendship, reciprocal patronage and shared political belief that clubs such as this fostered. WL

---

14 Black 2006, p.3.
15 Benn 1877, p.444, n. 1. For a longer discussion of the picture, and the issues of attribution surrounding it, see W. Laffan, 'The Adelphi Club', in Laffan 2002, pp.27-37.
16 *The Hibernian Magazine* (January 1773), see Millin 1932, p.168.
17 Bernard 1830, vol. 1, p.317.
18 Dermott 1782, p. xix.
19 Black 2006, p.5.
20 Dermott 1782, p.188.
21 Griffith 1788, p.65.
22 Powell 2005, p.82.

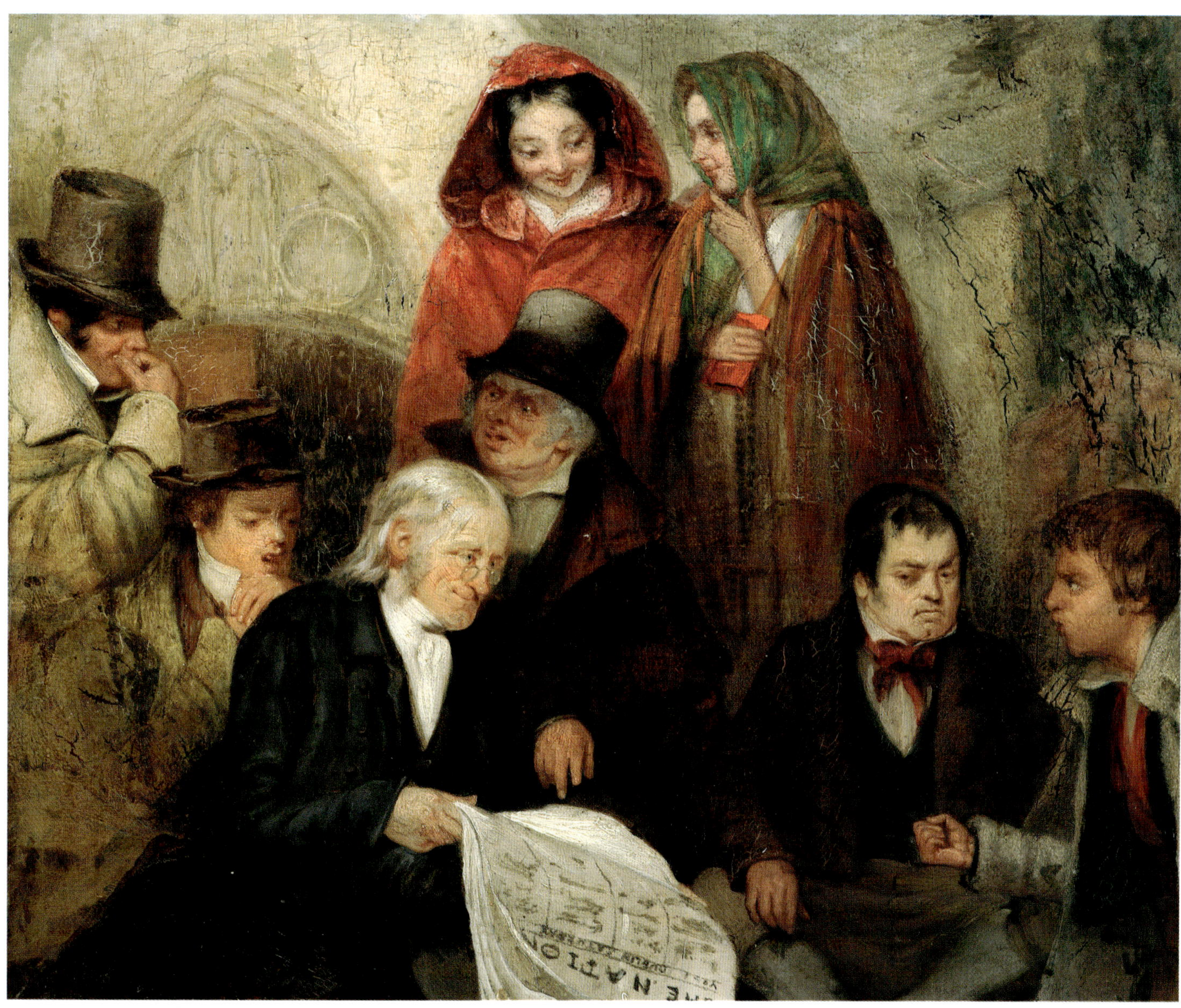

67. Reading The Nation

Henry MacManus

The Nation was a weekly newspaper founded in 1842 by three young barristers, Charles Gavan Duffy, Thomas Davis and John Blake Dillon, to promote the campaign for repeal and serve generally as the mouthpiece for the Young Ireland movement. It has been suggested that its inception was the result of a conversation between Duffy, Davis and Dillon as they strolled through the part of the Phoenix Park that later became People's Flower Garden.[23] John Mitchel was appointed editor of the paper following Davis's death in 1845, but resigned the post two years later due to political differences. *The Nation* was suppressed in 1848 for its revolutionary content, and though Duffy relaunched it the following year, it never recovered its radical cachet. By the mid 1850s it propounded a constitutional nationalist agenda and, having merged for a short period with the *Irish Catholic* in the 1890s, it merged with the *Irish Weekly Independent* in 1900 and closed down.

All three of the founders, Davis in particular, were interested in the arts, and discussions of literature, sculpture, music, painting and architecture became an important ingredient of the newspaper. Among those to contribute articles to it was the artist and antiquarian George Petrie. *The Nation* also featured comprehensive reviews of the annual Royal Hibernian Academy exhibitions. Duffy, Davis and

Henry MacManus (c.1810-78)
67. *Reading The Nation*
Oil on canvas
30.5 x 35.5 cm
National Gallery of Ireland

Dillon saw the arts as a means of regeneration and of bringing people of different religious backgrounds together. In fact, such was Davis's fervour that he even approached Frederic William Burton with a view to establishing a national school of painting, but the artist demurred on the grounds that it could not be done in the absence of an equivalent school of poetry. Henry MacManus was a close friend of Duffy who, like the artist, was from Monaghan.[24] MacManus's association with Duffy and the Young Irelanders led him to convert from Orangeman to nationalist. He helped to design the Milesian Crown, 'a sort of jellybag hat with a crown shaped brim, made of green velvet and embroidered with shamrock', that was presented to Daniel O'Connell in Mullaghmast in 1843.[25]

Through his picture MacManus has attempted to celebrate the appeal of *The Nation*, and more broadly to communicate both the character and culture of the Irish, qualities that Duffy and his allies were eager to promote. As a white-haired gent, possibly a clergyman, reads the cover page of what may well be the first issue of *The Nation*, an animated elderly man points at the text and the figures to his left look on contemplatively.[26] The young men on the other side of the reader seem even more roused by what they hear. The younger clenches his fist defiantly, while his associate glances at the paper and ponders its contents with an expression of barely suppressed agitation. None of the men receives the news passively. In the background, two women, one wearing a distinctive hooded cloak, survey the group with an almost serene piety, one of them clutching conspicuously the distinctly Catholic attributes of a prayer book and rosary beads. *The Nation*, however, sought to be inclusive, and the gothic pediment of a church door in the background emphasises a common religiosity and culture within the group and alludes to Ireland's medieval Christian past. MacManus's picture thus extols explicitly such perceived virtues as patriotism, piety, and erudition. Some years earlier, Thomas Crofton Croker had described rural Ireland as having a similarly learned and refined community, claiming that 'amongst the peasantry, classical learning is not uncommon; and a tattered Ovid or Virgil may be found even in the hands of common labourers'.[27]

MacManus's painting is, in short, a propagandist image presented in the guise of an orthodox genre picture.[28] Its message is delivered on the simple and accurate premise that newspapers and pamphlets attracted a significant audience in Ireland in the mid-nineteenth century. Over the subsequent century, artists illustrated in their work the key role played by newspapers in reporting events of personal and national import, reflecting shared experiences (such as emigration), garnering political support and mobilising the public. The artists' standpoints differ, so that while Helmick in *News of the Land League* (cat. 68) addresses the dissemination of information on the nationalist movement, Richard Thomas Moynan laments the death of Queen Victoria with his *The Street Arab's Tribute (The Death of the Queen)* (both NGI).[29] In Charles Lamb's *Hearing the News* of c.1920-22 (private collection), he continued the theme established by MacManus.[30] In that painting, in which a group of three Irish peasants, one of them an austere-looking matriarch in a western shawl, listen intently as a fourth reads to them from a paper, reinforces the perception of the Irish as a literate, informed and politicised people. BR

---

23 MacGowan n.d., p.11. The protracted conversation was concluded under an elm tree in the park.

24 MacManus's Monaghan origins have been deduced from the earliest addresses from which he exhibited.

25 Sheehy 1981, p.25.

26 One can make out at the top of the page 'THE NATION/VOL 1/DUBLIN/SATURDAY'.

27 Croker 1824, p.326.

28 Significantly, the painting was donated to the NGI by Charles Gavan Duffy's own family.

29 Other depictions of newspapers and newsboys include Samuel Rowan Watson's *Wud yeh?*, Jack B. Yeats's *Dublin Newsboys*, Lilian Davidson's *Here is the News*, and Charles Lamb's *Hearing the News* (all in private collections).

30 S.B. Kennedy 1991, p.230.

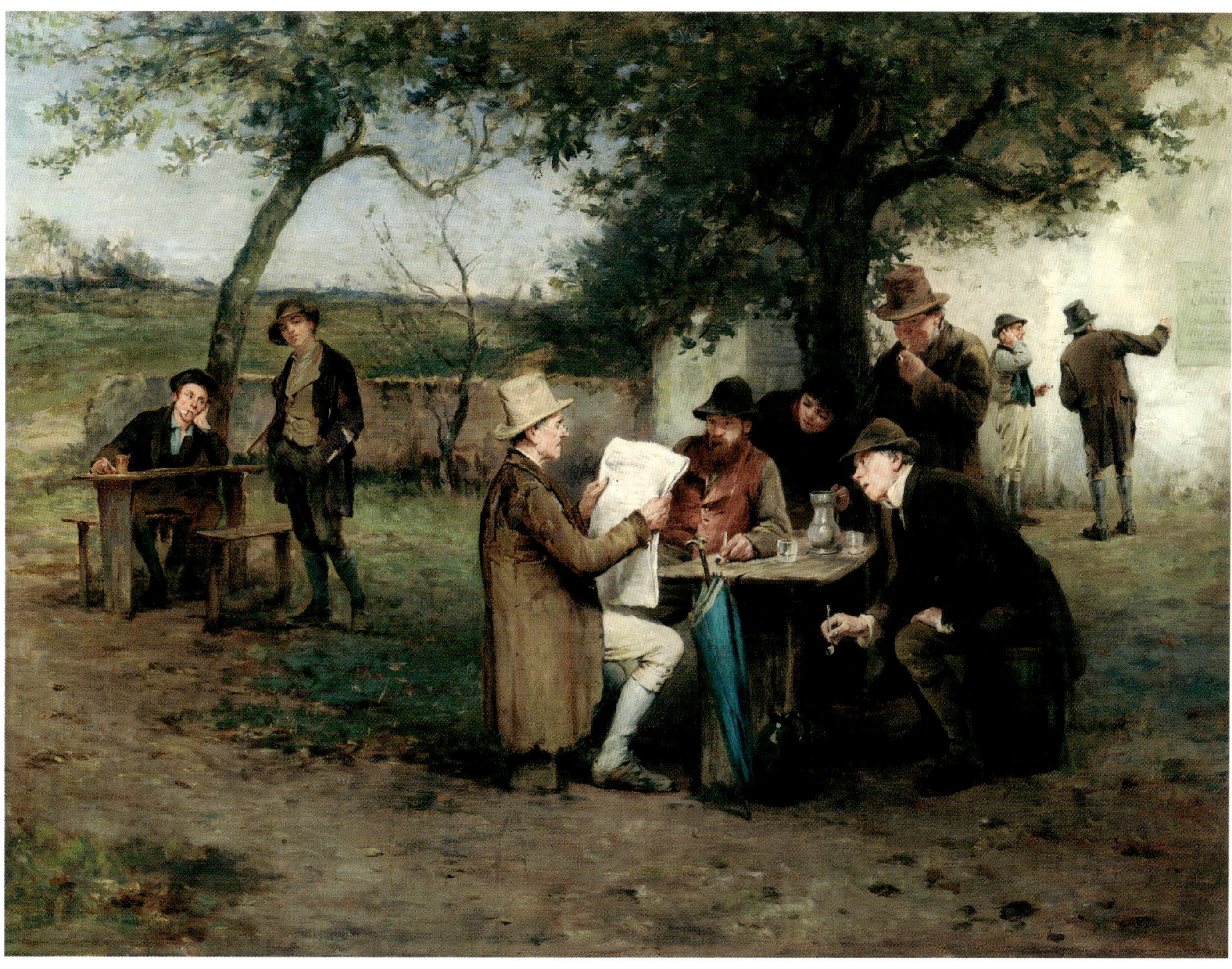

Howard Helmick (1845-1907)
68. *News of the Land League*
1891
Oil on canvas
80.5 x 105 cm
National Gallery of Ireland

68. News of the Land League

Howard Helmick

Howard Helmick visited Ireland repeatedly in the 1870s and 1880s to paint in studios in counties Cork and Galway. The resulting genre paintings shed light on aspects of rural life that native Irish painters often avoided as commonplace or controversial. Born in rural Ohio, Helmick grew to become an accomplished and successful painter, having trained at the École des Beaux Arts in Paris under Cabanel. He exhibited most of his Irish genre subjects in London at the Society of British Artists and the Royal Academy, but just a few at Dublin's Royal Hibernian Academy.

This topical political painting shows a man in a swallowtail coat reading a newspaper aloud to a country audience. In the background, a similarly well-dressed figure points out a poster, headed with the words 'Land League' and pasted to the back wall of a public house, to another man who scratches his head in puzzlement. The drinkers' expressions range from fascination to bemusement, while in the background two younger men seem interested yet aloof. The furniture is of an economical 'earth fast' construction, its legs held firmly in the ground, which was better known within primitive architecture.[31] Public houses were favoured locations for political discussions, and legislation was even passed to suppress this, by making it an offence to display 'any sign, flag, symbol, colour, decoration or emblem, except the sign of the house', a law that prevailed until 1960.[32]

Helmick's precursors in choosing this theme included David Wilkie, who introduced the subject of a newspaper being read aloud in his *Village Politicians* (private collection) of 1806. In John Boyne's watercolour *The County Chronicle* (private collection) of 1809, the artist adopted a pub setting for his richly symbolic narrative, in which a smart barber surgeon reads to country people about the perceived threat of French invasion.[33] Among the rural poor, newspapers were luxury commodities to be shared. The church door in the background of Henry MacManus's *Reading the Nation* (cat. 67), in which a more middle-class audience listen to one of their number reading from a nationalist newspaper, points to the role of religion within politics in the 1850s.

Literacy and politics were also central to James Brenan's powerful *Notice to Quit* (private collection) of 1880 and *Letter from America* (Crawford Municipal Art Gallery), the second of which Helmick doubtless noticed at the RHA in 1875.[34] Another less celebrated American painter, Mrs J. Lizzie Cloud, who exhibited twice at the same time and from the same address as Helmick, showed *Connemara Postman*, in which a letter is read aloud in a farm kitchen, at the Society of British Artists in 1872.[35] Several of Helmick's other gently satirical paintings, including *A Difference of Opinion* (private collection) of 1882 and *The Schoolmaster's Moment of Leisure*, exhibited at the Royal Academy in 1874 demonstrate his interest in politics and social issues.[36] His *News of the Land League* does not seem to have been publicly exhibited, and differs from MacManus's and Boyne's pictures, both of which show the papers' titles clearly. Instead he opts for ambiguity by literally brushing over the head of the newspaper to leave it as a grey area, when there was ample space for a legible title.

Founded in 1879, The Land League (under various names) led the exploited tenantry on a campaign for fair rents and rights, through years of agitation, boycotting and refusal of rents. In 1881, Gladstone's second land act (the Land Law (Ireland) Act) was passed in response to consistent demands for fair rent, fixity of tenure and free sale of holdings.[37] CK

---

31 Kinmonth 1993, p.31, fig.26.

32 Molloy 2002, p.57

33 Claudia Kinmonth in Laffan 2002, pp.38-42, cat.9.

34 Kinmonth 2006, figs. 116, 136 and 248. Erskine Nicol had painted his equally powerful *Notice to Quit* in 1862. Brenan continued to address the subject of literacy with *The Village Scribe* (1881) and *Bankrupt* (1881).

35 Kinmonth 2006, p.254, fig.247.

36 *ibid*, figs 215 and 246.

37 Before Independence, it was followed by the land acts of 1885, 1891, 1903 and 1909. Gladstone's first land act was passed in 1870.

69. A View of the Inn, Laytown, County Meath
William Sadler

70. A View of the Inn, Baldoyle
William Sadler

Though William Sadler's paintings at times lack the sophistication of works by his artist compatriots, his assiduous application to recording his native Dublin and its environs was remarkable. His pictures, such as *A View of the Inn, Laytown, County Meath* and *A View of the Inn, Baldoyle* (which count among many depictions of inns and guesthouses by the artist) are resolutely the product of a lifetime of looking.[38] One can imagine Sadler, perhaps more than any Irish artist of his generation, scouring the city for subjects, alert to local detail. With scenes from Donnybrook and Howth to the Phoenix Park, Sadler chronicled, as neither sentimentalist nor strict empiricist, the everyday life of the city.

Sadler worked predominantly on panel, which was less fragile than canvas, and consequently more portable. Indeed, some of his pictures have an immediacy that suggests that they were painted on the spot, and Sadler would have been able, if necessary, to place small panels on his lap rather than having to rely on an easel. The intricate detail that characterises much of his work would have been executed in the studio, but it seems highly likely that he sketched and composed his subjects outdoors. One presumes that Sadler also simply preferred working on panel. As a support, it certainly lent itself to the opaque, gouache-like effect that he favoured.

The wooden sign hanging from the seaward gable of the inn in Laytown, visible to passing boats, and the proximity of the building to the shoreline testify to the close relationship between coastal communities and the sea. Alarmingly exposed, but sturdily built, the inn is easily accessible by boat. Three figures enter the inn for sustenance and shelter, while another hauls his open boat onto the beach intending, one assumes, to follow them. The weather is closing in: storm clouds gather overhead and angry waves jostle boats moored by the shore. The smoke from the inn's two chimney stacks, and the advertisement for 'Best Wines' on the sign above the door hint at the comfort available within, while the loss of plaster from the façade indicates the regular punishment meted out to the building by winds off the Irish Sea.

The liberal nature of the alcohol licensing laws in nineteenth-century Ireland rendered setting up in the business a competitive but risky venture.

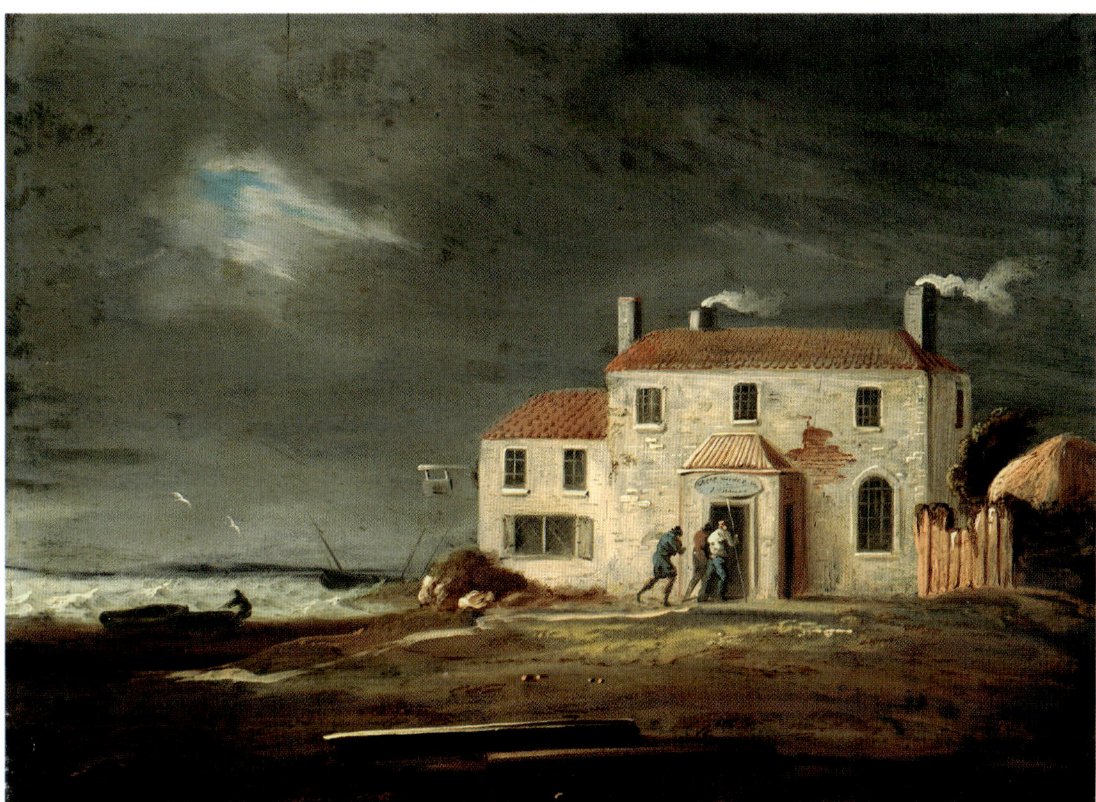

William Sadler (1782-1839)
69. *A View of the Inn, Laytown, County Meath*
Oil on panel
24 x 30 cm
National Gallery of Ireland

Moreover, the laws were not just relaxed, but notoriously impenetrable and poorly understood.[39] The Licensing (Ireland) Act of 1833 removed the limit on the number of licences that could be issued annually and restricted the grounds on which applications could be refused by a magistrate. The renewal of licences also became very straightforward. The Lord's Day Act of 1685, passed some 67 years after it had been in England, was the first formal restriction in Ireland of licensed trading hours. It prohibited the sale of alcohol on Sundays 'during the hours of divine service', allowed for the enforcement of this restriction by constables, and dictated that alcohol licences be renewed annually.[40] These regulations did not extend, however, to the setting up of beer stalls at fairs and other public events. Traders in those circumstances were merely obliged to have a certificate demonstrating that they had bought the beer and had paid the associated duty on it at a public brewery. Curiously, under the conditions of an Act of Parliament of 1760 the only parties denied the right to sell beer in this fashion were alehouse keepers who brewed their own beer. This ban lasted until 1825, when licensed brewers were allowed to trade alongside unlicensed competitors.[41] It was not until 1874 that an attempt to outlaw the unlicensed sale of alcohol was successful.

Inns and taverns had been in operation in Ireland since the Middle Ages as, under the influence of the Normans, commerce and trade became increasingly formalised and controlled.[42] The fortunes of the guesthouse industry oscillated over subsequent centuries and under various administrations,[43] but breweries, ale houses and taverns continued to flourish and proliferate. Both taverns (a term that originally had connoted establishments selling wine) and alehouses were being referred to collectively as 'public houses' by the seventeenth century, a term subsequently abbreviated to 'pub' during the nineteenth century. Pubs even saw off the competition of coffee houses so that by the 1790s, Dublin could boast around 1,300 pubs, with 50 on Thomas Street in the Liberties alone.[44] They were widely seen not just to provide refreshment and good company, but also as places where business could be conducted. A wide variety of beverages, both imported and local, would have been available in the pubs painted by Sadler.

Pubs and taverns on the outskirts of Dublin provided refreshment and shelter for travellers and became known as 'bonafides' or 'roadhouses'. By accommodating 'bona fide travellers', these establishments were afforded special licenses, allowing them to remain open into the early hours.[45]

William Sadler (1782-1839)
70. *A View of the Inn, Baldoyle*
Oil on panel
21 x 32 cm
National Gallery of Ireland

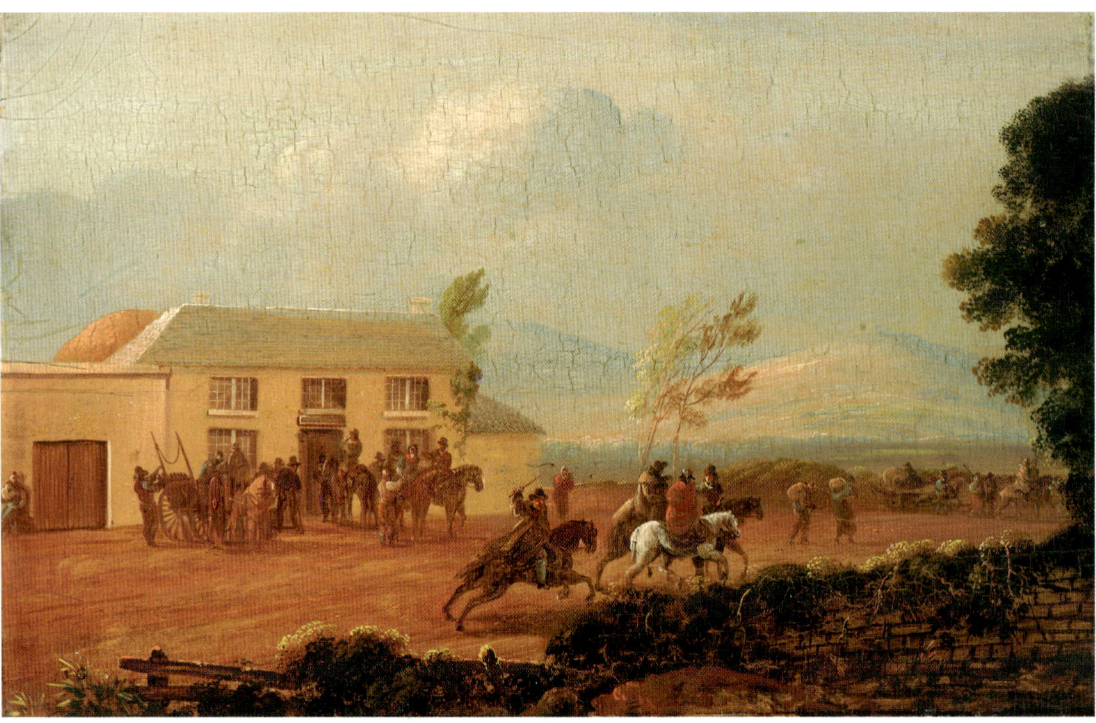

Their more liberal hours made them attractive to patrons frustrated by the closure of pubs elsewhere, particularly on Sundays.[46] The counterpoint to the growing popularity of the pub was the temperance movement, championed throughout the country by firebrand figures such as Fr Theobald Mathew and endorsed by, among others, Daniel O'Connell, whose own son founded a brewery in 1832.[47]

Samuel Lewis recorded in 1837 that Baldoyle, situated on an isthmus that connects Howth to the mainland, comprised 'about 200 houses, and is much frequented in summer for sea-bathing'.[48] It seems likely that as well as accommodating a healthy passing trade, as indicated by Sadler's picture, the inn would have been frequented by those employed, either directly or indirectly, in the fishing industry. According to Lewis, fishery at the beginning of the nineteenth century 'employed nine wherries belonging to this place, averaging seven or eight men each'.[49]

The early and sustained popularity of the public house was attributable to many factors including, in rural areas, its role as a social focal point for local communities and, in urban areas, to the fact that a significant proportion of the cities' lower socio-economic groups lived in cramped and squalid conditions far from conducive to socialising or relaxation. By the 1930s and 1940s, there was a large number of shebeens, kips and speakeasies (unlicensed drinking establishments) in Dublin's tenements and elsewhere, which attracted as regular a crowd as their legal equivalent.[50] Indeed, 'shebeening' became the main social outlet for many men in the poorer parts of Dublin. Equally, shebeens often provided the morning 'cure' for hangovers attributable to lengthy sessions in public houses the previous night. Relations between Dublin's reputable publicans and the operators of these illicit establishments were, understandably, often poor.[51] BR

38 For a discussion of Sadler's pictures of Dublin Bay, see Rooney 2004a.
39 Molloy 2002, pp.4-5.
40 *ibid*, p.31.
41 *ibid*, p.32.
42 Inns differed from taverns in that they provided overnight accommodation.
43 By the seventeenth century, there was a notable scarcity of accommodation throughout the country, including in the cities and large towns.
44 Powell 2005, p.8.
45 Kearns 1996, p.53.
46 The bonafide law was not abolished until 1960.
47 Fr Mathew claimed to have administered the pledge to some five million people, over half the population of Ireland.
48 S. Lewis 1837, vol. I, p.101.
49 *ibid*.
50 Kearns 1996, p.16.
51 See Kearns 1996, p.17.

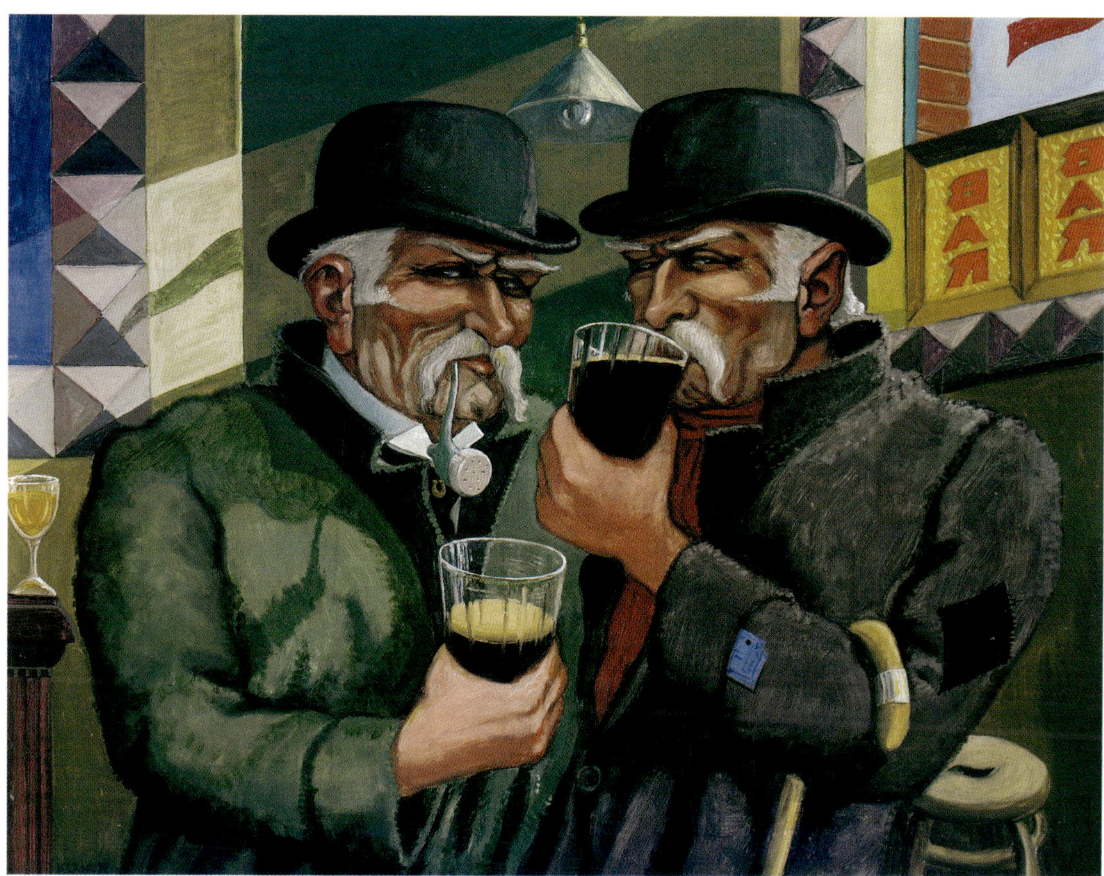

Harry Kernoff (1900-74)
71. *Twins. There's only a Few of Us Left*
Oil on board
61 x 75.5 cm
Private collection courtesy of Karen Reihill Fine Art

71. Twins. There's only a Few of Us Left
Harry Kernoff

72. In Davy's Parlour Snug
Harry Kernoff

Harry Kernoff executed many pub scenes, often of some of Dublin's best-known establishments, such as Davy Byrne's, The Bailey, The Palace Bar and The Brazen Head. He invariably presented them, either implicitly or explicitly, as places of both social and cultural importance, which were frequented by Dublin characters, where significant literary and artistic figures (often his friends) met, and where theatres like the Abbey and the Gate advertised their productions. In *Davy Byrne's, Duke Street, from the Bailey* (NGI), for example, two playbills, one for the Abbey, the other for the Gate, are clearly visible.[52] Kernoff often included himself in these pub interiors, wearing his distinctive wide-brimmed hat. In *In Davy's Parlour Snug*, the artist appears with Davy Byrne, proprietor of the eponymous pub, and Martin Murphy, set-maker at the Gate Theatre. Placing himself amongst such company, Kernoff asserts his position within Dublin's social, literary and theatrical circles, a position also implied by Maurice MacGonigal in *The Olympia, Dublin* (cat. 41). Through the Radical Club, founded by Liam and Tom O'Flaherty, Kernoff became a member of the Studio Club, which itself subsequently became Toto Cogley's Cabaret in Harcourt Street. Madam Cogley became one of the first directors of the Gate theatre, which provided Kernoff with a number of his notable sitters, including Mícheál MacLiammóir and Hilton Edwards.

The direct, engaging arrangement of the figures in *In Davy's Parlour Snug* is typical of Kernoff's portraiture (his sitters included such eminent literary figures as W.B. Yeats, James Joyce and Brendan Behan) but differs from what Crookshank and Glin have described appositely as the 'oblique' quality of his street scenes, exemplified by his *Forty Foot, Sandycove* (cat. 60).[53] In *Boon Companions* (Ulster Museum), an earlier watercolour, Kernoff, Byrne and Murphy are arranged exactly as they are in *In Davy's Parlour Snug*, but appear against a different background.

Kernoff was a regular patron of pubs like the Palace Bar, but not a heavy drinker. Indeed, his abstemiousness among his peers was admired, his friend Seán Gallagher writing from Liverpool 'you are the only man who can pressure an even keel. I don't know how you do it'.[54] Kernoff expressed his caution with regard to alcohol in 1960 with a poetic rebuttal to

'A pint of plain is your only man', the celebrated refrain from Flann O'Brien's *The Workman's Friend* :

> *Sheer escapism, of that there is no doubt.*
> *One wonders indeed what it's all about.*
> *Drink does not improve the work of a man,*
> *Moderation is the only right plan.* [55]

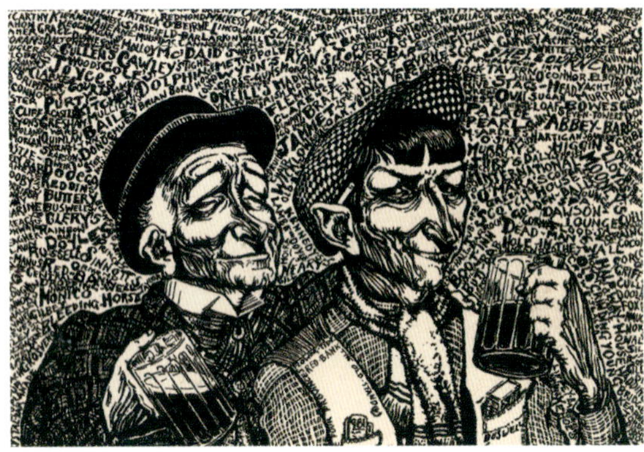

Fig.32. **Harry Kernoff,** *A Bird Never Flew on One Wing*, 1941, pen on paper, National Library of Ireland

Kernoff marked the central role of the public house in Irish society with *A Bird Never Flew on One Wing* (fig.32), in which two drinking companions toast their first drink (one wing) with a view to enjoying their next. The background of the drawing is filled to capacity with the names of Dublin Pubs that Kernoff had sourced from the telephone directory.[56]

Harry Kernoff (1900-74)
72. *In Davy's Parlour Snug*
1936
Oil on board
58.5 x 71.5 cm
Collection Lord Lloyd-Webber

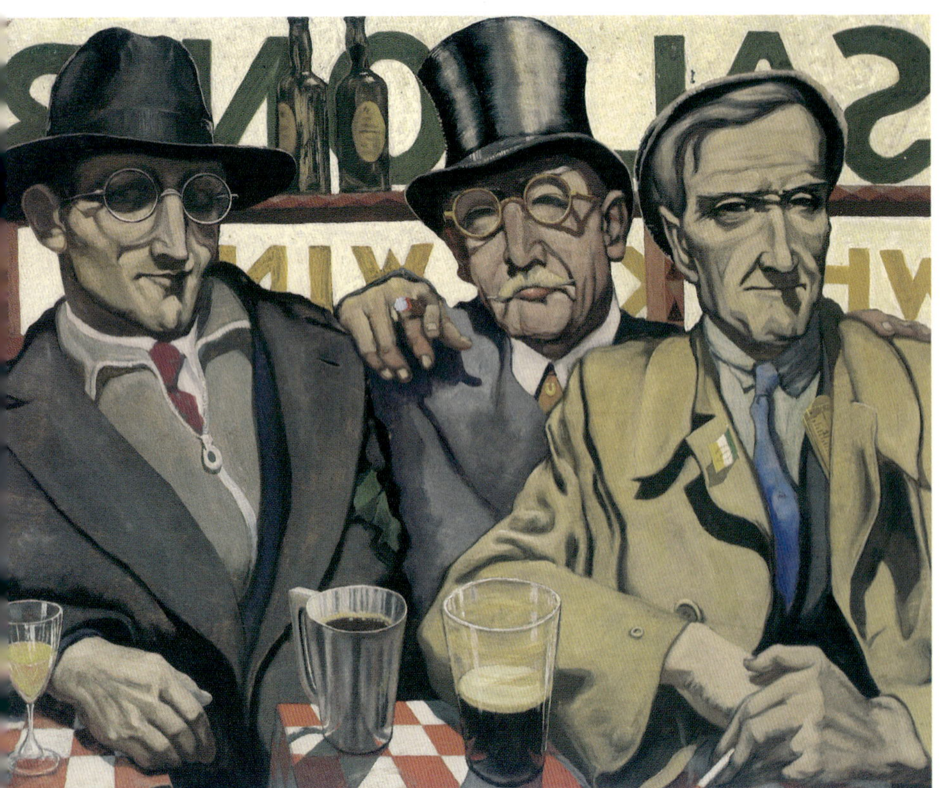

Davy Byrne's was one of a number of so-called 'Literary Pubs' in Dublin that were celebrated particularly between the 1930s and 1950s. Others included McDaid's, The Bailey, The Palace Bar, all of which are still in business in Dublin, and The Old Bull and Bush in Duke Street.[57] Here, Dublin's poets, writers, artists, journalists and intellectuals congregated regularly for 'stimulating conversation and social interaction'.[58] McDaid's regulars, for example, included Brendan Behan, Patrick Kavanagh, Austin Clarke, J.P. Donleavy and Liam O'Flaherty.[59] The society on show in the public house was also known to have informed the work of earlier writers, such as Synge, Joyce and O'Casey.[60]

Kernoff was among Davy Byrne's luminaries. Davy Byrne himself, indeed, was something of a celebrity, as implied by Kernoff's painting. Paddy O'Brien, head barman at McDaid's for over three decades, recalled that in 1937, Davy Byrne's was 'the only literary pub that was alive then'. 'It was,' he continued 'the 'in' place where you'd find St John Gogarty and those of his generation. They all drank there and made it a literary pub'.[61]

This association between literature and the public house may have its origins in the eighteenth century, as pamphlets, political publications, news sheets and the like were often launched in taverns and coffee houses and book auctions were frequently held there.[62] Furthermore, many printers and publishers shared buildings with taverns or were located adjacent to such establishments. Kernoff's views of pub interiors, perhaps unintentionally, affirm the status of the bar as a male domain, which it retained well into the 1960s. Indeed, many bars were explicitly (and legally) male only. BR

52 McConkey 1990, pp.172-73.
53 Crookshank and Glin 2002, p.292.
54 NLI, MS 20,917 (letter dated 1 May 1947). Quoted in McAuley 2003, pp.14-15.
55 NLI, MS 20,919.
56 McAuley 2003, p.14.
57 Journalists constituted a significant proportion of the clientele of the Palace Bar on Fleet Street.
58 Kearns 1996, p.5.
59 Other well-known pub characters were Miles na gCopaleen and the artist Sean O'Sullivan.
60 Kearns 1996, p.64. Yeats was a less enthusiastic patron of the Dublin pub, and like George Russell (AE) and George Moore, preferred to entertain privately.
61 *ibid*, p.65. McDaid's subsequently became synonymous with the bohemian set and could boast a volatile and entertaining coterie of artistic patrons.
62 *ibid*, p.63.

73. Invitation, Hesitation, Persuasion

Nicholas Crowley

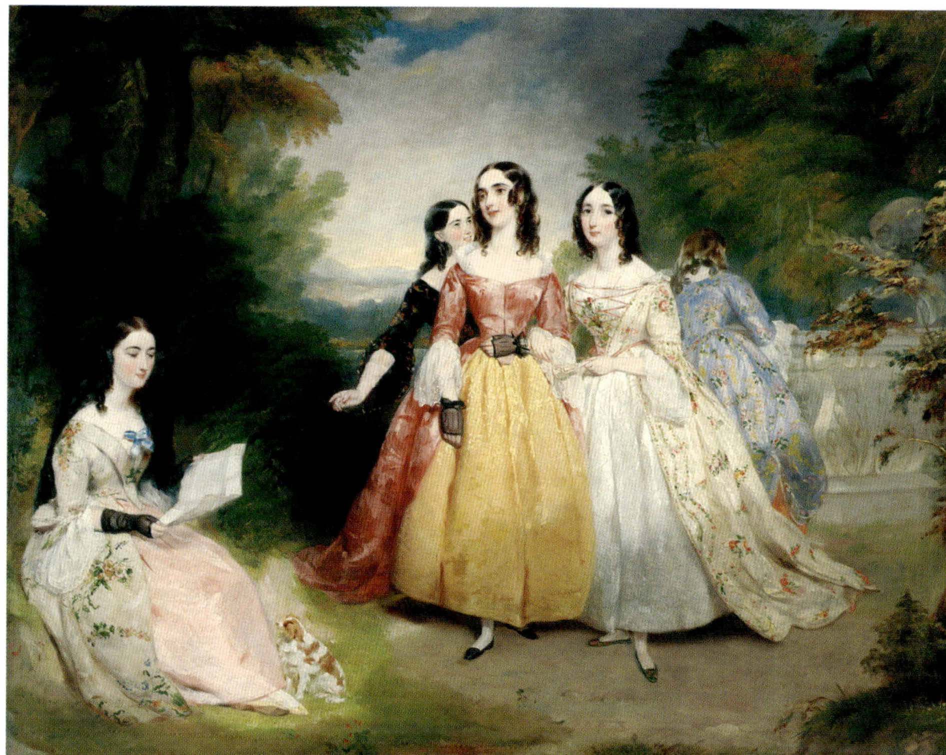

Nicholas Crowley (1813-57)
73. Invitation, Hesitation, Persuasion
Exh. 1846
Oil on canvas
102 x 127 cm
National Gallery of Ireland

Bearing an enigmatic title and unorthodox costume detail, Crowley's *Invitation, Hesitation, Persuasion* is a confounding picture. Though the title implies a distinct narrative, the detail of the picture does relatively little to elucidate it. It seems that the young woman at the centre of the composition arrives at a social event, closely attended by companions, one of whom links her arm protectively. The balustrade to the right, the verdant, picturesque background and the fact that all the young women appear without male or older escorts suggest that the event might be taking place in a rural, domestic setting, probably a large country house. One might infer, therefore, that the young woman has accepted her invitation to this society event, perhaps the celebration of a particular event such as a birthday, only following the intercession of friends. Furthermore, it seems likely that the event is a fancy dress party of a kind that was popular among the wealthy and upper classes in the nineteenth century in Britain and Ireland.[63]

Queen Victoria and Prince Albert helped to popularise fancy-dress as a relatively lighthearted alternative to the usual formality of upper-class entertainment in the nineteenth century by taking a prominent role in widely reported *bals costumés* at Buckingham Palace in 1842, 1845 and 1851. The second of these had a mid-eighteenth century theme.[64] Revival fancy dress was already, however, a well-established practice. Many eighteenth-century gowns (as well as other garments) were cut, reshaped or re-modelled decades later for fancy dress or other purposes. Indeed, the gown worn by Wolfe Tone's mother, which was modified for the centenary of the 1798 rebellion, resembles one of those gowns worn in Crowley's picture.[65]

It was well-known for revellers to dress in their ancestors' clothes for particular occasions, though party-goers did not necessarily adhere rigidly to period fashions. Significantly, the characters in Crowley's painting sport mittens, shoes and hairstyles that were fashionable for young middle or upper-class girls in the first half of the nineteenth century, but wear eighteenth-century gowns that may well have been retrieved from family attics. Typically, some of the skirts (petticoats) would have been made up for such occasions.

Much of Crowley's work betrays an interest in fashion and costume. Indeed, the prevailing taste in Ireland, following an English model, for historical, theatrical, religious and literary themes, as well as elaborate group portraiture, allowed Crowley and artists of similar sensibilities to indulge liberally their interest in costume. Crowley worked principally as a portrait painter, and some of his finest and most theatrical portraits, including *Tyrone Power as Connor O'Gorman in the Groves of Blarney* (Annaghmakerrig House) and *Taking the Veil* (St Vincent's Hospital, Dublin), display his modish fascination for costume and fabric.

Crowley's contrived, elaborate composition complements Mrs Hall's florid acclamation of Irish women, written just three years earlier. 'In writing of Irish women,' she says 'we refer to no particular class or grade; from the most elevated to the most humble, they possess innate purity of thought, word, and deed; and are certainly unsurpassed, if they are equalled, for the qualities of heart, mind, and temper, which make the best companions, the safest counsellors, the truest friends, and afford the surest securities for sweet and upright discharge of duties in all the relations of life.'[66] BR

---

63 The author is very grateful to Mairead Dunlevy for her assistance in the cataloguing of this picture.

64 See Baines 1981, p.129-30.

65 This gown is in the collection of the National Museum of Ireland at Collins Barracks.

66 Hall 1843, vol. II, p.315.

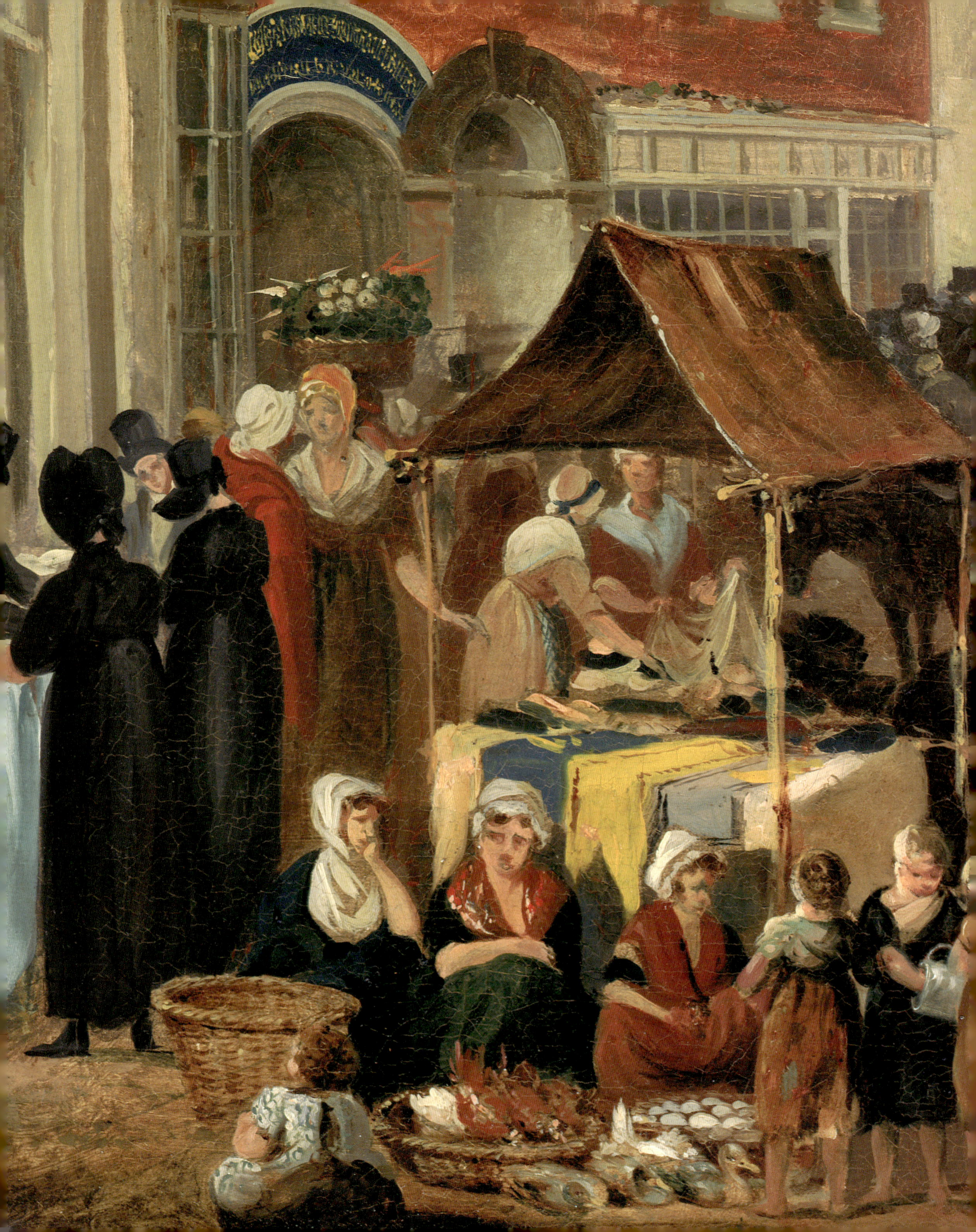

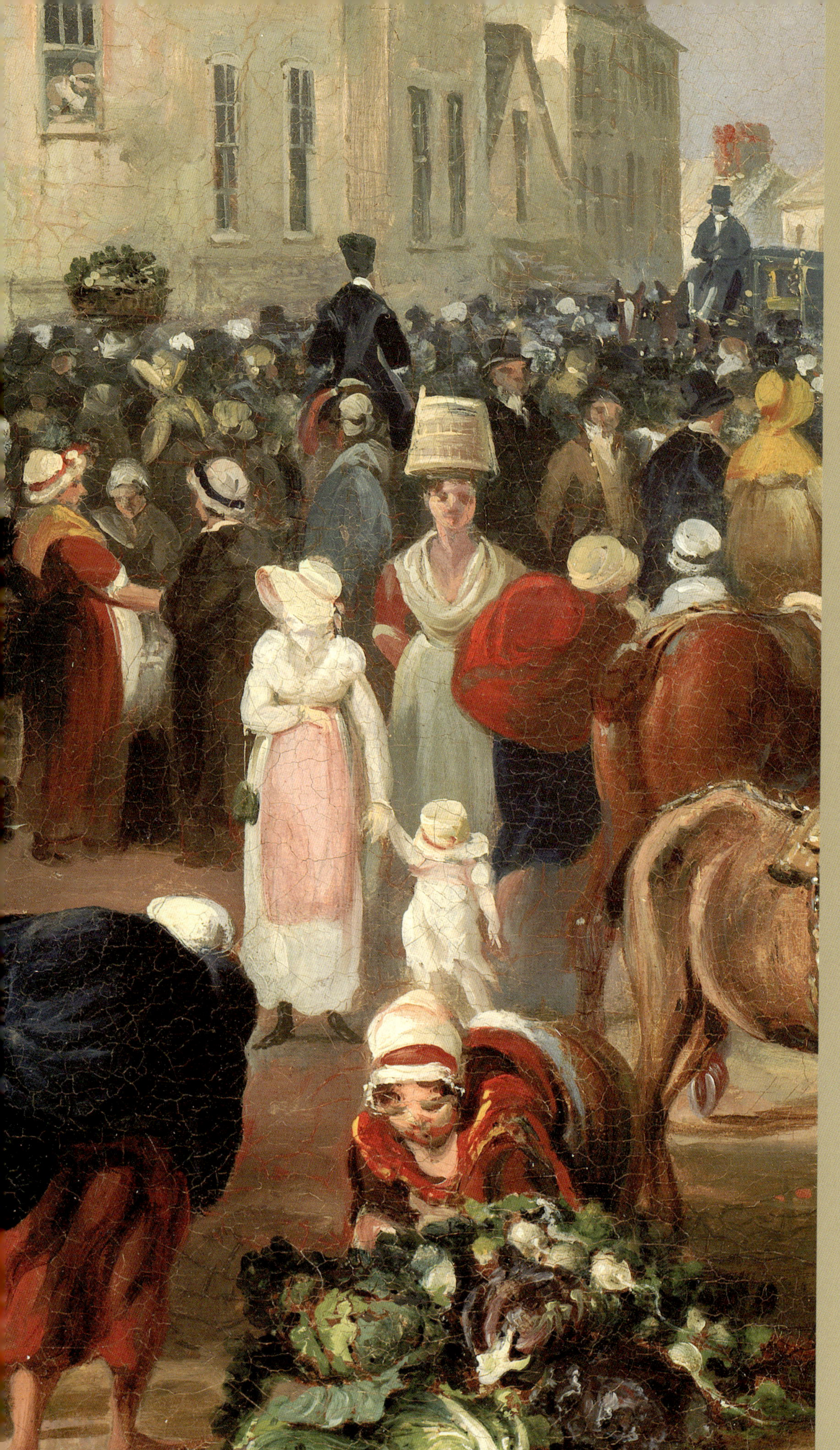

Fairs, Parades & Calendar Customs

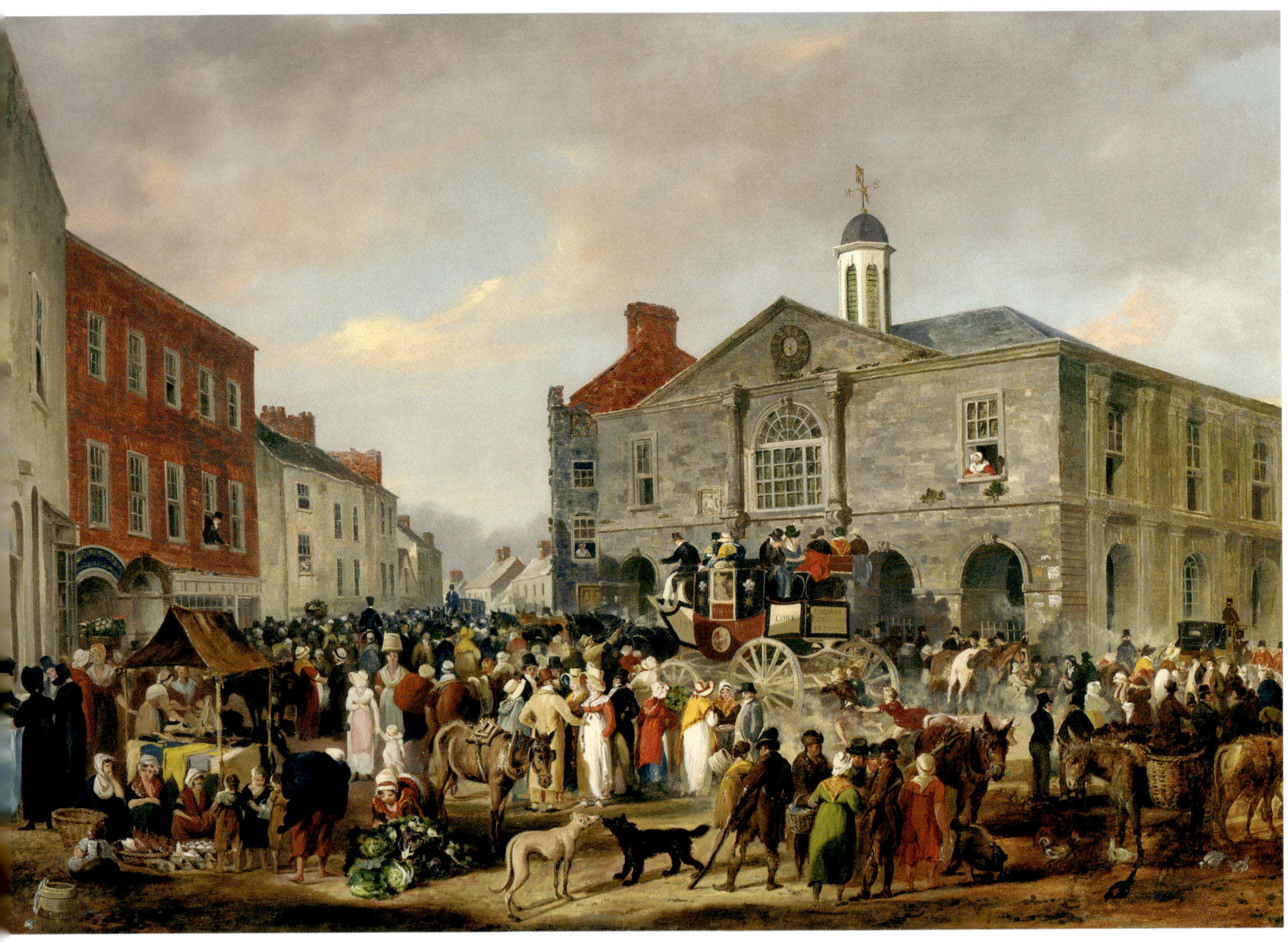

William Turner de Lond
(fl. c.1820-26)
74. *Market Day, Ennis*
c.1825
Oil on canvas
76.5 X 106.5 cm
Merrion Hotel Collection

74. Market Day, Ennis

William Turner de Lond

Crowded scenes within urban settings predominate among the comparatively few surviving paintings by William Turner de Lond. The suffix to his name indicates that the painter came from London, and in common with other artists visiting Ireland from abroad at that time, he provides valuable insights into aspects of material culture that are seldom described in words. The records of an art exhibition in Limerick held in 1821 inform us that Turner de Lond showed as many as twenty-five titles there amongst a total of sixty-four by professional artists. Ten of his pictures seem to have been of Irish subjects, possibly including this one. However, two closely similar versions of this painting have survived. The other one has three dogs in the foreground rather than two and an open window in the centre of the courthouse where this one is closed.[1] Otherwise, apart from minor changes such as the colour of one of the women's petticoats in the foreground, the two are essentially the same.

Turner de Lond has used artistic licence in the juxtaposition of classes, arranging the poor and labouring people in a crescent around members of the gentry, who in their clothes of pale creams, yellows and reds stand out in the sunlight. Such deliberate arrangement notwithstanding, details within the picture ring true and show us, for example, how the working women tied their shawls carefully behind their backs to their apron strings, and the way in which they carried pails of milk on their heads or huge creels of turf on their backs. In one instance, in the left foreground, a black shawl covers a woman's load. The painter again draws attention to the Irish country woman's role as tantamount to a beast of burden, by showing a donkey laden with turf (on the far right) immediately beneath a woman whose burden rope is looped around her forehead. The woman grips the rope behind her ears to balance the weight. A further contrast is provided by the immaculately dressed gentry above this vignette, riding horses with fashionably docked tails, and travelling in carriages. The contrast between the barefoot working women and the well-heeled ladies with their low-cut neatly fitted bodices and high bonnets could not be greater. Although market scenes had previously been painted by Nathaniel Grogan of Cork and Francis Wheatley, the portrayal of classes mingling so closely at such events was a relative novelty. Maria Spilsbury Taylor also brought an insightful outsider's view to the theme (cat. 81).

To the left the higglers and egglers, accustomed to travelling door-to-door to sell, lay out baskets of duck eggs, and assemble directly on the ground fowl that are alive or ready to pluck. An array of coloured linen, a more expensive commodity, is arranged behind them on a timber stall roofed with patchwork and against a shop-front, where elegantly dressed women in black gowns are being tempted by top-hatted salesmen. The courthouse appears to be the one built in 1733 on the junction of Jail Street by Francis Bindon (and subsequently demolished to make way for a statue of Daniel O'Connell). It was the commercial and social hub of the town, and functioned as a market exchange around its ground-floor arcade where 'produce could be weighed and traded on market days'.[2] By the early eighteenth century legislation was introduced to prevent local butchers from selling meat there, because of the inevitable blood, offal and mess. So instead we see the carcass of a pig being examined as it is slung across a horse's back, a convenient measure to sidestep such legislation. The clock on the courthouse façade tells us it is three thirty-five. This would have been eleven minutes ahead of Dublin, as Irish time was not standardised until 1859 with the introduction of railway timetables.[3] Each detail opens up an avenue of discovery, not least the historical importance of Ennis as a centre of market economy in the region. Its economic importance in County Clare was second only to neighbouring Limerick, to which it was conveniently linked by river as well as by the emerging network of stagecoaches, shown here as the centre of activity. The stage coach arriving is painted with its route 'Limerick, Ennis, Cork, Killarney' and is probably one of William Bourne's. He formed a network which by 1815 had to compete with that of Charles Bianconi, whose 'Bians' carried up to twenty passengers and came to dominate the network.[4]

Turner de Lond has captured with an actualist's attention to detail the congestion and commotion that attended market days in Ennis. Roy Foster has described the painting as a quintessential image of pre-Famine life, which presents a panoramic view of Irish society, and epitomises how life goes on in the interstices between major historical events (in this case, the Act of Union and the Famine).[5] CK

1 The other similar painting is now in the collection of the Knight of Glin. See Claudia Kinmonth, Judith Hill and William Laffan in Laffan 2006, pp.68-69, 106-08, fig.73, 190-97.

2 Brian Ó Dálaigh, 'The Origins, Rise and Decline of the Ennis Fairs and Markets', in Cronin et al 2001, p.54.

3 The corporation's responsibilities included maintaining the clock on the façade of the courthouse and the bell in the cupola. These served a crucial role in the management of the market as trading times were strictly regulated.

4 The coach from Limerick to Ennis travelled via Cratloe and Six Mile Bridge and terminated at the Coach Office on Church Street. Ó Dálaigh 1986, p.14.

5 Education Symposium, National Gallery of Ireland, 4 November 2005.

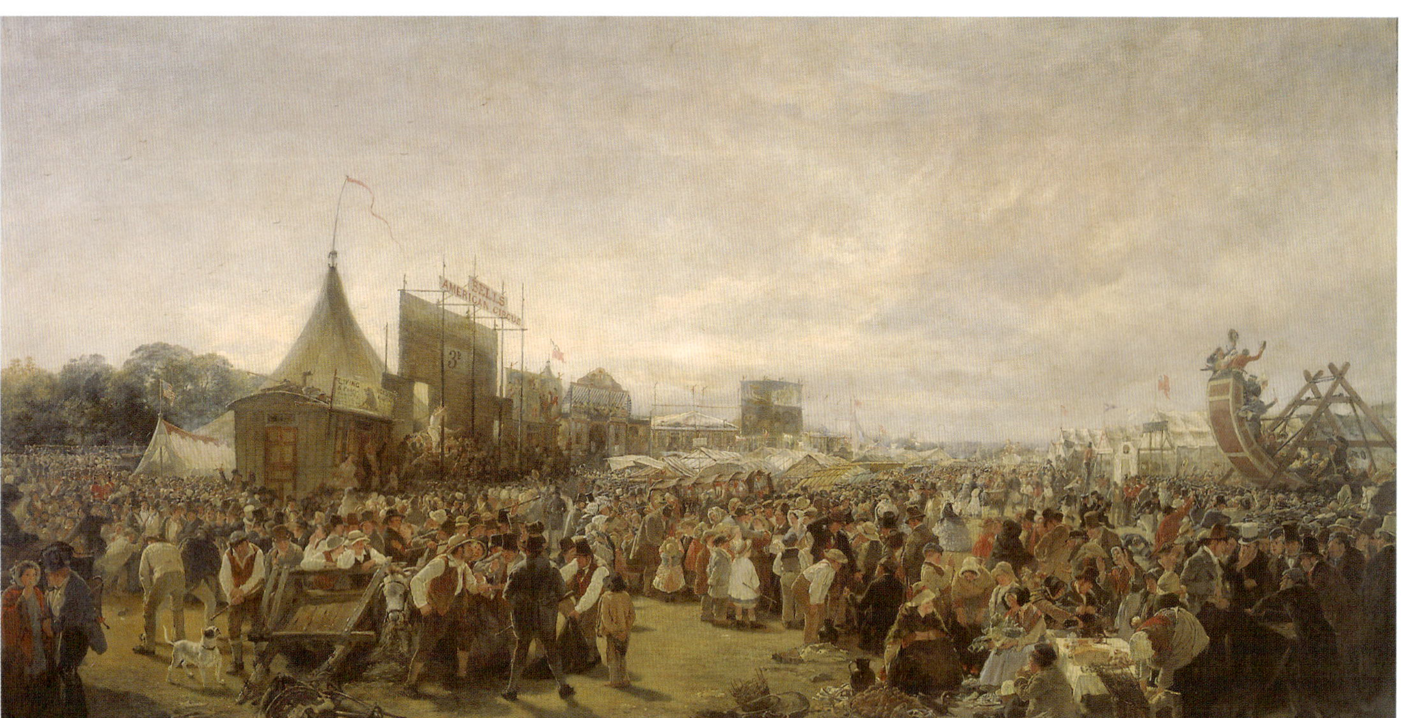

Erskine Nicol (1825-1904)
75. *Donnybrook Fair*
1859
Oil on canvas
102.7 x 210.8 cm
Tate. Purchased 1932
See Foldout opposite page 145

75. Donnybrook Fair

Erskine Nicol

Fairs and markets were a crucial element of the social and commercial life of Irish towns for centuries. While some of these were unruly, hedonistic affairs, most were relatively light-hearted and inclusive. Mrs Delany wrote that the fair in Killala in 1732 was to feature 'two horse races, one race to be won by the foremost horse, another by the last horse… a prize for the best dancer, another for the best singer, a third for the neatest drest [sic] girl in the company… tobacco to be grinned for by old women, a race run by men in sacks, and a prize for the best singing boy'.[6] 'Judge you', she enthused, 'if these will not afford us some good sport'.[7]

Donnybrook Fair, which dated back to the thirteenth century, commenced each year on the 26 August and ran officially for eight days. By the early nineteenth century, it often ran for over two weeks, but in 1837 Lord Mayor William Hodges, exercising his prerogative, restricted the fair to one week, excluding the Sabbath. For generations, the fair had drawn vast crowds from the country to the outskirts of Dublin for the sale of livestock and, more famously, the provision of entertainment. It was held on the green known as Madden's farm,[8] adjacent to the ancient graveyard in Donnybrook.

Nicol might be said to be indulging a certain nostalgia not just for Donnybrook Fair, which had been banned just four years earlier, but for fairs of its kind in general, which were in decline throughout Britain and Ireland. Brentford Fair, for example, was by 1860 a pale imitation of its old self, Nottingham Goose Fair was reduced in size in the 1870s, and Bartholomew Fair, like Donnybrook, was effectively abolished in 1855.[9] Interestingly, Nicol marked the demise of Donnybrook Fair elsewhere by including the poster announcing the ban in the background of *Whistling and Whittling* (private collection).[10]

Clearly legible in Nicol's picture is the sign above the entrance to a tent of the temperance movement. This may seem somewhat incompatible with the reputation of the fair for drunkenness and excess, but is consistent with that movement's strategy. Temperance rallies in the 1830s and early 1840s were themselves often elaborate affairs with floats, music and all manner of pageantry. Admittedly, by the 1850s, the movement was in decline and maintained only by a relatively small number of zealous members but Edward Lees Glew, a relatively little-known Irish painter, identified the movement as having played a pivotal role in the ultimate demise of Donnybrook Fair.[11] The 'peelers,' in his opinion, 'with the great temperance movement instituted by Father Matthew [sic], soon produced a reaction which materially interfered with the exercise of this privilege, and the renowned Donnybrook was eventually compelled to succumb to the march of intellect and morality, and take its place among the things that were'.[12]

Nicol's *Donnybrook Fair* represents the most elaborate and ambitious of many representations of the fair by successive artists from the eighteenth to the mid-nineteenth century. Wheatley, illustrating Donnybrook Fair in the 1780s, established a tradition that was to be continued by the likes of William Sadler, Daniel Maclise, George du Noyer, Samuel Watson, Samuel Lover, and numerous contributors to the illustrated press.[13] Such was the attraction and popularity of the subject that the abovementioned Glew copied and updated an existing painting of the fair by Samuel Watson and wrote a lengthy self-congratulatory pamphlet about his efforts.[14]

The 'fair-under-canvas' depicted by the likes of Wheatley and Sadler seems rather ramshackle when compared to Nicol's panorama of wooden-framed attractions and ordered lines of tents. In fact, it is curious that while the former type celebrates social order taking place in a haphazard environment, Nicol presents the viewer with a scene of chaos and unruliness in an altogether more ordered setting. Admittedly, these physical differences might also be attributable to the fact that poorer tents appear to have predominated around the fringes of the fair.[15] In any case, contemporary accounts of behaviour at the fair suggest that neither representation can be taken as wholly reliable.

Like many of his predecessors, Nicol has been careful to make legible as many of the signs and hoardings as possible. On the right hand side of the picture the 'temperance' tent sits incongruously between vintners 'Michael Costigan Stoneybatter' and 'T. Geoghegan', and opposite their colleagues 'Doherty' and 'Murphy from Rath[gar]'. More exotic are the names of the larger entertainments further back on the left, among them the 'Royal Menagerie', 'Bells American Circus' and, most curious of all, 'Living Wonders & Paddy Maguires Learned Pig Toby who can tell the hours of the day & discourse like a Christian'. Elsewhere, the stars and stripes of the United States billow above another entrance to Bells Circus. These colourful canvasses, signs, flags and painted hoardings were often carefully designed to accommodate low levels of literacy.[16]

Earlier paintings and illustrations indicate that theatre companies, menageries and circuses were an integral part of the activity by the 1830s. Many menageries, like Polito's and Wombwell's, travelled from Britain and elsewhere, no doubt attracted by the burgeoning numbers of visitors to the event.[17] These companies changed over the years, but the nature of their entertainment remained the same as the fair became a predominantly social event. Their initial representation coincided with the foundation of the Zoological Gardens in Dublin in 1830 (see cat. 49-52). One erstwhile visitor, writing in the *Dublin University Magazine* after the abolition of the fair, recalled the lions, tigers, snakes and even an orangutan that adorned elaborate hoardings at the fair, but lamented that the wretched animals themselves bore little resemblance to these advertisements.[18]

Clearly visible on the right hand side of the composition, heavily loaded with revellers as it careers upwards, is a swingboat very similar to the one placed equally conspicuously but rather more irreverently in Charles Lamb's much later *Pattern Day* in *Connemara* (cat. 82). Further back, the scarlet tunics of soldiers stand out amidst the throng. According to Glew, such characters, 'from the brave grenadier to the dashing dragoon' were a regular and popular presence at the fair. 'It is worthy of remark', he maintained 'that, not withstanding the natural antipathy existing in Ireland to Saxon rule, the British soldier is nowhere a more general favourite, especially with the fair sex, a red-coat being an almost certain passport to the heart of an Irish lady'.[19] Their presence was not necessarily benign, however. While the police force had responsibility for day-to-day matters of law and order, the army was deployed regularly at fairs, markets, political meetings and any other public gatherings 'at which breaches of the peace might be expected'.[20] Moreover, as a significant proportion of those who enlisted in the nineteenth century were of a rural background and/or in desperate circumstances, fairs and other 'haunts of dissipation and inebriation' were fruitful recruitment grounds for the army.[21] The writer in the *Dublin University Review* claimed that while press-gangs would not venture into Donnybrook during fair time, 'crimps and recruiting sergeants improved the occasion by treating unwary peasant or smoked city-tradesman to the villainous potations of the tents, and regaling their ears with the stirring patriotic songs of the day, so redolent of devotion to the Crown of England, and of hatred and contempt for the

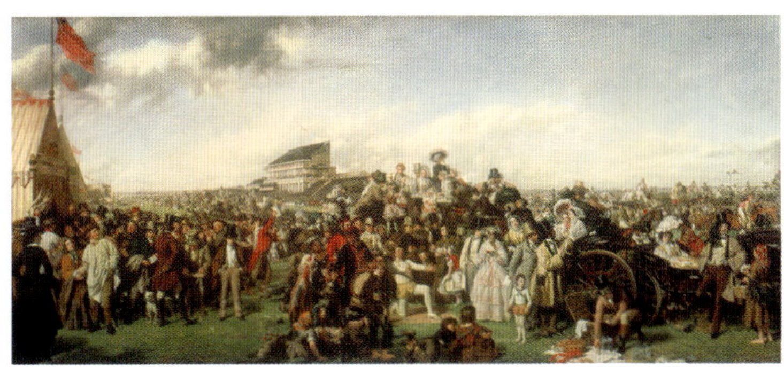

Fig. 33. **William Powell Frith,** *The Derby Day*, 1858, Tate Britain

Mounseers and Boney'.[22] Some believed, indeed, that recruitment was one of the crucial reasons for the survival of the fair.

This painting can by read reasonably as Nicol's response to William Powell Frith's seminal painting *The Derby Day* (fig. 33), which had been exhibited to great acclaim at the Royal Academy in London the previous year.[23] Admittedly, Nicol's painting does not feature the diversity of character, or more specifically, the cross-section of class that is evident in Frith's, but nevertheless represents a large portion of Irish society. While it would be overstating the case to claim that *Donnybrook Fair* divulges 'essential information as to the moral, intellectual and social standing' of each of its characters as Frith's had done, Nicol's painting, when considered in the context of all the textual and pictorial descriptions of the fair over decades does reflect a peculiarly Victorian, analytical approach to the subject.[24] It lacks the comprehensive and anthropological qualities of Frith's *The Derby Day* and *The Railway Station* (Royal Holloway Collection), but however superficial its kinship with Frith's paintings might be, even the most summary review of Nicol's representation of the Irish peasant will demonstrate that he was *au fait* with the current and modish perceptions of particular physical and physiognomic types.

A curious etiquette often prevailed at Donnybrook Fair despite the event's rather hedonistic reputation. Several nineteenth-century accounts record that it was common practice among those attending the fair to don their finest clothes before indulging wholeheartedly in the large variety of consumables available. Nicol's picture corroborates this, but elsewhere departs from those contemporaneous accounts and illustrations that lampooned the event and those who attended it. The artist's perceived predilection for the 'stage Irishman' may appear to be in evidence in many areas of the composition, but is contradicted elsewhere and is at odds with his elevation of the subject to such a grand scale. With a painting of unmistakably salon dimensions, Nicol successfully communicates the remarkable popularity of the fair by the nineteenth century. In 1841, for example, John and Peter Madden, owners of the patent to the fair, recorded the attendance on one day alone, the 26 August, as 74,792.[25]

Regrettably, perhaps, a constant in representations of Donnybrook and other fairs and patterns are the raised cudgels of faction fighting. Glew pronounced that 'a fight in Donnybrook fair was regarded as an indispensable pastime',[26] Thomas Crofton Croker declared that 'a fair, patron or other public meeting seldom concludes without a pitched battle, and the loss of three or four lives',[27] and William Carleton's story 'The Battle of the Factions' provides an alarmingly matter-of-fact outline of the ideal Irish cudgel, including the stipulation that it should 'leave, if possible, the smallest taste in life in the pit of the skull'.[28] Mr and Mrs Hall display the same curious combination of outrage and fascination in their lengthy description of faction fighting in Ireland.[29] Their interest in the role of women in such encounters in particular betrays a confused sensibility.[30]

Despite melodramatic and other florid descriptions of the supposed saturnalia at Donnybrook, alternative accounts of the fair suggest that the abolition of the event was at least premature. The physical arrangement of the event, if not commensurately the behaviour that prevailed there, became noticeably more orderly in the 1830 and 1840s.[31] Mr and Mrs Hall maintained that under the influence of the temperance movement and a more conspicuous and efficient police presence conduct at Donnybrook had improved markedly by the 1840s. Visiting the fair twice, they 'heard nothing, and noticed nothing that could offend the most scrupulous…'.[32] They encountered 'no quarrel approaching to a brawl' nor 'a single intoxicated person of either sex'. [33] Indeed, to the best of their knowledge, the police had not made a single arrest.

Gambling, much of it illegal, was engaged in liberally at the fair, and features in a number of depictions. Attractions ranged from relatively innocuous fairground games of chance like the wheel-of-fortune and trick o'the loop to more clandestine activities. Roulette often took place in privately hired premises near the fair which, like shebeens, were under constant threat of discovery by parties of the Dublin Metropolitan Police. A tense coexistence persisted each year between the legal and the illicit, with mountebanks, cardsharps and charlatans eager to exploit the high spirits and lack of vigilance of the crowds. Evenings at the fair were dominated by music, dance and song as pavilions were filled with revellers. Musicians would play a requested tune for a fee and couples would sometimes engage at one end of a tent in the 'door dancing' recorded elsewhere by Nicol (cat. 5).[34] Meanwhile, ballad singers might be heard 'wheezing out their ditties, mournful or merry all over the fair green'.[35] To some extent, Donnybrook Fair was the victim of its own popularity, outlived by fairs that were more local and more modest in scale.

Ultimately, the *dramatis personae* in Nicol's panorama represent an accumulation of the figures in his other paintings, rather than a microcosm of Irish society *per se*. Here revellers, burly labourers, listless sots and handsome youths mingle with fops, refined beauties and crones. The picture amalgamates Nicol's previous Irish subjects while anticipating those to come. BR

---

6 Llanover 1861, p.369.
7 *ibid*.
8 Glew 1870, p.23.
9 Leach 1985, p.97.
10 Nicol painted at least two versions of this subject.
11 By the 1860s, the main focus of the movement had shifted from abstinence to the closing of public houses on Sundays. Kearns 1996, p.21.
12 Glew 1870, p.24.
13 Wheatley also depicted Palmerstown Fair, another large, popular event which traditionally took place the week immediately before Donnybrook Fair.
14 See Rooney 2002, p.100-04.
15 *Dublin University Review* 1861, p.498. Daniel Maclise's drawing of the fair of c.1826 (Victoria & Albert Museum) demonstrates that large wooden hoardings and theatre fronts featured at that time.
16 See Ó Maitiú 2001, p.171.
17 Transporting these shows was a risky affair. Polito's Menagerie, established in 1758, lost almost its entire show in a shipwreck en route to Ireland in 1835 or 1836. Wombwell's Menagerie was founded in 1805 and became a regular feature at Donnybrook.
18 *Dublin University Review* 1861, p.500.
19 Glew 1870, p.39.
20 Virginia Crossman, 'The Army and Law and Order in the Nineteenth Century', in Bartlett and Jeffery 1996, p.359.
21 E.M. Spiers, 'Army Organisation and Society', in Bartlett and Jeffery 1996, pp.336-39.
22 *Dublin University Review* October 1861, p.498.
23 Nicol exhibited *Donnybrook Fair* at the Royal Scottish Academy in 1860.
24 Cowling 1983, p.462-63.
25 Ó Maitiú 2001, p.171.
26 Glew 1870, p.35.
27 Croker 1824, p.231.
28 Carleton 1990, p.132-33.
29 Hall 1843, vol.I, p.429.
30 *ibid*, p.427.
31 For discussions of the evolution of the fair, see Ó Maitiú 1995 and Ó Maitiú 2001, pp.164-179.
32 Hall 1843, vol.II, p.340.
33 Not everyone was of this opinion. A writer in the *Dublin University Review* welcomed its abolition, citing the 'evil effects of street education on children' and describing the descent into anarchy that took place as the night approached. *Dublin University Review* 1861, p.502.
34 Ó Maitiú 2001, p.176.
35 *ibid*.

76. Above the Fair

Jack B. Yeats

From the time Jack B. Yeats lived in Devon in his mid-twenties, fairs were for him a constant source of inspiration and he produced numerous works in watercolour and subsequently in oil on the

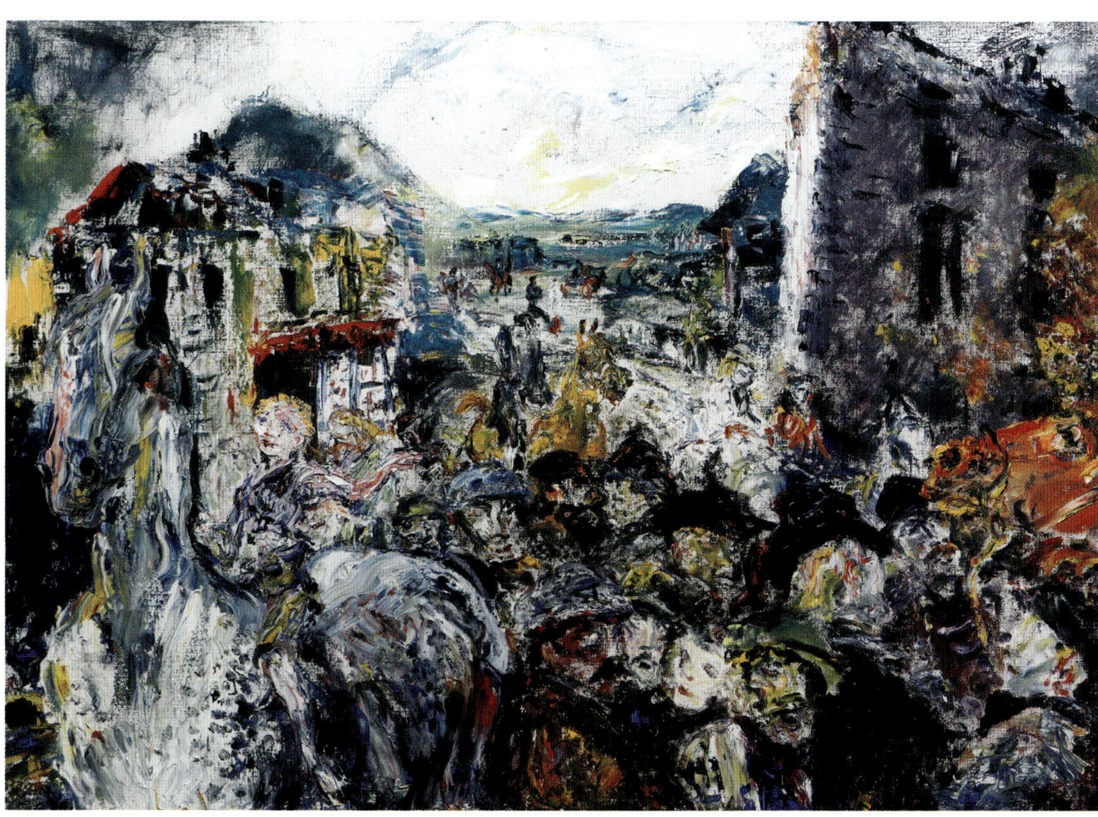

Jack B. Yeats (1871-1957)
76. *Above the Fair*
1946
Oil on canvas
91 x 122 cm
National Gallery of Ireland

subject.[36] For his earlier images of Irish fairs, Yeats appears to have drawn heavily on his memory of travelling in North Mayo with his friend J.M. Synge. Synge's recollections, published in the *Manchester Guardian*, record the central importance of the fair to the social and commercial life of local communities. 'In Swinford,' he wrote 'which may be taken as a good example of these market towns, there are seven roads leading into the country, and it is likely that a fair was started here at first, and that the town as it is now grew up afterwards'.[37] Yeats produced illustrations to accompany Synge's articles.

It is interesting to compare *Above the Fair* with Yeats's *A Fair Day, Mayo* (fig.34), painted two decades earlier and described by Hilary Pyle as 'perhaps his last straight painting of the bustle and excitement of a country fair'.[38] *A Fair Day, Mayo* is set in Ballycastle, a small town near Ballina that Yeats knew well. Conspicuously, no place name in the title of *Above the Fair* threatens to diminish its more universal quality. Similarly, no lovers exchange glances; no young boys talk; and no stalls display their wares. Instead, the fair becomes a dynamic whole, in which all these elements lie hidden in an amorphous mass. Appropriately, the *leitmotif* of horses and riders raised above the crowd alone remains. Horses featured in Yeats's earliest drawings of hunting scenes and fairs, and had assumed a central importance in his later work as a symbol of physical and emotional freedom.

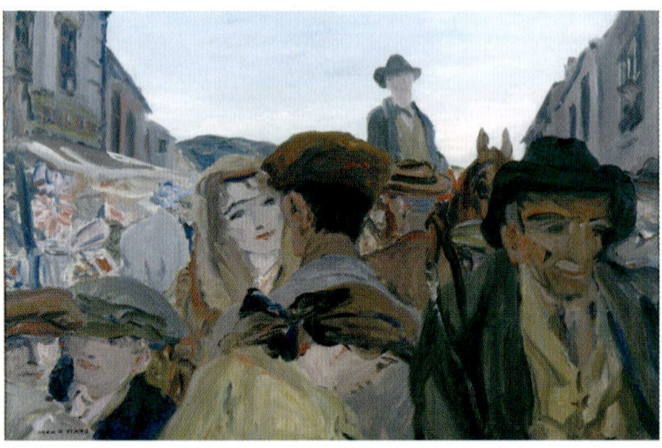

Fig.34 **Jack B. Yeats,** *A Fair Day, Mayo*, 1925, private collection

Though this picture, among others, including Yeats's *Islandbridge Regatta* (NGI), is essentially expressionistic, it is 'still consciously rooted in recognisable experience'.[39] Moreover, this recognisable experience is not some obscure point of reference for the artist alone but something familiar to both artist and audience. Though Yeats does seem to have had an unerring belief in the importance of everyday events, other works of the period are, by comparison with *Above the Fair*, almost impenetrably metaphorical and/or literary.[40] From his time as an illustrator in London and throughout his career, Yeats had been drawn to scenes from everyday life. An adherence to the local often transcended more complex considerations in his work as boxing matches, horse races, country assizes, harvests, hurling matches and a myriad of other episodes occupy his paper and canvas.

Above the Fair is, however, a more loaded image than some of his earlier, more empirical records. Pyle has suggested that the title of the painting derives from the manner in which the diminutive, golden-haired child on the horse to the left of the composition is 'raised symbolically' *above the fair*. The title can reasonably be understood as a literal reference to the raised vantage point from which the scene is viewed but is more likely, when considered in the context of Yeats's later work, as Pyle suggests, to refer to the young boy on the horse who has been elevated, separated and consequently freed from the maelstrom of people below him. The notion of freedom from constraint applies equally to the subject and to the painting process as Yeats employs a vigorous but controlled hand in applying the paint in thick impasto to the canvas. His use of colour is similarly liberal and expressive, barely conceding to orthodoxy. As a result, subject-matter and facture coalesce so that the product at once harks back to Yeats's earlier themes (and by extension those of Taylor, Nicol etc) while responding to more esoteric, Modernist sensibilities. BR

36 Yeats moved with his wife Mary to Strete, near Dartmouth, in 1897. Mary was herself from Devon.

37 Price 1966, vol.II, p.334.

38 Pyle 1990, p.31.

39 *ibid*, p.33.

40 See Pyle 1993a, pp.86-101.

77. Fashions at the Fair

Lilian Davidson

Lilian Davidson's work bears some resemblance to the early figurative social themes of Jack B. Yeats, whose portrait she painted in 1938, but is overall more sombre in tone and promotes pattern over the sheer virtuosity of draughtsmanship in evidence in Yeats's work. Davidson does not break the picture surface down into a mass from which shapes slowly emerge, as Yeats does in *Above the Fair* (cat. 76) but rather allows certain figures to stand out, by dint of colour (a bright petticoat), shape (a woman carrying a creel under her shawl) or gesture (a hand with splayed fingers). Here, certain elements, such as bands of colour on a shawl or a piebald calf, allow her to exploit locally the tonal contrast that she achieves elsewhere through the juxtaposition of separate elements. It is not surprising that Davidson excelled in painting night scenes, as these allowed her to indulge her evident fascination in tone (eg *Night in Claddagh* (private collection) and *Cottages, Keel, Achill* (private collection)) and the fragmenting potential of light. Davidson was also a gifted watercolourist with a deft touch, and was a committed contributor to the Water Colour Society exhibitions over some forty years.

Despite its stylised arrangement and painterly quality, *Fashions at the Fair* does suggest genuine experience. Indeed, the bustling presence of the old women in the midst of the crowd calls to mind the familiar type remembered by Patrick Kavanagh in his poem *In Memory of My Mother*:

And I see us meeting at the end of a town
On a fair day by accident, after
The bargains are all made and we can walk
Together through the shops and stalls and markets
Free in the oriental streets of thought.

The heavy, durable attire of the people attending the fair in this picture certainly lent itself to the bold modelling that Davidson preferred and that recurs throughout her oeuvre, regardless of setting.[41] She achieved this same weighty, textured effect in such disparate works as *Fair Day in Miss O'Dowd's* (private collection), a view of the crowded interior of a shop in Roundstone, *Here is the News* (private collection), a record of a group of working men reading the cover page of the *Irish Times* outside the newspaper's offices in Westmoreland Street and *Hanging out the Washing, Rathmines Back Streets* (private collection), a thickly-painted view over cottage rooftops in that Dublin suburb.

Lilian Davidson (1879-1954)
77. *Fashions at the Fair*
Oil on canvas
71 x 92 cm
National Gallery of Ireland

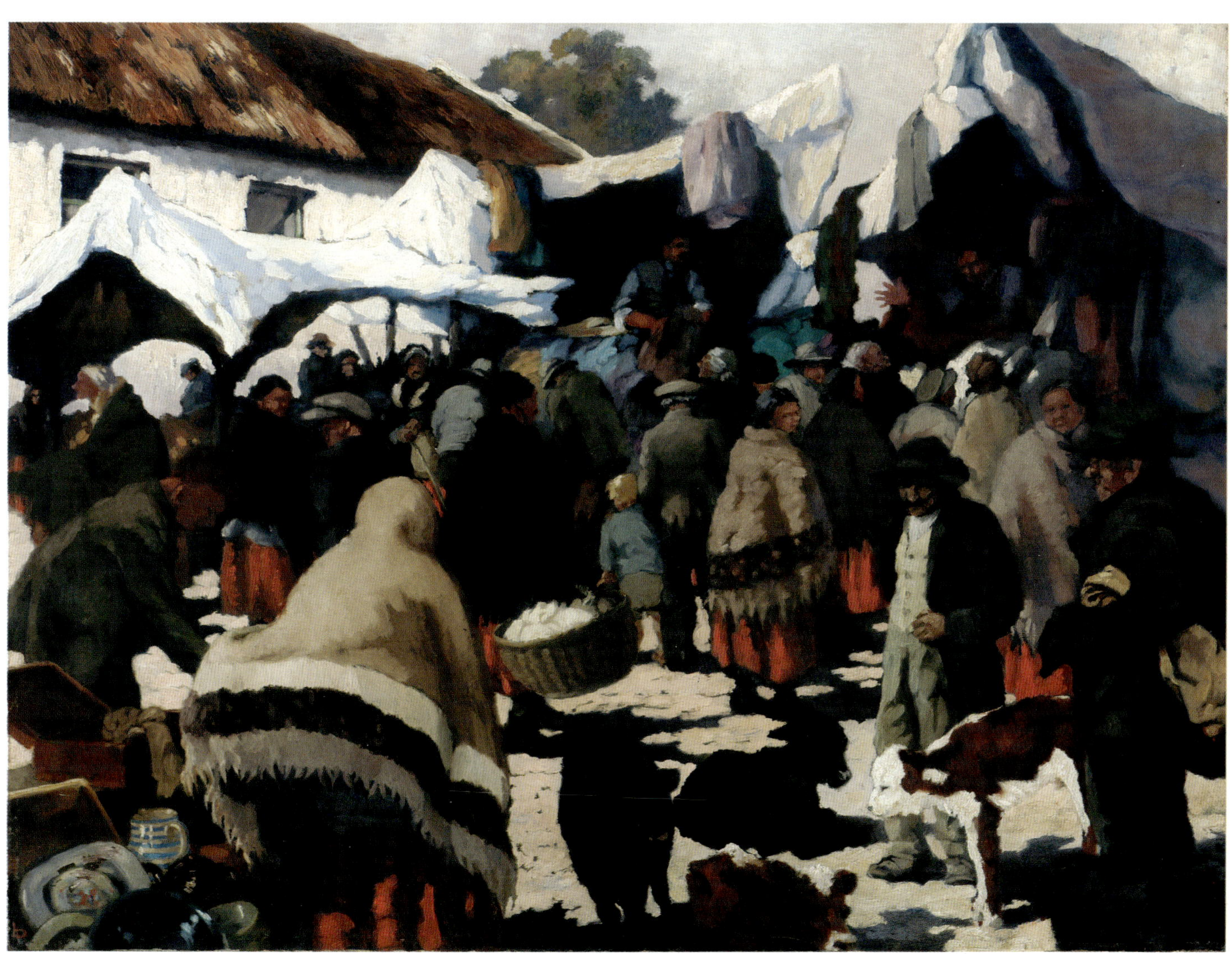

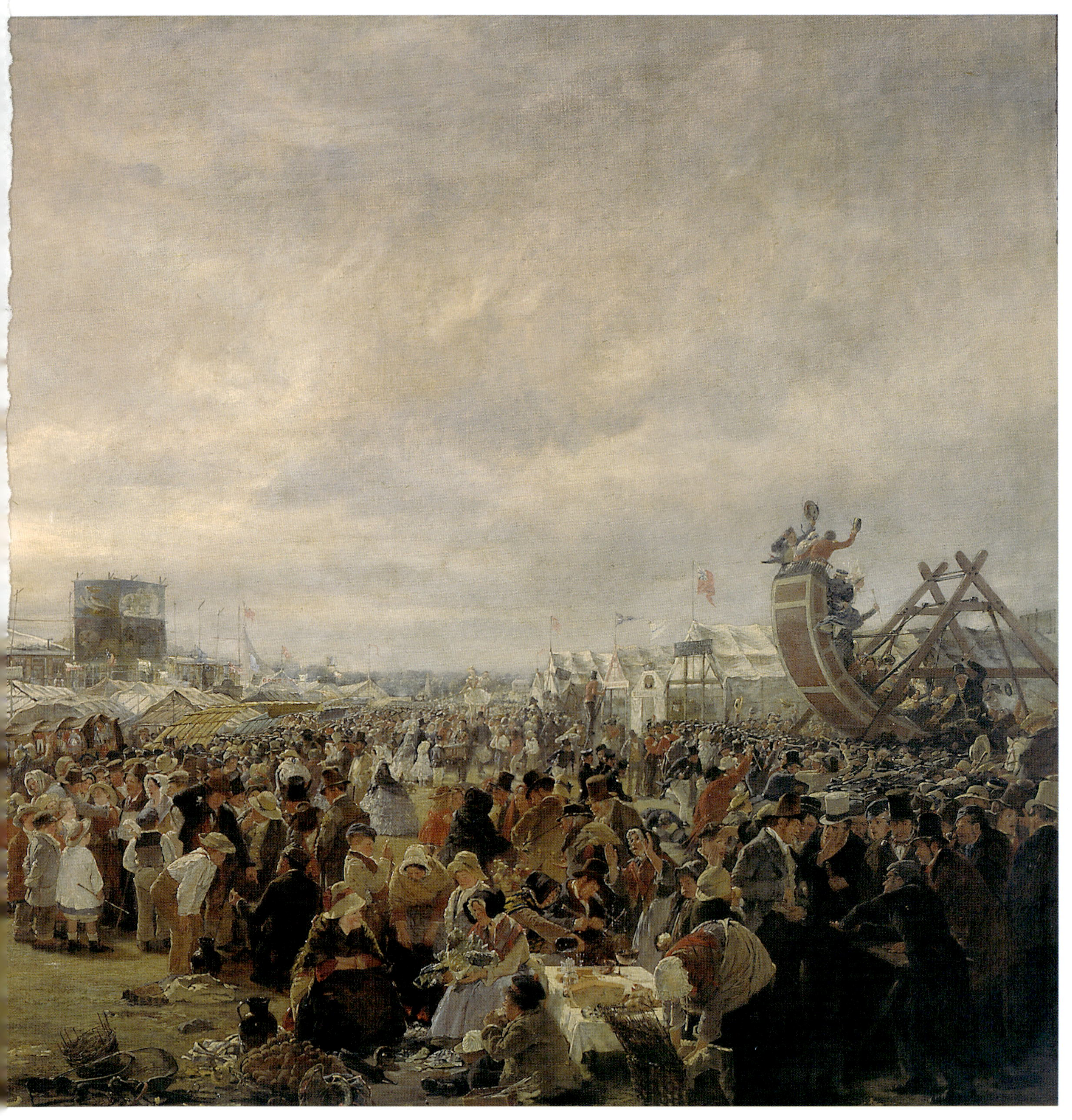

Erskine Nicol (1825-1904)
75. *Donnybrook Fair*
1859
Oil on canvas
102.7 x 210.8 cm
Tate. Purchased 1932
See page 141

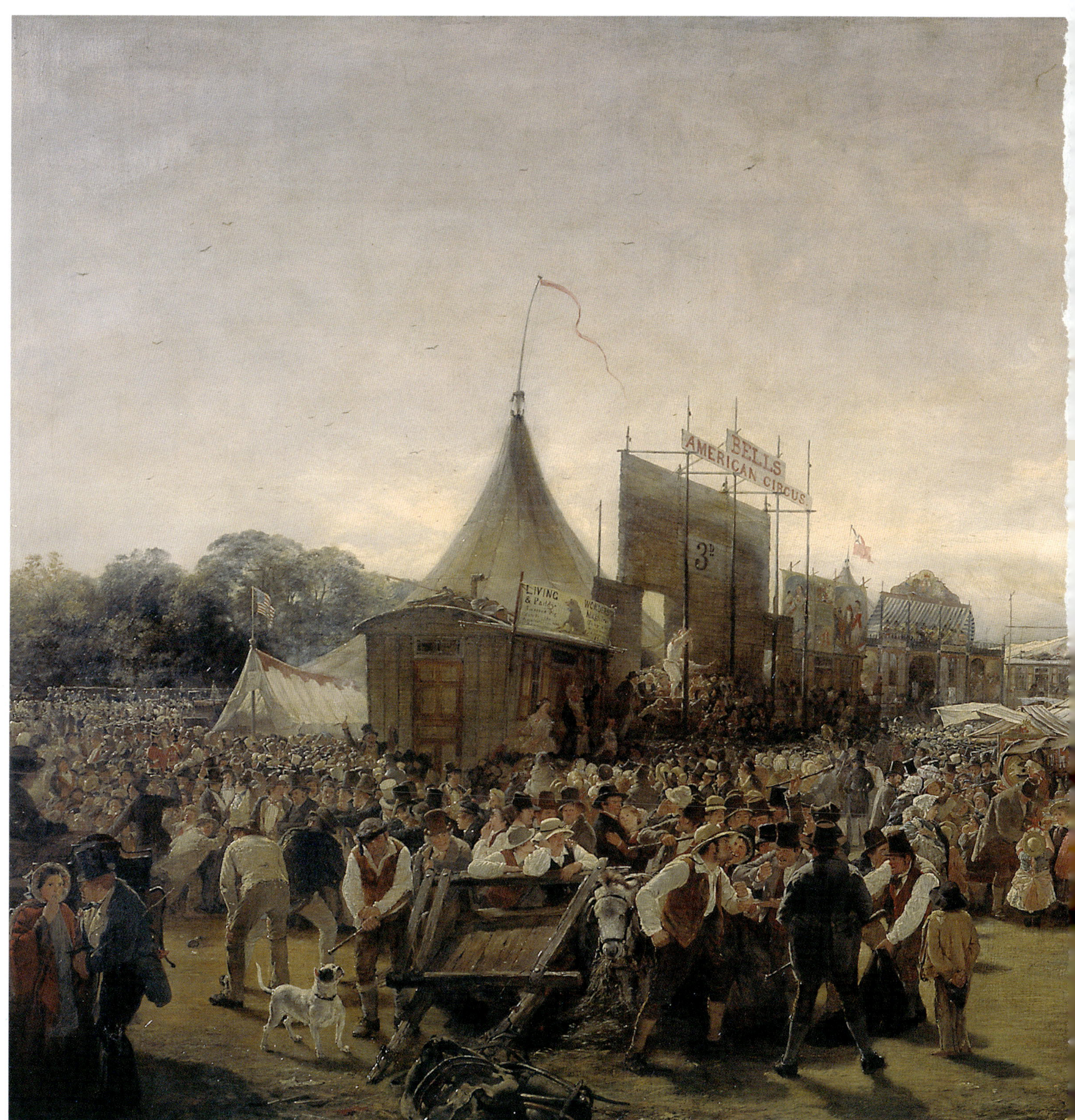
BELLS
AMERICAN CIRCUS
3d
LIVING
& Paddy

Fashions at the Fair could almost be seen as the exterior equivalent of *Fair Day in Miss O'Dowd's*, in which men can be seen through the door of the shop negotiating a sale, perhaps of livestock.[42] Davidson's style seems ideally suited to her choice of quotidian subjects and the robust, earthy characters that animate them. She did manage to create strong, intensely tonal images, in which the figures appear as solid as the man-made and natural environments they inhabit. Davidson's figures, wrapped in heavy shawls or oversized jackets call to mind Grace Henry's similarly stocky peasants (see for example *The Top of the Hill* (Limerick City Gallery of Art)). Crowded in front of the clothing stall, they seem like a collage of colour and shadow. This sophisticated, coherent pattern-making also serves as an alternative means of conveying the sense of community that one can identify throughout this exhibition. More superficially, perhaps, the tapestry-like effect Davidson achieved in this and other works complements the variety of fabric with which they are often replete.

Though she did visit France, Belgium and Switzerland, Davidson was unable to spend lengthy periods on the Continent. Instead, she travelled widely within Ireland, journeying to Donegal first in the 1920s and subsequently making productive trips to Achill and Connemara. Davidson was also among a number of early twentieth-century artists, including Maurice MacGonigal, Harry Kernoff and Jack B. Yeats, to execute work for the Dublin theatre, designing sets and programmes for the Dublin-based Torch Theatre, of which she was a founder. Significantly, her involvement in the theatre went further, however. As well as poetry and prose, Davidson wrote for the theatre under the *nom-de-plume* Ulick Burke, and her play *Bride* was performed at the Gate Theatre in Dublin in 1931.[43] When one combines this distinction with the fact that some of her paintings, *Fair Day at Miss O'Dowd's* in particular, are strikingly theatrical in composition, analogies with the work of J.M. Synge are arguably as fitting as in the case of any single other Irish artist. When parallels are drawn between the work of Irish painters and Synge, they are normally qualified in terms of equivalency. For example, the *Northern Whig*, in reviewing Paul and Grace Henry's work on view in Belfast in 1911, admired the manner in which they had flung away 'accepted formulas as boldly as Synge did when he began to do in drama what they have set themselves to do in colour'.[44] Davidson also worked as an art teacher in various places, most notably from her address at Earlsfort Terrace in Dublin, and was popular with her students. BR

41 For an account of Davidson's life and discussion of her work, see Cahill 1999, pp.34-45.

42 See Kinmonth 2006, pp.234-35.

43 Hilton Edwards directed the play while Micheál McLiammóir designed the sets and costumes.

44 'Paintings of Irish Life', *Northern Whig*, 13 March 1911. Paul Henry had met Synge with W.B. Yeats by chance in Paris in about 1898/99 and was greatly impressed by him.

78. Donkeys

Letitia Hamilton

Throughout her career, Letitia Hamiliton returned regularly to the subjects of fairs and market scenes. Travelling in Ireland, she recorded in sensitive and undramatic terms the activities in many local markets, including those of Clifden, Mitchelstown, Roundstone and Castlepollard. The last of these, which appears to have been painted from a first-floor window, presents a view over the entire market and demonstrates, as does *Donkeys*, Hamilton's unobtrusive approach to painting such busy scenes. In *Donkeys*, one views the canopies and stalls of the market place at a distance. Although the donkeys in the foreground occupy a significant portion of the painting, the work is not a study of the animals but rather an integrated view that reveals Hamilton's interest in composition, the flattening of surfaces, and the influence of her travels abroad.

Raised in Dunboyne, County Meath, Hamilton enrolled at the Metropolitan School of Art at the age of twenty-nine. Although this was a late age to begin her formal artistic training, she was fortunate to have been raised within an artistic family,[45] and her training at the college merely marked her determination to study art in more depth.[46] She attended the School of Art with her sister Eva during the period when William Orpen was working there as a visiting teacher. However, as Hilary Pyle points out, while she must have owed her strong graphic line and mastery of architectural detail to Orpen's instruction,[47] the freshness and spontaneity of technique with which she produced her outdoor scenes is far removed from Orpen's academic style.

It has been suggested that Hamilton's interest in Impressionist painting stemmed from a visit to Northern France while a student at the Chelsea Polytechnic and her sojourn in Belgium under the tuition of Frank Brangwyn, who influenced her consideration of pattern and broadness of technique.[48] On her return to Dublin, she successfully applied these teachings to her depiction of Irish rural scenes and in 1920, with a group of artists including Paul Henry, she became a

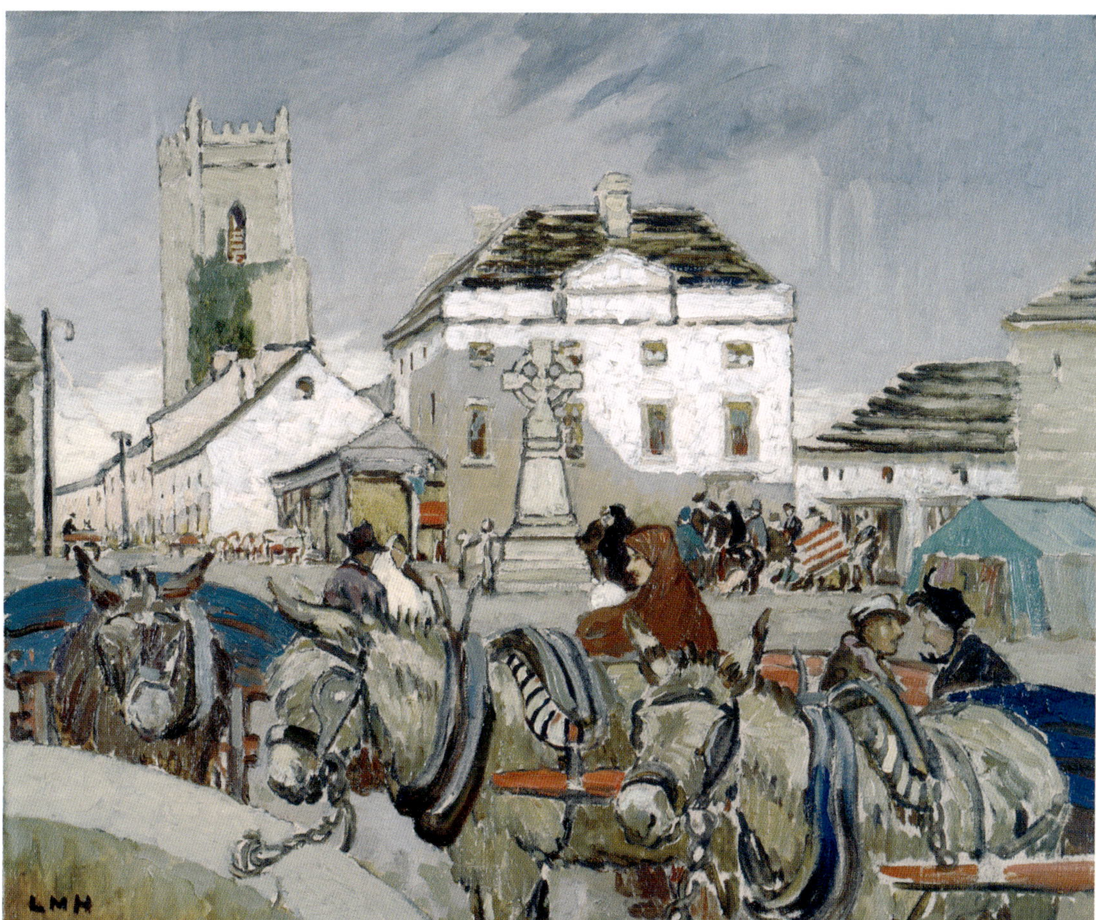

Letitia Hamilton
(1878-1964)
78. *Donkeys*
Exh. 1932
Oil on board
55.9 x 66 cm
Collection Ulster Museum, Belfast

founding member of the Dublin Painters' Society. Henry's characteristic flat surfaces, outlined forms and broad brushwork were a significant influence on Hamilton's style and became clearly visible in much of her work.[49] There is, perhaps, something reminiscent of Henry's mountains in the large white building that dominates the centre of *Donkeys* and, set against a large overcast sky, presides over the activity in the square.

As Hamilton did not date her work it is often difficult to ascertain when specific paintings were executed. To date, this example has been taken to be *Donkeys*, a picture exhibited at the RHA Annual Exhibition in 1932. However, the subject and technique of the painting suggest that it may be an earlier work. The market square depicted is that of Monasterevin, County Kildare, where the Hamilton sisters lived from 1917 to 1918. During this period, Letitia painted the town and the surrounding areas and exhibited a number of these paintings at the RHA, including one entitled *The Market at Monasterevin* in 1918.

Although the picture features some aspects of the fluid, painterly style that Hamilton developed later in her career, there is no evidence of the use of a palette knife, which she began to favour in the 1920s. The manner in which this picture is executed is certainly comparable with other earlier works she produced in Monasterevin. In particular, her 1917 painting *Monasterevin* (private collection), a view of the town from across a river, features a large cloud that looms over the houses and was undoubtedly inspired by Henry.[50]

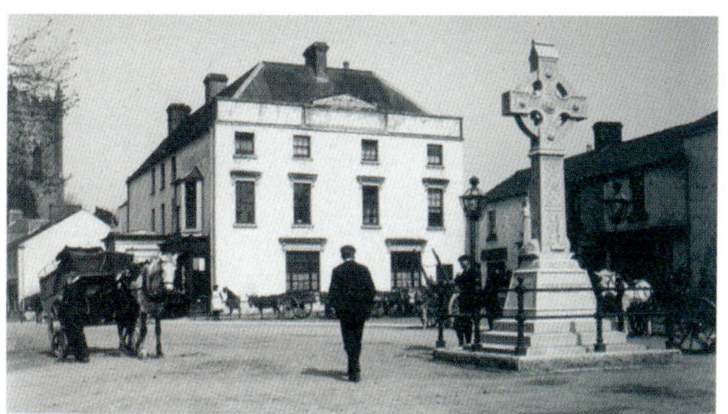

Fig.35. Anonymous, *The Market Place at Monasterevin*, 1902, University of St Andrews

Usually produced on-the-spot, Hamilton's early paintings were characterised by a simplification of forms and shapes and the use of a limited palette.[51] *Donkeys* is painted primarily in neutral tones of white and grey, with shades of blue. Hamilton uses red, the richest colour in the composition, sparingly, cleverly highlighting various points of focus for the viewer: the donkey carts (in the foreground and in the distance) and the group of people gathered in the square. This use of colour complements her appreciation of pattern and the decorative impulse that she expressed through her vigorous application of paint. Her flattening of the sky with broad brushstrokes, rendering of the buildings with thick dabs of white, and description of the donkeys with short strokes at various angles may be attributable to Hamilton's awareness of the work of Roderic O'Conor.

The perspective of Hamilton's picture allows one to appreciate the entire market square and its position within the small town. Punctuating the centre of the picture is a replica of a Celtic cross, erected in 1899, which is a monument to Fr Prendergast, a curate of the parish who was hanged during the 1798 Rebellion. The large three-storey building in the background was Flemming's Inn and subsequently the General Stores Co. Building,[52] and to the right is the market house, built by the Droghedas in 1905.[53] The white gable-end belongs to a pub called the Drogheda Arms (now Gahan's) and the tower is that of St John's Protestant Church (fig. 35). As with most Irish towns the market was primarily a site for commercial exchange and provided a venue for the sale and distribution of produce and livestock from the surrounding areas.[54] However, it also functioned as much as a site of social exchange as the pub or church. Market areas were usually located outside the town centre to allow easier access. In 1832, the Monasterevin market was divided in two, due to the realignment of Dublin Street following the construction of the Town Bridge, which crossed the River Barrow. DM

45 As children, Letitia and her sister Eva were aware of the work of their grandmother Caroline Hamilton and cousin Rose Barton.

46 Pyle 1997a, p.126.

47 *ibid.*

48 *ibid.*

49 Dalsimer and Kreilkamp 1996, p. 80.

50 See Pyle 1997a, p.130, fig.10.

51 S.B. Kennedy 1991, p.29

52 The building was certainly the General Stores Co. Building by 1922.

53 The author is very grateful to Barry Walsh of the Monasterevin Historical Society for his assistance.

54 Lalor 2003, p.370.

79. The O'Connell Centenary Celebrations

Charles Russell

Though essentially a panoramic image of a political event, Russell's painting also records a celebration promoted by its organisers and reported by the press, with varying degrees of enthusiasm, as a social occasion. Over their three-day duration, the O'Connell celebrations were to include a solemn requiem at the Pro-Cathedral ('a foil to the lighter scenes that are to follow', according to *The Times*),[55] a grand banquet at the Exhibition Palace, the procession, a fireworks display in the Phoenix Park, an opera, and a boat race on the Liffey and 'other entertainments for the populace'.[56]

The turn-out at the commemoration, consistent with Daniel O'Connell's ability to mobilise the public during his own lifetime, was huge. In the mid-century, 'the age of crowds', mass demonstration was common, notwithstanding attempts by the Tory press to understate it or, conversely, nationalist commentators' capacity to exaggerate.[57] One of the principal achievements of O'Connell's monster meetings of the early 1840s was to galvanise local communities, regardless of individuals' knowledge of or interest in politics. As neutral observers at a meeting in Lismore in 1843 commented, 'these people are, evidently, little acquainted with the question of Repeal. But they are ready, when directed, to join in a quiet display, and enjoy the pleasure of a day of recreation'.[58] Attempts were made in the late 1860s and 1870s to regenerate the fervour for public demonstration that had existed in the 1840s. Indeed, the Amnesty Association did so to great effect, their efforts culminating in the assembly of a crowd of some 200,000 at a demonstration in Cabra in 1869.[59] Four years later, the organisation's meetings in Clontarf and Glasnevin were attended by an estimated 250,000 and 300,000 respectively.[60] In the 1870s, Fenian funerals, such as that of John O'Mahony, who had died in America, also attracted very large numbers.

Stating that the procession would be 'memorable as the greatest event of its kind which has ever occurred in this country' *The Times* estimated cautiously that between 30,000 and 50,000 people joined it on its five-mile course round the centre of the city.[61] The *Irish Times* was less conservative in its estimate and prone to hyperbole in its general description of proceedings. The route was lined from the start, the paper claimed, 'with hundreds of thousands of spectators, quite orderly and manifestly interested in the highest degree in the proceedings they had

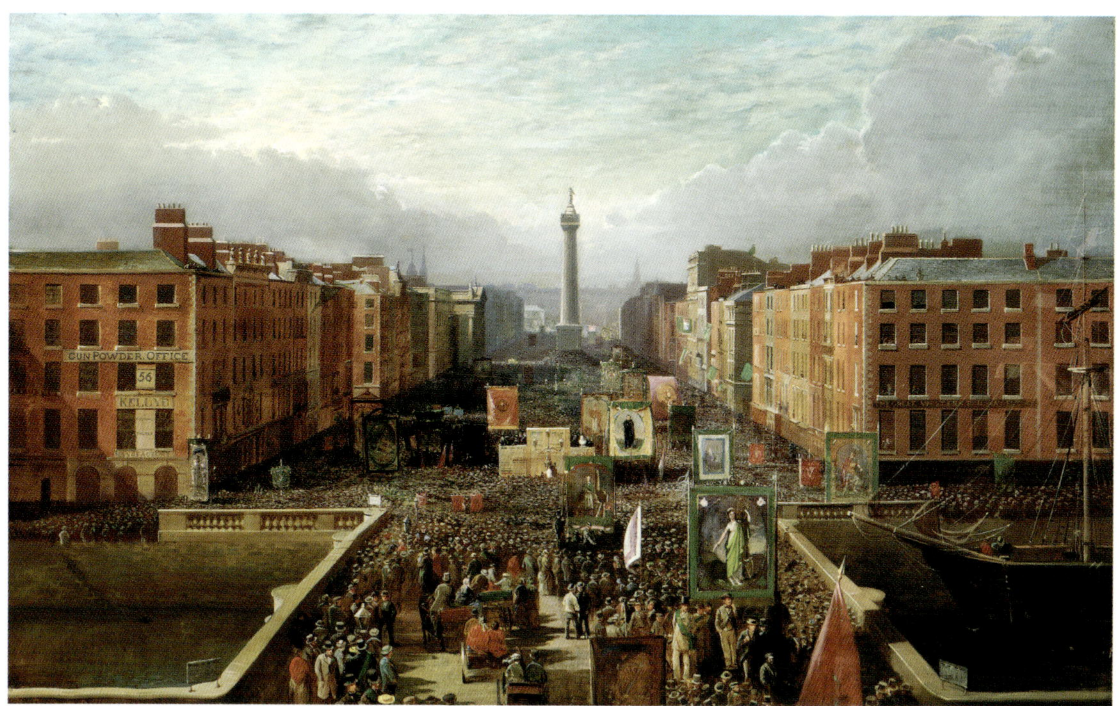

Charles Russell (1852-1910)
79. *The O'Connell Centenary Celebrations*
1875
Oil on canvas
104 x 163 cm
National Gallery of Ireland
See Foldout opposite page 155

assembled to witness'.[62] Onlookers assumed every vantage point so that 'from kerb stone to roof top they were to be seen, old and young, rich and poor'.[63] It was a measure of the scale and popularity of the celebrations that the City of Dublin Steamship Company made its entire fleet of twelve vessels, including the *Leinster* (cat. 55), available to transport travellers from Liverpool to Dublin.[64]

Charles Russell, himself the son of a painter, came to Ireland from Scotland at the age of twenty-two, just a year before painting *The O'Connell Centenary Celebrations*. Significantly, he was employed in painting portraits from photographs for S. [John] Chancellor, whose premises were located at 55 Lower Sackville Street, a building clearly visible in the painting.[65] Other important photographers, including William Lawrence, the Stark Brothers and Adolph Lesage had studios at the same time on Sackville Street.[66] Russell's large painting was therefore not just an elaborate record of an historic event in nineteenth-century Dublin but also of part of the city with which Russell himself would have been intimately familiar. It bears therefore a self-referential quality not unusual among photographers. Robert French, for example, one of the principal photographers working for William Lawrence, often included himself in his photographs.[67]

O'Connell Street (formerly Sackville Street) was and still is depicted regularly from this same raised viewpoint. Indeed, Russell was not the first to exploit this vantage point at the junction of of D'Olier Street and Westmoreland Street. Exactly a decade earlier, for example, the *Illustrated London News* printed an illustration of the laying of the foundation stone of the O'Connell Monument that is identical to Russell's in all but local detail. It too depicts the street and bridge thronged with crowds and even features a banner of O'Connell to the right of the monument foundations as one appears in Russell's oil painting. The ceremony of the laying of the foundation stone in 1864 also attracted vast numbers of people to Sackville Street.

These public displays were evidently statements of a changing Ireland and the increasingly coherent organisation of the unions, but were also opportunities for celebration and levity eagerly exploited by the public. The O'Connell centenary celebrations of 1875 have been referred to as the moment when 'processional fervour of Irish trade unions reached its height' and Russell has made sure to pay particular attention to the description of banners in his painting. Interestingly, *The Times* reserved its criticism for what it perceived as the grotesque amount of money spent on the banners behind which the respective organisations marched.[68] Indeed most of the banners were commissioned specially for the occasion and those few that were not new had been retouched, revarnished or regilded. Many, according to the *Irish Times*, were 'masterpieces in design and execution'.[69] Among the banner details identifiable in Russell's painting are the figures of Brian Boru, O'Connell himself and Isaac Butt, leader of the Amnesty Association, who was actually present at the procession.[70] A myriad of trades and interests was represented among the crowd, from coal porters and chimney cleaners to the Regular Boot Makers, the Hackney Car Owners Association, the Limerick Pig Buyers, the Fishermen of Ringsend, the Cork Harbor Shipwrights, the Dublin Skinners Society and the Regular Cart and Wagon Builders Society.

On the day of the procession, shops were closed, and even cab and tram drivers (who normally had to toil harder on festive days) were prevented or dissuaded from working. A carnival atmosphere prevailed throughout the day and there were no notable outbreaks of violence. All those attending appeared to embrace the good humour and *The Times* recorded that 'in the thickest parts of the throng, where it was difficult to thread one's way by slow and sinuous steps, women were carrying infants in their arms without the slightest fear'.[71] Such was the good humour at the procession that The *Irish Times* expressed confidence that 'a glorious future must await the nation which is at the same moment so impulsive and yet so docile'.[72] BR

55 *The Times*, 10 July 1875.
56 *ibid*, 7 July 1875.
57 Maura Cronin, "Of One Mind'?: O'Connellite Crowds in the 1830s and 1840s', in Jupp and Magennis 2000, p.140.
58 Chief Secretary's Office Registered Papers (National Archives of Ireland), OR 1843, 19/10165, 20/13315, 29/19515; *Belfast Commercial Chronicle*, 30 September. 1843. This refers to the campaign for the repeal of the Act of Union.
59 See Clare Murphy, 'Varieties of Crowd Activity from Fenianism to the Land War, 1867-79', in Jupp and Magennis 2000, pp. 173-86.
60 The main objective of the Amnesty Association was the release of prisoners jailed following the abortive rising of 1867. The movement's final rally took place in Glasnevin on 23 November 1873.
61 *The Times*, 7 August 1875.
62 *Irish Times*, 6 August 1875.
63 *ibid*.
64 *ibid*, 30 July 1875.
65 Strickland 1913, vol. II, p.313. Chancellor's offices were in the second building on the left of Sackville Street.
66 Chandler 2001, p.97. Grafton Street and Westmoreland Street could also boast a number of photography firms during this period, in response to the demand for *cartes de visite*. A Charles Russell is recorded as practising as a commercial photographer in Belfast in the 1890s.
67 Chandler 2001, p.61.
68 *The Times*, 7 August 1875.
69 *Irish Times*. 7 August 1875.
70 Loftus 1978, p.22.
71 *The Times*, 7 August 1875.
72 *Irish Times*. 7 August 1875.

80. Procession Day

Muriel Brandt

It is not certain what specific procession, if any, Brandt records in this painting. Though dating back over seventy years, the St Patrick's Day parade in Dublin was a solemn, rather understated affair until its expansion in the 1970s and An Tóstal was not inaugurated by the government until 1953.[1] Brandt's picture oscillates between the general and the specific. Out of the colourful, animated crowd one can pick out individuals of note, such as the girls running their bikes along the street, the man in the hat looking up, perhaps in admonishment, more likely in curiosity, at the children climbing the lamppost, or the young boy whose rigid Wellington boots afford him little purchase as he tries to join his friends. However, the crowd remains an integrated mass, whose common purpose is defined by their orientation in one direction and by the bunting that flies above their heads. The work exemplifies the 'nice free style' identified in Brandt's work by the *Irish Times* in its review of the RHA exhibition of 1949, in which this painting featured.[2]

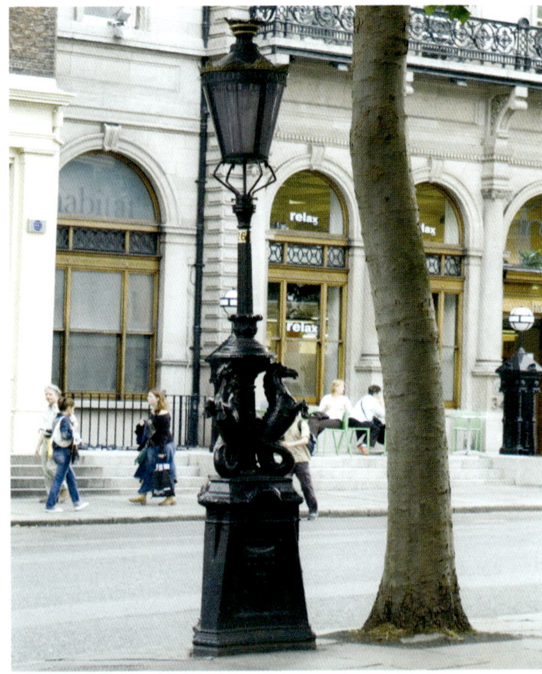

Fig.36. College Green, Dublin

A comparative photograph taken on College Green (fig.36) demonstrates that Brandt manipulated the view and simplified the detail to facilitate her composition. The arched windows and engaged columns in the background belong to the former Union Bank on Dame Street, and provide a rhythmical and harmonious background to the scene, but Brandt chose not to include the building's first-storey cast-iron balcony. The inclusion of the phone box also appears to be fanciful, and even suggests an alternative view from College Green towards Trinity College. Brandt was less circumspect in her description of the ornate lamppost, which bears much of the intricate detail of the original, most notably the hippocamps (mythical seahorses) at its base and the crowning design. A version this distinctive cast-iron lamp design is also to be found on Grattan Bridge in Dublin. Brandt's truncation of space, by which the principal elements of the composition are brought close together, contributes to the atmosphere of bustle and excitement that pervades her picture.

Children were among Brandt's favourite subjects, as reflected in *The Procession* and the more conventional *Charleville, Enniskerry, with three Children, two on Ponies*.[3] Significantly, in 1949, she designed a postage stamp commemorating the international recognition of the Republic of Ireland. Some years later, she provided the illustrations for Donal O'Sullivan's book *Irish Folk Music and Song*

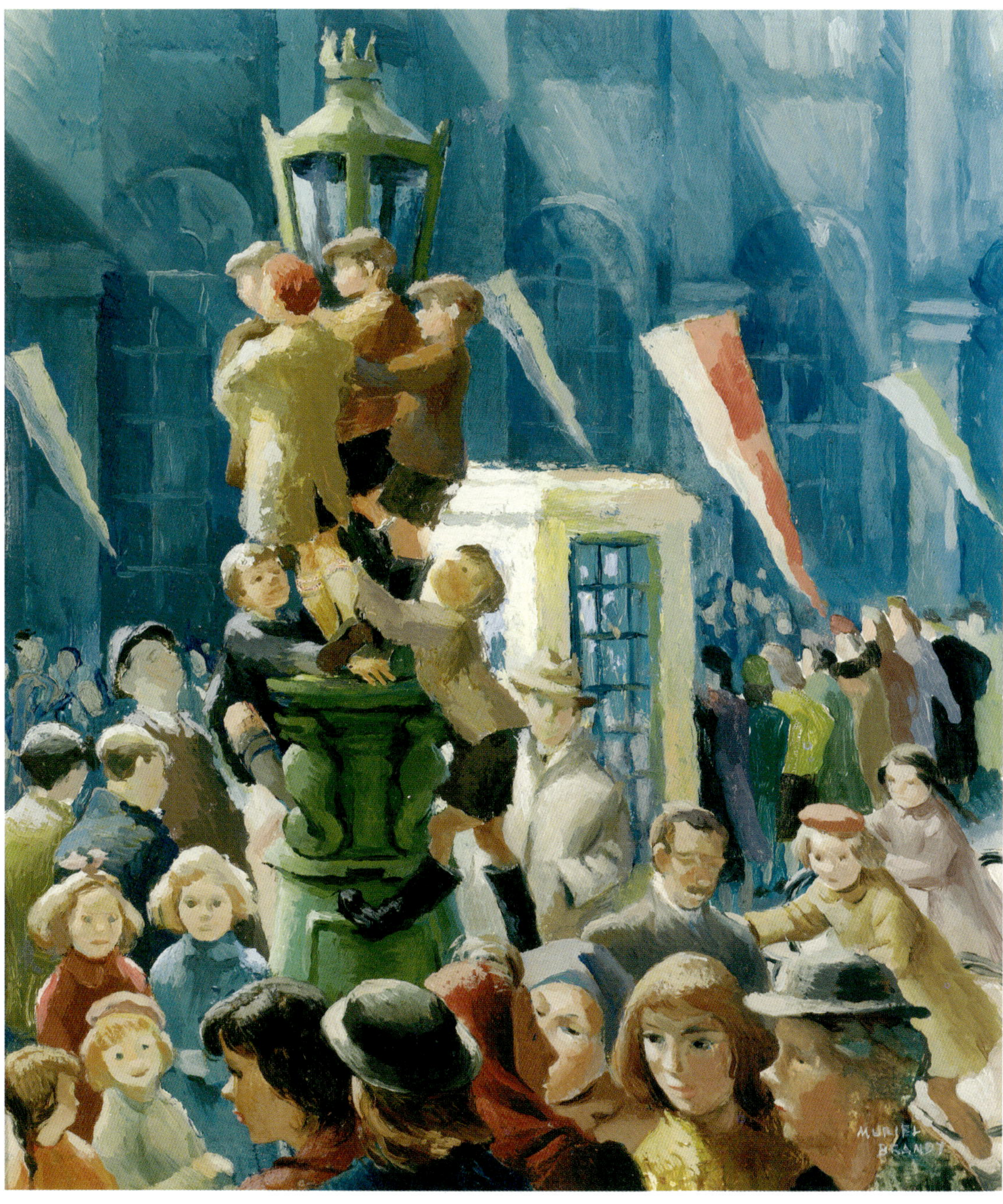

Muriel Brandt (1909-81)
80. *Procession Day*
Exh. 1949
Oil on canvas
38 x 31 cm
Courtesy Gorry Gallery

(1956). Brandt is associated closely with Dublin, chiefly on account of the seven scenes of the life and miracles of St Anthony she painted for the Church of the Franciscan Friars on Merchant's Quay,[4] and another series she painted for the nearby Adam and Eve Church. She also contributed some 63 works to the RHA exhibitions over forty years. BR

73 An Tóstal was a spring festival introduced by the government to attract tourists to Ireland.

74 *Irish Times*, 25 April 1949.

75 See James Adam and Bonhams, 31 May 2000, lot 96.

76 This was Brandt's first major commission. The largest of these paintings, measuring approximately eleven square metres, was destroyed by fire shortly before the artist's death.

81. Pattern at Glendalough, Co. Wicklow

Maria Spilsbury Taylor

This is the last of three paintings of Glendalough produced by this London-born artist. The Prince Regent commissioned the first, as he wanted Taylor's first Irish picture. Of the three, this one concentrates less on the devotional reasons for this fundamentally religious gathering than on its social and convivial aspects. Glendalough is an ancient monastic site at which each year on 3 June pilgrims gathered to celebrate St Kevin, whose relics were believed to have been held there since the 9th century.[77] Taylor's view looks up the valley, with the river dividing the crowd, and the exagger-

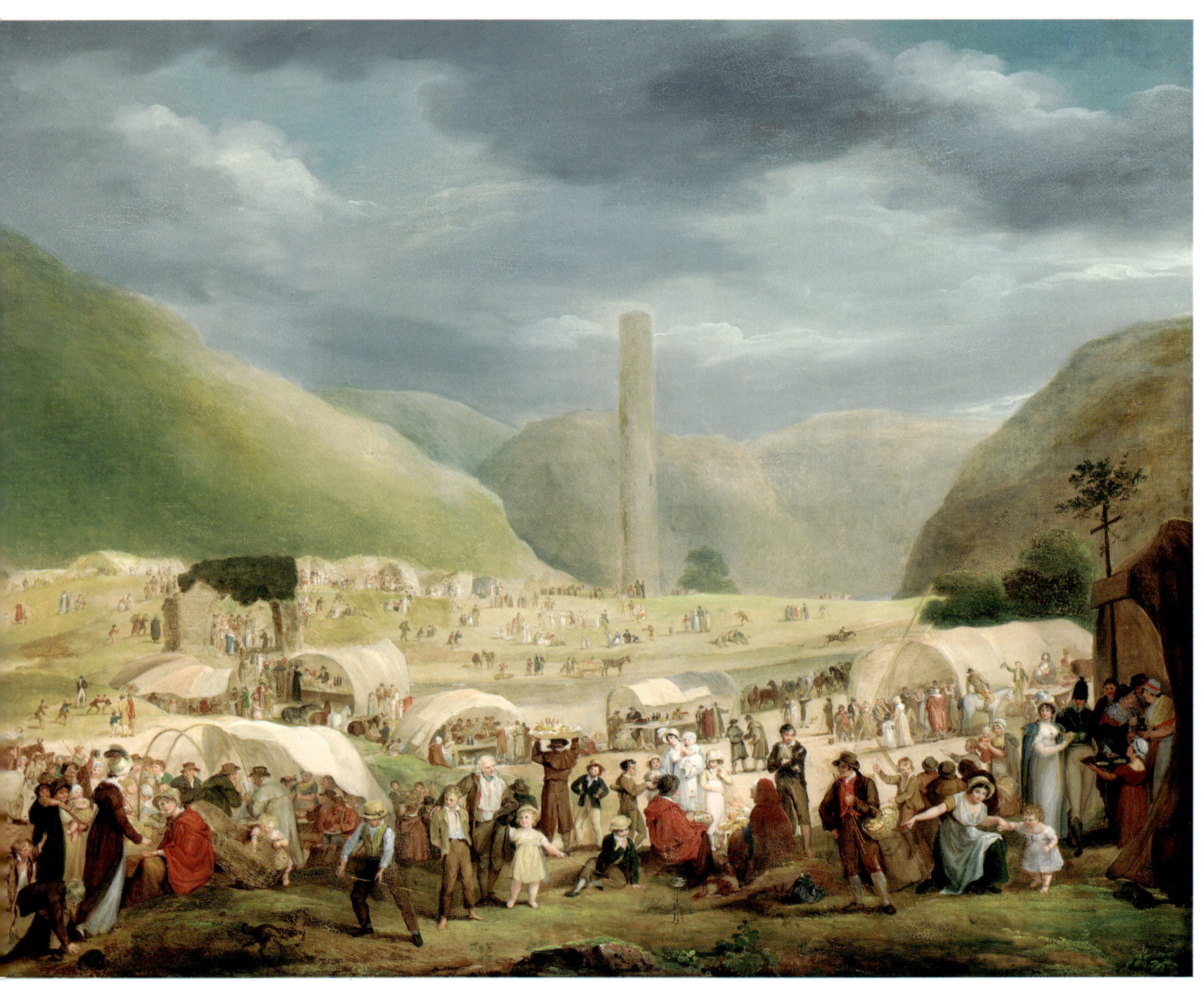

Maria Spilsbury Taylor
(1776-1820)
81. *Pattern at Glendalough, Co. Wicklow*
c.1816
Oil on canvas
102 x 124 cm
UCD, Delargy Centre for Irish Folklore and the National Folklore Collection

atedly tall round tower encircled by the 'remarkably smooth and high mountains'.[78]

Following her marriage to John Taylor, Maria settled in Wicklow, where her father, the engraver Jonathan Spilsbury, had worked as drawing master to the Tighe family. Meticulous pencil sketches of family life, often featuring children and indoor scenes in school rooms and cottages, reveal her delight in portraiture and genre that also predominate here. Other artists focused on such lively fair scenes and Joseph Peacock's impressively detailed vision of *The Patron, or Festival of St Kevin at the Seven Churches, Glendalough* (Ulster Museum) provides the same viewpoint but is more stereotypical in its depiction of drunkenness and violence, with a mass of people fighting beneath the tower. As if to emphasise the darker social side of these events, which were increasingly the subject of repression by Catholic authorities, Peacock puts both activities in shadow.[79] Taylor's subsequent version shows compositional similarities, but is notably lighter in shade as well as subject. Her tone is distinctly positive, and she is one of few artists to show ladies giving money to the poor, as can be seen here in the foreground. Within a few years Turner de Lond was showing the mingling of the rich and poor at a market (cat. 74), but Taylor lavishes far more attention on the detail of the most fashionably dressed. In the centre she depicts a woman wearing a high-waisted blue and white dress and holding a baby in matching colours literally above the poor, and such detail gleams like a miniature painted within the larger scene. The woman reaches out to give money to a beggar boy leaning on a crutch, while beneath her two women sit in red hooded cloaks, selling toys and food from their baskets. A doll is held up, which is dressed in the same fashionable clothes as the mother, even to the point of having plumes like the feathers on its bonnet. The toy seller has a man's hat placed over her white bonnet and the same arrangement is worn by a countrywoman on the far right.

Equally fascinating insights can be gleaned from the baskets of ribbons and food being sold. Oatcakes, ready to eat and easy to keep, were favoured by travellers and may be what is piled in the man's basket on the right. A linen-lined basket contains apples, twists of red and white barley sugar and what may be red sweets or fruits displayed on sticks. The artist draws aside the patched cloth covers of the booths to reveal the people dancing in pairs within, and the tables laden with food and bottles. A throwing game occupies the families in the foreground. Horses with their tails fashionably docked are assembled in the background for sale. To the right a soldier steps out, accompanied by a lady in a low-cut dress with transparent sleeves and adorned with ribbons.

There is a sense of reality within the contrasts of rich and poor and their symbioses. Charlotte Yeldham's research suggests that Taylor's concern for such charity and communality is consistent with her connections with the Methodist and Moravian churches.[80] This is a certainly a more ordered and sedate assemblage of Irish types than that is on show in Nicol's later painting of Donnybrook Fair (cat. 75). Whether such themes reflect myth or reality, the aspects of material culture depicted are valuable visual records.

As well as being a focal point for local communities on days such as that recorded by Taylor and Peacock, Glendalough was also from an early stage a much celebrated attraction for tourists and visitors from other parts of the country. 'After the Eagle's Nest at Killarney,' claimed Mr and Mrs S.C. Hall 'the beauty and sublimity of which should be free from human intrusion, and the Giant's Causeway, where the wonders of creation press so strongly upon the mind as to demand silence from all things, except the ocean- after these, we would wish to be alone at Glendalough'.[81] CK

---

77 Ledwich 1808, pp.180-81.

78 *ibid*, pp.176-79. Ledwich's illustrated description of the seven churches refers to the river Avonmore with its stepping stones, and to the Ivy clad Church, which may be what Taylor shows here to the left of the scene, behind the tents.

79 For further discussion of stereotypical behaviour depicted in fairs and patterns, and on the associated links between Peacock's and Taylor's paintings, see Dunne 2006, pp.56-57.

80 Yeldham 2005, p.204.

81 Hall 1843, vol.II, p.231.

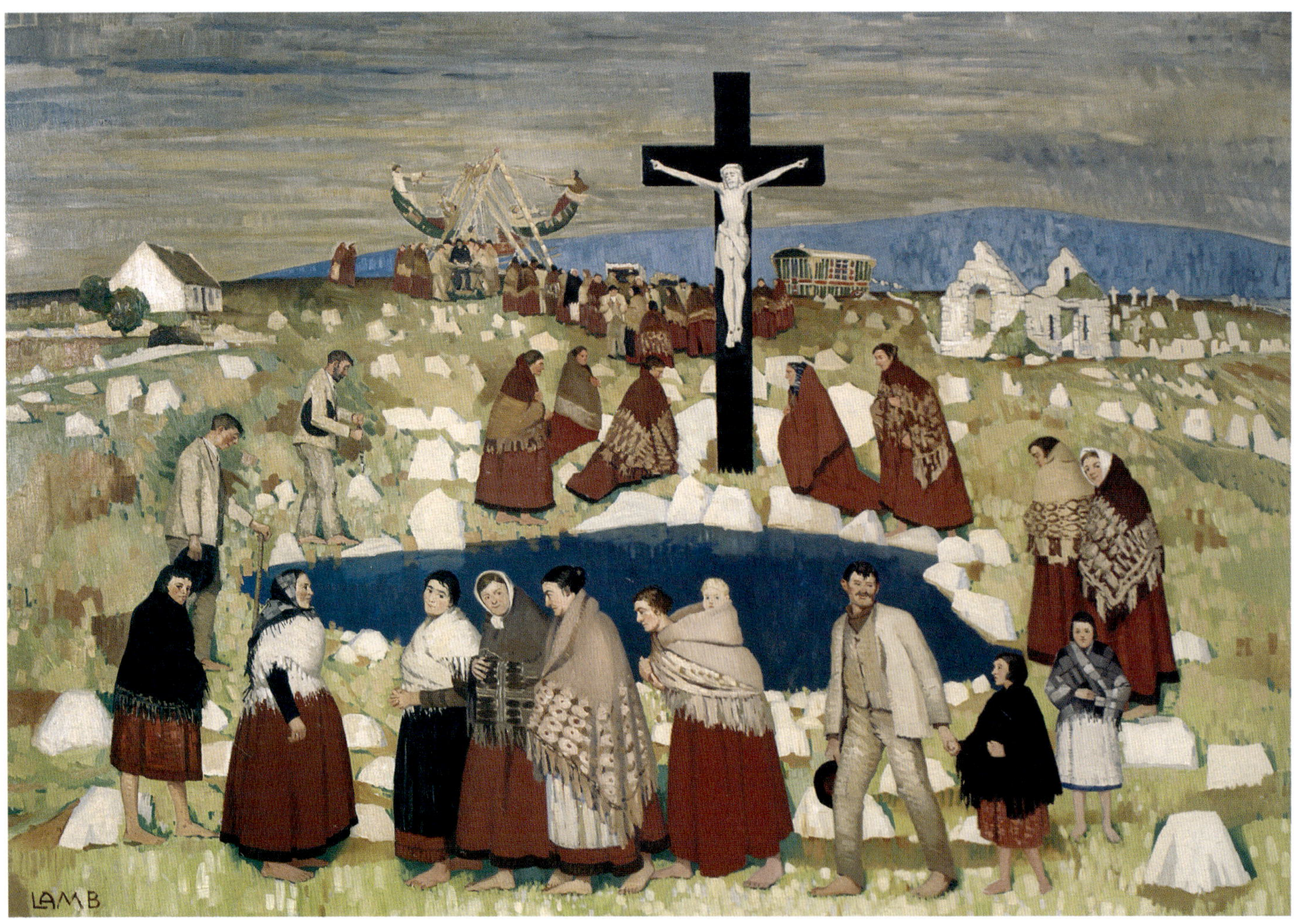

Charles Lamb (1893-1965)
82. *Pattern Day in Connemara*
1934
Oil on canvas
200.0 x 270 cm
National University of Ireland, Galway

82. Pattern Day in Connemara

Charles Lamb

There are aspects of surprising continuity between descriptions and portrayals of Irish rural customs by nineteenth-century visitors and artists of the early Free State such as Charles Lamb. Although he, like Paul Henry, chose to live among the subject matter of his choice, there is often the sense that he still paints as an outsider. This comes across both in a quasi-anthropological approach to depicting local customs and artifacts, but also more generally in a somewhat uncritical use of west of Ireland subject matter to bear allegorical significance, which must have bemused the inhabitants of Carraroe. If paintings by Lamb such as *Pattern Day in Connemara* and *Dancing at a Northern Crossroads* (cat. 7) do not have the same blatantly didactic, even propagandist intent, apparent in much of Sean Keating's work, there is often a latent sense of 'message' and general feeling of import.

Here Lamb continues the nineteenth-century tradition of portraying the ancient religious rite of the pattern, the gathering at a holy well or other holy site on the feast day of a saint. The religious aspect of the custom had merged with social, business and distinctly impious activities which led to several of the most popular patterns being banned by the Catholic hierarchy. William Carleton noted how it was 'quite usual to see young men and women devoutly circumambulating the well or lake on their bare knees with all the marks of penitence and contrition strongly impressed upon their faces; whilst again, after an hour or two, the same individuals may be found in a tent dancing with ecstatic vehemence to the music of bagpipe or fiddle'.[82] In this context Lamb's tall crucifix and swing-boat seem not such a strange juxtaposition.

The famous pattern at Glendalough had been portrayed on a number of occasions in the nineteenth century by Maria Spilsbury Taylor (cat. 81) and Joseph Peacock (Ulster Museum). In these examples commercial and societal impulses are placed in the foreground. Lamb's work however, also picks up on the antiquarian thrust of George Petrie whose *Last Circuit of the Pilgrims at Clonmacnoise* (NGI) has a distinctly allegorical feel, a final dawn for an ancient society and its values. In all of these pictures there is emphasis on Catholic belief at ancient monastic sites dominated by Round Towers and High Crosses. However, in Petrie's *St Brigid's Well* the holy site is unmarked by any symbol of Christian belief suggesting the continuity with pre-Christian holy places.[83]

The religious customs surrounding holy wells and pattern days were explored by Philip Dixon Hardy in 1840. 'I pressed a very old man...to state what possible advantage he expected to derive from the singular custom of frequenting in particular such wells as were contiguous to an old blasted oak, or an upright unhewn stone... his answer, and the answer of the oldest men, was that their ancestors always did it; that it was a preservative against Geasa-Draoidacht, ie the sorceries of Druids; that their cattle were preserved by it from infections and disorders; that the daoini maethe, ie the fairies, were kept in good humour by it!'[84] No doubt to protect from the continuation of such pagan associations, the well in Lamb's picture is dominated by a huge crucifix which stands out as a modern intrusion on this ancient site and which is studiously ignored by all of those participating in the circular precession around the well.

If Hardy's tone is mocking, Lamb seems to have believed in the innate spirituality of the west of Ireland, and saw in a return to its culture the opportunity for a spiritual cleansing of the nation. To Lamb, these people were, in Arthur Power's words, 'the seed, root and branch of this country; from whom everything proceeds, and to whom it seems now, everything must return'.[85] This perception is redolent of that shared by artists visiting Brittany in the late nineteenth century, who felt that local Breton communities they encountered, and among whom they lived, represented a world of tradition and piety that was primal and dignified but gradually disappearing. Lamb himself visited Brittany in the mid 1920s, producing such works as *Breton Peasants at Prayer* (Garter Lane Art Centre, Waterford) of related subject matter. It is interesting in this regard to note that Elizabeth, countess of Fingall likened Irish patterns to *pardons* in Brittany but conceded that though both had a religious association, or had done originally, 'the religious part had lapsed and the "Pattern" had become a purely frivolous occasion'. Similarly, she recalled that patterns in Galway featured dancing competitions, fair booths with oranges, apples, sweets and gingerbread 'all mixed together gaily for sale'.[86]

Lamb's painting is remarkable for its size alone. In the catalogue accompanying the memorial exhibition of Lamb's work at the Municipal Gallery of Modern Art in Dublin in 1969, the organisers acknowledged that it was not possible to show the painting 'due to transport difficulties' and this is the first time it has been exhibited in Dublin.[87] *Pattern Day in Connemara* was commissioned by the Haverty Trust, established in 1930 to encourage contemporary Irish art. In subject matter it accords well with other commissions by the Trust such as the series of pictures illustrating the life of St Patrick commissioned from Leo Whelan, Sean Keating and Margaret Clarke.

By the time Lamb was commissioned to paint the picture in 1934/35, he had developed a somewhat reductive vision of the west of Ireland. While earlier essays such as *Dancing at a Northern Crossroads* (cat.7), *Connemara Harvesters* (private collection) and *The Quaint Couple* (Crawford Municipal Art Gallery) were studio-bound, staged studies in the tradition of Orpen and Keating, here to a large extent Lamb appears to have relinquished naturalism in favour of a more coded, abstracted approach. The feeling of ancient rite is reinforced by the circularity of the figures and essential symmetry of the composition. The roofless ruins to the right contrast with the white modern cottage to the left as if indicative of different dispensations on either side of the crucifix. Lamb simplified his forms over time so that the figures that occupy his later compositions are shadowy by comparison with the angular characters in such paintings as *Dancing at a Northern Crossroads* (cat.7). Both in the flattened form of the pictorial space and in the stylised west of Ireland figures, with their suggestion of mystical rather than just political import, Lamb here begins to move from the Keating tradition to anticipate the Connemara work of Gerard Dillon in the next two decades. WL

---

82 Carleton 1911, p. xxiv.

83 Murray 2004, p.23.

84 Quoted in Murray 2004, p.145.

85 Power 1969.

86 Fingall 1991.

87 Municipal Gallery of Modern Art 1969.

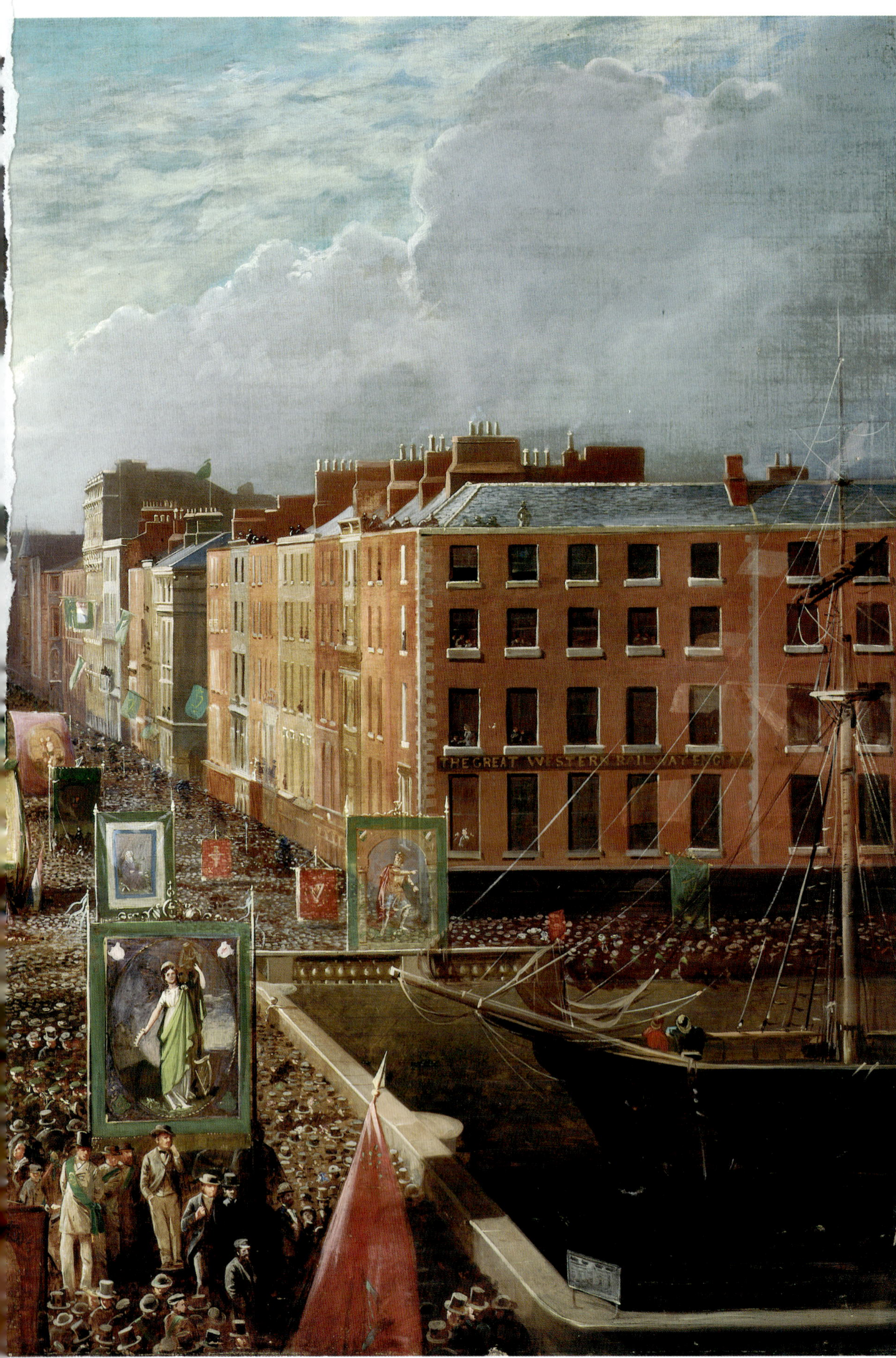

Charles Russell
(1852-1910)
79. *The O'Connell Centenary Celebrations*
1875
Oil on canvas
104 x 163 cm
National Gallery of Ireland
See page 150

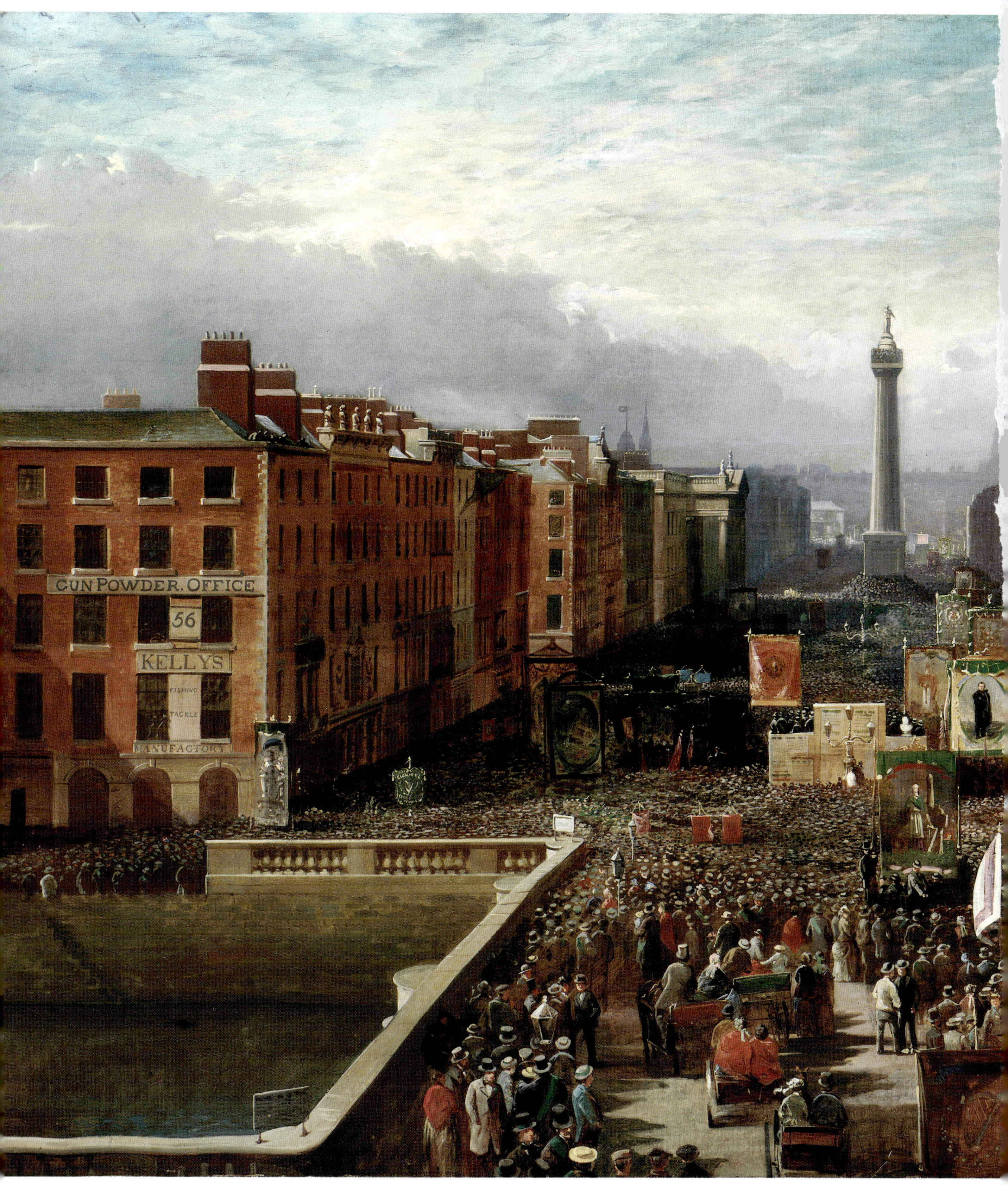
GUN POWDER. OFFICE
56
KELLYS
FISHING
TACKLE
MANUFACTORY

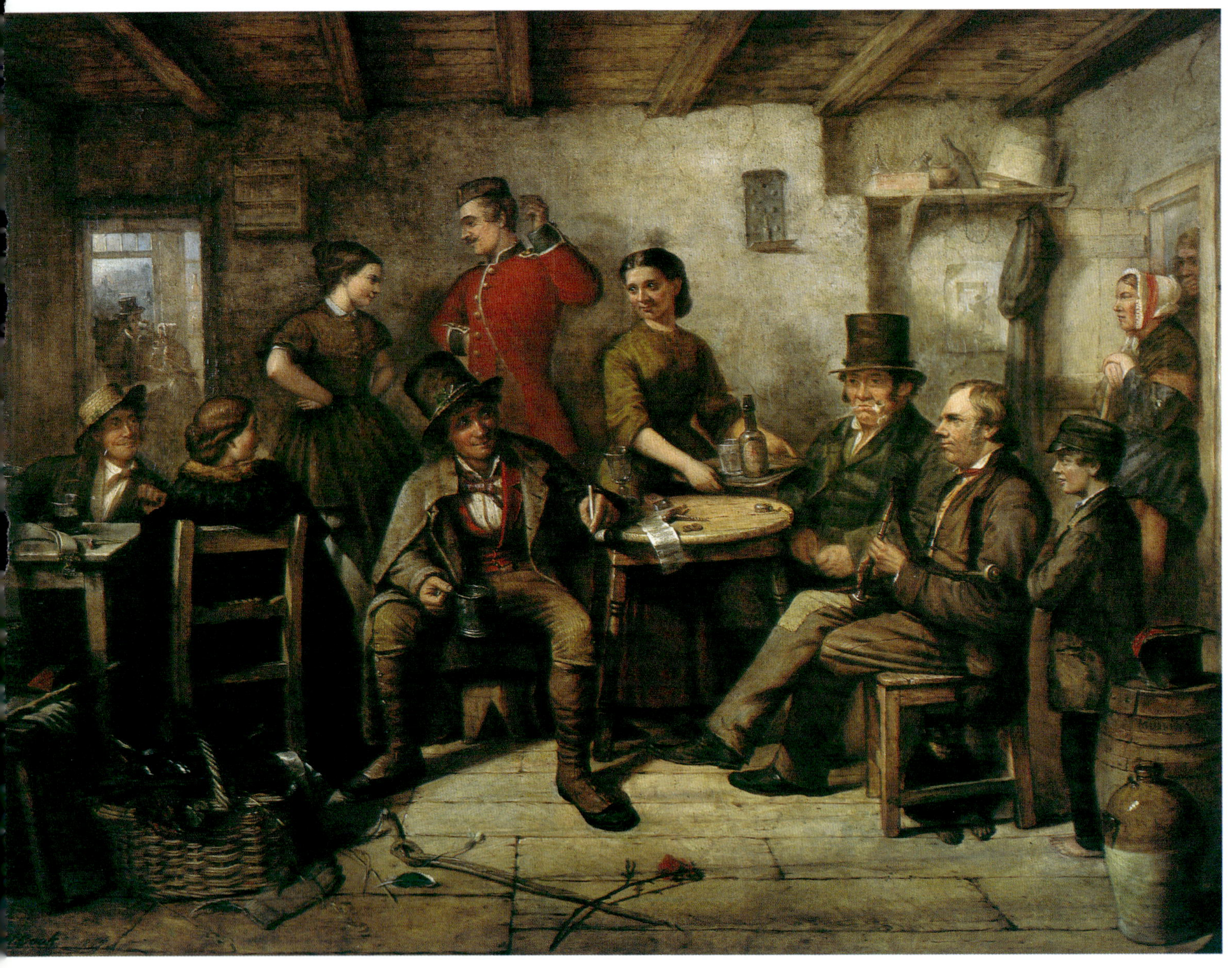

Charles Henry Cook
(c.1830-c.1906)
83. *St Patrick's Day*
1867
Oil on canvas
86.4 x 111.7 cm
Courtesy of the National Library of Ireland

83. St Patrick's Day

Charles Henry Cook

Charles Cook was born in Bandon, and subsequently lived in Cork, from where he later emigrated to England, settling in Bath. Records indicate that he exhibited about fifteen pictures in Cork and Dublin from 1851 onwards, including some at the RHA. This painting is likely to be the one entitled *St Patrick's Day* lent to the Cork Industrial Exhibition in 1883, as four of the men sport shamrock in their hats.[88] Cook's other works include similarly rounded figures, and usually depict scenes of rural life, featuring musicians, dancers, themes of romance and especially of emigration.[89]

The setting is the shady backroom of a country pub where the thematic, if not pictorial, focus is on a young woman who dances daringly with a soldier. With this character, Cook introduces the topic of rebellion from the marriages of economic convenience which were commonly arranged by farmers for their daughters. He employs an array of artistic symbolism, inconspicuously woven within the functional accoutrements of the room, to provoke debate over such a controversial match. As if the curtain had been raised for the central act of a play, the contemporary audience was tempted to debate the dancers' togetherness and its possible consequences. Upon the sloping stage-like floor lies a lovers' knot in twisted willow under a red rose with battered petals: a symbol of imperfect romance. Through time the language of flowers had various meanings, but the primrose often meant early youth, and the daisy here on the table to the left beside the discarded guardsman's belt represented innocence.

The dancing girl's clothing, a full petticoat and a shirt beneath a fitted bodice, and her hairstyle are more fashionable than those of the barmaid in the centre. The dancers are symbolically represented by the two dead fowl draped decorously over each other in the wicker basket on the floor. A mallard, blood dripping from his beak, has green and white plumage that matches the soldier's collar and cuffs. A red hen lies beneath the mallard, wild oats protrude from between their bodies, and an open bottle and a vine leaf rest beside them. The soldier's open uniform is meticulously portrayed, and in detail represents accurately a specific regiment that visited Cork's Victoria Barracks during the artist's youth.[90] The infantryman has risen from the stool on the left, leaving his cane and his gloves scattered carelessly. In the seventeenth century, the diarist Samuel Pepys mentioned that gloves were a customary marriage gift, yet here one is discarded on the floor. A small casket with a scarlet lining lies on the stool, open yet symbolically empty of its precious contents. On the wall to the left of our errant dancer hangs a birdcage, which provided wild birdsong in many households. However, close examination reveals that the bird has flown along with the young woman's chances of a respectably arranged marriage, with its attendant dowry of goods and chattels. The wall sconce on the right holds an unlit candle, symbolising the dark side of life. The women's hooded cloaks, the carpenter's chairs and the barrel in the foreground emblazoned with the name Murphy's are all objects characteristic of Cook's native Cork.

Relaxation and conviviality were customary for this annual holiday, when the abstinences of Lent were cast aside to celebrate Ireland's patron saint. Significantly, the first substantial change to licensing legislation made by the government of the Free State was to close pubs on St Patrick's Day from 1927 to 1960. Above the uilleann piper, and beneath a dangling Catholic rosary, an unframed print is pinned to the wall. It shows a widely reproduced lithograph called 'Outward Bound' after a painting by Scottish painter Erskine Nicol, which depicts 'Paddy' on the Dublin docks pondering advertisements for steamships to New York, Quebec and the 'New World'. Nicol was sufficiently well known for this picture within a picture to be recognised as an icon of emigration.[91] Emigration and a new start abroad, together or alone, was one option for those who contravened the strict conventions of rural communities. CK

---

88 When this painting was conserved in 2005, the name Flynn was found chalked repeatedly on the back of the canvas and stretcher, matching the name of the lender of this title to the Cork Industrial Exhibition in 1883.

89 Julian Cambell discusses *Awaiting the Emigrant Ship* (Cork City Library), painted in 1867, the same year as *St Patrick's Day* in Murray 2006, pp.128-29.

90 Kinmonth 2006, pp.188-89.

91 *ibid,* fig.187.

H. Allingham 1906
Hugh Allingham, 'Extracts from John Wesley's Journal- A Wonderful Clock' in *Ulster Journal of Archaeology*, vol.12, second series (January 1906), pp.47-48.

W. Allingham 1854
William Allingham, *The Music Master*, (London 1854).

W. Allingham 1860
William Allingham, *Day and Night Songs and The Music Master*, (London 1860).

Arnold 1991
Bruce Arnold, *Mainie Jellett and the Modern Movement in Ireland*, (New Haven and London 1991).

Arnold 1998
Bruce Arnold, *Jack B. Yeats*, (New Haven and London 1998).

Baines 1981
Barbara Burman Baines, *Fashion Revivals from the Elizabethan Age to the Present Day*, (London 1981).

Ball 1903
Francis Elrington Ball, *A History of the County Dublin*, vol. II, (Dublin 1903).

Ballard 1998
Linda May Ballard, *Forgetting Frolic, Marriage Traditions in Ireland*, (Institute of Irish Studies, Belfast, 1998).

Banim and Banim 1825
John Banim and Michael Banim, *Tales of the O'Hara Family*, (London 1825/1826).

Barnard 1998
Toby Barnard, *The Abduction of a Limerick Heiress: Social and Political Relations in Mid-Eighteenth-Century Ireland* (Maynooth 1998).

Barnard 2004
Toby Barnard, *Making the Grand Figure: Lives and Possessions in Ireland, 1641-1770*, (New Haven and London 2004).

Barrett 1973
Cyril Barrett, 'Michael Angelo Hayes, RHA, and the Galloping Horse', *The Arts in Ireland*, vol.1, no.3 (1973), pp.42-47.

Barrington 1827
Sir Jonah Barrington, *Personal Sketches of his own Times*, (New York 1827-32).

Bartlett and Jeffery 1996
Thomas Bartlett and Keith Jeffery, eds, *A Military History of Ireland*, (Cambridge 1996).

Battersea 1922
Constance Battersea, *Reminiscences*, (London 1922).

Bell 2002
Jonathan Bell, *Conor. Drawing from Life*, (Belfast 2002).

Benn 1877
G. Benn, *A History of the Town of Belfast* (Belfast 1877).

Berkeley Art Museum 1998
When Time Began to Rant and Rage. Figurative painting from twentieth-century Ireland, exh. cat. University of California, Berkeley Art Museum, (London 1998).

Bernard 1830
John Bernard, *Retrospections of the Stage*, 2 vols, (London 1830).

Black 2006
Eileen Black, *Art in Belfast 1760-1888. Art Lovers or Philistines?*, (Dublin 2006).

Blake 1991
Raymond Blake, *In Black and White. A History of Rowing at Trinity College, Dublin,* (Dublin 1991).

Bourke 1999
Marie Bourke, 'An Image Reflecting National Identity. Charles Lamb (1893-1964) and life in the west of Ireland', *Céide*, vol.2, no.4, (March/April 1999), pp.19-22.

Bourke 2000
Marie Bourke, 'A Growing Sense of National Identity. Charles Lamb (1893-1964) & the West of Ireland', *History Ireland*, vol.8, no.1, (Spring 2000), pp.30-34.

Bourke and Bhreathnach-Lynch 1999
Marie Bourke and Sighle Bhreathnach-Lynch, *Discover Irish Art*, (Dublin 1999).

Bowen 1955
Muriel Bowen, *Irish Hunting*, (Tralee 1955).

Boylan 1968
Lena Boylan, 'The Connollys of Castletown: A Family History', *Bulletin of the Irish Georgian Society*, vol. XI, no.4 (October-November 1968), pp.1-46.

Brady and Simms 2001
Joseph Brady and Angrett Simms, ed., *Dublin Through Space and Time*, (Dublin 2001).

Brennan 1999
Helen Brennan, *The Story of Irish Dance*, (Dingle 1999).

Brooks 1999
Denis Brooks, 'Irish Bellows-Pipes', *The Pipers' Review*, vol.xviii, no.3, (Summer 1999).

Brown 1990
Terence Brown, *Ireland. A Social and Cultural History 1922-1985*, (London 1990).

Cahill 1999
Katherine Cahill, 'In the Mainstream of Irish Naturalism. The art of Lilian Lucy Davidson, 1879-1954', *Irish Arts Review*, vol.15 (1999), pp.34-45.

Campbell 1984
Julian Campbell, *The Irish Impressionists*, exh. cat. National Gallery of Ireland, (Dublin 1984).

Campbell 2004
Julian Campbell, *Walter Osborne in the West of Ireland*, (Dublin 2004).

Carleton 1911
William Carleton, *Traits and stories of the Irish Peasantry*, 4 vols. (Boston 1911). First published 1830.

Carleton 1990
William Carleton, *Traits and Stories of the Irish Peasantry*, (Gerrards Cross 1990).

Chabanais and Goldberg 1994
Paula Chabanais and David Goldberg, 'Sidney Smith: Painter and Muralist (1912-1982)', *Irish Arts Review*, vol. 10, (1994), pp. 235-44.

Chandler 2001
Edward Chandler, *Photography in Ireland. The Nineteenth Century*, (Dublin 2001).

Clarke 1995
Liam Clarke, *Memories of Lehaunstown Races*, (Foxrock Local History Club 1995)

Jn Coleman 1988
John Coleman, 'A Painter of Living Art: Jack P. Hanlon 1913-1968', *Irish Arts Review*, vol.5, (1988), pp.222-28.

Js Coleman 1893
James Coleman, 'The Story of Spike Island', *Journal of the Cork Historical and Archaeological Society*, vol.II, no.13 (January 1893), pp.2-8.

Collier 1872
John Payne Collier, *An Old Man's Diary, Forty Years Ago*, vol. 4, (London 1872).

Corballis 1891
James Henry Corballis, *Forty-Five Years of Sport*, (London 1891).

Cowling 1983
Mary C. Cowling, 'The Artist as Anthropologist in Mid-Victorian England: Frith's Derby Day, the Railway Station and the New Science of Mankind', *Art History*, vol.6, no.4 (December 1983), pp.461-77.

Croker 1839
Thomas Crofton Croker, *The Popular Songs of Ireland*, (London 1839).

Croker 1969
Thomas Crofton Croker, *Researches in the South of Ireland*, (London 1969). First published 1824.

Croker 1998
Thomas Crofton Croker, *Fairy Legends and Traditions in the South of Ireland*, (London 1998). First published 1825.

Crofts 1997
Sinéad Crofts, 'Maurice MacGonigal PRHA (1900-79) and his Western Paintings', *Irish Arts Review*, vol.13, (1997), pp.135-42.

D. Cronin et al 2001
Denis A. Cronin, Jim Gilligan and Karina Holton, eds, *Irish Fairs and Markets. Studies in Local History*, (Dublin 2001).

M. Cronin 1999
Mike Cronin, *Sport and Nationalism in Ireland. Gaelic games, soccer and Irish identity since 1884*, (Dublin 1999).

M. Cronin 2002
Mike Cronin, *The Wearing of the Green. A History of St Patrick's Day*, (London 2002).

Crookshank 1966
Anne Crookshank, *Louis Le Brocquy. A Retrospective Selection of Oil Paintings 1939-1966*, Municipal Gallery of Modern Art, Dublin and Ulster Museum, Belfast, (Dublin 1966).

Crookshank 1992
Anne Crookshank, 'The Conversation Piece in Irish Painting in the Eighteenth Century', in A. Bernelle, ed., *Decantations, A Tribute to Maurice Craig*, (Dublin 1992), p.16-20.

Crookshank and Glin 1969
Anne Crookshank and the Knight of Glin, *Irish Portraits 1660-1860*, exh. cat. National Gallery of Ireland, Dublin , National Gallery London and Ulster Museum Belfast, (1969).

Crookshank and Glin 1978
Anne Crookshank and the Knight of Glin, *The Painters of Ireland*, (London 1978).

Crookshank and Glin 1994
Anne Crookshank and the Knight of Glin, *The Watercolours of Ireland*, (London 1994).

Crookshank and Glin 2002
Anne Crookshank and the Knight of Glin, *Ireland's Painters*, (New Haven and London 2002).

Dalsimer 1993
Adele M. Dalsimer, ed., *Visualizing Ireland. National Identity and the Pictorial Tradition*, (Boston and London 1993).

Dalsimer and Kreilkamp 1996
Adele M. Dalsimer and Vera Kreilkamp, eds, *America's Eye: Irish Paintings from the Collection of Brian P. Burns*, exh. cat. Boston College Museum of Art, (Boston 1996).

Day 1991
Angelique Day, ed., *Letters from Georgian Ireland*, (Belfast 1991).

D'Arcy 1992-93
Fergus D'Arcy, 'A Horse called Flyar: a problem of Irish art history', *Journal of the Kilkenny Archaeological Society*, vol. XXVIII (1992-93), pp.92-95.

Darcy 1991
Fergus D'Arcy, *Horses, Lords and Racing Men. The Turf Club 1790-1990*, (Curragh 1991).

Dermott 1782
Laurence Dermott, *Ahiman Rezon, or a Help to a Brother*, (Belfast 1782).

Dillon-Malone 2001
A. Dillon-Malone, *Historic Pubs of Dublin*, (Dublin 2001).

DNB 2004
Oxford Dictionary of National Biography, 60 vols, (Oxford 2004).

Dolan 1998
Terence Patrick Dolan, *A Dictionary of Hiberno-English. The Irish use of English*, (Dublin 1998),

Doyle 1935
Lynne Doyle [Leslie Alexander Montgomery], *Spirit of Ireland.* (London 1935).

Dublin University Review 1961
Anon., 'A Stroll over Donnybrook Fair-Green', *Dublin University Review*, (October 1861), pp.492-503.

Dunlevy 1989
Mairead Dunlevy, *Dress in Ireland. A History*, (London 1989).

Dunlevy and Ó Gráda 2003
Mairead Dunlevy and Cormac Ó Gráda, 'A Bowling Match in Castlemary, County Cork', in David Dickson and Cormac Ó Gráda, eds, *Refiguring Ireland. Essays in honour of L.M. Cullen*, (Dublin 2003), pp.224-29.

Dunne 2006
Tom Dunne'The Dark Side of the Irish landscape' in Peter Murray, ed., *Whipping the Herring. Survival and celebration in nineteenth-century Irish art*, exh. cat. Crawford Municipal Art Gallery, (Cork 2006), pp.46-59.

Edgeworth 1999
Maria Edgeworth, *Castle Rackrent*, (Oxford 1999). First published 1800.

Essex 1728
John Essex, *The Dancing Master*, (London 1728). Translation of Pierre Rameau, *Le maître à danser*, (1725).

Everett 1994
Nigel Everett, *The Tory View of Landscape*, (New Haven and London 1994).

Fielding 1985
Henry Fielding, *Tom Jones*, (London 1985). First published 1749.

Figgis and Rooney 2001
Nicola Figgis and Brendan Rooney, *Irish Paintings in the National Gallery of Ireland, Volume I*, (Dublin 2001).

Fink 1990
Lois Marie Fink, *American Art at the Nineteenth-Century Paris Salons*, (Cambridge 1990).

Fingall 1991
Elizabeth Mary Margaret Plunkett countess of Fingall, *Seventy Years Young. Memories of Elizabeth, Countess of Fingall; told to Pamela Hinkson*, (Dublin 1991). First published 1937.

Fitz-Simon 2003
Christopher Fitz-Simon, *The Abbey Theatre: Ireland's National Theatre. The First Hundred Years*, (London 2003).

Fleeton 1984
G. Fleeton, ed., *A Seat Among the Stars. The Cinema and Ireland*, (London 1984).

Flower 1973
Robin Flower, *The Western Island or The Great Blasket* (Oxford 1973).

Geary and Kelleher 2005
Laurence M. Geary and Margaret Kelleher, eds, *Nineteenth-century Ireland. A Guide to Recent Research*, (Dublin 2005).

Gilligan 1988
H.A. Gilligan, *A History of the Port of Dublin*, (Dublin 1988).

Glennie et al 1996
Sarah Glennie, Roisin Kennedy, Brenda McParland and Alistair Smith, *Louis le Brocquy 1939-1996*, exh. cat. Irish Museum of Modern Art, (Dublin 1996).

Glew 1870
Edward Lees Glew, *Life in Dublin or Donnybrook Fair in its Palmiest Days. As Illustrated in Glew's Mammoth Picture*, (Newark 1870).

Griffith 1788
A. Griffith, *Miscellaneous Tracts*, (Dublin 1788).

Gwynn 1938
Stephen Lucius Gwynn, *Dublin Old and New*, (Dublin 1938).

Hall 1843
Mr and Mrs Samuel Carter Hall, *Ireland: Its Scenery, Character &c*, 3 vols (London 1843).

Hall n.d.
Mrs S.C. Hall, *Popular Tales of Irish Life and Character*, (London n.d.).

Hall 1855
Mrs S.C. Hall, *Sketches of Irish Character*, 5th Edition (London 1855).

Hawthorne 1928
Julian Hawthorne, *Shapes that Pass*, (London 1928).

Hempton and Hill 1992
David Hempton and Myrtle Hill, *Evangelical Protestantism in Ulster Society 1740-1890*, (London 1992).

Henry 1951
Paul Henry, *An Irish Portrait*, (London 1951).

Hewitt 1977
John Hewitt, 'Conor's Art', in Judith Wilson, *Conor 1881-1968: The Life and Work of an Ulster Artist*, (Dundonald 1977), pp.107-27.

Hill et al 1988
John Hill, Luke Gibbons and Kevin Rocket, *Cinema and Ireland*, (London 1988).

Hunt Museum 2005
Shades of Light- evocations of summer, exh. cat. Hunt Museum, Limerick, (Limerick 2005).

Hutchinson 1983
John Hutchinson, *AE. George Russell and his Circle*, exhibition brochure, Arts Council of Northern Ireland, (Belfast 1983).

Hutchinson 1985
John Hutchinson, *James Arthur O'Connor*, exh. cat. National Gallery of Ireland, (Dublin 1985).

IMMA 1991
Mainie Jellett 1897-1944, exh. cat. Irish Museum of Modern Art, (Dublin 1991).

Ireland 1986
John de Courcy Ireland, *Ireland and the Irish in Maritime History*, (Dun Laoghaire 1986).

Ireland 1992
John de Courcy Ireland, *Ireland's Maritime Heritage*, (Dublin 1992).

Ireland 2001
John de Courcy Ireland, *History of Dun Laoghaire Harbour*, (Blackrock 2001).

Irish Traditional Music Archive 1992
'The Uileann Pipes in Irish Traditional Music', in *Irish Traditional Music Archive*, (1992), p.5.

Jupp and Magennis 2000
Peter Jupp and Eoin Magennis, eds, *Crowds in Ireland, c.1720-1920*, (Basingstoke 2000).

Kearns 1996
Kevin Kearns, *Dublin Pub Life and Lore*, (Dublin 1996).

B. Kennedy 1993
Brian P. Kennedy, *Irish Painting*, (Dublin 1993).

P.Kennedy 1863
Patrick Kennedy, 'Irish Dancing Fifty Years Ago', *Dublin University Magazine*, vol. LXII (1863), p.430.

R. Kennedy 1999
Róisín Kennedy, *Dublin Castle Art. The Historical and Contemporary Collection*, (Dublin 1999).

S.B. Kennedy 1989
S.B. Kennedy, *Elizabeth Rivers*, exh. cat. Gorry Gallery, (Dublin 1989).

S.B. Kennedy 1989-90
S.B. Kennedy, 'Paul Henry: An Irish Portrait', *Irish Arts Review*, vol.6, (1989-90), pp.43-54.

S.B. Kennedy 1991
S.B. Kennedy, *Irish Art and Modernism 1880-1950*, (Belfast 1991).

S.B. Kennedy 1999
S.B. Kennedy, 'An Enduring View of Irish Identity. Paul Henry and the Realism of Fiction', *Irish Arts Review*, vol.15, (1999), pp.98-107.

S.B. Kennedy 2003a
S.B. Kennedy, 'An Enduring Presence: Paul Henry and the Irish Landscape', *Irish Arts Review*, (Spring 2003), pp.58-60.

S.B. Kennedy 2003b
S.B. Kennedy, *Paul Henry*, exh. cat. National Gallery of Ireland (Dublin 2003).

Kennelly 1967
Brendan Kennelly, 'AE. His Work', *Irish Times*, (10 April 1967).

Kenny 1928
Thomas J. Kenny, *Tour of the Tipperary Hurling Team in America*, (London 1926).

Kinmonth 1993
C. Kinmonth, *Irish Country Furniture, 1700-1950* (New Haven and London 1993). Republished 2006.

Kinmonth 2001
Claudia Kinmonth, 'Rags and Rushes: Art and the Irish Artefact, c. 1900', *Journal of Design History*, vol, 14, no. 3, (2001), pp. 167-186.

Kinmonth 2006
Claudia Kinmonth, *Irish Rural Interiors in Art*, (New Haven and London 2006).

Krause 1972
David Krause, ed., *The Dolmen Boucicault*, (Dublin 1972).

Laffan 1999
William Laffan, ed., *Masterpieces by Irish Artists 1660-1860*, Pyms Gallery, (London 1999).

Laffan 2001
William Laffan, ed., *The Sublime and the Beautiful. Irish Art 1700-1830*, Pyms Gallery, (London 2001).

Laffan 2002
William Laffan, ed., *The Art of a Nation: Three Centuries of Irish Painting*, Pyms Gallery, (London 2002).

Laffan 2003a
William Laffan, ed., *The Cries of Dublin. Drawn from the Life by Hugh Douglas Hamilton, 1760*, (Tralee 2003).

Laffan 2003b
William Laffan, ed., *A Year at Churchill*, (Tralee 2003).

Laffan 2005
William Laffan, ed., *Miscelanea Structura Curiosa by Samuel Chearnley*, (Tralee 2005).

Laffan 2006
William Laffan, ed., *Painting Ireland. Topographical Views from Glin Castle*, (Tralee 2006).

Lalor 2003
Brian Lalor, ed., *The Encyclopaedia of Ireland*, (Dublin 2003).

Lavery 1940
John Lavery, *The Life of a Painter*, (London 1940).

Lawrence 1905
W.J. Lawrence, 'Punch and Judy: A Famous Dublin Show', *Irish Independent*, 29 August 1905.

Leach 1985
Robert Leach, *The Punch and Judy Show. History, Tradition and Meaning*, (London 1985).

Le Brocquy 1996
Louis le Brocquy, *The Head Image: interviews with the artist*, (Dublin 1996).

Ledwich 1808
Edward Ledwich, *Antiquities of Ireland*, (Dublin 1808).

Le Harivel 1983
Adrian Le Harivel, *National Gallery of Ireland. Acquisitions 1982-83*, (Dublin 1983).

Le Harivel and Wynne 1984
Adrian Le Harivel and Michael Wynne, *National Gallery of Ireland. Acquisitions 1982-1983*, (Dublin 1984).

Leslie 1772
J. Leslie, *Phoenix Park: A Poem*, (London 1772).

C.A. Lewis 1975
Colin Andrew Lewis, *Hunting in Ireland: An Historical and Geographical Analysis*, (London 1975).

S. Lewis 1837
Samuel Lewis, *A Topographical Dictionary of Ireland*, 2 vols, (London 1837).

Llanover 1861-62
Lady Llanover, ed., *The Autobiography and Correspondence of Mary Granville, Mrs Delany*, 6 vols, (London 1861-62).

Loftus 1978
Belinda Loftus, comp., *Marching Workers. An exhibition of Irish trade banners and regalia*, exh. cat. Arts Council of Ireland, (Dublin 1978).

Longmate 1968
Norman Longmate, *The Waterdrinkers. A History of Temperance*, (London 1968).

Lynd 1912
Robert Lynd, *Rambles in Ireland*, (London 1912).

Lyons 1979
F.S.L. Lyons, *Culture and Anarchy in Ireland 1890-1939*, (Oxford 1979).

McAuley 2003
Rosemary McAuley, *A Fresh Way of Seeing. Harry Kernoff in his Times*, (Dublin 2003).

McBride and Flynn 1996
Stephen McBride and Roddy Flynn, eds, *Here's Looking at You Kid! Ireland Goes to the Pictures*, (Dublin 1996).

MacCarvill 1958
Eileen MacCarvill, ed., *Mainie Jellett. The Artist's Vision. Lectures and Essays on Art*, (Dundalk 1958).

McConkey 1990
Kennth McConkey, *A Free Spirit. Irish Art 1860-1960*, (Woodbridge 1990).

McConkey 1993
Kenneth McConkey, *Sir John Lavery*, (Edinburgh 1993).

McElligott 1971
Tom J. McElligott, 'Handball. A Game for Idle Hands?', *Ireland of the Welcomes*, vol.20, no.2 (July-August 1971), pp.6-10.

McElligott c.1984
Tom McElligott, *The Story of Handball: The Game, The Players, The History*, (Dublin c.1984).

MacGonigal 1976
Ciarán MacGonigal, *The Harry Kernoff Memorial Exhibition*, The Hugh Lane Municipal Gallery of Modern Art, (Dublin 1976).

MacGowan n.d.
Kenneth MacGowan, *The Phoenix Park*, (Dublin n.d.).

MacNeill 1971
D.B. MacNeill, *Irish Passenger Steamship Services, Volume 2; South of Ireland*, (Newton Abbot 1971).

Maume 1999
Patrick Maume, *The Long Gestation: Irish Nationalist Political Life 1891-1918*, (Dublin 1999).

Mayes and Murphy 1993
Elizabeth Mayes and Paula Murphy, *Images and Insights: Hugh Lane Municipal Gallery of Modern Art*, (Dublin 1993).

Millar 1852
T. Millar, *Picturesque Sketches of London Past and Present*, (London 1852).

Millin 1932
Samuel Shannon Millin, *Sidelights on Belfast History* (Belfast and London 1932).

Molloy 2002
Cian Molloy, *The Story of the Irish Pub. An Intoxicating History of the Licensed Trade in Ireland*, (Dublin 2002).

Morash 2002
Christopher Morash, *A History of Irish Theatre, 1601 -2000*, (Cambridge 2002).

Morrow 1941
H.L. Morrow, 'The Art of Paul Henry', *Irish Times*, (1 November 1941).

Mulholland 1889
Rosa Mullholland, 'Irish Painters in this present Year' in *The Irish Monthly*, vol.XVII (September 1889), pp.481-84.

Municipal Gallery of Modern Art 1969
Charles Lamb 1893-1964, exh. cat. Hugh Lane Municipal Gallery of Modern Art, (Dublin 1969).

Murray 1993
Peter Murray, 'Art Institutions in Nineteenth-Century Cork', in Patrick O'Flanagan and Cornelius G. Buttimer, eds, *Cork. History and Society*, (Dublin 1993).

Murray 1997
Peter Murray, ed., *Irish Art 1770-1995. History and Society*, (Cork 1997).

Murray 2004
Peter Murray, *George Petrie (1790-1866). The Rediscovery of Ireland's Past*, (Cork 2004).

Murray 2005
Peter Murray, *Maritime Paintings of Cork and associated historical material 1700-2000*, (Cork 2005).

Murray 2006
Peter Murray, ed., *Whipping the Herring. Survival and celebration in nineteenth-century Irish art*, exh. cat. Crawford Municipal Art Gallery, (Cork 2006).

NGI 1987
Irish Women Artists. From the eighteen century to the present day, exh. cat. National Gallery of Ireland and The Douglas Hyde Gallery, (Dublin 1987).

NGI 1988
National Gallery of Ireland. Acquisitions 1986-1988, (Dublin 1988).

Ní Shuilleabháin 1992
Eibhlís Ní Shuilleabháin, *Letters from the Great Blasket*, (Dublin 1992).

Nicholson 1851
Asenath Nicholson, *Annals of the Famine in Ireland*, (New York 1851).

Norton 1991
James Norton, 'The Ward Union's Most Famous Field Master, Leonard Morrogh', *Hounds*, (October 1991), pp.28-29.

Nulty 1978
Oliver Nulty, *James Humbert Craig RHA (1878-1944)*, exh. cat. Oriel Gallery, (June 1978).

O'Brien and Piercy 2003
Gerard O'Brien and Sioban Piercy, *Imaging Ireland: selected works from the collection of National University of Ireland Galway*, (Galway 2003?)

O'Keefe and O'Brien 1902
James George O'Keefe and Art O'Brien, *A Handbook of Irish Dances*, (Dublin 1902).

Ó Dálaigh 1986
Brian Ó Dálaigh, 'An Early Nineteenth-Century Painting of Ennis', *The Other Clare*, x (1986), pp.12-14.

Ó Dálaigh 1995
Brian Ó Dálaigh, *Ennis in the Eighteenth Century. Portrait of an Urban Community*, (Blackrock 1995).

Ó Gaoithín 1982
Micheál O Gaoithín, *A Pity Youth Does Not Last*, (Oxford 1982).

Ó Maitiú 1995
Séamas Ó Maitiú *The Humours of Donnybrook. Dublin's Famous Fair and its Suppression,* (Maynooth 1995).

Ó Maitiú 2001
Séamas Ó Maitiú, 'Changing Images of Donnybrook Fair' in Denis A. Cronin, Jim Gilligan and Karina Holton, eds, *Irish Fairs and Markets. Studies in Local History*, (2001), p.164-179.

Open 1985
Michael Open, *Fading Lights and Silver Screens: A History of Belfast Cinema*, (Belfast 1985).

O'Regan 2004a
Maebh O'Regan, 'Military Manoeuvres: The making of a masterpiece', *thoughtlines 7. An Anthology of Research*, National College of Art and Design, Dublin (2004), pp.17-28.

O'Regan 2004b
Maebh O'Regan, 'Richard Moynan: Irish Artist and Unionist Propagandist', *Éire-Ireland*, vol.39, nos 1-2 (2004), pp.59-80.

Ó Suileabháin 1983
Muiris Ó Suileabháin, *Twenty Years A-Growing*, (Oxford 1983).

O'Sullivan 1999
Niamh O'Sullivan, *Aloysius O'Kelly. Paintings, Politics and Popular Culture*, exh. cat. Hugh Lane Municipal Gallery of Modern Art, (Dublin 1999).

O'Sullivan 2000
Niamh O'Sullivan, 'The Priest and the People: Mass in a Connemara Cabin', *Circa*, (Summer, 2000), p.16-18.

O'Sullivan 2002
Niamh O'Sullivan, 'The Mystery of the Lost Painting', *The Irish Times,* (2 November 2002), p.6.

Otway 1839
Rev. Caesar Otway, *Sketches in Ireland, descriptive of interesting portions of Donegal, Cork, and Kerry*, (Dublin 1839).

Pakenham 2000
Valerie Packenham, *The Big House in Ireland*, (London 2000).

Piggott 1906
W.J.P. [William Jackson Pigott], 'Miller Family of Lurgan' in *Ulster Journal of Archaeology*, vol.12, second series, (1906), pp.141-42.

Powell 2005
Martyn J. Powell, *The Politics of Consumption in Eighteenth-Century Ireland*, (London 2005).

Power 1969
Arthur Power, 'Charles Lamb 1893-1964. A Memoir', in *Charles Lamb 1893-1964*, exh. cat. Hugh Lane Municipal Gallery of Modern Art, (Dublin 1969).

Price 1966
Alan Price, ed, *J.M. Synge: Collected Works, vol.II, Prose*, (London 1966).

Pückler-Muskau 1987
Hermann Pückler-Muskau , *Puckler's Progress. The Adventuress of Prince Pückler-Muskau in England, Wales and Ireland as told in letters to his former wife, 1826-9*, (London, 1987). Translated by Flora Brennan.

Pyle 1970
Hilary Pyle, *Jack B. Yeats. A Biography*, (London 1970).

Pyle 1986a
Hilary Pyle, *Estella Solomons. Works from an Artist's Studio*, exh. cat. Crawford Municipal Art Gallery, (Cork 1986).

Pyle 1986b
Pyle, Hilary, *Jack B Yeats in the National Gallery of Ireland*, (Dublin 1986).

Pyle 1990
Hilary Pyle, *Images in Yeats. An exhibition of the work of Jack B. Yeats*, exh. cat. National Gallery of Ireland, (Dublin 1990).

Pyle 1992
Hilary Pyle, *Jack B Yeats: a catalogue raisonné of the oil paintings*, (London 1992).

Pyle 1993a
Hilary Pyle, 'Jack B. Yeats- 'A Complete Individualist", *Irish Arts Review*, vol.9, (1993), pp.86-101.

Pyle 1993b
Hilary Pyle, *Jack B. Yeats: His Watercolours, Drawings and Pastels*, (Dublin 1993).

Pyle 1994
Hilary Pyle, *The Different Worlds of Jack B. Yeats: his cartoons and illustrations*, (Dublin 1994).

Pyle 1997a
Hilary Pyle, 'The Hamwood Ladies: Letitia and Eva Hamilton', *Irish Arts Review*, vol.13, (1997), pp.122-34.

Pyle 1997b
Hilary Pyle, *Yeats: Portrait of an Artistic Family*, (London 1997).

Pyle 1999
Hilary Pyle, *Estella Solomons HRHA (1882-1968)*, exh. cat. The Frederick Gallery, (Dublin 1999).

Pyms 1993
an Ireland… imagined, exh. cat. Pyms Gallery, (London 1993).

Pyms 1986
Pyms Gallery, *The Irish Renascence- Irish Art in a Century of Change*, (London 1986).

Rameau 1725
Pierre Rameau, *Le maître à danser*, (Paris 1725).

Rivers 1946
Elizabeth Rivers, *Stranger in Aran*, (Dublin 1946).

Robinson 1884
Lionel G. Robinson, 'English Art as Seen Through French Spectacles. III- The Modern School', *The Art Journal*, (October 1884), pp.342-44

Rockett et al 1987
Kevin Rockett, Luke Gibbons and John Hill, *Cinema and Ireland*, (London 1987).

Rooney 2002
Brendan Rooney, 'All the Fun of the Fair. Images of Donnybrook Fair by Glew and Watson', *Irish Arts Review*, (Summer 2002), pp.100-04.

Rooney 2004a
Brendan Rooney, *Sadler's Wall*, (Bethesda, 2004).

Rooney 2004b
Brendan Rooney, 'Seitenblick: German Influence on Nineteenth-Century Irish Painting', in B. Maaz, ed., *A German Dream. Masterpieces of Romanticism from the Nationalgalerie Berlin*, exh. cat. National Gallery of Ireland (Dublin 2004), pp.32-39.

Sayers 1974
Peig Sayers, *The Autobiography of Peig Sayers of the Great Blasket Island*. Translated into English by Bryan MacMahon, (Dublin 1974).

Scott 2005
Yvonne Scott, *The West as Metaphor*, exh. cat. Royal Hibernian Academy, (Dublin 2005).

Seigne 1928
John William Seigne, *Irish Bogs: Sport and Country Life in the Irish Free State*, (London 1928).

Sheehy 1981
Jeanne Sheehy, *The Early Celtic Revival, exh. cat. National Gallery of Ireland*, (Dublin 1981?).

Slide 1988
Anthony Slide, *The Cinema and Ireland*, (London 1988).

Smith 1996
Alistair Smith, *Louis le Brocquy: Paintings, 1939-1996*, exh. cat. Irish Museum of Modern Art, (Dublin 1996).

Smyth 1984
Hazel Smyth, *The B&I Line: a history of the British and Irish Steam Packet Company*, (Dublin 1984).

Snoddy 1996
Theo Snoddy, *Dictionary of Irish Artists. Twentieth Century*, (Dublin 1996).

Snoddy 2002
Theo Snoddy, *Dictionary of Irish Artists. Twentieth Century*, (Dublin 2002).

Solkin 1993
David Solkin, *Painting for Money. The Visual Arts and the Public Sphere in Eighteenth-Century England*, (New Haven and London 1993)

Stairs 1990
Susan Stairs, *The Irish Figurists and Figurative Painting in Irish Art*, (Dublin 1990).

Stewart 1990
Ann Stewart, *A Dictionary of Irish Art Loan Exhibitions 1765-1927*, 3 vols (Dublin 1990).

Stuart 1819
James Stuart, *Historical Memoirs of the City of Armagh*, (Newry 1819).

Strickland 1913
Walter Strickland, *A Dictionary of Irish Artists*, 2 vols, (Dublin 1913).

Synge 1911
John M. Synge, *In Wicklow, West Kerry and Connemara*, (Dublin 1911).

Teehan 2004
Virginia Teehan, ed., *Jack B. Yeats. Master of ceremonies*, exh. cat. Hunt Museum, Limerick (Limerick 2004).

Tinney 1998
Donal Tinney, ed., *Jack B. Yeats at the Niland Gallery Sligo*, exh. cat. Niland Gallery Sligo, (Sligo 1998).

Toal 1996
Brian Toal, *Road Bowling in Ireland*, (Armagh 1996).

Turpin 1988-89
John Turpin, 'The National College of Art under Keating and MacGonigal', *Irish Arts Review*, vol.5, (1988-89), pp.201-11

Tyers 1998
Padraig Tyers, ed., *Blasket Memories*, (Dublin 1998).

Tynan 1888
Katherine Tynan, 'Irish Types and Traits', *The Magazine of Art*, vol. II, 1888.

Ua Maoileoin n.d.
Pádraig Ua Maoileoin, *The Blaskets*, (Dublin n.d.).

UCD 1993
Amharc Oidhreacht Éireann. Folk Tradition in Irish Art, exh. cat. Department of Irish Folklore, University College Dublin, (Dublin 1993).

Irish Traditional Music Archive 1992
'The Uileann Pipes in Irish Traditional Music', in *Irish Traditional Music Archive*, (1992).

Vallely 1999
Fintan Vallely, ed., *The Companion to Irish Traditional Music*, (Cork 1999).

Vickers 2000
John A. Vickers, *Dictionary of Methodism in Britain and Ireland*, (Peterborough 2000).

Waddington 1940
Victor Waddington, comp., *Twelve Irish Artists*, (Dublin 1940).

Waldron 1968
Ethna Waldron, 'Joseph Malachy Kavanagh', *The Capuchin Annual*, (1968), pp.314-27.

Walker 1997
Dorothy Walker, *Modern Art in Ireland*, (Dublin 1997).

Walker 2003
Dorothy Walker, 'Paul Henry, an alternative view', *Irish Arts Review*, (Spring 2003), p.61. Reprint.

Walker Art Gallery 1976
American Artists in Europe 1800-1900. An Exhibition to Celebrate the Bicentenary of American Independence, exh. cat. Walker Art Gallery, (Liverpool 1976).

Wall 1962
M. Wall, *Forty Foot Gentlemen Only*, (Dublin 1962).

Wallace 1987
Peter Wallace, *Multyfarnham Parish History*, (Mullingar 1987).

Warburton et al 1818
J. Warburton, Rev. J. Whitelaw and Robert Walsh, *History of the City of Dublin*, vol. 2, (London 1818).

Watson 1969
Sydney J. Watson, *Between the Flags. A History of Irish Steeple Chasing*, (Dublin 1969).

Weinberg 1991
H. Barbara Weinberg, *The Lure of Paris: Nineteenth-century American painters and their French teachers*, (New York 1991).

White 1994
James White, *Gerard Dillon. An illustrated biography*, (Dublin 1994).

Whitefield 1771-72
Rev. George Whitefield, *The Works of the Reverend George Whitefield*, 6 vols, (London 1771-72).

Whyte-Melville 1872
George John Whyte-Melville, *Songs and Verses*, (1872).

Williams 1963-65
H. Williams, ed., *The Correspondence of Jonathan Swift*, 5 vols, (Oxford 1963-65).

J. Wilson 1977
Judith Wilson, *Conor 1881-1968: The Life and Work of an Ulster Artist*, (Dundonald 1977).

K. Wilson 1995
Kathleen Wilson, *Sense of the People: Politics, Culture and Imperialism in England, 1715-1785*, (Cambridge 1995).

Wright 1820
G.N. Wright, *A Guide to the county of Wicklow* (London 1820).

Wynne 1983
Michael Wynne, *Fifty Irish Painters*, National Gallery of Ireland (Dublin 1983).

Yeldham 2005
Charlotte Yeldham, 'A regency artist in Ireland: Maria Spilsbury Taylor (1776-1820), *Irish Architectural and Decorative Studies. The journal of the Irish Georgian Society*, vol. VIII (2005), pp.187-219.

Young 1892
Arthur Young, *Arthur Young's Tour in Ireland 1776-1779*, (London 1892).

INDEX

This is a select index, principally of people and places mentioned in the text. Names in bold are those of artists and photographers. Numbers in bold denote subjects represented, discussed in detail and/or illustrated.

A

B

C

D

E

F

G

H

P

Q

R

S

T

U

V

W

Y

Z

Photo Credits

Illustration page iii © The Artist's Estate. Photo © The National Gallery of Ireland. Photographer: Roy Hewson

Figs 1, 3, 5, 6 Photographs courtesy of the Sean Sexton Collection

Fig. 2 Photo courtesy of Edward Chandler

Figs 4, 8 © Fr. Browne S.J. Collection. Photographs courtesy David Davison & Associates Ltd

Figs 7, 11 Photographs © 2006 Getty Images Inc. (Hulton Getty Picture Collection)

Fig. 9 Photo © National Museums and Galleries of Northern Ireland, Ulster Folk and Transport Museum

Fig. 10, cat. 83 Photographs courtesy of the National Library of Ireland

Figs 12, 13, cats 2, 6, 39, 53, 66 Photographs by kind permission of the owner

Figs 14, 16, 19, 23, 24, 26, 28, 36, cats 4, 10, 16, 23, 29, 30, 45, 46, 65, 67-70, 73, 74, 77, 79, 81 Photographs © National Gallery of Ireland. Photographer: Roy Hewson

Fig. 15 Photo © V&A Images

Fig. 17 Image courtesy of the Gorry Gallery

Fig. 18, cats 19, 42, 63 © The Estate of William Conor. Photographs reproduced with the kind permission of the Trustees of the National Museums of Northern Ireland

Fig. 20 © The Artist's Estate. Photo © The Crawford Municipal Art Gallery, Cork

Fig. 21, cats 25, 28, 49-52, 76 © Estate of Jack B.Yeats/DACS, London 2006. Photographs © National Gallery of Ireland. Photographer: Roy Hewson

Fig. 22, cats 15, 27, 41, 44, 78 © The Artist's Estate. Photographs reproduced with the kind permission of the Trustees of the National Museums of Northern Ireland

Fig. 25 © The Estate of John Luke, 2006. Photograph reproduced with the kind permission of the Trustees of the National Museums of Northern Ireland

Fig. 27 Photo © NMPFT/Science and Society Picture Library

Fig. 29 © The Estate of Jack B. Yeats/DACS, London 2006

Fig. 30 Civica Raccolta dell Stampe A. Bartarelli Collection. Photo courtesy of Fabio Saporetti, Sapretto Immagini d'Arte Snc

Fig. 31 Photo © The National Gallery, London

Fig. 32 © The Artist's Estate. Photo courtesy of the National Library of Ireland

Fig. 33, cat. 75 Photographs © Tate, London 2006

Fig. 34 © The Estate of Jack B. Yeats/DACS, London 2006. Photo courtesy of Karen Reihill Fine Art

Fig. 35 Photo courtesy of the University of St. Andrews Library

Cat. 1 Photo courtesy of the Courtauld Institute of Art

Cat. 3 Photo © Irish Linen Centre & Lisburn Museum Collection

Cat. 5 Photo courtesy of the Gorry Gallery

Cat. 7 © The Artist's Estate photo by kind permission of the owner

Cat. 8 Photo © Prudence Cumming Associates Ltd

Cat. 9 Photo © Bryan Rutledge

Cat. 11 © The Estate of William Conor. Photo © The National Gallery of Ireland. Photographer: Roy Hewson

Cat. 12 Photo courtesy of UCD Delargy Centre for Irish Folklore and the National Folklore Collection

Cat. 13 © The Artist's Estate. Photo courtesy of James Adams Salesrooms

Cat. 14, 60 © The Artist's Estate. Reproduced courtesy of the AIB Group. Photographer: John Kellett

Cat. 17, 71 © The Artist's Estate. Photographs courtesy of Karen Reihill Fine Art

Cat. 18 © The Artist's Estate. Photo courtesy of Dublin City Gallery The Hugh Lane. Photographer: John Kellett

Cat. 20 © Estate of Jack B. Yeats/DACS, London 2006. Photo courtesy of Dublin City Gallery The Hugh Lane. Photographer: John Kellett

Cats 21, 48, 54 Photographs courtesy of the Crawford Municipal Art Gallery, Cork

Cat. 22 Photo © Christies, London

Cat. 24 © The Artist's Estate. Photo by kind permission of the owner

Cat. 26 © The Estate of William Conor. Photo courtesy of Whyte's Auctioneers, Dublin

Cats 31, 56, 57 Photographs reproduced with the kind permission of the Trustees of the National Museums of Northern Ireland

Cat. 32 Photo courtesy of John Wesley's House & The Museum of Methodism London

Cat. 33 Photo courtesy of the owner

Cat. 34 © The Artist's Estate. Photo © The National Gallery of Ireland. Photographer: Roy Hewson

Cat. 35 © The Artist's Estate. Photo courtesy of Crawford Municipal Art Gallery, Cork

Cat. 36 © Courtesy of Felix Rosentiel's Widow and Son., London. Photo courtesy of Dublin City Gallery The Hugh Lane. Photographer: John Kellett

Cat. 37 © Estate of Jack B. Yeats/DACS, London 2006. Photo courtesy of Sligo Municipal Collection, The Model Arts & Niland Gallery Sligo. Photographer: Denis Mortell

Cat. 38 © The Artist's Estate. Photo © The National Gallery of Ireland. Photographer: Roy Hewson

Cat. 40 Photo courtesy of Karen Reihill Fine Art

Cats 43, 72 © The Artist's Estate. Photographs © Sotheby's, London

Cat. 47 Photo courtesy of Whyte's Auctioneers, Dublin

Cat. 55 Photo courtesy of Pyms Gallery, London

Cats 58, 59 © Heirs and Successors of Mainie Jellett. Photograhs © The National Gallery of Ireland. Photographer: Roy Hewson

Cat. 61 © The Artist's Estate. Photo by kind permission of the owner

Cat. 62 © Pierre le Brocquy. Photo © The National Gallery of Ireland. Photographer: Roy Hewson

Cat. 64 © The Estate of William Conor. Photo © Sotheby's, London

Cat. 80 © The Artist's Estate. Photo courtesy of the Gorry Gallery

Cat. 82 © The Artist's Estate. Photo courtesy of NUI Galway